The Emancipist

THE EMANCIPIST

Daniel O'Connell

1830–47

Oliver MacDonagh

WEIDENFELD AND NICOLSON
London

© 1989 Oliver MacDonagh

First published in Great Britain by
George Weidenfeld and Nicolson Ltd
91 Clapham High Street, London SW4 7TA

ISBN 0 297 796372

Photoset by Deltatype Ltd,
Ellesmere Port, Cheshire
Printed in Great Britain by
Butler & Tanner Ltd, Frome

Contents

For Honor and Paddy McSweeney

Illustrations

Preface

The Emancipist describes O'Connell's life from the achievement of Catholic Emancipation in 1829 to his death in 1847. To some degree, it differs in pitch and emphasis from its predecessor, *The Hereditary Bondsman*. Before 1829, O'Connell had been pre-eminently a barrister-agitator, a political outsider who was forced to operate extra-murally. From 1830 on he was a fully professional popular politician – perhaps the first of his line – a leading British as well as Irish liberal, a first-rank member of the House of Commons, and the main sustainer of the whigs in office down to 1841. He ceased to practise regularly as a lawyer – with the incidental (though to the historian very heavy) loss of his close correspondence with his wife while he was on circuit, this correspondence being the most revealing single source for his personal and family affairs.

Thus the second book is inevitably more 'public' than the first. It is also more complex. *The Hereditary Bondsman* was an essentially simple story of a single supreme achievement. *The Emancipist* tries to describe a lengthier and more arduous ascent, in which the mountaineer can give a name to, but never clearly see, the summit at which he aims; nor can he always know which is the upward path. The book does not pretend, however, to being a general political history of the period 1830–47. An O'Connell-less account of Irish politics in these years would truly be a *Hamlet* without the Prince; he was their centre and almost their sole point of reference. Even the British politics of the day would be quite inexplicable without him. None the less, *The Emancipist* is a biography. It is concerned with what concerned O'Connell. It tries to measure things only as they were measured out to him, or as he measured them himself. Goethe once wrote of the 'high perspective' of the popes, 'who see the great as great, the small as small'. Contrariwise, in the biographer's perspective, what was great in his subject's life is great, and what was small, is small. This particular bias is enjoined.

At the same time, the life of O'Connell was, in certain senses, more than one man's life. He was a very extraordinary individual who did many extraordinary things and he underwent a much grander and more varied range of the everyday experiences than most of us. But it is not for this reason that we must regard him as 'larger' than himself. It is rather that he was in part the faithful reflector, and in part the actual shaper, of the emergent Irish nationalist Catholic culture. O'Connell's own history is a vital constituent of the history of this development. As Sean Ó Faolain put the point, with magnificent extravagance, 'He was interesting in a hundred ways, but in no way more interesting than in this – that he was the greatest of all Irish realists who knew that if he could but once define, he would thereby create. He did define, and he did create. He thought a democracy and it rose. He defined himself, and his people became him.' A Heidelberg horseboy once put it more simply. When a traveller asked him whom he thought O'Connell was, he answered, 'The man who discovered Ireland.'

'Discovery' may seem a word ill-suited to O'Connell, most of whose ideology was derivative and whose career was strewn with abandoned initiatives. Yet he was perhaps the greatest innovator in modern democratic politics, as well as the originator of almost all the basic strategies of modern Anglo-Irish constitutional relations. Faced with the problems (and opportunities) of turning the deeply aggrieved from their endemic violence; of concentrating and deploying purposefully the force inherent in their numbers; of turning to his own account the established juridical and parliamentary systems; and of exploiting the new levels of literacy and communications, he became, perforce, a tireless political experimenter and gadgeteer. Over decades of trial and error, he worked out a new programme of public affairs and of mass organization and mobilization, which was to have universal application. Simultaneously, he developed a methodology peculiarly appropriate to colonial counter-attack, in situations where violence was eschewed and the imperialist power a constitutional government. Well might Lecky acknowledge 'the splendour and originality of the genius' which could devise such things. But the very magnitude and permanence of this achievement adds another supra-personal dimension to the biography.

The title of this book derives from an Australian word coined to describe those released, whether conditionally or absolutely, from their servitude. They had another struggle ahead of them, to turn their formal into *real* civic equality and to gain, in their own eyes as well as the eyes of the 'exclusives', parity of social esteem. From 1830 until his death, O'Connell saw himself as engaged in much the same kind of endeavour for his people.

I have provided references for all direct quotations; more general attributions may be found in the Bibliographical Note; and Biographical Notes are also supplied to furnish additional information on individuals.

One vitally important acknowledgement which I made in my earlier preface to *The Hereditary Bondsman* applies with equal force to *The Emancipist*. 'It would not have been possible to write a book like this at all without the publication from 1972 onwards of the magisterial new collection of the O'Connell correspondence edited by Professor M. R. O'Connell with the assistance of Mr Gerard J. Lyne. My debt to Professor O'Connell, however, far exceeds the opportunity to use this fundamental source. He made the letters not yet in print available to me in transcript or proof form; in addition I had, of course, his own important writings on O'Connell to draw on.'

I owe much to other people too, my heaviest debts being to Dr Tom Dunne of University College, Cork, and Dr Iain McCalman of the Australian National University, who read almost all my chapters with kind care; to Mrs Pamela Crichton who foraged and checked for me tirelessly; to the gallant secretarial staff of the History Department in the Research School of Social Sciences and, in particular, Mrs Beverly Gallina; and to Dr B. J. O'Neil who has furnished me with an Assessment of the causes of O'Connell's death. I have also to thank the Royal Bank of Scotland for permission to draw on their records; their archivist, Miss Alison Turton, for supplying me with material; and Dr Pauric Travers and Mrs Finola Collins for helping me to verify overseas sources.

I have run out of ways of trying to express adequately my gratitude to my wife. But there will never be an end to my appreciation of her loving patience with it all.

Canberra, December 1988   O. MacD.

CHAPTER 1

A Sort of Plateau

1830

I

At the beginning of 1830, O'Connell was well into his fifty-fifth year, his wife, Mary, being three years younger. He was still remarkably handsome – in the Kerry style – and tall, powerful and heavy. He had long worried about his burliness, and striven against it by undereating. But, as usual, Mary reassured him. 'As you are well, darling', she wrote on 1 March 1830,

> I care little for your *increasing* size, the more particularly as you always exaggerate your size. *It* can't at all events be unwholesome. It does not proceed from inactive or sedentary habits. You are neither an epicure nor a hard drinker. Indeed if you were . . . large and a gormandizer, I should then be unhappy about you. [But you] have the best of constitutions and may God continue it to you is my constant prayer.[1]

Certainly, he had the best of constitutions. He was seventy years old before he showed the first sign of failing. Apart from mention of some mysterious malaise in mid-1832, the sole surviving reference to his being doctored in the entire decade of the 1830s is an order for 'a box of the seasickness pills' to be sent to him *'at once . . . to Dublin'*,[2] before he faced again the Irish Sea. Meanwhile he worked the same cruelly long hours, often fourteen or fifteen in a day, as he had done since early manhood. It was also true, and perhaps pertinent to his capacity for torrential labours, that he drank only moderately. For eighteen months in 1840–1 he even became a total abstainer under the banner of Fr Mathew; but he did so only to meet a challenge to practise what he preached, and doubtless the practice became tedious with time. Although the entertainment at his home in co. Kerry, Derrynane, where he kept more or less open house throughout the autumns, was wildly generous, it stopped well short of flowing drink. For even O'Connell's holidays were layered with work.

During his long vacations at Derrynane, in addition to his evening hours of reading, account casting and letter-writing, the morning hours of hare-hunting were interspersed with business. He dispensed seigneurial justice, and caught up with the great world's happenings, on the run. As W. T. Fagan described it.

> He delighted in playing the Irish Tanist amongst his dependents. He was Judge, Jury and Executive in all their disputes . . . and like the Court of Law in England in former days, his Court moved about wherever he went. Often, on the top of some mountain crag, while the hounds were at fault, would he sit on one of nature's rude imperishable benches to hear and determine the disputes . . .
>
> His mountain sports never turned him from his absorbing pursuit of POLITICS. He was in the habit of proceeding on his hunting expeditions early in the morning and on foot; wearing thick *brogues* and bearing a substantial *wattle* in the hand. Breakfast was taken out, and at the usual hour, in some convenient spot, it was laid out *al fresco*. Then the post-boy arrived with letters and newspapers. No editor ever had so many at his command or ever read them with more attention . . . letters were read and opened and thrown down. Newspapers were read and flung aside; and when the repast was over, the huntsman's horn was sounded, and the fine pack of beagles summoned to their day's work.[3]

This was his joyous time; it was the loss of the days on the mountains with his dogs that he grieved for most when he was held back in, or torn away to, his parliamentary or agitatory duty. It was in part an exultation in bodily well-being and the physical challenge, but still more a form of reconsummation of his union with his native landscape. O'Connell's sense of place was very powerful, and nowhere could he satisfy this as fully as on the foot-hunt along the uplands behind Derrynane. Half-way about the compass towered higher mountains, jagged in outline or lost, across a line, in mist or rain. Southward lay the vast stretch of Kenmare Bay, with its broken near-coast and dreaming or tortured sea, and in the distance, the dark mass of the opposing ranges in west Cork. Love of country was at once O'Connell's political stock in trade and deepest passion. It was a love of Ireland's earth and skies no less than a constitutional idealization, and the epicentre of its physical expression was the matchless stretch of territory about Derrynane.

His wife, though also born and bred in Kerry, was far from sharing this enthusiasm. For her, Kerry carried memories of an impoverished childhood in the 'prying, curious *busy*' county town, Tralee.[4] It also symbolized a provincialism which she wished her own children, and in particular her daughters, to escape. Moreover, all through her married life, it had drawn her husband away from her for much longer than she would have sanctioned were his movements really under her command. He kept being caught – a most willing fly – in the webs of relations, connexions, clients, flatterers and friends spun all about the county in the years of his boyhood and during his three decades of practice at the Munster bar. Mary chafed, and even remonstrated occasionally at the resultant absences; but she knew that the lures of Kerry could never be altogether overcome. Worst of all for her was being immured in Derrynane in winter. As a counter, she had for years pleaded her 'delicacy' in a wet, wild climate: she was, she insinuated, healthier in almost any other place, and in particular in the cities, Dublin and London. Conversely, O'Connell tried to undermine her resistance to the place, as in writing to her from Tralee on 13 March 1832,

> I wish to God we were together, darling, and that Derrynane agreed with you as well as London. But I hope, darling, that you will come back so stout as to be able to *run about*. I am getting a road from the end of the kennel road to the chapel which will greatly extend your usual drive and thus give you a little *circuit* of your own. I will take care to have a good car horse for you, love.[5]

There is little to suggest that she lived much 'in society' in either of the capitals. In 1830 she forwent even accompanying the O'Connell family party to that great event in the Dublin calendar, the 'Patrick's Ball' on 17 March, with the easy comment, 'Going out by day and going out by night are very different to those who are apt to take cold as I am'.[6] We do not know how she spent her months in London whenever she joined O'Connell for the parliamentary sessions. But certainly she entertained and was entertained there little, if at all. None the less, whether in her home in Dublin, 40 Merrion Square, or in London lodgings, she liked urban life. It offered modest luxury; it had style; it might open the door to good matches for her unmarried daughters. When in March 1830 she was about to join O'Connell in London for the first time she wrote,

> My dearest Love,
> . . . If you think that lodgings will answer, why not take them? Perhaps those you have might answer with some additional rooms. Of all things let the rooms be large and airy. They must consist of three best sleeping rooms with one for James [O'Connell's manservant] and his wife and a servant man's apartment. Richard [O'Connell's coachman] is very anxious I should send him and the horses by the *steamer* from this to London. We must have him and the horses at expense in Ireland and be obliged to have job horses and coachmen in London which, from what I can learn, will [be]

dreadfully expensive . . . Perhaps if James would be on the look out he may be able to get a small house on reasonable terms with coachhouse and stable for the time we may be in London. All this I leave to your consideration . . . my wish is to be as saving as possible both here and elsewhere but I am anxious to make a good appearance in London for the sake of our girls. It might be of great advantage to them.[7]

Despite their covert tug-of-war over where and at what level to live, O'Connell and Mary were still, as they had always been, in fundamental unison and harmony. Their love-match of 1802 had never worn thin. After almost thirty years of time's abrasions, its lineaments still showed out clearly in the rubbed brass. On 24 July 1830 Mary wrote to her husband,

This is the eight-and-twentieth anniversary of our wedding day – the day of the week too – which to me was the commencement of a happiness that through your fault [never] was and never will be decreased. I have been the happiest of women since I first knew you and I feel that if you don't love me more, you do not now, in my old age, love me less. And oh darling how dear, how very dear are you to my fond and grateful heart![8]

According to Fagan, who knew her well, Mary's intellect was 'of the masculine order',[9] critical and strong. But all this flew out the window when it came to her *vision* of O'Connell. At various times during 1830, she wrote fondly to him in London, 'At this rate I expect one of these days to be the wife of the Prime Minister of England, Daniel O'Connell. Really, love, it is what you may look forward to without sacrificing one inch of your principles. They will see they cannot do without you';[10] 'I fancy [you] . . . looking as independent as if you were already Prime Minister of England . . . Darling you have brought a blessing upon yourself and your family, and your example has done more for the Catholic Church than ever was done by a layman at any period';[11] and 'My heart overflows with gratitude and pride for being the wife of such a man.'[12]

O'Connell was not the man to be outdone in any language, least of all that of endearment. Typical were the salutations of successive letters in mid-1831, 'My own sweetest love' and 'My own darling Mary'. Equally typical were his preface to the first, 'I have the Corporation case [a major malversion suit] to argue this day at the Rolls and I ought not to consume time from it *even in writing to you*, my own sweetest darling Love',[13] and the expression of his solicitude in the second, 'Darling, my own darling, why will you injure your health by fretting [about a formerly threatened duel]? . . . I should be as happy as *the day is long* if I could overcome your uneasiness. Mary,

I have a plan to go down with you to Windsor before the business of the House actually commences.'[14] All this was private discourse, between the two, meant to be read only by one another. But we can at least claim, in defence of intrusion, that it also had profound 'public' implications. When they were apart (now relatively rarely) the O'Connells interchanged letters almost daily, and in these O'Connell revealed his inner fears and triumphing, sure of a responsive sympathy or delight. Nor was Mary's mere blind support. At a certain level – that provided by O'Connell himself, the newspapers and Catholic Dublin's *on dits* – her grasp of politics was clear and sure, given her steady bias in O'Connell's favour. By her intelligent sympathy, she took some of the incessant strain off O'Connell's shoulders, and in return his self-revelation and dependence on her approval and applause warmed her by the assurance of her own indispensability and filled her with a sense of vicarious achievement. They also made her feel loved. 'All our children', she wrote to him on 5 December 1830, 'quiz me not a little upon the regularity of your letters. I suppose they are surprised you should think so much of a little old woman as to write to her every post. It is a doubt to me however if even [R.L.] Sheil, who has got so much by his lovely wife [Sheil had recently married an heiress], is as much attached to her as my darling old man is to his fond and grateful old woman.'[15]

Only one of O'Connell's children, his eldest daughter, Ellen, was as yet 'settled' in 1830. Five years earlier she had married Christopher Fitz-Simon, to O'Connell's ultimate benefit, as Fitz-Simon was to prove a tactful and painstaking political supporter and intermediary. It is true that the older boys, Maurice and Morgan, born in 1803 and 1804 respectively, were apparently launched upon careers, Maurice at the Irish bar and Morgan as a cavalry officer, in the Austrian Hussars. But Maurice never practised law energetically and soon ceased to practise it at all, while the charming feckless Morgan had neither the abilities nor the persistence which a poor Irishman required to fight his way upward in a foreign aristocratical profession. O'Connell's other sons, John (born in 1810) and Daniel (born in 1817), were still students, the first reading law in London and the other a schoolboy at the Jesuit college, Clongowes Wood. His daughters Betsey and Kate were as yet unmarried; if they were to be placed on a par with Ellen each would have to be provided with a dowry of £5000.

Thus O'Connell carried as heavy a familial burden as ever in 1830, although it was of course accompanied by the usual complex of parental emotional engagement, itself impossible to quantify exactly in terms of pains and pleasures. Certainly, O'Connell's children cost him dearly in time and care as well as money. He was an effusively affectionate father, especially towards his daughters. He might express his feeling with characteristic lack of reticence or commonplace decorum, as when, at a public meeting, he declared, 'I know what it is to respect as well as love those whom, in parental language, I call my angel daughters . . . whatever storms I may be engaged in abroad, when I return home, I have, as it were, attendant angels waiting about me, and cheering me on to renewed exertion.'[16] But he could also treat them with great sensitivity, as when after Betsey's wedding in 1831 he sent this message to her sister (now the only unmarried girl though Betsey's elder), 'Tell my sweetest Kate I hope to live to see her love a husband more than she loves her father though she may rely on it that her father will never love her less than he does at present.'[17] O'Connell also indulged his sons, even if less exuberantly. He defended Daniel's neglect to write home from school with, 'Darling, why do you fret yourself about Danny? If he was in the slightest degree unwell the Jesuits would write to you at once and, as to the sweet fellow himself, a letter necessarily takes away the play hours of a day.'[18] When Mary changed her mind about his sending a thunderbolt to his sons, he agreed with his usual easy grace, 'I recognized with delight your *mother's heart* in your retracting the *scolding* I meant to give my poor boys.'[19]

At the same time – at any rate, at this time – O'Connell's sons caused him more difficulties than his daughters, and Maurice the most difficulty of all. He had charm and cleverness, but was also lazy, expensive and cursed with the widespread expectation that he would measure up to his father in achievement. Sadly, he was still attempting to imitate O'Connell in his public bearing and even vituperation, like the small boy repeating the conjurer's movements – but without the conjuror's effects – after the party. Whether in despair of Maurice's making a living at the bar or in the hope that his eldest son would turn into his political as well as his legal heir, O'Connell decided in 1830 to introduce him to his own new trade, that of parliamentary politican. He put him forward for Drogheda at the general election of that year, and though Maurice failed both at the polls and in subsequent petitions against his successful opponent, O'Connell found him a seat, albeit at the cost of savage local quarrels, at a by-election for co. Clare in March 1831. O'Connell would never have serious difficulty in finding a compliant Irish constituency for Maurice – or indeed any of his sons; the crux was the cost of a parliamentary career. O'Connell and his wife had long been on the hunt for a rich wife for Maurice, and their efforts became strenuous once again about the time of the by-election. The girl in sight was a daughter of George Bourke Kelly, who had acted as chairman of the English Catholics committee of the O'Connell Testimonial in 1829. The 'principals' negotiated first, O'Connell writing from London to Mary, who was in Dublin, on 5 March 1831, 'Maurice had better remain with you until I see the Kellys [again]'.[20] The second meeting appears to have gone well, and on 26 May 1831, O'Connell complained to Mary (now in London while he was in Dublin), 'You have not said anything of the young lady of Acton [Miss Kelly]. If she does not *forbid*, it is sufficient. Recollect *that*, darling.'[21] Nothing came of the affair. Perhaps Maurice resisted an arranged marriage. Certainly, he was to leap in the opposite direction sixteen months later.

Meanwhile, O'Connell had inadvertently launched himself on a 'solution' to the problem of his sons' futures. At the 1832 general election, Maurice's brothers, Morgan (who had abandoned the Austrian cavalry) and John, together with their brother-in-law, Fitz-Simon (by now virtually another of O'Connell's sons), joined him in the House of Commons; and eventually even Daniel, whom O'Connell set up in business after he left school, also became an MP. To some extent, this indicated their incapacity to make their own way in the world. But it also manifested O'Connell's new determination to establish a core of totally obedient parliamentary supporters, who could also be deployed at will across the Irish constituencies, as so many pieces in his game of parliamentary nominations and substitutions. A family party within a party was cruelly expensive to maintain and more or less reduced the young O'Connells to the level of political automata, as well as perpetual dependents on their father. But it also helped to make O'Connell himself a parliamentary leviathan – even the greatest British magnate of the day 'owned' fewer members – and, Maurice perhaps apart, seems to have deepened rather than alienated his boys' loyalty and love. After all, his children could scarcely help being minnows to his Triton when it came to public things. Even the arrival of Betsey's first child was announced to the world in terms which did at least as much justice to her father as herself: 'Birth at Darrynane Abbey, the lady of N. J. Ffrench, of Fort William, in the county of Roscommon, Esq., and youngest daughter of Daniel O'Connell, M.P., of a son and heir.'[22]

II

In 1829 O'Connell abandoned his regular practice as a barrister. During the 1830s he toyed at least once with the notion of returning wholeheartedly to his old profession, and occasionally accepted briefs which carried high fees or promised political *éclat*. Sometimes he picked up a few additional cases during a visit to an assize town on special retainer. When in very low water financially in 1839–40, he actually sought business. 'I will give opinions in Dublin', he wrote wryly to P. V. Fitzpatrick on 14 December 1839, 'to any persons unwise enough to pay for them',[23] and in the following summer he appeared in some rather inglorious cases on the unfamiliar western circuit, at Galway and Castlebar. This seems to have been his swansong at the bar. His practice between 1829 and 1840 would not have accounted for more than a tenth of his time or income.

None the less, his thirty years as a prodigiously busy, versatile and successful advocate had shaped him permanently. There seems to be no question that he stood in first rank of counsel. Retrospectively, the *Law Magazine* compared him favourably with the two leading English advocates of his own generation.

> It is impossible to conceive a more powerful advocate than Mr. O'CONNELL was, before a Judge and Jury. They who have heard him in Parliament only, can form no notion of the man, such as he was, whilst wielding men's minds in his natural sphere of action. Impassioned and vigorous as BROUGHAM, discreet, argumentative, and zealous for his client, and forgetful of himself, as LYNDHURST, he had a playfulness of humour, a readiness of wit to affix an irresistibly ludicrous epithet, or apply some story fraught with ridicule, in an appalling degree, where he pleased – a power, moreover, of the deepest pathos, to which the former two were strangers. No man that ever spoke, did probably possess the power of moving the feelings and passions of a Jury in the same degree as Mr. O'CONNELL.[24]

His Irish contemporaries were unanimous that, while others might excel him in particular specialisms, none matched him as a professional, all round. 'Every requisite for a barrister of all-work', wrote W. H. Curran in his critical *Sketches of the Irish Bar* in 1823, 'is combined in him; some in perfection – all in sufficiency.' He was a master of procedure and the practical application, on an instant, of general legal principles; he was almost without a rival 'in a vehement and pertinacious talent with which he contends to the last for victory, or, where victory is impossible, for an honourable retreat'. Although his chamber business was immense, his forte was jury cases, and in particular as defence counsel in criminal proceedings. Curran observed that he was unerring in choosing the line best adapted to his auditors.

> But, in addition to the art of heating the passions of his hearers to the malleable point, O'Connell manifests powers of observation of another, and, for general purposes, a more valuable kind . . . Throw him upon any particular class of men, and you would imagine that he must have lived among them all his life, so intuitively does he accommodate his style of argument to their particular modes of thinking and reasoning. He knows the exact quantity of strict logic they will bear, or can comprehend. Hence, (where it serves his purpose) instead of attempting to drag them along with him, whether they will or no, by a chain of unbroken demonstration, he has the address to make them imagine that their movements are directed solely by themselves . . . This of course, is not to be taken as O'Connell's invariable manner, for he has no invariable manner, but as a specimen of that dexterous accommodation of particular means to a particular end, from which his general powers as a nisi-prius advocate may be inferred. And so, too, of the tone in which he labours to extort a verdict; for though, when compelled by circumstances, he can be soft and soothing . . . yet on other occasions, where it can be done with safety, he does not hesitate to apprise a jury, whose purity he suspects, of his real opinion of their merits, and indeed, not unfrequently, in the roundest terms, defies them to balance for an instant between their malignant prejudices, and the clear and resistless justice of the case.[25]

This may be taken as an epitome of his public method. In politics no less than law, his art of persuasion had many tones, including, paradoxically, the defiant and the denunciatory; and not just in the trial room but in everything O'Connell strove for the verdict, rather than effect. Forensically, he was indivisible.

It is curious that O'Connell, who was pre-eminently an efficient counsel, also became a mythical figure through his profession. The folk-hero of Irish legend was preternaturally cunning, dextrous in laying traps for his opponents, adroit in uncovering their deceits, endlessly audacious and resourceful – and of course ultimately triumphant. The popular image of O'Connell as a lawyer was essentially the same, and it was, in part, the secret of his power over the rural masses. A great cross-examiner is a sculptor carving in snow; only on the rare occasions is he extensively reported. O'Connell's last great performance as a criminal barrister, in a case which apparently validated and certainly enlarged his heroic reputation, was one such occasion. It is worth considering in detail.

On Saturday 24 October 1829, a first batch of prisoners, Patrick O'Leary, a well-to-do 70-year-old farmer, and three others, were convicted at Cork of conspiring to murder several landlords living near Doneraile. O'Connell, who had already decided to reduce severely if not abandon entirely his legal practice, and was then holidaying at Derrynane, had refused the prisoners' brief. But after the conviction of O'Leary and his co-defendants a messenger was sent ninety miles on horseback to Derrynane to implore O'Connell to take up the cause of the remainder. In keeping with the melodrama already infusing the affair, O'Connell responded to the desperate appeal by driving himself from Derrynane throughout the night of 25–6 October, breaking his journey only at Macroom for three hours' sleep. In the mysterious country fashion, the word of his dash for Cork had got abroad, and there were knots of people to cheer him on at every crossroads and straggle of cabins along the way. The court, sitting at 9 am on 26 October, refused an application for an adjournment until O'Connell should arrive, although he was expected within the hour. As the swearing in of the jury reached its end, however,

> there was a buz in the avenues to the Court, produced by the appearance of Mr O'Connell, who . . . was received, as usual, with unequivocal demonstrations of applause by the populace. The learned gentleman's outward appearance testified that he had been travelling all night, but after throwing off his top covering, he seemed quite fresh and ready for business, and some refreshment being sent to him, he seemed in a few minutes to forget everything but the case he had undertaken.[26]

The fables of the subsequent encounter were built around O'Connell's superior command of law, protracted and vituperative duel with John Doherty (the solicitor-general, who led the prosecution), and confounding of the crown's witnesses by a cross-examination which seemed to read their secret purposes as if through glass. Stripped of their embellishments of witty and plangent exchanges, the popular stories showed a real grasp of the progress of the trial. O'Connell's repeated objections soon halted the stream of hearsay and leading questions which had slipped by in the course of Saturday's hearing; his every objection was upheld. His sustained assault upon Doherty's affectations and unprofessional conduct of the case told in the end on the attitudes of even the bench, the fellow-counsel and the jury. During O'Connell's second day in court, the presiding judge Pennefather and the other prosecuting barristers – with a decided air of 'the lady doth protest too much' – took the extraordinary step of vouching publicly *seriatim* for Doherty's probity. Later the court refused to entertain a counter-affidavit from Doherty after O'Connell had charged the prosecution 'with a suppression of evidence, and a withdrawal of witnesses for the prisoners'. 'Perchance', the court ruled, 'the reading of the replying affidavit might militate against the prisoners at the bar'.[27] By that stage the compact front of judges and prosecuting counsel, then usual in cases of agrarian crime, was in complete disarray.

But O'Connell's *chef-d'oeuvre* was the breaking down of the prosecution's four chief witnesses, whiteboys who had turned king's evidence. The newspaper summary of some of the passages of cross-examination of the first witness, Daniel Sheehan, will suffice to illustrate O'Connell's method of entanglement: the lines of questioning can be readily inferred.

[Witness –] I cannot recollect how often we [Patrick Daly and he] met together; I was once in a house drinking porter with him, but I do not recollect how often we were drinking together; . . . I do not recollect that I swore I was not in company with Daly.

Mr O'Connell – You are a great fellow at recollection; you are a perfect *non mi ricordo*.

It was Colonel Hill who sent me to Dublin; I was sworn in a whiteboy only five or six years ago; the third time I was sworn in was about twelve months ago; my second swearing in was in winter, and of a Sunday . . . I cannot say what time I was last sworn in as a whiteboy . . . I do not recollect from one year to ten when I was last sworn in a whiteboy.

Mr O'Connell – Well, what am I to do with this fellow? Witness – On the trial last Friday I thought I was not bound to Mr M'Carthy, since I was not sworn a witness for him; I am not as honest a man to-day as I was on Friday; I know I am obliged to answer you, Sir; . . . I do not recollect how long this Doneraile business is going on; I know what a month is, but I do not know how many there are in a year; I don't recollect when Dr Norcott's carriage was fired at; I know Michaelmas and Christmas; I can't say whether Mr Low was fired at before or after Christmas; Mr Low was fired at before the attack on Dr Norcott's carriage; I do not recollect which was fired at; the Doneraile meeting was the first; I know not how many years ago the Doneraile business happened; at the meeting held there, Leary, Magner, Hickey, Wallis, Shine, and William Nowlan were present; these are the same names I told Sergeant Goold; Michael Nowlan was also there; he was a relation of William Nowlan's.

After Mr O'Connell had, with considerable perseverance, and much time been occupied in endeavouring to obtain from the witness an answer as to whom Michael Nowlan was, he acknowledged that there was no such person.[28]

The evidence of the other whiteboy witnesses was similarly trans-muted by O'Connell in a babel of contradiction and inconsequenti-ality; one of them was driven in his misery to cry out, "'tis little I thought I'd meet you here to-day, Counsellor O'Connell!'[29] The discrediting cross-examination proved crucial. The juror who held out against conviction, in the teeth of sustained pressure from his fellows and the bench, told the judges, 'My Lords, . . . I cannot agree with them [his brother jurors], for the character given by the witnesses for the prosecution of themselves was such, that I would not believe a single tittle of their evidence.'[30] With a hung jury, the second set of defendants (less one acquitted already) was discharged – ostensibly to be retried later, but in reality for good.

In the third trial, which followed immediately, O'Connell held the initiative throughout, and so pursued his earlier onslaught on the crown's evidence that even Pennefather, in his summing-up, described its witnesses, variously, as 'wretches', 'miscreants, who have steeped their hands in repeated acts of blood', 'monsters' and 'base'. The jury took only twenty minutes to find the latest contingent of defendants 'not guilty'. Thereupon the prosecution announced that it would not proceed with the charges against those still untried, primarily because of 'the character of the evidence'[31] – that is, the evidence after it had passed through O'Connell's mangle.

The *Freeman's Journal* reported that 'every tongue was loud in praises of Mr O'Connell, to whose exertions the result is universally attributed'.[32] The accolades were well-earned. There can be little doubt that more than a dozen men would have been hanged had he not taken command of the defence. As it was, the lives of even the first four prisoners were saved as, retroactively, his devastating cross-examination caused their sentences of death to be commuted to transportation. O'Connell's role as the almost magical deliverer was confirmed in the popular conception. He stood forth as the peasants' bulwark against the state, even when, as was almost certainly the case at Doneraile, they attempted to defend their means of living by a scheme of selective assassination. It was advocacy in such agrarian *causes célèbres* which cemented his union with the rural masses. Yet, once the verdict was in, he addressed the people in the tones of the sheriff of Nottingham rather than Robin Hood, and aligned himself firmly with the cause of public order. He made his peace with the opposing counsel (Doherty excepted), discountenanced any overt celebration of his triumph and told the peasantry to take warning from the trial of the utter ruin into which Whiteboyism and any similar excursion into conspiracy and violence must lead them. The final courtroom exchanges were mutually congratulatory.

> Mr O'Connell . . . If ever the people had an opportunity of witnessing the pure administration of justice, it has been afforded to them on this occasion; and if ever there was a practical lesson held out to the perpetrators of crime that there is no fidelity to be placed in their companions in guilt – no matter what obligations of secrecy were entered into by the confederacy – the present Commission has fully demonstrated it; while what I cannot but call the majestic impartiality with which justice has been administered by the bench must inspire confidence in all. I beg pardon, my Lords, for having thus intruded, but I could not help saying so much.
>
> Baron Pennefather – Those trials have been brought forward by the Crown, and defended by the counsel for the prisoners, in a manner which, in the name of the Court, and I think I may say in the name of the public, has been most satisfactory . . . It is right too, to say, that while the prisoners have been defended with great power and ability, that defence has been conducted with perfect regard for the due administration of the laws.
>
> Mr O'Connell bowed to the Court.[33]

In several ways, O'Connell the counsel provides us with keys to understanding O'Connell the public man. In both roles he combined aggression and dauntlessness in the popular cause with a most careful adherence to the rules and conventions governing the system in which he was operating. In both, he threw himself into the 'case' of the moment, but, win or lose, proceeded to the next with undiminished appetite for, and commitment to, the succeeding struggle. No one had more settled general principles than he, but neither was anybody more absorbed in the immediate. In both roles, O'Connell was fertile and variable in tactics, loud and eager in the thick of conflict, yet ready and even anxious to settle for lesser gains the moment the larger ones appeared unattainable. In both, he alternated the gravely responsible and demotic notes, as need suggested. He treated, for instance, the judges in the Doneraile trials with all formal respect, making his submissions with professional decorum. But every so often he played to the groundlings in the courtroom, as in mimicking Doherty's mincing dismissal of a witness, 'You may go down, sir', with 'Naw! daun't go daune, sir',[34] or in adding to his supporters' treasury of remembered sallies with

> Court – Mr O'Connell, from whence do you take your definition of perjury?
>
> Mr O'Connell – My Lord, I take it from the Catholic cathechism.[35]

In changing his occupation from law to parliamentary politics in 1830, O'Connell merely exchanged one forum for another. His methodology and mental predisposition remained the same. They had been stamped into him by virtually a lifetime's practice at the bar. Not that there was any reason for him to try to put on a new man at the age of fifty-five. He had already mastered the arts of popular domination, and of working within – often just within – the bounds of official structures. He had forged and tempered an extraordinary range of tools for public use; they would do practically as well in one place as another.

III

In abandoning his regular practice at the bar O'Connell lost the staple of his income. In money terms, he probably sacrificed about £6000–£7000 per annum, and came to depend instead on Irish public subscription – a species of 'compensation' – to provide him with the bulk of his resources. This soon became settled into a more or less annual 'Tribute' to himself; sporadically, a 'Rent' was also collected for various political movements or emergencies. It is impossible to say exactly how much these levies raised; the sums varied significantly from one phase of activity to another. But an annual average of some £12,000 would seem a reasonable estimate for 1831–45. His landed and other income was probably £4000–£5000 per annum.

None the less O'Connell found it almost impossible to make ends meet. He was chronically extravagant and careless with money, and drew no real distinction – if indeed there were any to be drawn – between his 'public' and his 'private' funds. His political expenditure was in itself enormous. As well as supporting his family party of MPs, he contributed heavily to his own associations and campaigns and the dissemination of information and propaganda. Even the maintenance of a third residence in London – a set of rooms in lodgings or a rented house, during the parliamentary session – and his incessant travel between Ireland and Great Britain and within both countries, were considerable burdens. General elections were the worst of all. He had sometimes to meet the costs of several contests, two or three of them for ruinously expensive county seats, and then to defend his gains, once more from his own pocket, against the inevitable petitions.

It is not surprising that with steady drains and sudden large demands on an income partly dependent on the caprice of the Irish public, O'Connell should have fallen from time to time into terrible financial trouble. It was no novelty for him to be close to bankruptcy. In fact, this might be said to have been his usual condition before, first, the legacies falling into his lap on the death of his uncle Maurice (Hunting Cap) O'Connell in 1825, and then the national testimonial raised for him on the attainment of Catholic Emancipation in 1829, lifted him for a short while well above the slough. After 1830 things were still worse in certain ways. A man in his later fifties – even an O'Connell – could not sustain the buoyancy of spirit, and the hope of somehow or other working his way out of calamity, which had been so remarkable a feature of his early manhood and middle age. Besides much more – in the form of still proliferating family charges, the expectations of benefaction deriving from his higher social station, and, above all, the carriage of what was virtually a separate political system on his own shoulders – now hung on his remaining solvent. Yet although O'Connell was still to suffer occasional desperate crises and days (and once or twice a week or so) of dark despondency, he was free of the near-constant financial frets and fears of the years before 1830.

This wonderful relief is chiefly to be explained by O'Connell's acquiring a financial manager in 1830. Patrick Vincent Fitzpatrick, born in 1792, was the son of Hugh Fitzpatrick, a Catholic bookseller and publisher who had been imprisoned for libel in 1813 in the course of an attempt by Peel to destroy O'Connell's agitation. P. V. Fitzpatrick, as a young barrister, became a member of O'Connell's entourage at the Catholic Association in the mid-1820s; and it was actually he who induced O'Connell to stand for co. Clare in the fateful by-election of 1828. He also – happy augury – undertook to raise sufficient money for the contest, and well over the required sum was speedily gathered in. This led on to Fitzpatrick's appointment as an organizer of the O'Connell testimonial in the following year – again with remarkable success, O'Connell sending him on 10 May 1830 his 'most sincere and cordial thanks . . . some occasion may arrive when I may be able to show you how deeply obliged I am, and how sensibly I feel my debt of obligation to you'.[36] Apparently off his own bat, Fitzpatrick next proposed that a 'Tribute' be raised regularly; for on 24 June O'Connell assured him, 'Your plan of a "Collection Sunday" I highly approve of'.[37] Fitzpatrick had thoroughly made his way into O'Connell's confidence and affection. In August 1830 O'Connell wrote to his brother James in Kerry,

This will be handed to you by my very kind and particular friend Mr P. V. FitzPatrick. He is the eldest son of the late Mr Hugh FitzPatrick. He has been one of the most useful, if not the most perseveringly useful, of the managers of 'the Fund'. All the articles in the [*Dublin Evening*] *Post* on that subject have been written by him. I cannot describe to you how grateful I am to him. He is now going to the South of Ireland. I recommend him to you in the strongest terms. Invite him to your house whilst he remains in Kerry. Show this letter to John [O'Connell's other brother], and take care to *forward* him throughout the kingdom of Kerry.

I leave this letter open that he may show it in Cork to our friend Charles Sugrue, Tom Fitzgerald, etc.[38]

Fitzpatrick demonstrated his mastery of his craft when raising the successful Tribute of 1831. He proved to be patient, prudent, tactful, systematic and wonderfully informed. Thereafter not only was he charged with the organization of the national collections (on a percentage basis) but he also took over, step by step, the management of O'Connell's own finances. The second task called for all the considerable calm, resourcefulness and powers of persuasion at his command; but he never failed his master. Fitzpatrick was much more than O'Connell's man of business. He rapidly became a sort of general adviser and arranger, and, especially after Mary O'Connell's death in 1836, O'Connell's chief confidant and nearest friend. But his vital role was that of shield between O'Connell and financial trouble. He could not insulate him completely from the consequences of over-spending and the reckless extension of commitments. But he saw to it that O'Connell was hauled out of each successive scrape. He gave him the opportunity to concentrate, almost all the time, upon the primary business of his life. He was Mazarin to O'Connell's Louis XIII, except that his loyalty was not to an abstract kingship but to a hero of his own. He was often called, even in his lifetime, O'Connell's *fidus Achates*; and so he was.

IV

In most, though not all, forms of political and cultural ideology, O'Connell was in the advance guard in 1830. During his remaining seveteen years of life, he moved further up the van in certain places; in others he fell back. Often it was the world about him that changed position rather than himself. Generally his views were constant.

Outside politics and morals, he tended to follow the drift of the day. Let us take creative literature as an illustration. Here his shifting taste was always conventionally good. Like most educated people, he somehow accumulated a wide knowledge of Shakespeare, perhaps in the style of Henry Crawford in *Mansfield Park*, 'Shakespeare one gets acquainted with without knowing how'.[39] As a young man, he was deeply impressed by the quintessential novel of sensibility, Mackenzie's *Man of Feeling*. A decade and a half later, he was taken with Byron and Scott. Byron's biting critiques of contemporary society and politics often matched his own, and Scott both resembled O'Connell remarkably in background and disposition and responded in much the same way, imaginatively, to the past. 'There never was such a novelist', O'Connell observed after re-reading all Scott's works in succession in 1841, 'and there never again will be another such.'[40] O'Connell's retrospective romanticism focused, however, on religion quite as much as – or perhaps more than – pageantry or the hierarchy and mutuality of traditional Gaelic society. He was 'an enthusiastic admirer of the cathedrals of England', especially Canterbury; in fact, he commissioned a painting of Becket's martyrdom to be hung in his Dublin parish church. It was at Canterbury that, according to his own account, he astounded the 'female guide' with the information that every prelate interred in the great 'pile' was a papist.

> 'Bless me!' cried the woman, in astonishment, 'I never knew that before.' – I then described the effect of the high altar lighted up for the celebration of mass in Catholic times; when the great aisle, now boxed up into compartments by the organ loft, stretched its venerable and unbroken length from the altar to the portal, thronged with kneeling worshippers. The picture delighted the woman. 'Oh!' cried she, clapping her hands, 'I should like to see that!' – 'God grant you may yet,' returned I.[41]

Like thousands of other readers, O'Connell became immediately enamoured of Dickens's early books. On 4 September 1837 he demanded that the new issue of *Bentley's Miscellany* be sent to him at Derrynane at once. 'The story of "Oliver Twist" is continued in [it], and I am most impatient to see it.'[42] Again like thousands of readers, he was, however, infuriated by the death of Little Nell, and in a storm of outraged sentimentality threw the volume which had recounted it away. Bulwer Lytton was among his later favourites.

He admired most of the leading Irish writers for the contemporary London market, chiefly Moore whom he virtually idolized for both his 'melodies' and his political novels such as *Captain Rock*, which was 'to the struggle for Catholic Emancipation what *Uncle Tom's Cabin* was to the abolition of slavery'.[43] But he also warmly praised the books of the Banim brothers and Gerald Griffin. Griffin's *Collegians* had a particular appeal, for O'Connell had defended the murderer unsuccessfully in the case on which the novel was based. (It was a rare instance of his rejoicing in an adverse verdict: 'I do not feel any the most slight regret at his conviction', O'Connell told his wife, 'It is very unusual with me to be *so* satisfied, but he is a horrid villain'.[44]) Significantly, the Irish authors whom O'Connell particularly liked – Moore, Griffin and the Banims – had Catholic backgrounds and, however prudently concealed or muted, nationalistic instincts similar to his own. Contrariwise, Maria Edgeworth's *The Absentee* jarred on him, ostensibly because he saw in it a covert attack upon himself, but more probably because he divined that by the 1830s Edgeworth had reverted to the standard Ascendancy condescension towards and suspicion of his class.

V

Thus, with a few Irish aberrations, O'Connell's pleasure reading generally followed the mainstream as it flowed. But the doctrine of one comparatively obscure novel, which had much impressed him when he was young, suffused his public conduct all his life. The novel was William Godwin's *Caleb Williams*, and the doctrine, as developed systematically in Godwin's *Political Justice*, was to provide him with the two master principles of his politics. The first of these was epitomized by O'Connell himself in the proposition that that government was best 'which laid fewest restraints on private judgment'.[45] The second was an absolute repudiation of violence in seeking political or any other ends. By itself, Godwin had argued, human reason was capable of producing infinite social amelioration; bloodshed halted progress, or rather drove things back. Public opinion was the ultimate source of every power; change that opinion, and accordingly government was changed. In a letter of advice of 16 February 1830 to Thomas Attwood, who had just set up the Birmingham Political Union, O'Connell translated Godwin's visionary philosophy into the language of the practical agitator.

> There are two principal means of attaining our constitutional objects which will never be lost sight of. The first is the perpetual determination to avoid anything like physical force or violence and by keeping in all respects within the letter as well as the spirit of the law, to continue peaceable, rational, but energetic measures so as to combine the wise and the good of all classes, stations and persuasions in one determination to abolish abuse and renovate the tone and strength of the representative system. The other is to obtain funds by the extension of a plan of collection which shall *accept* from no man more than he can with the utmost facility spare even in these times of universal distress. The multiplication of small sums, of very small

sums, should be the proper as it would be the efficacious popular treasury
... The people should incessantly call for reform until their cry is heard
and *felt* within the walls of Westminster.[46]

Godwin's first principle, the utmost freedom from restraint, virtually subsumed the whole range of O'Connell's political objectives; it
also classified O'Connell's type of early-nineteenth-century radicalism. It was no chance that by 1830 he was commonly termed
'liberator' or 'emancipator'. These terms indicated precisely how
O'Connell saw his general task – as the unshackling of people from all
the fetters imposed by ascendancy, discrimination or prejudice, as well
as by tyranny itself. O'Connell did not follow Godwin to the uttermost
limits of *Political Justice*; he did not seek, for instance, the eradication
of such 'coercive' institutions as monarchy, aristocracy or the law of
contract. But overall he adhered to an extreme programme of
individual rights. This programme was essentially negative in character, a grand procession of 'freedoms from'. But it could also be
regarded positively, as the steadfast pursuit of civil equality.

With much justice, O'Connell claimed the name of universal
egalitarian. He represented his struggles to achieve parity for
Catholics and Irish as mere particular manifestations of a general
aspiration. Typical was his powerful and consistent advocacy of
Jewish 'emancipation'. As he assured the leader of English Jewry, Isaac
Goldsmid, towards the close of 1829, 'you will find in me the constant
and active friend to every measure which tends to give the Jews an
equality of civil rights with all other the king's subjects, a perfect
unconditional equality. I think every day a day of injustice until that
civil equality is attained by the Jews.'[47] He was as good as his word.
Although Jewish relief was a highly unpopular cause in Britain (it was
opposed even by many radicals, including Cobbett), O'Connell was
foremost in support of the removal of Jewish disabilities bill in the
House of Commons in 1830. He made short shrift of the cant which
commonly clothed racial prejudice. He would have none of the
arguments that equality for Jews would de-christianize the state and
establish an 'alien' body in the polity. During the debate of 22
February 1830, he declared that instead

> of separating the Legislature from Christianity, by conceding the claims of
> the Jews, we should prove ourselves still more Christian by doing as we
> would be done by, and carrying into effect the principle of perfect freedom
> of conscience, – a principle that already manifested its beneficial tendency,
> and which would be the more beneficial the more widely it was extended.[48]

Later, on 17 May 1830, he dealt masterfully with the attack on Jews for their outer loyalties. A Jew 'might still remember the traditional home of his father . . . [but] he was still obedient to our laws. Let them not, therefore talk of the name of Christianity, when it was used to do evil instead of good.'[49]

Racial prejudice or exclusion he attacked with cold reason, but colour prejudice and slavery he attacked with passion: these fired him to savage and contemptuous denunciation. He would never visit the United States: it was a slaveholding country. He would never shake the hand of an American who in any way – even by mere residence in a 'bond' state – condoned the abomination. 'I should be sorry to be contaminated by the touch of a man from those States where slavery is continued', he told an anti-colonization meeting in London in 1833.[50] His earnestness cannot be doubted. During 1843–5 he persisted in his public condemnations of slavery in the United States. Even at the cost of ultimately destroying his entire support system in the United States, he did not yield to the sustained pressure of the American Repealers either to maintain silence on the subject or to declare Irish independence to be the political priority. The Young Ireland faction, and indeed many others within his home movement, generally argued that Ireland's need for overseas sympathy and resources should be paramount. O'Connell would have none of this. A deeply entangled politician, he sometimes hedged initially. But from the start to finish he never really deviated from the line that the American Declaration of Independence was a lie before God, while men, women and children were bought and sold, used and looked upon, as chattels: he would, he said, recognize no man as an Irishman who failed to repudiate this institution. Moreover, O'Connell's 'brotherhood of man' embraced all victims of Western colonialism. In a speech to the Aborigines Protection Society in 1840, for example, he denounced colonialism in Australia and New Zealand as carrying ruin and genocide in its train; 'no other human event led to evils so multitudinous'.[51] 'There', he once declared, 'are your Anglo-Saxon race! Your British blood! your civilizers of the world . . . the vilest and most lawless of races. There is a gang for you! . . . the civilizers, forsooth, of the world!'[52] His hatred of supremacism, colour-discrimination and servitude had been formed and settled long before 1830. From early in the century he had been a leading figure in the main European abolitionist organization, the British and Foreign Anti-Slavery Society, and during the years 1830–3, he was to play a critical part in the successful campaign for West Indian 'emancipation'. Despite the compensation of the former slaveholders (which he deplored) he later 'looked upon [this victory] . . . as one of the glorious acts of nineteenth-civilization, a symbol of the inevitable progress of man'.[53] His last decade in politics was the same; he continued to pour out time, words and political powers in the cause of black and other 'coloured' liberation. Small wonder that he was already in 1830, and would remain until his death, a hero of heroes to the American negroes and many abolitionists.

What of that other great body of deprived, women? As a young man, O'Connell had reasoned himself into an affirmation of full sex equality on general individualist principles. But in the world in which he was to live, female 'emancipation' was scarcely even a debated issue; and, more or less automatically, O'Connell accepted the dominant concept and practice of sharply separated spheres for men and women. When, however, he was suddenly forced to decide on a question of women's public rights, his inherent individualism conquered conventionality. On 17 June 1840, Lucretia Mott, an American delegate to the General Anti-Slavery Conference then taking place in London, asked O'Connell for his opinion on the conference's rejection of women delegates on the grounds 'that the admission of women being contrary to English usage [it] would subject them to ridicule, and that such recognition of their acknowledged principles would prejudice the cause of human freedom'.[54] O'Connell's lengthy reply was testimony to his ultimate candour as well as his underlying liberality.

I should premise by avowing that my first impression was strong against that admission, and I believe I declared that opinion in private conversation. But when I was called on by you to give my personal decision on the subject, I felt it my duty to investigate the grounds of the opinion I had formed; and upon that investigation I easily discovered that it was founded on no better grounds than an apprehension of the ridicule it might excite if the Convention were to do what is so unusual in England – admit women to an equal share and right of the discussion. I also, without difficulty recognised that this was an unworthy and, indeed, a cowardly motive and I easily overcame its influence.

My mature consideration of the entire subject convinces me of the right of the female delegates to take their seats in the Convention and of the injustice of excluding them . . . Mind has no sex; and in the peaceable struggle to abolish slavery all over the world, it is the basis of the present Convention to seek success by peaceable, moral and intellectual means alone, to the utter exclusion of armed violence. We are engaged in a strife not of strength but of argument. Our warfare is not military; it is Christian. We wield not the weapons of destruction or injury to our adversaries. We rely entirely on reason and persuasion common to both sexes . . .[55]

O'Connell never spoke, nor was he ever called on to speak, on women's political rights, and certainly, following the orthodoxy of the day, he took their role to be essentially domestic. But he did discern that the voting powers of women shareholders in the East India Company and the Bank of England made nonsense of the notion that women had no place in public affairs; and the rigour of his individualist principle renders it likely that, had he entered politics in 1860 instead of 1830, he would have been among the first to press women's suffrage and their constitutional equality in general.

All in all, his claim to universality as a liberator can be sustained. Gladstone's posthumous tribute was essentially just.

> He was an Irishman, but he was also a cosmopolite. I remember personally how, in the first session of my parliamentary life [1833], he poured out his wit, his pathos, and his earnestness, in the cause of negro emancipation. Having adopted the political creed of Liberalism, he was as thorough an English Liberal, as if he had had no Ireland to think of. He had energies to spare for Law Reform, for Postal Reform (a question of which he probably was one of few to discern at the time the greatness), for secret voting, for Corn Law Repeal, in short for whatever tended, within the political sphere, to advance human happiness and freedom.[56]

VI

In his letter of late 1829 to Goldsmid, O'Connell wrote:

> To my mind it is an eternal and universal truth that we are responsible to God alone for our religious belief and that human laws are impious when they attempt to control the exercise of those acts of individual or general devotion which such belief requires. I think not lightly of the awful responsibility of rejecting true belief but that responsibility is entirely between man and his creator, and any fellow being who usurps dominion over belief is to my mind a blasphemer against the deity as he certainly is a tyrant over his fellow creatures.[57]

This was his proclaimed position on religious toleration in 1830, as it had been in 1813 when he declared that 'perfect liberty of conscience [was] . . . eminently, almost exclusively the hope of liberty' in Ireland,[58] and as it was to be in 1841 when he told the Earl of Shrewsbury that the 'respect which each person would claim for his own opinion would require of him to treat with equal justice the opinion of others'.[59] In general O'Connell lived up to his professions.

His normal state of bitter struggle with 'Orangeism' and the church establishment in Ireland was truly, as he claimed, an opposition to a political ascendancy based on confessional allegiance. He even strove for compensation for Protestants displaced in the course of Irish reforms. 'I want to work out political changes', he declared, 'but I am equally desirous to avoid inflicting individual injury. I war against systems, not against men'.[60] At one level, O'Connell was a hot religious partisan. He eagerly counted up Catholic converts and hailed the advance of Puseyism as an inadvertent tribute to Catholic principle; he exulted that his religion was 'daily making progress – it receives an impulse from various and opposite quarters'.[61] But this was a far cry from deviating from public impartiality or abating his innate magnanimity towards persons.

It was characteristic that O'Connell should have warmly supported, in April 1830, the re-instatement of an Anglican army officer who had been dismissed from the service for refusing to fire signals at a Catholic ceremony in Malta, and equally that, in a sect-torn society, O'Connell should have himself employed a Protestant attorney, a Protestant land-steward and at least one Protestant manservant. He was a tireless advocate of the English dissenters' causes, from the abolition of religious tests for office to the abolition of church rates, and despite the chasms in creed he remained on good terms with almost all, and in particular with the Society of Friends. 'Friend O'Connell', the Quaker veteran, Joseph Pease, once told him on parting, 'I have for many years watched thine actions closely; I have kept mine eye upon thee, and I have never seen thee do aught that was not honest and useful.'[62] The solitary blemish on O'Connell's non-conformist record was an outburst of 1 August 1839 against 'the filthy slime of Wesleyan malignity'.[63] The Methodists were perhaps the bitterest contemporary assailants of Catholicism, and the issue at stake was perhaps the most inflammatory of all, proselytization. Besides, O'Connell was despondent at the time. None the less, he lapsed equally in charity and taste.

For a nineteenth-century Catholic, O'Connell was as remarkable for his commitment to the total separation of church and state as for his unqualified defence of the individual's liberty of conscience. On 11 September 1830, he wrote, in a letter intended for the public eye, of the recent revolution in France whereby the Bourbon monarchy had been superseded:

There is one feature in this great and satisfactory change which as a Catholic I hail with the most profound conviction of its utility – it is the complete severance of the church from the state. Infidelity, . . . which has deluged France with the blood of the Catholic clergy, was losing ground by degrees since the concordat obtained by Napoleon but the progress of Christian truth and of genuine piety was much impeded since the return of the Bourbons, by the unhallowed commixture of zeal for religion with servile attachment to the Bourbons. 'La religion et le Roi' were put in juxtaposition . . . Religion was thus placed in a false position. Catholicity in France was situate somewhat as Protestantism has been, and to a certain extent still is, in Ireland. It was considered to be the enemy of the people and of liberty.

I heartily rejoice that the last glorious revolution has altered the position. Religion left to its own intrinsic merits may sustain some slights and will certainly be exposed to many calumnies but those merits and the heavenly beauty of its precepts and practices will be likely to win their way with more facility now that they cannot be ranged with any hostile party . . . France has set the great and glorious example . . . [64]

This remained O'Connell's credo. He was later to dismiss the Orleanists in France as false liberals. But this he regarded as confirmation rather than contradiction of his principles; their active anti-clericalism and repressive legislation represented, in his eyes, an invasion of religious liberty by the state.

It was no wonder that O'Connell had become already the paladin of the nascent Catholic liberal movements on the Continent. In fact, at the very time that he wrote his manifesto of 11 September 1830, the young Comte de Montalembert had arrived as a pilgrim at Derrynane, to make obeisance to the great champion of Catholic liberty. When, however, Montalembert, together with his fellow-liberals Lamennais and Lacordaire, sought papal approbation of their advocacy of freedom of conscience and the separation of church and state, the new pope, Gregory XVI, elected in 1830, rejected them and their journal, L'Avenir, out of hand. His encyclical Mirari vos, promulgated in 1832, condemned most liberal tenets including unlimited freedom of assembly, of speech and of the press, and 'the erroneous and absurd opinion – or rather, derangement – that freedom of conscience must be asserted and vindicated for everyone'.[65] Moreover, to the embattled defender of the papal states, the separation of civil and spiritual authority seemed the very emblem of irreligion.

Yet, although Rome obliquely reproved O'Connell's political activity from time to time, by forbidding the Irish clergy to engage in any form of agitation against established government, O'Connell himself remained unscathed. No censorious line or word ever issued from the Curia. On the contrary, during 1838 Gregory XVI, as marks of particular regard, granted two special indulgences to the O'Connell family, another indulgence to any person who prayed in O'Connell's private chapel at Derrynane, and the privilege of a portable altar to O'Connell himself – this last being normally reserved for heads of state. For his part O'Connell, to counter doubts cast upon his orthodoxy, had written in the preceding year,

> I revere in all things the authority of the Holy See. I really believe (in so far as I know myself) that there is not a single person who pays more sincerely than I do, and with all my heart, the submission – in the widest sense of the word – to the Holy See which the Catholic Church demands of her children. I have never said and shall never say a single word which I would not subject to her authority with profound obedience. I am attached to the centre of unity with the most ardent desire never to separate myself from it either in thought or word or action, and if I should ever deceive myself in the opinions I express, I hope that they will be interpreted according to my sentiments because my submission to the authority of the Church is complete, whole and universal.[66]

How is O'Connell's high favour, let alone his exemption from censure, to be explained? He had several advantages: he was a layman; he was devout; he made no pretence to knowledge of theology; he had long struggled for, and ultimately won, the most famous Catholic victory of the age; he was sincerely, as well as prudentially, deferential to the Church; most Irish bishops were on most occasions his admirers. Secondly, the principal 'error' of contemporary liberalism, singled out for special condemnation in *Mirari vos*, was religious 'indifferentism'. Here O'Connell was orthodox beyond all question. He fully accepted the precept 'no salvation outside the Church', even if, characteristically, he also held that no one had a 'right to judge his neighbour's conscience'[67] or to suggest that a rejection of Catholicism might not be serious and sincere. Finally, the most important difference between the contestants may well have been which way, on the time scale, they faced. Whereas Gregory XVI and his kind were still fighting the intellectual battles of the *ancien régime*, O'Connell's was the prophetic role: poles apart, a line yet ran straight between the two. Grounded in benign individualism and universal concepts of human rights, O'Connell anticipated the sort of theology which was to be released in the Roman Church by the Second Vatican Council. As Helen Coldrick puts it, he had 'adopted the advanced view that religious freedom possessed a positive moral content . . . Because man was rational and free, he enjoyed the right to decide for himself ultimate matters of belief and commitment.'[68]

It is true that, during his last years, O'Connell seemed increasingly rigid in religious – or, more strictly, ecclesiastical – concerns; there were also suggestions of clericalism in some of his public utterances and stances. But these were largely the product of circumstance. The O'Connellite party among the Irish episcopate (on whom he depended politically from 1840 onward) was also, doctrinally, the narrowest and most truculent. Moreover, Peel's ministry (1841–6) deliberately raised divisive religious issues in the hope of alienating the more 'moderate' or 'broader' section of the Irish Catholic prelacy from O'Connell's movement. In such conditions, politics demanded that O'Connell bend a little to the ultramontanist wind. In any case, his every instinct would have warned him against Greeks – in the shape of English tories – bearing gifts. He was also led to the edge of sectarian asperities in 1845–6 by Young Ireland insinuations that he headed a 'priests' party' and that some at least of his lieutenants were striving, by fair means or foul, for Catholic ascendancy in Ireland. Again, however, O'Connell was essentially responding to a political challenge, with the additional provocation – as he saw it – of being lectured or patronized by Johnny-come-lately recruits to his cause, some young enough to have been his grandsons, others as suspicious of popery as any of his Exeter Hall assailants. All things fairly considered he adhered remarkably to his earliest definitions of individual and institutional rights in matters of religion. He was as truly tolerant, both by nature and deliberate endeavour, as might reasonably be asked of anyone – not only of his own but also of almost any other time.

VII

In general, in the fields of human rights and religious freedom, O'Connell held positions analogous to those attained by most Western liberals by the 1960s. *Pari passu*, he became, if anything, a more rather than a less 'advanced' radical during 1830–47, for in these years reactionary opinion clarified and conservative opposition hardened at certain points. Economic freedom was, however, a much more complicated business. By upbringing and inheritance, O'Connell was a lesser Irish landlord of the indulgent, non-improving, uncommercial kind. He occasionally supported agrarian reforms in the tenant interest, and his native kindliness and *quieta non movere* attitudes certainly earned him universal or near-universal popularity on his estates. But, practically speaking, he had no clear policy towards Irish land beyond the encouragement of residency, and of his own particular type of paternalism and chieftainship, among proprietors at large. It would scarcely be an exaggeration to approximate his landed philosophy to the Dickensian 'spirit of Christmas'. Correspondingly, although he repeatedly visited industrial towns and cities in the English north and midlands, he understood little of the fundamental structure or implications of British industrialism. He was at home in the old world of craftsmen and artisans, but that was all.

On the other hand, O'Connell applied his radical individualism as confidently and rigorously to the commercial and manufacturing as to any other fields. He was a doctrinaire free trader and the keen enemy of all constraints on trade or the supply of labour. Before 1830 this had little significance in his public life; it led to nothing more than occasional *obiter dicta* on distant things. Thereafter, however, in consequence of O'Connell's being both a leading member of the House of Commons, and a close ally of English middle-class and artisan radicals, his economic principles had a considerable bearing on politics on both sides of the Irish Sea. He had warmly approved the repeal of the Combination Acts (which had in effect rendered trade unions illegal and strikes criminal offences), but only because he was committed to the principles of the 'free contract' and personal liberty of choice and action. He did not favour trade unions as fighting forces, for the very same principles led him also to assert every individual's right to enter into his own wage contract. Hence O'Connell's firm backing for the prohibition by the Trade Unions Act of 1825 of 'intimidation', 'protestation', 'obstruction', the 'closed shop' and even peaceful picketing – a concatenation which made it extremely difficult to conduct a lawful strike. 'It was fair for them [workers] to combine . . .', he was to declare in 1838, 'but the moment they attempted to coerce others, the moment that they carried the effect of their combination to any other individuals, that instant crime commenced, and they were not only guilty of a crime in the eye of the law, but also of a moral crime, and they inflicted a robbery upon others.'[69] O'Connell was unconcerned by working-class denunciation, when it came, for 'he felt satisfied in his own conscience that he was acting as their best friend'.[70] By this he meant that restrictive labour practices were inimical to employment, and thereby ultimately to wages too. 'They [workers] were not entitled to wages out of capital; they were only entitled to them out of profits, and if their employers made no profits the wages must decrease. Wages, which were the price of labour, must depend upon the demand.'[71] Such reasoning was later to be execrated as Gradgrindism, and would eventually seem 'gothick' to the enlightened. But, to keep perspective, we should recollect that O'Connell was merely repeating the most advanced economic precepts of the day, and that he was to be in his grave for almost thirty years before (by means of the Conspiracy and Protection of Property Act of 1875) the law ceased to uphold most strictly the attitudes towards unionism which he expressed. Nor can it be doubted that he believed that his was the humane as well as the scientifically proven answer to the labour problem of the 1830s.

There are, however, other fields of ideas in which, after 1830 and still more after 1840, O'Connell began to seem a man of the past rather than the future or the present. Ideologically, he had been bred, as we have seen, a rationalist and a universalist, with an essentially atomistic view of society. Certain trends in Ireland and, to some extent Great Britain, worked against all three during his final years. They had made no great headway before he died, yet quite enough for his unease with, and resistance to, them to become apparent.

First, extra-rational politics broke the surface. If only in a half-hidden way, several of O'Connell's fundamental presuppositions came under challenge. The Germanic type of romanticism and idealism which infused the *Nation* newspaper and the more ardent element in Young Ireland placed the emphasis on the race rather than the person, the group rather than the individual, instinct and emotion, rather than reason, cultural rather than constitutional liberation, and a subjective and creative rather than a formal and negative concept of independence. Secondly, in part because of the passion generated by such a view of nationality, but also because there were few left who, like O'Connell, had had direct experience of the French Revolutionary turmoil and the Irish risings of 1798 and 1803, doctrines of armed resistance – if only in hypothetical form – began to circulate in Ireland once again before O'Connell died. To him, they were anathema. He was not himself above administering the heady stuff of ancient violent glories to his public. He even chose as the motto for his *Memoir on Ireland, Native and Saxon*, Moore's braggart lines,

> On *our* side is Virtue and Erin,
> On *theirs* is the Saxon and Guilt,

which, every Irish reader would have known, followed directly

> But onward! – the green banner rearing,
> Go, flesh ev'ry sword to the hilt.[72]

But this was merely to use the long-dead past as a momentary intoxicant. It could not – horror of horrors! – have any current or future reference.

In the third place, the new concept of 'the nation' was accompanied by a new notion of its supremacy. For O'Connell, the Irish nation meant simply all the inhabitants of Ireland, 'Catholic, Protestant and Dissenter'. In its political manifestation, it existed primarily to ensure fair play for all its members. Each denomination should have equal claims, in law and civil rights, within its bounds. But 'the nation' conceived of as a spiritual entity demanded much more of its component individuals, and this was to become of increasing importance as the public domain expanded in the third and fourth decades of the nineteenth century. Again some of O'Connell's basic presuppositions were under challenge. Let us take education, which was now becoming a governmental or partly governmental concern, as an example. Was it 'the nation's' function to facilitate the individual, be he Catholic, Protestant or Dissenter, in exercising his 'right' to educate his own children, or was 'the nation' to be itself responsible for inculcating 'national' values in the young, relegating their Catholicism, Protestantism or Dissent to the region of private instruction and belief? Did 'the nation' ultimately imply the secular state? These were the sorts of issues suddenly confronting O'Connell before he died. Finally, there was the surreptitious advance of incipient collectivism. Who in 1830 would have dreamt that, by 1847, public health, arterial drainage, industrial safety and factory hours would have been among the leading domestic issues of the day? Certainly not O'Connell, whose idea of the state was largely confined to the staples of late eighteenth-century central government – national defence, national revenue, foreign affairs, constitutional arrangements, and law and order in their largest aspects.

Thus, in his final phase, O'Connell anticipated in many ways our modern world. But there were other things in which he followed faithfully in the main line of contemporary thought, and yet others where he stayed deaf to the first whispers of the future. Meanwhile, he stood, in 1830, on a sort of plateau. Emancipation was behind him, Repeal before. The climb would be more difficult than ever.

CHAPTER 2

The Houseman

1830–1

I

'Othello's occupation's gone!': so men thought of O'Connell on the eve of his entry into the House of Commons in February 1830. For a quarter of a century he had been an agitator outside the walls of the legitimate political system. It was hardly to be expected that, approaching the age of fifty-five, he should take up successfully a new business, which was, so to speak, the very inversion of his old. He had, moreover, forced himself into a closed circle by hateful means. In the eyes of the British political classes, he had recklessly aroused the passions of the mob, and dangerously weakened the barriers to violence, licence and dispossession. As a popular agitator, he seemed to personify the force which threatened their hereditary domination. As Irish, as Catholic and as a mere bullyragging counsel, he was regarded as an intruder upon a company of gentlemen all the more so as he would no longer accept challenges to duels. As a public man, his intempterate vilification and open passion were adjudged 'low', and he was generally regarded as unprincipled. Charles Greville, a faithful reflector of upper-class reactions, summed him up in his journal at the end of 1830:

> Utterly lost to all sense of shame and decency, trampling truth and honour under his feet, cast off by all respectable men, he makes his faults and his vices subservient to the extension of his influence, for he says and does whatever suits his purpose for the moment, secure that no detection or subsequent exposure will have the slightest effect with those over whose minds and passions he rules with such despotic sway. He cares not whom he insults, because, having covered his cowardice with the cloak of religious scruples, he will resent no retaliation that can be offered him.[1]

Correspondingly his 'party', when it came to be formed in the Commons, was despised as cads. Even Le Marchant, an advanced and well-informed young liberal, noted in his diary in 1833:

His [O'Connell's] immediate followers are not [a] very creditable looking set. Fergus O'Connor has the appearance of a country attorney. He was involved some time ago in a charge of robbing the mail, and he did not come off with very clean hands . . . Daunt and O'Dwyer have more of the ruffian about them. Lalor shews that he has never been in gentleman's society before. I believe it was only last year that Sir Henry Parnell . . . presented [him] with a coat, being the first he had ever been the owner of, to appear in. Some of the others are not a whit better.[2]

Much of this was simple vulgar prejudice of the type more economically displayed by Wellington in his celebrated complaint about the 'shocking bad hats' to be found in the first 'Reformed Parliament'. But it also expressed the inveterate resentment of the elite, for O'Connell had ranged against him the peculiar combination of insolence and frightened ruthlessness which marks a privileged order under threat.

None the less Othello did make his way. O'Connell became one of the handful of men who came late to Parliament with a large reputation, and retained it undiminished. When one adds to his name those of Cobden, Joseph Chamberlain and Ernest Bevin, one has practically exhausted the category. With his marvellous plasticity, he caught 'the tone of the House' at once. Even his first appearance on the parliamentary stage, arguing the case for his own admission at the bar of the House on 18 May 1829, had been adjudged 'in manner and tact beyond what could have been conceived, and all that it should be';[3] and the following passage from his maiden speech proper on 4 February 1830 coruscates with the irony, clarity and deceptively simple art which rendered him immediately effective in the Commons:

What did it [the King's speech] contain? The first point was, that foreign nations continued to speak in terms of peace; but did they ever do otherwise when a war was on the point of breaking out, or even when the war itself had actually commenced? The next information was, that the Russian war was at an end. That was an important discovery, indeed; and, of course, none of them knew that before. They were then told that nothing was determined as to Portugal. And why? Ah! they were not told that. Was the character of Don Miguel then doubtful? Did any one doubt that he had usurped the throne of another, and endeavoured to cement his seat by the spilling of innocent blood? If so, why did the government of England shrink from the decision to which it ought to come? They were next told of the partial distress of the country. But was that a fact? He thought that the expressions which had fallen from the three hon. members on the other side who had supported the Address, were – the one, that the distress was general; the second, that the distress was extraordinary; and the third, that the distress was overwhelming. The chancellor of the Exchequer, however, had made one happy discovery; he had found an 'Oasis in the desert' – a country where no distress at all existed: and, who would have thought it? – that country was Ireland.[4]

It had been generally believed that a demagogue who fed on adulation would fail before an inimical, intimate and sophisticated club. Far from it: he could strike the right note at once. After his appearance at the bar of the House in May 1829, Lord Lansdowne told him, through Tom Moore, 'that from report he had conceived that, however suited to a popular assembly or mob, [O'Connell's] eloquence would not answer for the *refinement* of Parliament, but that he was now decidedly convinced of the contrary'.[5] Correspondingly, Greville reported on his maiden speech in a journal entry of 5 February 1830, 'O'Connell [made] his *début*, and a successful one, heard with profound attention, his manner good and his arguments attended and replied to.'[6] Nor was that speech an isolated oratorical piece. Four days later, he assured his friend James Sugrue that he was rapidly learning to handle the House and would soon be 'a constant speaker'.[7] In fact, during his first week in the Commons he spoke briefly or intervened at almost every sitting, and J. C. Hobhouse, an old parliamentary hand, observed that he invariably performed 'sensibly';[8] in context, there was probably no higher praise. From this beginning until three months before his death in 1847, O'Connell was a major (though often execrated) parliamentary figure. Some even considered him, in his prime, the most complete speaker in the Commons. One American observer wrote after visits to England in 1834 and 1837 during which

> I made it a point of professional duty . . . to hear the leading orators of the age; and . . . I would place the illustrious living in the following order of precedence. O'CONNELL, I think, is the finest orator of the age, for his rare concentration of intellectual gifts. He is logical, profound, sarcastic, bitter, humorous, playful, – and has a masterly command of all the earnest and touching passions. I have heard him at least fifty times, and in every variety of question; and every new display gave me a higher opinion of his varied, astonishing, and exquisite powers. In the commons, next to him, I would rank Lord STANLEY; then, Sir ROBERT PEEL . . . they are master of debate.[9]

As telling a tribute to O'Connell's personal dominance as any of the laughter and huzzas and howls which accompanied his speeches in the 1830s were the silence and murmurs of pretended agreement with which his final broken rambling was heard when he last addressed the House, a trembling, piteous shadow of his former self.

In many respects O'Connell was fortunate in the timing of his entry into Parliament. In British terms, 1830 represented one of those formative moments when one type of politics is in final disarray, with its successor still obscurely in the making. The eighteenth-century political system, in which the use of crown patronage and influence provided the basis of government, had lost its mainspring by 1815. The decay was not only virtually complete but also universally apparent after the death of Lord Liverpool in 1827. O'Connell's victory in the Clare by-election of 1828 had, therefore, a significance quite beyond either the immediate Catholic question or Irish disaffection. It seemed to sound the beginning of the end of the effortless ascendancy of the nobility and squirearchy in national politics. It was this aspect of the result which most deeply impressed such men as Wellington and Peel. What was to follow no one knew. But it seemed clear that some degree of power-sharing with other classes was inevitable, that the representative principle would advance, and that party would gradually shift its base from self- or family interest towards sectionalism and ideology, and ultimately supplant patronage as the main supplier of guaranteed House of Commons votes. As a conventional British radical on all these matters, O'Connell had at once a clear programme to push and a considerable body of potential allies.

In terms of Irish politics as well, 1830 marked a formative moment. The constitutional implications of the Act of Union were by now fully apparent. On the one hand, the Protestant interest as a whole had moved over to support the Union; a quasi-colonial government for Ireland, in the form of a lord lieutenancy and its surrounding apparatus, had, contrary to the original expectations, been retained; and successive British cabinets had opted for a species of 'indirect rule' based upon a privileged position for, and the near-monopoly of office and favours by, the loyalist minority. On the other hand, the Catholic Relief Act of 1829 had weakened and, in a limited sense, even broken into this redoubt; O'Connell had established independent sources of power, both by capturing county seats and by gathering and organizing intimidatory masses; and, in the process of attaining these objectives, he had succeeded in associating the Catholic Church with agitation, hostility to British rule and pressure for denominational equality. Thus, he occupied an interesting bridgehead. In which direction he would try to move, and how, and with whom, were still dark questions. But never since 1801 had Irish circumstances been nearly so uncertain or unfixed.

II

O'Connell spent his first two months in parliament learning his new craft. Generally, he made his own openings by getting up petitions in Ireland. This was not difficult; as he himself had said three years earlier, 'really we are so used to petition that we can get them drawn in every village by men from the highest to the poorest classes among us'.[10] During February and March 1830 he arranged through various Irish friends and agents for a large number to be forwarded to him for presentation in the House of Commons. These inspired petitions, which constituted the majority he received, reveal his initial strategy. Most of them concerned the exactions of the established church, municipal corruption or Catholic needs, though a few raised politically neutral grievances about bridges, market places and the like. Significantly, only two of the petitions related to Repeal of the Act of Union.

The matters which first engaged O'Connell closely were, however, different from these. On 4 February 1830 he procured a petition for a new and comprehensive legal code from his old ally, Edward Dwyer, the former secretary of the Catholic Association. Dwyer had gathered 10,000 signatures for him. 'Rational' legal reform had long been to the forefront in O'Connell's programmes. As he said of himself a few days after he had received Dwyer's petition, 'there never lived a more complete, entire, unchangeable enemy to law abuses as they exist – a more determined advocate for the *domestic* instead of the *factitious* – the *summary* in contradistinction to the *technical* form of procedure'.[11] This brought him close to the English radicals, in particular Bentham. O'Connell's other leading concern in his first session in the Commons was an Irish bastardy bill brought in by the government to equalize Ireland and England in this regard. O'Connell opposed the bill fiercely, arguing that to enable unmarried women to secure maintenance for their children from whichever unmarried man they nominated as the father would undermine Irish (as it had already undermined English) sexual morality. He even appealed directly to at least two Irish bishops for their aid in denouncing the proposed measure. All told, his opening parliamentary campaign may have been busy and eccentrically radical, but it was certainly not nationalistic.

On 6 April 1830, while in Dublin for the Easter recess, O'Connell set up the Society of the Friends of Ireland of all Religious Persuasions to promote the causes for which he had gathered petitions earlier in the year, as well as a handful of new issues. Repeal was one of the objectives, but the Society's initial emphasis was on financial rather than political 'Justice for Ireland' – the abolition of the malt, paper and coal duties and resistance to the government's proposed increase in the taxes on newspapers and spirits. Though its programme was generally moderate (with Repeal half-lost in the multitude of other appeals), the Society was suppressed by vice-regal proclamation within three weeks of its inauguration. Wellington's government had determined well beforehand to leave O'Connell no square of agitatory ground to stand on. The experience of the Catholic and New Catholic Associations of 1824–9 had steeled it against all cries of 'arbitrary rule'.

Possibly because of this gross provocation, possibly because he had learned while in Ireland that his mild conduct in the Commons was unpopular – his election agent in Clare thought it 'right . . . to tell you that people here seem to think you have made "a bad fight" in Parliament'[12] – O'Connell took the offensive upon his return to London. This took the form of virtually individual combat with his old court-room antagonist, the Irish solicitor-general, John Doherty. At the beginning of May 1830 O'Connell brought the Doneraile Conspiracy, and another recent case, in which Doherty had been accused of professional misconduct in his zealous pursuit of verdicts for the crown, before the Commons. In the sympathetic arena of the House, Doherty had the better of the first exchanges; O'Connell withdrew one motion and lost a second heavily. Doherty counter-attacked when, a little later, O'Connell appealed publicly for a run on the banks in Munster in the hope of weakening the Wellington administration. Proud of attaining and retaining office, Doherty mocked O'Connell as a strolling player who would wreck the theatre because the company refused to hire him. Proud of his own capacity as a lawyer and contemptuous of Doherty's incompetence, O'Connell, in return, mocked the 'stage trick, scenic skill and forensic manage-ment'[13] with which the solicitor-general strove to hide his professional inadequacy. O'Connell declared himself pleased with his own performance. 'I assure you', he told his friend, R. N. Bennett, on 25 June 1830, 'I taunted him very successfully upon his sore point – his ignorance. I also flung off the attack upon me gaily and with sufficient contempt for all parties concerned in it.'[14] But jousting with Doherty was a futile exercise, all too likely to be dismissed as a slanging-match of Dublin coal porters by supercilious English members. However ready a learner and effective a speaker O'Connell had proved himself to be, he had still not settled upon a profitable track to follow in the House of Commons.

A leading reason for his uncharacteristic tentativeness during the first half of 1830 was the supposed imminence of George IV's death, for this would precipitate a general election and a fresh parliament. Even before he entered the Commons, O'Connell had evidently planned, to some extent, for this occurrence. On 4 February 1830 Dwyer forwarded to him in London proposals for particular election agents for himself in co. Clare, his son Maurice in Drogheda, his son-in-law Christopher Fitz-Simon in co. Wicklow, and his admiring young supporter, Michael Quin, in co. Tipperary – evidence, as well, that, even at this early stage, O'Connell had hopes of building up a parliamentary 'connection' of his own after the eighteenth-century fashion. No one could predict how long the king would last. On 21 April O'Connell told Bishop Doyle of Kildare and Leighlin, 'the dropsy in his chest is believed quite incurable. He may live these four or five months – he may die in a week.'[15] Two months later he reported, 'There is nothing new. The Ministry, tottering, despised and despicable. The King lingering beyond expectation.'[16] In fact the king died on 26 June, almost immediately after this was written; but during the long months of waiting and uncertainty O'Connell had more or less mirrored the House of Commons as a whole in being both directionless and loth to make commitments.

Curiously, his dealings with his own constituency, Clare, took on something of the same colour. The achievement of Emancipation had transformed Irish electoral conditions. The disenfranchisement of the 40s. freeholders in the counties had suddenly swept away at least three-quarters of the voters. The Catholic hierarchy had solemnly enjoined their priests, on 3 February 1830, to refrain from any further political activity. Above all, the movement which O'Connell had constructed in the 1820s had achieved its specific goal and was practically demobilized. Rev. John Kenny, parish priest of Kilrush and (despite the episcopal prohibition) still a zealous electoral agent for O'Connell, told him frankly on 20 April 1830, 'Though the landlords could not secure the return of two [members for co. Clare] they could by threats, bribery etc. certainly return one.'[17] Kenny believed that O'Connell could retain the remaining seat, but also that he was unaware of the difficulties in the way of his success. In the first place, James O'Gorman Mahon intended to stand for the county, and although he was unlikely to defeat O'Connell, he could certainly embarrass him. O'Gorman Mahon's local following was considerable and he was prepared to spend a fortune (his new wife's dowry) both legally and illegally on a campaign. But, much worse, O'Connell had promised his friend Major William MacNamara in 1829 that he would back him in the next Clare election. O'Connell claimed that MacNamara had subsequently absolved him from this undertaking. This MacNamara denied, and since he had O'Connell's promise in writing and O'Connell could appeal only to a private conversation, the Major had the upper hand throughout. Tangled and increasingly public and bad-tempered exchanges culminated in a challenge from O'Connell's son, Morgan, which MacNamara, though a noted duellist, refused. By 9 July 1830 O'Connell had decided that the game was up in Clare: 'I am bound . . . too strictly', he privately confessed, 'that is the fact.'[18]

With the general election pressing, he wished desperately 'to be able to take a *decisive* course'.[19] Almost three months earlier he had prepared a fall-back position at Drogheda where Maurice would stand down in his favour should he decide to contest that seat. Since then he had either made or responded to electoral overtures in no less than six counties other than Clare – Wexford, Waterford, Cork, Galway, Louth and Meath – and would have gone for Kerry had not Lord Kenmare's brother been standing there. Finally, for whatever reason, O'Connell chose co. Waterford, although this placed him in direct competition with Thomas Wyse, the architect of the Catholic Association's crucial electoral victory there in 1826, for the popular vote. On 13 August 1830, after two days' polling, O'Connell proposed to retire in favour of Wyse, so disastrous were the consequences of dividing the liberal camp. Wyse took the hint, and instead retired in O'Connell's favour; at last, the 'Liberator's' return to parliament was assured. From beginning to end, it was a lamentable performance by one who had set up to be a professional politician. O'Connell had disturbed arrangements, strained supporters' loyalties, alienated Wyse and offended potential colleagues in at least half a dozen constituencies – and his son lost Drogheda into the bargain. Whatever parliamentary skills he had already demonstrated and however deep his reservoir of public gratitude in Ireland, it was high time for him to work out definite purposes and *modi operandi* outside as well as within the House of Commons.

III

Meanwhile, help came adventitiously. The 'July Revolution' in 1830 in France seemed not only to O'Connell but also to all other Irish liberals both a model and a confirmation that even more oppressive regimes than Wellington's might be suddenly and almost bloodlessly superseded. On 3 October one of his young supporters exulted in the 'aid that you [O'Connell] *must* derive from the exhilarating events that are every day springing up, an almost miraculous illustration of your principles and doctrines'.[20] Two days later, O'Connell congratulated himself on the latest turn of events: the 'Belgic revolution' against the Dutch was proving even 'more important than the French',[21] for – to him, at least – Belgium provided the additional analogy of a Catholic people freeing itself from an enforced union with a more populous, despotic, Protestant power. The British government saw things in much the same light as O'Connell. Although this augmented O'Connell's practical problems (in the increased use of vice-regal power to stifle agitation) it was none the less encouraging to learn that Peel was looking down the same vista as himself and seeing Dublin following the same insurrectionary road as Paris, unless restrained or diverted by one means or another.

Heartened by all this, O'Connell in effect launched a new campaign at a public dinner in Killarney on 7 October 1830. The original object was the celebration of the French and Belgian revolutions, but O'Connell turned it 'in truth, [into] a meeting for the repeal of the Union'.[22] Soon after, he set out his programme and priorities in a letter to Michael Staunton, editor of the *Morning Register*:

> The Union should now be agitated in every possible shape . . . [including] the formation of a permanent society. A permanent society is absolutely necessary in order to collect funds *in primo loco*, to collect funds *in secundo loco*, and to collect funds, thirdly and lastly, because we have both mind and body within us and all we want is the means of keeping the machine in regular and supple motion. Corruption was said by Burke to be the oil that makes the wheels of government go. Money is as necessary to keep in due operation the springs of popular excitement . . .
>
> On Friday [8 October] we got up a most numerous meeting in honour of the French and Belgic revolutions in the court house of Tralee and passed many honest resolves. On Saturday another meeting in the same court house, and resolutions in favour of petitions against the Subletting and Vestry bills, for radical reform and the Repeal of the Union. Today [11 October] I attend a dinner . . . at Kanturk; tomorrow I get a public dinner in Cork; on Wednesday [13] October], a meeting for redress of grievances in Youghal; on Thursday, a public dinner in Waterford; on Friday, a meeting in Waterford for redress of grievances . . .

AGITATE! AGITATE! AGITATE!²³

It was a measure of O'Connell's determination to end the hesitancy and uncertainty of the spring and summer of 1830 that he should, in the space of ten days, have addressed nine public meetings or banquets –for he immediately continued his 'progress' from Waterford to New Ross and Enniscorthy. Never before had he canvassed so intensively; never before had he given up so much of his sacrosanct 'vacation month', October, to work of any kind. Everywhere he was met with adulation. 'The manner', a contemporary observed, 'in which he was received during the journey from Darrynane [sic], until his arrival in Cork, was beyond anything he had ever before experienced. On the roads as he passed, crowds of peasantry met him, cheering for REPEAL as his carriage drove by.'[24] Everywhere, Repeal was in the forefront of the political demands; the city and county meeting at Waterford had been summoned for the sole purpose of getting up a petition in its favour. Dublin Castle responded on 18 October with a proclamation against an 'association . . . formed, or . . . about to be formed in the city of Dublin, under the name of the Irish Society for Legal and Legislative Relief, or the anti-union Association'.[25] It may also have inspired the 'Leinster Declaration' of 29 October (so-called because the Duke of Leinster chaired the meeting at which it was drawn up) repudiating the current agitation for Repeal and supporting 'the permanence of the British connection'.[26] O'Connell was producing not only a fresh agitation but also a fresh political polarization in Ireland; many of the 100 peers and MPs who signed the Declaration were whigs or liberals.

As soon as Parliament reassembled, Peel carried the war into O'Connell's camp. On 2 November 1830 he told the Commons that, through his Repeal agitation, O'Connell intended to sever Ireland's links with Britain by force, and that his movement must end in a revolution like that which had just overthrown the Bourbon regime in France. O'Connell of course denied that Repeal implied either violence or repudiation of the crown; and in the end he was unexpectedly supported. His letter to Dwyer next day described his triumph.

The scene last night in the House was a most extraordinary one. There never was yet any man so beset as I was when I went into the House and, during the first speeches, every allusion to me of an unkind nature was cheered. Although Peel attacked me directly, he sat down amid rapturous applause. I got up at once. They at first were disposed to slight me but I rebuked them with indignation and certainly took my wicked will of them fully and to my heart's content. I cannot be a judge of my own speaking but

I know that I threw out in my old [Catholic] Association style. I also know that the result was most cheering for me for the men who had been standing off from me before, and were not only cool but hostile, became of a sudden most cordial in their manner and confidential in their declarations. One perceives a change of this description better than one can describe it, and the change was complete.[27]

The change probably owed as much to the whigs' need of his support to bring down the tory government – he had pointedly described himself as the representative of Ireland rather than Waterford alone – as to his eloquent self-defence. O'Connell was about to be wooed politically, brief though the initial courtship proved to be.

Meanwhile, although he devised a series of 'Repeal breakfasts' in Dublin to circumvent the prohibitory proclamation of 18 October, there was little O'Connell could do immediately towards building up a permanent political organization. But he could pursue the other major objective set out in his letter to Staunton, collecting funds. He did not, however, follow the course which this letter had implied, the initiation of a 'Repeal Rent' after the pattern of the 'Catholic Rents' of 1824–9. Instead, as we have seen, on the advice of his new Admirable Crichton, P. V. Fitzpatrick, he decided to renew and render permanent the personal 'tribute' to himself, the O'Connell Testimonial of 1829. On 31 August 1830 he told Fitzpatrick, 'The elections are over . . . The harvest is getting in. The periodical distress is for the present over. This is the time to do something for the Fund. This, of course, is confidential; that is, it must not be known to come from me.' He warmly approved the scheme which Fitzpatrick had sketched out already for a designated Sunday (varying from diocese to diocese) when an annual collection would be taken up at the church doors. This was a variant of the method used in collecting the Catholic Rent, but O'Connell's financial goal remained exactly what it had been in 1824: 'one shilling each from one seventh of the Irish Catholics would be one million of shillings or £50,000; more, in fact, than could be necessary'.[28] Fitzpatrick assured O'Connell that he had 'never for a moment . . . lost sight of the fund', and in particular approved of O'Connell's suggestion that it was best to begin at Waterford, if its new bishop, Abraham, who was a whig and an enemy of Repeal, could be manoeuvred into sanctioning a diocesan collection. A 'select deputation' could then be mustered to beard Archbishop Murray of Dublin: 'his cooperation. . . , if obtained, will almost beyond doubt secure the rest of the bishops'. The final step would be a visit to each important district before the appointed Sunday 'to put the collectors in harness'. Fitzpatrick concluded with a foretaste of his skill as political manager, not least in his tactful management of his 'master':

> The idea of the shilling subscription is good but its promulgation must be immediately antecedent to the day of actual collection. It must apply to the 'great public' and by no means be permitted to interfere with the contribution of larger sums from those able and willing to give such. It was my intention this morning to have suggested to you to write some letters to the journals on attractive topics or declaratory of your intended course of proceedings in the next Parliament. Such things are useful stimulants and I am happy to perceive you have anticipated me by a communication to the Waterford papers . . . You will of course appear in the shape of an eloquent eulogy [by public letter] on the French Revolution . . . It may be well timed to pay a compliment in some of your earliest papers to the bishops and clergy. There will be little difficulty in doing this from the general admission that no praise can in their regard savour of flattery.[29]

Already we can see why Dr Angus Macintyre concluded that 'In O'Connell's political machine, the discreet, efficient and charming Fitzpatrick ... played an unobtrusive but vital part, the full significance of which is missed if he is described simply as O'Connell's faithful supporter or as his financial agent.'[30] Early in October 1830 he proceeded to execute the first part of his plan in Waterford. He worked on Abraham, not directly, but through friendly priests at a diocesan assembly at Cahir. Lest Abraham suspect that he was being manipulated, Fitzpatrick 'quarter[ed] myself at Clonmel where I shall have it in my power to canvass quietly some of the influential clergy as they pass to the meeting'. Characteristically, he did not confine himself to the matter immediately in hand. Having noticed that O'Connell had recently offended J. M. Galwey and his supporters, who were important in Waterford politics, by a chance reference in a public letter, he suggested 'the *possible* good policy of your dropping in upon Mr. Galwey on your route from Cork. He may be and I believe *is* worth "whistling back", particularly as I find "the unfriendly" in this district in somewhat greater force than I was prepared to expect.'[31]

It was clear that, in Fitzpatrick, O'Connell had at last found answers to the problems of financing his agitation and monitoring and maintaining a national political machine. At the same time he had found in the Parliamentary Intelligence Office which he set up in Dublin and its 'curator', Dwyer, a metropolitan centre and management safe from repression even under the current laws and exercise of vice-regal discretions. In short, O'Connell had rapidly acquired or thrown together the nucleus of a major movement before he returned to the House of Commons in the late autumn of 1830.

IV

'I attend the House constantly from its sitting to its rising', O'Connell wrote on 3 December 1830.[32] This claim to assiduity was thoroughly justified; and between being assailed as a demagogue and charlatan for raising the Repeal cry in Ireland, and himself assailing the Irish administration (and especially Doherty) as brutal and unscrupulous, he had been the storm centre of many a debate during the preceding month. In a typical exchange, on 9 November, a junior minister, George Dawson, called him 'a man of vulgar mind and mean ideas';[33] while O'Connell rejoined that he would not be intimidated by 'placeholders, who revel on the hard earnings of the people'.[34] When, however, Wellington resigned on 16 November 1830 and the whigs under Earl Grey took office after decades in the wilderness, it looked for a while as if O'Connell might become a regular government supporter, or at least be politically neutralized. After all, when his entry into the Commons had first seemed imminent, he had observed to the Knight of Kerry, 'I need not tell you that if I get in I will be a Whig but certainly one "des plus prononcés" because my opinions upon reform are of the most strong description'.[35] Moreover, it was still generally assumed in the British governing circle that O'Connell was in politics for money and other personal ends. Accordingly, an attempt was made to buy him off as soon as – or possibly just before – the whigs gained office.

The Marquess of Anglesey, destined to be the new Irish lord lieutenant, interviewed O'Connell at least twice in London about this time. 'Lord Anglesey', O'Connell wrote later, probably with reference to a meeting between them in mid-November, 'sent for me and talked to me for two hours to prevail on me *to join* the Government, . . . he went so far as to discuss my private affairs in order to prevail on me to repair my fortunes.'[36] Rumour had it that O'Connell was offered the Irish mastership of the rolls and other judgeships (including the chief justiceship of Calcutta!), and his own statement seems also to imply an invitation to accept a political office. The mastership of the rolls, with a knighthood and perhaps ultimately a peerage, would certainly have been attractive earlier in his career. For years O'Connell (and still more Mary) had looked forward to his ending in eminence on the bench, with a large, secure income, an elevated social standing and ample leisure. But by now he would have been generally condemned at home as the betrayer of his country had he taken the king's shilling in any form – and by no one more grievously than Mary. 'My dearest love', she wrote to him on 1 December 1830,

> Thank God you have acted like yourself, and your wife and children have more reason to be proud of you now than they ever were. Had you acted differently from what you have done it would have broken my heart. You cannot abandon the people who have always stood by you, and for whom you have sacrificed so much . . . Had you been betrayed into an acceptance of the terms offered by Government you would die of a broken heart before six months expired. You now stand firmly on the affections and on the love of your countrymen, and when that country is aware of the *splendid sacrifice* you have made for them, . . . they will strain every nerve to reward you. I shall hold up my head higher than ever I did. I shan't be afraid to look at the people as I certainly should if you were a titled pensioner of the Government . . . I never saw anything like the pleasure that danced in their [his children's] eyes when assured of your refusal. May God bless you, my own love! Words are inadequate to tell you how I love and respect you for this late act, so like and so worthy of yourself.[37]

The government, however, gave him no credit for principle. Even Anglesey, who probably judged O'Connell more charitably than any other of the whig leaders, concluded that he was 'flying at higher game than a judgeship . . . he is secure of a better income from the deluded people than *any Government* can venture to give to *any Person* whatever'.[38] Anglesey also attributed the reason given by O'Connell for rejecting whig pleas for support – that is, their retention of Doherty as Irish solicitor-general – to pique and fear of '*his Master* (for so Doherty certainly was in the H. of Commons)'.[39] Despite, or perhaps because of, this, no less than three separate attempts were made between mid-November and mid-December 1830 to win O'Connell over to the whigs' side. After the failure of the last, however, Anglesey decided that there was nothing for it but war to the death against O'Connell in Ireland, and accordingly began to strike military postures before himself and others, even prior to his setting sail for Dublin. 'I saw him [O'Connell] yesterday, for an hour and a half', he wrote to the Irish whig Lord Cloncurry on 16 December 1830,

> I made no impression upon him whatever; and I am now thoroughly convinced that he is bent upon desperate agitation . . . For the love of Ireland I deprecate agitation . . . But if the sword is really to be drawn, and with it the scabbard is to be thrown away – if I, who have suffered so much for her [Ireland], am to become a suspected character, and to be treated as

an enemy – if, for the protection of the State, I am driven to the dire necessity of again turning soldier, why then I must endeavour to get back into old habits . . .[40]

Conversely, O'Connell blew hot and cold in his attitude towards the whigs over the same period. At one point he endorsed a plan 'for a procession to meet the Marquess of Anglesey' upon his landing at Dublin.[41] But almost immediately he changed his mind. 'I decidedly think', he re-instructed Dwyer on 1 December, 'the anti-unionists ought not to give him any *glorification*. This is the result of my deliberate judgment.'[42] Six days later, in response to a fresh government overture asking him to state his demands other than Repeal, he re-iterated his refusal to accept any office or favour for himself and set out an alarming catalogue of twelve political 'wants'. Significantly, several of these were specifically 'Catholic' in character, while others aimed at breaking the exclusive Protestant hold upon the Irish corporations and grand juries. O'Connell may well have decided, before he returned to Ireland for the parliamentary break, that the Catholic card was now the one to play. From London, he tried to stir Archbishops Curtis and Murray, as well as MacHale of Killala and perhaps other Irish bishops, into raising publicly the issue of Catholic education.

From the moment that he reached Dublin, Anglesey seemed set upon a policy of destroying O'Connell's Repeal movement in all its manifestations. Between 26 December 1830 and 13 January 1831 he issued no less than four proclamations suppressing meetings in favour of Repeal, the 'Repeal breakfasts', the Parliamentary Intelligence Office and the long-promised 'permanent organization' for the agitation, which O'Connell attempted to institute on 6 January. Anglesey also tried to forestall any repetition of the various legal manoeuvres by which O'Connell had kept the Catholic Association alive by proclaiming – blanket-wise – 'any adjourned, renewed, or otherwise continued meetings of the same, or of any part thereof, under any name, pretext, or device whatsoever'.[43] Finally on 18 January 1831 he had O'Connell and five of his lieutenants arrested on thirty-one charges of 'evading' either the recent proclamations or the Proclamation Act itself.

All this was sailing very close to arbitrary government. Shortly before he left England, Anglesey himself had stated publicly that, although he was a determined opponent of Repeal, he considered agitation on its behalf perfectly allowable. In the same vein, Melbourne, the home secretary, told the lord lieutenant that, while any attempt to revive the methods of the Catholic Association should be stamped on, the historic constitutional rights to discuss and petition must not be infringed. Thomas Wallace, a leading Irish liberal lawyer, who disapproved strongly of both the Repeal movement and O'Connell's current conduct, none the less spoke of Anglesey's charges as 'savour[ing] strongly of *illegality* and *oppression* . . . to an extent which *greatly* endangers public liberty'.[44] Given the whigs' self-image as the party of civil and religious freedom, and the consequent embarrassment if they persisted for long with government by ukase in Ireland, it seems likely that the real purpose of the repression was to force O'Connell to abandon Repeal and compose his differences with the government. Similarly, it is difficult to credit that O'Connell believed his own repeated assertions that Repeal was imminent. It seems much more probable that he was trying, through whipping up a campaign for Repeal, to bring the whigs to more satisfactory terms on Irish issues – and, equally important in his eyes, in the filling of Irish offices. Viewed in this light, the apparently dramatic series of events, set in train by the respective arrivals of O'Connell and Anglesey in Ireland, may perhaps best be interpreted as the continuation – by other means – of the bargaining of November-December in London.

At any rate, in the game which followed his arrest, O'Connell 'proceeded to outwit and outmanoeuvre his opponents'.[45] He worked on several fronts. Former Irish liberal and whig allies were used to canvass in London and Dublin on his behalf. Two of them, Cloncurry and Lord Meath, were pressed to join in a reform campaign, in which the issue of Repeal would be omitted. A run on the banks in Munster was attempted, though only tentatively, lest the provincial economy be really injured. More important, O'Connell used all his legal lore and ingenuity – ultimately successfully – to find a way out of the dilemma, a course by which he himself might escape all penalties without the government having to lose face by dropping the prosecutions. His secret negotiations with the ministry – which neither side would admit to having initiated but which began soon after his arrest – make it certain that he was well aware of, and prepared to allow for, the government's difficulties, and also that his price for dropping the Repeal agitation was an official programme of Irish amelioration. But his most effective move of all was his decision to oppose his close friend, the minister Lord Duncannon, in a forthcoming by-election in co. Kilkenny, should the government persist with its prosecutions. 'Lord Duncannon', he wrote to the go-between, R. N. Bennett, on 7 February 1831, is a man for whom I have the highest respect, esteem and regard but he is now 'one of my prosecutors' and as the Ministry are determined to *crush* me, I must carry the political war into their quarters. He must expect opposition if the prosecutions go on. I have arranged materials for a powerful opposition. I have entered into the details of finding money and attornies and I believe he will find it a hard task to succeed, coming forward in the shape of one of my prosecutors.[46]

O'Connell had left it much too late to defeat Duncannon. But his intervention even at the eleventh hour reduced the majority – on Duncannon's home ground – to a mere sixty-one votes. As Dwyer claimed on 26 February, 'Had a committee been formed a week earlier or had you not been prevented by other arrangements from going to Kilkenny, there can be no doubt but the Colonel [Butler, Duncannon's opponent] would be the sitting member.'[47] The lesson for the whigs was unmistakable: that they might well lose up to twenty Irish seats in a general election, should O'Connell oppose them, and that meanwhile it would be dangerous to appoint any Irish county member to ministerial office since this would bring on a by-election. O'Connell's readymade solution to their problem was now tacitly accepted. He pleaded guilty to certain of the charges in the knowledge that he would not appear for judgment until after the Proclamation Act had expired and the measure under which he had been prosecuted become inoperative. When the case came up again in May, it simply fell to the ground as lacking any current legal basis.

For his part, O'Connell was freed from the obligation of attempting to renew the Repeal agitation by the introduction of a widesweeping parliamentary reform bill on 1 March 1831. This he could hail (in a letter to the 'People of Ireland') as a measure deserving 'the ardent and decided support of every friend of national liberty';[48] its passage was now the foremost political objective. The whigs reciprocated by welcoming O'Connell's return to the Commons. 'You cannot conceive', he told Mary on 5 March, 'what a change there is already towards me in the House.'[49] None the less he feared for his reception when his turn would come to speak upon the bill. 'Only think', he wrote to her again on 8 March, the sixth day of the debate, 'of my being so absurd as to feel nervous in the rascally House. Yet so it is . . . My own darling heart, my fame as a parliamentary orator depends on this day and I am speaking to an exhausted subject.'[50] But he triumphed. Next day Greville noted, 'O'Connell was very good, and vehemently cheered by the Government, Stanley, Duncannon, and all, all differences giving way to their zeal.'[51] Congratulations poured in, but the praise which he seems to have valued most was that of the English attorney- and solicitor-general who pronounced his to have been the most effective and magnanimous speech in the entire debate. At last, he and the whig government were effectively in alliance. In the general election of May 1831, which followed the House of Lords' rejection of the first reform bill, O'Connell worked in complete harmony with and for the ministry, parcelling out Irish candidatures, helping to secure the return of ministers such as Parnell and Duncannon, and even suggesting to Duncannon that he should be supported from whig party funds if he abandoned his safe county seat and used his name to try to wrest some borough from the tories. It is not surprising that he should have been swept up in the enthusiasm for reform (one of his life-long political passions) or happy to find himself flattered and courted by the administration. But neither was it altogether wise to have responded so unreservedly. In particular, in his eager pursuit of reform in Britain, he failed to exploit his current power, which was very great, to secure an equivalent advance in Ireland.

V

O'Connell was necessarily a Janus-faced politician. He was a member of Parliament because he was supported by the masses; his power in the House of Commons derived ultimately from their compacted power. Grey observed in 1831 that O'Connell's mastery of the Irish people had provided him 'With the greatest opportunities & the most powerful means that almost any man ever possessed of raising his own character, & serving the Publick',[52] and such an influence over millions needed to be constantly cultivated. But it would not do for *vox populi* to employ the same accent or forms of speech inside as outside the House of Commons. O'Connell's other political role was that of a gentleman in an assemblage of gentlemen, governed by complex rules of conduct, and (in the strict sense) highly conventional in its mode of debate and acceptable tone of oratory. Like many others, Stanley made much of the contrast between the O'Connell of Westminster and the O'Connell of the Dublin public meeting, who 'habitually bespattered' his opponents 'amongst the mobs'.

> For no two persons could be more different from each other than the hon. member for Waterford speaking in that House, and the same hon. Member elsewhere, or rather somebody who bore his name, for he could scarcely

believe it to be the same person, when 'courting the most sweet voices of the rabble'.[53]

It is worth exemplifying the dualism at length; it goes to the heart of O'Connell's difficulties in blazing the trail of the democratic parliamentary representative. First let us take an extract from his speech in the debate of 12 May 1830 on the Doneraile conspiracy trial. O'Connell's accusations were grave. He charged Doherty with tampering with or manufacturing evidence in order to secure convictions (and with them death sentences) in a murder trial, and the British government with appointing a juvenile incompetent, Lord Francis Leveson Gower, as Irish chief secretary, with the task of defending these malpractices. Yet O'Connell's language never crossed the bounds of controlled derision and disdain and licensed parliamentary invective.

What care I, then, for the unwise arrogance – the unfounded presumption – the overweening vanity of his [Leveson Gower's] censure. May I continue to deserve it! His office is, indeed, one of great promise. It is part of his public career. He is on his road (for such is the miserable destiny of this country) to still higher station. He is an apprentice in politics, and he dares to censure me, a veteran in the warfare of my country. His office is a mere apprenticeship. The present premier [Wellington] was Secretary in Ireland – the present Secretary of State [Peel] was Secretary in Ireland – so was the present Chancellor of the Exchequer [Goulburn]. Their juvenile statesmanship was inflicted upon my unhappy country. I have heard that barbers train their apprentices by making them shave beggars. My wretched country is the scene of the political education of our statesmen, and the noble Lord is the shave-beggar of the day for Ireland. I have done with the noble Lord – I disregard his praise – I court his censure – I cannot express how strongly I repudiate his pretensions to importance – and I defy him to point out any one act of his administration to which my countrymen could look with admiration or gratitude, or with any other feelings than those of total disregard. His name will serve as a date in the margin of the history of Dublin Castle – his memory will sink in contemptuous oblivion.[54]

This was classical public speaking. The short, driving sentences; the triple flourishes, the epigrammaticism and antitheses; the banked fire and finely calculated satire; the precision of terminology – 'proper words in their proper places'[55] – all manifest O'Connell's eighteenth-century training. The *beau ideal* of his boyhood had been Grattan; Douai and St Omer had grounded him in Cicero and Renaissance exercises for forming public men, in 1791–3. But form and dexterity apart, the passage was aglow with a master-image. 'Shave beggar' expressed both perfectly and passionately Ireland's resentment of the contemptuous relegation of its government to the second or third level of significance, and of the contemptuous assumption that it harboured merely a mendicant and subjected race. For nearly two decades, the phrase was to be wielded, often with deadly effect, in Irish assaults upon British policy and administration.

The contrasting declamation was occasioned by a proclamation for the suppression of dangerous societies issued by the then Irish chief secretary, Sir Henry Hardinge, in the absence of the lord lieutenant, on 18 October 1830. At a public dinner in Dublin four days later O'Connell, to the accompaniment of 'cheers and laughter', denounced 'English soldier-scribes, illegal proclamations and tall, raw-boned Scotchmen'.

> I arraign that paltry, contemptible little English soldier [Hardinge], that had the audacity to put his pitiful, and contemptible name to an atrocious Polignac Proclamation (loud cheers) – and that too in Ireland, in my own country – in this green land – the land of Brownlow – the country of Grattan – now in his grave – (hear) – the land of Charlemont and of the 70,000 volunteers – the heroes of the immortal period of '82 (cheers). In that country it is that a wretched English scribe – a chance-child of fortune and of war, urged on by his paltry, pitiful lawyerlings – puts his vile name to this paltry proclamation putting down freemen (cheers). I would rather be a dog and bay the moon, than the Irishman who would tamely submit to so infamous a proclamation. I have not opposed it hitherto, because that would implicate the people and give our enemies – the English Major-General and his lawyerling staff – a triumph (hear, hear, hear). But I will oppose it; and that too, not in the way that the paltry castle scribe would wish – by force. No; Ireland is not in a state for repelling force by force. Too short a period has elapsed since the cause of contention between Protestants and Catholics was removed – too little time has been given for healing the wounds of factious contention, to allow Ireland to use physical force in the attainment of her rights or the punishment of wrong . . . as yet the progress of reconciliation is not completed, and until it is, Ireland – being divided – would be too weak for the physical force of her enemies. I do not advocate the display of physical force at any time. God forbid that such a desire should influence my conduct. I only allude to the circumstance to show that even were physical force justifiable, Ireland is not now in a condition to warrant its display (cheers). Well, I obeyed – the people obeyed the proclamation – they did not submit to the base mandate of a paltry Englishman (cheers). No; I never will submit to such audacity; and I here promise that I will never cease to pursue the – miscreants shall I call them? – no, that would be too hard a phrase; – but I will call them the despicable, base, miserable, paltry creatures, with bad heads and worse

hearts, who issued that nefarious proclamation (cheers) – in that place, where, and at that period when, reason shall be listened to. I do not mean to say that I shall be attended to in the rotten, borough-mongering Parliament. But I trust the day is not far distant when reason shall be heard, and when fine and imprisonment shall mark the foul conduct of Secretary Major-General Sir Henry Hardinge (loud cheers).[56]

The audience being predominantly middle class, this was a higher order of bombast than O'Connell used at outdoor popular meetings. None the less, it might be dismissed, at first sight, as rhodomontade. It was pitted with apparently meaningless abuse – 'paltry', 'base', 'vile', 'lawyerling' and the like. It shamelessly thumped the sentimental-patriotic drum, with scarcely a pretence of relevance. It was, practically speaking, self-contradictory – the audience was enjoined to obey but not to submit to the proclamation, and O'Connell promised to 'pursue the miscreants' in Parliament, but not until after it had been reformed!

Yet it would be quite mistaken to write off such a speech as mere rambling braggadocio. On the contrary, it was calculated rhetoric. In effect, O'Connell was instructing his followers to conform to the proclamation and abstain from violence. But it would not do for an order of this kind to be issued in plain language. Demagogues need their own sort of tact. O'Connell had therefore to cover the retreat, by vague – in fact, illusory – indications of future legal and parliamentary challenges to the proclamation, and by working up his audience to a sense of their unimpaired power and pride by references to the glories of 1782 and the force at Ireland's command once sectarian divisions were obliterated. It did no harm to hint that this force might be physical, before rapidly repudiating such a thought. Still more to the purpose, the degradation of opponents through personal abuse, in order to diminish their seeming formidability, or if possible render them ludicrous instead of fearsome figures, was part of O'Connell's stock-in-trade. This explains his strange antistrophes upon the unfortunate Hardinge, whom he and his audience alike must have known to be the mere instrument of official policy in this case.

It was only to be expected that the Aunt Sallies of these affairs should resent the rain of verbal missiles. In accordance with the accepted code, Hardinge desired 'satisfaction' for the insults heaped upon him. O'Connell had, however, long made it clear that he would fight no further duels. They were, he now argued, against both conscience and reason – an exchange of pistol shots being quite irrelevant to the rights and wrongs of any political dispute. He was, he said, always ready to disavow an established *error of fact*, but nothing more. All this was rehearsed in O'Connell's reply to Hardinge, published in the Dublin newspapers on 24 October 1830. But his principal defence was that he had spoken of Hardinge only as an official, not as an individual. 'He [O'Connell] spoke of Sir Henry Hardinge in his *public* capacity as an instrument of despotism. He did not say one word of him in his private capacity.'[57] It was natural enough that O'Connell should take this line. From his standpoint, the scurrility ladled upon Hardinge was purely in the line of business. It had nothing to do with Hardinge personally. Simply, the exigencies of agitation demanded that any relevant officer of the crown should be so assailed. But it was also natural that Hardinge, learning that he had been paraded in public as a 'paltry, contemptible little English soldier . . . a wretched English scribe, a chance-child of fortune and of war', should feel that he had been intolerably affronted. If not the horsewhip, at least the challenge was the ordained response. O'Connell's refusal to conform to the most elementary rule governing 'satisfaction' exposed him to the scorn of his social equals. Cowardice was the usual explanation of his conduct, counter-scurrility and slander its common consequence. Worse still, his attitude tended to place him in – to use the contemporary phraseology – the blackguardly as against the gentlemanly class. During 1832, for instance, the Irish chief secretary, E. G. Stanley, and the former Irish solicitor-general, Philip Crampton, declared that O'Connell had no claim to being a gentleman because he insulted opponents while refusing the consequent challenges to duels. Nothing could be more hurtful to his *amour propre*, or more harmful to him in the high politics of Westminster, than to be pronounced *déclassé*.

Yet O'Connell's two voices, the parliamentary and the popular, were not really disconnected. Each was a means of attaining and exercising influence. Largely by his forensic skill, he accumulated political capital in Ireland, and largely by his forensic skill, he spent it judiciously in the House of Commons. It was, in the last analysis, a single process. Unfortunately for O'Connell, his particular popular and professional techniques, although well-tried and proven over quarter of a century, necessitated his playing contradictory public roles, with contradictory lines, styles and intonations. But to abandon either would have impoverished, perhaps even rendered nugatory, his performance.

CHAPTER 3

Systole and Diastole

1831–2

I

In the general election of 1831, O'Connell fought something akin to a national campaign. He did not, however, fight on his own behalf but, as has been said, made common cause with the 'Reformers' generally. He busied himself arranging 'liberal' candidatures and electoral committees in at least nine of the Munster and Leinster counties, as well as in several boroughs; and almost uniformly he succeeded. His dealings reveal a remarkably close knowledge of, and capacity to manipulate, the local power-systems. Correspondingly, his zeal in 1831 extended his range of influence. Perhaps the most striking instance of his control of things was his response to Lord Duncannon's plea for an uncontested re-election in co. Kilkenny. At a word from O'Connell, Duncannon's opponent withdrew, although O'Connell modestly disclaimed all the credit. 'Col. Butler', he told Duncannon on 29 April 1831, '*put* the compliment on me of having declined in consequence of my letter to him. But I am too candid to do so by you. All, however, is safe in that quarter.'[1] He acted in such a masterful fashion in this case because Duncannon was his main link with the government in London. It was through Duncannon that he pressed (not always in vain) requests for minor return-favours. Duncannon was also the conduit for his demands that the Irish administration cooperate in securing the return of members favourable to the reform bill. Here he was less successful. Anglesey and Stanley appear to have allowed their dislike and distrust of O'Connell to outweigh the normal duty and interest of a government at election times, which was of course to use its official influence on behalf of 'friends'.

O'Connell's manoeuvres created difficulties for himself. In his current constituency, co. Waterford, he attempted a complex play in order to increase the 'Reform' representation all round. This involved securing the Hon. George Lamb, a junior minister, for his running mate. When Lamb refused to stand, O'Connell too withdrew from Waterford and at the eleventh hour plumped instead for co. Kerry, although this offended some of his warmest Waterford admirers. When it seemed as if he might have a dangerous contest on his hands in Kerry after all, he worked might and main for an invitation (duly received) to stand for co. Tipperary. In the end, however, he and another 'Reformer' won Kerry easily, after he had put the family political machine into rapid operation by writing to his brother John on 2 May 1831,

> You must now instantly begin to work. You must ransack the county. Speak to the bishop. Engage every voter. Write every priest. Send Maurice and Charles Brenan [O'Connell's cousins] in every direction where a voter can be had. Write to James [O'Connell's brother] to come home at once and assist us. Do not deceive yourself as to my majority . . . I suppose the members of the [Tralee] Chamber of Commerce will become my committee. If proper arrangements can [be] made the expense will be as nothing.[2]

Significantly, O'Connell's platform in Kerry was limited to two specific issues, the great reform bill and the abolition of negro slavery. Neither in public nor in private did he so much as mention Repeal – or any other specifically Irish matter – during the entire campaign. If his opponent, the Knight of Kerry, is to be believed, however, O'Connell's supporters did not hesitate to enlist religion on their side. In excusing his own early withdrawal from the contest, the Knight reported,

> The Priesthood were marshalled under a Jesuit Bishop. I was depicted as a traitor at once to King and Country . . . my vote [against] Reform was an attack on the People and their Religion . . . – the effect was a general fury equal to that raised against Vesey [Fitzgerald] in Clare [in the by-election of 1828] and with much more of personal rancour. The effect would have been the detaching of almost every Catholic freeholder from even the best Landlords – and in the conflict I should have polled little more than the Protestants giving Dan a universal triumph . . .[3]

Only slowly did O'Connell's informal alliance with the whigs (who triumphed in the general election, most of all in Ireland) begin to crumble. He forbore to resent Stanley's repulsive formality both during and immediately after the electoral campaign, and returned to Westminster at the beginning of June 1831 in high hope that the government would reward his loyalty by a more conciliatory approach to Irish issues. But after interviews in London with both Anglesey and Stanley, he concluded that although 'they desire to do good to Ireland' their leading principle was 'English domination . . . [and] as the control of Ireland *must* be obtained as the *primary* object, everything Irish is looked at through that medium'.[4] This reading of official policy was vindicated all too soon. When a new version of the Irish parliamentary reform bill was presented, it ran on lines markedly different from those designed for the remainder of the United Kingdom. The government gave Ireland only five additional seats whereas Scotland received eight. This left Scotland with almost twice as high a parliamentary representation per head of population. The new English and Welsh representation was more than twice as high as the Irish – indeed, in terms of county seats (in general the most 'open' and 'popular' part of the system) the disproportion was almost 5:1. Meanwhile, several Irish boroughs with electorates well below the new British minimum were retained intact. Franchise reform showed a similar disparity. The 40s. freeholder was enfranchised in England and Wales but remained unenfranchised in Ireland; and the English registration machinery was now incomparably superior. But even the lack of uniformity was not uniform. The government insisted upon a £10 household suffrage in English and Irish boroughs alike, although it was well recognized that the true Irish equivalent would have been a £5, and not a £10, valuation. This correspondence had, however, precisely the same motivation as the various distinctions. The ministry was determined to avoid, wherever possible, changes which would increase either the democratic or the Catholic element in the Irish electorate. The whigs' desire to do Ireland (or even their own party) 'good' was indeed secondary to their desire to keep Ireland secure under Britain's domination.

O'Connell, unpleasantly surprised when Stanley re-presented the Irish parliamentary reform bill in the Commons on 1 July 1831, described the few changes from the original measure (minor concessions on the county leasehold franchise), as 'Stanley's humbug "improvements" '.[5] But he was inhibited from pressing home his attack by his own tactical error in having welcomed the first Irish bill warmly in the course of his 'generous' reform speech of 8 March. He compounded this mistake by parleying privately with various ministers during the summer and early autumn of 1831. By the end of the parliamentary session, he had gained nothing more than further trivial amendments in the leasehold franchise clauses. All the great matters – the number and size of the Irish constituencies and the principal qualifications for enfranchisement – remained untouched. O'Connell blamed Stanley exclusively for this failure; he believed that the other members of the cabinet whom he had seen were genuinely sympathetic to his representations. Meanwhile Stanley had given further offence by introducing an Irish arms bill, also on 1 July 1831. 'It is an atrocious act . . .', O'Connell wrote next day, 'if passed, [it] would just come to this that whilst the Orange Yeomanry got arms from Government, the people were to be deprived of all means of preventing their throats from being cut with impunity.'[6] At this stage, still counting on his utility to and his cordial relations with the whigs, he was as confident of securing the withdrawal of the arms bill as he was of winning substantial modifications in the Irish reform proposals. He had no doubt that Stanley and 'the hare-brained and vain Anglesey' would have to retreat 'under the pressure of public opinion'.[7] But once again the government yielded little; the arms bill was eventually enacted with only one significant amendment.

Gradually, the enmity between O'Connell and Stanley deepened. On O'Connell's side, the seeds of rancour were probably first sown at the time of his arrest in January 1831 when (as he later put it), under Stanley's directions from Dublin Castle, 'common thief-takers were sent to his house, to drag him from the bosom of his family'.[8] Stanley's hauteur, contempt for 'inferiors', dexterity in debate and unconcealed support for the continuance of Protestant Ascendancy in Ireland, perfected O'Connell's enmity. For his part, Stanley resented O'Connell's incessant attacks upon the partiality, corruption and incompetence of his administration in Ireland; on 10 August 1831 he broke out against O'Connell's 'coming down there [the House of Commons] night after night and without proper notice charging the Irish Government with having acted unfairly in this case, in that case, or in the other case'.[9] Correspondingly, O'Connell scarcely exaggerated when he spoke of 'the anti-Irish party which he [Stanley] commanded in the Cabinet'.[10] Their parliamentary exchanges soon became virtually individual combat.

None the less, O'Connell did not yet break with Grey's government, and the Lords' rejection of the second (or 'great') reform bill on 8 October 1831 brought him back, immediately and fully, to its support. Even before this happened the more liberal faction in the cabinet, led by Lords Brougham and Holland, had been pressing hard to win (or rather buy) O'Connell over to a permanent alliance with the whigs. Grey himself, though he loathed both O'Connell and his politics, admitted that his power was extraordinary, and his backing necessary for the carrying of reform. The details of the government's consequent offers and approaches to O'Connell are once more obscure. But we can guess something of their nature from two letters to Richard Barrett, editor of *The Pilot*, in which O'Connell wrote, on 5 October 1831, '*Strictly, strictly private* and most confidential. I COULD be Attorney-General – in one hour',[11] and on 8 October, 'Expect to see me about Tuesday week [18 October], *not* Master of the Rolls nor Sir Daniel but honest and true and your sincere friend'.[12] We know certainly that, at the request of Sir Henry Parnell, the secretary-at-war, Bishop James Doyle proffered him some post or other about this time, and on 26 October he actually received a patent of precedence admitting him to the inner Irish bar – an honour and advantage which he had coveted for twenty years. A few days earlier Grey had expressed the hope that this favour (already in train) together with the promise of a post for one of his sons-in-law (probably Nicholas Ffrench who had recently married his daughter, Betsey) would prove 'only preliminaries to a more useful connection with him [O'Connell]'.[13]

Although Doyle told Parnell on 17 October 1831 that his interview with O'Connell was 'more successful than I anticipated',[14] there is no evidence to suggest that O'Connell seriously considered accepting either political or judicial office at this time. But he was certainly ready to enter into an informal concordat with the whigs in return for the introduction of a sort of spoils system in the Irish administration. He expected it to be systematically 'liberalized'. As he put the point to Duncannon on 19 October,

> The government [at Dublin Castle] is, in point of fact, as essentially anti-Irish and Orange as it was in the days of Peel or Goulburn . . . allowing, as I readily do, that the intentions of the ministry are good, of what value is that when all their appointments are almost without exception from the ranks of their present and *continued* enemies? . . . I can now pledge myself that if the government will act with vigour on their own principles, Ireland will be a source of strength and comfort to them.[15]

A subsequent speech by a member of the ministry, Lord Ebrington, was taken by O'Connell to have given the necessary assurance that the Irish administration would be thoroughly 'reformed' according to his wishes, and with that he proceeded to put his part of the supposed bargain into effect. He himself described the sequel thus in a letter of 4 December 1831:

> I did think that Lord Ebrington spoke *advisedly* and that, therefore, my principles would be adopted in the management of Ireland and my popularity transferred to the King and the King's government. So far I was

not only ready to assist, but I did assist. For on my arrival there [Dublin], I found a formidable Anti-Union organization complete, called the Trades' Union, headed by a man [Marcus Costello] of popular qualifications and capable, I fear, of misleading. I took them out of his hands. I not only turned them but I can say I turned the attention of the rest of the country from the overpowering question of Repeal to the suitable one of Reform, and I actually kept matters in suspense in this state for a month after my arrival.[16]

This was a reasonably accurate abridgement of the story of O'Connell's activity after his return to Ireland on 18 October 1831. He found that the artisans of the capital had been organized into a powerful combination, the Dublin Trades Political Union, radical in tendency and wholeheartedly committed to Repeal. Immediately, he established a corresponding middle-class association, the National Political Union, with the much more moderate programme of assisting the ministry to carry through reform, and — instead of Repeal — the achievement of all the 'benefits . . . which could possibly be procured by a domestic and local legislature'.[17] Next, he attacked the D.T.P.U. as divisive (in setting the working and middle classes against each other), and proceeded to infiltrate it with his own supporters. Within a month, he had in effect captured it for his own purposes. The artisans' association changed both its constitution and its name (to the National Trades Political Union), threw Repeal overboard and endorsed O'Connell's current collaborationist policy. Thus he was fully justified in telling Duncannon on 4 December that he had brought the divergent agitation into line in support of the whig government. It was true of course that he was also serving his own political ends in subordinating a potentially independent movement and crushing a potential rival for popular leadership in Dublin, Marcus Costello. But this did nothing to diminish the whigs' obligation to him for his strenuous political exertions.

Thus he had good reason to feel aggrieved when the government failed to provide a quid pro quo. As he pointed out to Duncannon on 4 December, there had been no change whatever in either the manning or the conduct of the Irish administration during the previous two months. The Irish legal establishment had, similarly, been left intact. Perhaps naively, O'Connell had expected the process of Irish concilia-tion to begin with the replacement of Stanley as chief secretary. Instead, 'Mr. Stanley, the snappish, impertinent, overbearing High Church Mr. Stanley, Mr. Stanley of Crimes Bill notoriety, who spoke of the "tried loyalty" of the Orange Yeomanry, was sent over again to be chief and only real governor.' O'Connell now menaced the ministry directly.

> Mr. Stanley MUST be put out of the government of Ireland . . . or the ministry *must* expect to lose the support of the Irish members . . . I say six [members] because so many have actually put themselves into my hands. If I, however, said twelve and went on to twenty, perhaps I would be nearer the truth. I know how easy it is for the friends of Earl Grey in England . . . to *bravely* exclaim against dictation. But all that is folly. The people of Ireland must have a party to support their interests; that party cannot certainly be the Tories. Alas! It is not the Whigs. Who are to be the friends of Ireland? We must form – I am forming – an Irish party, a party without religious distinction.[18]

He gave immediate substance to his threat by announcing that he would not return to the Commons when parliament reassembled on 6 December 1831, but instead devote himself to the more important business of building up the National Political Union at home. He also publicly condemned Bishop Doyle's current support of Anglesey's administration, adding, sadly, that his lordship had been taken in by 'Castle smiles'.[19] These were comparatively daring steps, and O'Connell tried to cover himself by also proclaiming his willingness to return within forty-eight hours to Westminster should the reform bill really be endangered, and by assuring Doyle that he had not meant to insult him personally. But Doyle, who evidently retaliated by threatening O'Connell with the loss of the Catholic Church's backing, was never fully reconciled.

Eventually, O'Connell retreated and agreed to attend the Commons again after the Christmas recess of 1831. Duncannon's earlier, anxious flattery – 'I need not assure you how necessary your presence here will be and how great a triumph your absence would give to the opponents of the Reform Bill'[20] – may have had some effect. But, more important, a prolonged absence would have damaged O'Connell's own cause. He had a vital interest in the achievement of parliamentary reform in Britain; he also believed that his best hope of altering the Irish bill lay in operating himself in the House of Commons. He considered that he had gone as far as he safely could in teaching the government that his support was not automatic, but must be paid for, politically. At the same time, his moves towards forming an independent Irish party, however accidental in origin, were by now seriously meant. Indeed, they were a logical development of his entire parliamentary experience of 1831.

II

Both the whigs and O'Connell had been exploring unknown terrain throughout the year. The systematic, continuous interaction of parliamentary and extra-parliamentary power was a new phenomenon. Isolated events or issues, such as the Wilkes episode or the anti-slavery campaign, had produced interesting specific novelties in the past. But a separate, or potentially separate, group in the House of Commons, with an unchallengeable leader, secure constituency bases and mass popular support, was quite unprecedented. How were the traditional parties to deal with such a group? How was *it* to traffic with *their* system? The whigs swung from the extreme of attempting to imprison or at least intimidate O'Connell to that of trying to recruit him to the ministry or remove him to a judgeship. They also set his 'political price' much too low, for they refused even to weaken significantly the 'Orange' hold upon Irish government. Duncannon pleaded, on 26 December 1831, that 'you [O'Connell] make no allowance for the situation in which they [the cabinet] came into power and the difficulty of altering old habits and prejudices'.[21] But the truth was that men like Grey and Stanley had no intention of advancing O'Connell's influence at the expense of that of the Ascendancy. Correspondingly, between May and December 1831, O'Connell moved from campaigning furiously for a whig victory in the general election to withdrawing from the Commons in protest against their inactivity. He, too, overvalued his hand. It was altogether unrealistic to expect that Stanley would be removed from Ireland, or even that Irish bills would be materially amended, at his *ipse dixit*.

None the less, each party was gradually learning the grammar of the new sort of politics. The main lesson drawn by O'Connell was that, having nothing to hope for from the English tories at Westminster, he must endeavour to increase his bargaining power *vis-à-vis* the whigs, and that, paradoxically, the best means of doing so was to create and control an independent Irish party. At the same time, he was prepared to ally, if he could, with the Irish tories against the two main British groupings. The purpose of this improbable combination would be to dictate, or at least profoundly influence, the Irish policy of whichever of the major parties happened to be in power. Throughout 1832 O'Connell was to oscillate between these strategies – or, more precisely perhaps, to pursue the first while trying also to knit into it something of the second.

O'Connell's parliamentary performance in 1831 is also worth

consideration as a whole for it reveals the range not only of his participation but also of his techniques and tactics in the business of the House of Commons. There is point moreover in looking to the beginning of whig rule in considering O'Connell as a parliamentarian. Only when the liberals were in power was he a true believer in – or at any rate a true practitioner of – 'the parliamentary method' in Irish politics. Under conservative rule, he instinctively assumed that progressive legislation would dry up, that the government's Irish policy would be unpalatable, and that the power of the state would be thrown behind the Protestant Ascendancy. For good measure, Peel (almost as deeply antipathetic to O'Connell as O'Connell was to him) was master of the tories almost to the end of O'Connell's period in the House. During phases of tory government, therefore, O'Connell turned towards extra-parliamentary agitation and attempts to organize pressure from without. His attendances at parliament during Peel's second ministry, 1841–6, were meagre and his performances perfunctory. Only when, in late 1845, the prospects of the liberals' return improved was 'the parliamentary method' once more in the ascendant.

On the seventy-seven sitting days on which he attended the Commons in 1831, O'Connell spoke 283 times. Some of these were mere interjections, but more were considerable, often very considerable, speeches. Almost all were powerful or telling. The meaning of the parliamentary method for him was immediately apparent in his approach to the dominant issue of 1831, parliamentary reform. He was of course committed to the full radical programme, down to universal male suffrage, the secret ballot, triennial parliaments and equal electoral districts. Lord John Russell's original bill fell very far short of this. Yet O'Connell accepted it – and on suggestive and prophetic grounds: first, as an instalment, and secondly, on trial for its capacity to provide radical political ends by other than radical political means. As he later observed, 'This measure gave none of these [the radical demands] . . . but it was in other respects so liberal and so extensive, that . . . it would demonstrate one of two things – either that further Reform was not necessary . . . or that it would give all these at a further period, . . . safely, certainly, and rationally.'[22] His entire handling of such an issue as Repeal was already foreshadowed here. Other expressions of O'Connell's radicalism also had revealing accompaniments. He was second only to Joseph Hume in pressing for reductions in public expenditure, and especially for the abolition of useless offices, both to save money and to limit government support resting on patronage. But his drive for municipal reform in Ireland soon passed from pressure to suppress offices in the gift of Irish local bodies to pressure for a share in them. Similarly, he warmly supported freedom of expression, and this became a significant issue in 1831 because of proposed curbs upon the press. But O'Connell formulated his opposition to controls in terms of counter-productivity rather than of principle. The threatened *Republican* and *Poor Man's Guardian* were, he said, 'ridiculous and disgusting trash'. They would be the only gainers from a prosecution. 'It was an excellent puff for . . . seditious publications, and the author must be much obliged to him [the Minister] for having pitied the sorrows of a poor old libeller who must otherwise have starved.'[23]

Foreign affairs were pressed into the background during 1831, but the aftermath of the Continental revolutions of 1830 occasionally engaged parliament's attention. Whereas, in as well as out of the House of Commons, O'Connell warmly supported the Belgian and Polish struggles for independence, he now strongly opposed the new Orleanist regime in France. The explanation of the disjunction, and of the sudden turnabout in his attitude to the government of Louis Philippe, was of course the anti-clericalism which the Second Monarchy had soon displayed. Since 1810 at least, O'Connell had distinguished French *liberaux* from true liberals in this regard. To some extent, his attitude towards the Belgians and Poles was determined by a romantic approbation of peoples striking for liberty: he spoke of their revolts as classic cases of 'the cause of poor downtrodden Man'. But they also illustrated 'this lesson, that one nation cannot continue with impunity to wrong and oppress another'.[24] What could be more apropos Ireland? In the cases of both Belgium and Poland, unions with more powerful alien states had been forced upon them; in both, Catholic peoples had been subjected to heretical or schismatic overlords. Finally, slavery apart, his approbation of the United States – 'the meridian splendour of American independence',[25] as he had called it in 1829 – was constant. His old vision of the whole western world engaged in a supra-national conflict between the forces of tyranny and freedom was far from dissipated.

When attention turned towards Ireland directly, the House's time and O'Connell's interventions were devoted mainly to affairs of the moment, such as affrays over tithes or malign crown prosecutions, or to the interests of specific groups which he was asked to support, such as turnpike trustees, tobacco growers or whisky distillers. But when on one occasion he raised the larger political question of Repeal in a debate, he repeated substantially the pattern of argument which he had used for parliamentary reform. First, he asserted his fundamental principle: 'if the Union were not repealed, Ireland would indeed soon cease to be a constituent part of the British Empire. It was necessary to the welfare and happiness of Ireland that she should have a domestic Legislature.'[26] Almost in the same breath, however, he hinted at a 'Justice for Ireland' experiment. Let them see whether a liberal, reforming government could and would provide Ireland with the same benefits which she might hope to gain from parliamentary independence:

> the object of those who advocated the Repeal of the Union was, to obtain a cheap government, and a just administration of the laws . . . The Repeal of the Union was merely a means to attain an end, and those who advocated that measure, expected now to attain their object without going through that ordeal . . . they were now willing to try the effects of a reformed House of Commons.[27]

In turn, this line of argument led into a demand for equal treatment for Ireland under the Act of Union, for standardizing practices in Ireland and Great Britain, for substituting a true marriage of kingdoms for a form of subordination. Such flexibility epitomized O'Connell's dialectical manoeuvres in the house, for his early 'moves', like opening gambits in chess, were often substantially the same.

The other striking characteristic of O'Connell's Irish 'policy' in parliament in 1831 was his relentless hostility to the influence of the Ascendancy. One curious corollary of this was a predilection for direct British rule as against sub-government by the loyalist minority. Even at the cost of open conflict with Hume, and despite his unvarying hostility towards the current incumbent, Anglesey, he argued for the retention of the lord-lieutenancy in Ireland as a brake on Castle influence. A constant theme in O'Connell's speeches during the year was denunciation of the Irish yeomanry as a partisan, 'Orange' force – ill-led, ill-conducted, cruel and vindictive – and the desirability of replacing them by regular British troops. Again, he pressed repeatedly for filling the Irish offices hitherto monopolized by the 'Orange faction' by a counter-balancing number of Catholics and liberal Protestants. Thus, although O'Connell's formal demand was full self-government for Ireland, his 'provisional position' amounted to a threefold demand for, first, the reduction of the power, privileges and monetary rewards of the Ascendancy, secondly, the advancement of Catholics in their place, and thirdly the maintenance of British and central authority in Dublin as the best hope of attaining these objectives.

It was only at the close of 1831, when he had temporarily abandoned the House of Commons, that he began to consider a fundamental change in his parliamentary tactics. Meanwhile, throughout the year he had laid down a new pattern at Westminster, whereby 'the Irish question', backed by popular agitations at home, would engross much of the time, and shape much of the business and many of the outcomes in the House of Commons. He had achieved this almost single-handedly and in particularly unfavourable conditions in that the sessions were dominated by a single, essentially non-Irish issue, the reform bill. Although his specific political successes were few and small in scale, he had succeeded generally as a politician, in a chill climate and an unfamiliar place.

III

O'Connell did his duty by the great reform bill in the spring parliamentary session of 1832 – but little more. He appears to have spent a mere five weeks in London, from late January until 1 or 2 March. Before he left for Westminster he had busied himself with inspiriting and developing his National Political Union in Dublin, and he broke his journey from Holyhead to London to visit Staffordshire and Warwickshire, the heartland of contemporary English radicalism. The Wolverhampton Political Union had sent him a flattering invitation to accept an address after he had been escorted into the town by a promised ten thousand working men:

> the Council of the Wolverhampton Political Union [wishes] to express our sentiments of approbation and esteem for the uniform, zealous and uncompromising exertions you have ever evinced in the cause of Reform and to mark our admiration at the vastness of your genius and the magnificence of your eloquence. Grateful for what you accomplished time past, the *emancipation of the seven millions*, for which and your patriotic efforts to restore us to our political rights, we earnestly desire to express our feelings of unfeigned thankfulness, and humbly solicit an opportunity to present an address as a memorial of our gratitude to the *Great Liberator* of religious disabilities.[28]

Having been duly fêted at Wolverhampton on 19 January 1832, O'Connell proceeded to a still larger reception arranged by the more celebrated Political Union at Birmingham: the Birmingham crowd was reported to have been 15,000–20,000 strong.

O'Connell, who was also being courted at this time by other Political Unions, was ready to champion the English radicals' demand for 'the whole Bill, and nothing but the Bill', in return for equal treatment for Ireland in terms of parliamentary reform. This meant, as he told the crowd at Birmingham, an increase of twenty-five members in the Irish representation, the elimination of the most scandalous Irish pocket and rotten boroughs, and the restoration of the 40s. freehold franchise. Although he was backing the government's own measure for England and Wales, the whigs were none too pleased at O'Connell's alliance, however temporary, with the English 'democracy'. Even the 'advanced' liberal Col. Leslie Grove Jones wrote to him from London on 22 January, 'You have not shown and have, I fear been making a *dinner* speech at Birmingham. I like you best in the House of Commons.'[29] But O'Connell was in no mood to be flattered into complaisance.

It is not clear whether he had already planned a popular campaign in Ireland when he returned to Dublin on 4 March 1832. One reason for his leaving the House of Commons so early in the session, and with crucial debates on the Irish tithes question due shortly to come on, seems to have been legal engagements during the spring assizes on the Munster circuit. He was involved in at least one case in Tralee and probably in other suits in Cork a little later. He was apparently contemplating at this time – perhaps only in an hour or two of gloom – the abandonment of parliamentary politics and a return to the Irish bar. On 11 February 1832 he had written to Fitzpatrick of the time 'When I leave the House and return to my profession'[30] in a context which suggested that this would happen comparatively soon. But whether it developed out of his going on circuit or had been long designed, a popular campaign in Munster dominated O'Connell's 'vacation' from parliament in March and April 1832.

It began with a wildly enthusiastic reception, on much too large and complex a scale to have been merely improvized, when he entered Tralee on 11 March. This was followed by a public dinner in his honour two days later. From Tralee he progressed – no lesser word will do for O'Connell's quasi-royal journeying – through Mitchels-town and Cahir to another grand reception and public dinner at Clonmel. Everywhere the pattern was the same. For miles outside the towns the roads were lined with people, and throngs of horsemen, carriages, bands and banners accompanied O'Connell to and from each main street or square. As he had prophesied to his wife on 13 March, 'You will hear a flaming account of my various receptions.

Everything is arranged for a most *amazing* entry into Cork [on 18 March]. If the day be fine we shall have one hundred thousand persons in my train.'[31] In fact, Cork's greeting exceeded even O'Connell's high expectation: on a wretched wet windy Sunday more than 200,000 people assembled for his welcome. O'Connell stayed ten days in Cork, and then embarked upon another round of processions and public dinners at Cahir, Cashel, Roscrea and Athlone between 29 March and 2 April.

The receptions were striking even when O'Connell was only passing through some little place. For example, the Millstreet correspondent of the *Cork Chronicle* reported,

> On Thursday morning [15 March], it having been known in Mill-street that the Liberator was to drive in from Killarney and breakfast at Murphy's hotel, on his way to Clonmel, which place he was to reach that day, the people of this town, with the Rev Mr Fitzpatrick, P.P., about seven o'clock went on about three miles on the Kerry road to meet him. When, after anxious expectation for some time, the Liberator appeared, he was received with deafening shouts. On two occasions the people almost insisted on taking the horses from his vehicle, but on no account would he admit them to do so. Having reached Mill-street, the crowd of people amounted to a large multitude. After breakfast, Mr O'Connell, having procured a chair on which he stood outside the door of the Hotel, addressed the people. Every sentence of his address was received by the people with loud cheers and every demonstration of pleasure and gladness.[32]

The massive Cork demonstration required very considerable organization – even more perhaps than it received, for there was confusion at some of the assembly points. The cortege took nearly four hours to reach the centre of the city from the point on the outskirts at which O'Connell's travelling carriage was met by the procession; it took about one hour and a half to pass any given station along the way. Not only was the entire route lined on either side, but also the river, to the left, was thronged with small craft and every street window and 'even the house-tops themselves' were crammed with people. The 'Morality Societies' and nearly fifty of the trades of the city mounted elaborate displays; they had drawn lots for their places in the parade. The trades' displays provide the clearest indication of the elaborate behind-the-scenes orchestration of the affair, for almost all of them were decked in orange and green, thus symbolizing the motifs which O'Connell now wished to be in evidence, union between Irish Protestants and Catholics and their common interest in the causes of

Reform and Repeal. The majority of the banners specified this in one form or another, generally linking O'Connell with Repeal. Typical were the mottoes on the Glass Makers and Glass Cutters flags: 'William IV and Reform' and 'O'Connell and Repeal'. Equally significant was the legend borne by the little company of the Cotton and Worsted Weavers, 'Twenty-eight Protestants – eighty Catholics', for O'Connell was also bent on presenting his current agitation as supra-denominational. But the artisans were only one element in this great manifestation of O'Connell's drawing-power. The celebrants ranged from beggars and labourers to the richest provision merchants and local manufacturers.

It is worth quoting O'Connell's speech in Cork extensively, for it perfectly exemplifies both his mastery of the demagogue's craft and his mode of signalling to the masses his current political priorities. O'Connell, reported the *Cork Chronicle*, 'came forward on the handsome platform of green and orange . . . and thus addressed the countless thousands that heaved and stirred like the waters of an ocean in an earthquake, beneath him . . .':

I have not . . . the presumptuous vanity to suppose, that I am master of any language that could possibly be adequate to express the sentiments and feelings that are overflowing in my bosom at this moment, at that mighty exhibition of national strength and national determination (cheers). But there is one thought which rises to my mind, above all others, and to which I must give utterance. It is the heartfelt gratification – the delightful feeling – the exquisite consciousness of knowing that the magnificent and undeserved compliment is paid me, not alone by the liberated Catholic, in requital for his freedom, but by my fellow-countrymen of all classes and creeds, and shades of religious opinions (tremendous cheering for some minutes). Yes, the compliment is enhanced by the fact of my Protestant fellow-countrymen joining with their Catholic brethren in paying it (loud and long continued cheering). Catholics (he continued, leaning his folded arms on the railing of the balcony, and addressing with the ease, affection, and familiarity of a father the stirless and silent immensity of human life below him) – Catholics, you and I are even (cheers). I did you a favour, and you do me another – and what a favour! – in requital. But, Protestants! in what terms can I thank you? What words can give expression to my feelings of gratitude for the honour you have done me this day? But I will do you a service too, for I will elevate your beloved country – our beloved country – (cheers) – into a powerful kingdom. I will take her from the position of a paltry province, and I will make her once again a kingdom, and independent (tremendous cheering) . . . I'll ask Lord Grey whether with such a shout ringing in his ears he should have selected such a man as

Stanley to rule this country? Stanley of tithe-system notoriety – Stanley, merely because he is an aristocrat in temper and habits, and the son of a peer . . . the shouts of the men of Cork many of whom are Orangemen – see I am a piece of an Orangeman myself, for I wear an orange lily in union with the shamrock (and he exhibited his green travelling cap, on the broad band of which were orange lilies and green shamrocks interwoven – while the repeated shouts of the thousands below him showed their satisfaction at the proceeding) – I say the tradesmen of Cork – the people of the country have spoken the word, and tithes are no more in Ireland (tremendous cheering). My friends, the meaning of the meeting to-day is this, that Ireland is too much oppressed – that she feels herself too much trampled upon to be so any longer (cheers) . . . we will once more have a parliament of our own in College green (tremendous cheering for many minutes). That is no sectarian meaning; that is no sectarian object (cheering); it is one in which every Irishman should feel a vital interest; it is one in which every Irishman does feel an interest (cheers); it is one in which we are all equally concerned, for it is one which comes home to every tie of our hearts and spirits (awful cheering).[33]

O'Connell was not presenting a precise programme but attempting to generate political excitement and expectation; and it was an additional advantage that his annual Tribute was being collected at this time. In so far as his Cork speech – like all the others delivered during his spring campaign of 1832 – had a major chord, it was Repeal. But this was blended with an appeal for continued support for parliamentary reform, a denunciation of alien rule in Ireland (and in particular, Stanley's) and the celebration, albeit premature, of the death of Irish tithes. The supposed victory on the tithes issue was coupled, once again, with a diatribe on Stanley's malignancy. In Cork, O'Connell embellished these basic themes with several references to the decline in the city's trade caused by the Act of Union; he usually found some local manifestation of depression to drive home the lesson that the Union was destroying Irish employment or reducing Irish incomes. But this too fitted into the final general demand for the restoration of Irish parliamentary independence. Thus O'Connell kept Repeal in the foreground but surrounded and interlinked it with other slogans; nothing was really pressed home. As he explained his strategy in a letter of 17 May 1832:

I do not urge on the Repeal when it could interfere with Reform but I utterly decline making any bargain on this head. I will not postpone the Repeal by contract although I tacitly allow it to stand over for a fitter season which is now very near. The English Reform Bill will be law in ten days [in fact, this did not occur until 7 June], and from that moment the

Repeal will be our cry; it will serve every purpose. In the first place it will compel a better Reform Bill for Ireland in order to disarm some of those who would otherwise join in the Repeal. Secondly, it will prepare the English mind for the more direct and constant agitation of the Repeal measure. It is absurd to suppose anything else could serve Ireland.[34]

Most noteworthy of all in his 1832 campaign was O'Connell's deliberate wooing of the Irish Protestants. No longer did he assail the Orange engrossment of public offices, honours and favours in Ireland. He was even silent on the subject of Dublin Castle's own mismanagement, as against Stanley's and the British government's oppression. All this was of course designed to persuade Protestants to make common cause with him in the forthcoming Repeal campaign. O'Connell believed that he was making headway. After his processional entry into Cork on 18 March, he boasted to Fitzpatrick of 'the respectable and *considerate* thousands who shouted for it [Repeal] yesterday – Protestants, Catholics and Presbyterians'.[35] Soon afterwards he stated publicly that, in supporting a motion on the Irish freeman vote earlier in the year, he had not been deterred by the fact that it favoured Protestant as against Catholic artisans. 'I think that if the Orangemen of the North understood my views', he added, 'there would be little difficulty in reconciling all Irishmen to each other and thus becoming so strong in our mutual cooperation as to be soon able to restore to Ireland legislative independence.'[36] In July, O'Connell's protracted and arduous efforts to secure recompense for an old Orange enemy, Sir A. B. King, who had been dismissed abruptly from his official post when the whigs came to power, at last succeeded. O'Connell had been moved to act primarily by his own good nature and pity for an aged man's sudden destitution. But he was also a political calculator. 'I do not think the act will be thrown away when we come to our next effort for conciliation', he told Fitzpatrick on 19 July 1832.[37] He ensured that the Dublin Protestants knew of his magnanimity when he was courting them later in the year. 'Are you aware', he asked William Scott, the former city sheriff,

> that it was I who fought out Sir A. B. King's pension for him? I can positively assert that he never would have got it but for me. I tell you these things to show the freemen that, although King was Deputy Grand Master of Orangemen and had, on the king's visit, behaved treacherously to myself yet I got an act of justice done for him when his own party literally threw him overboard.[38]

There is some evidence that O'Connell's large-mindedness was not politically wasted. King himself, who was still a respected figure in

Dublin Orangeism, wrote in gratitude, 'To *you*, Sir, to whom I was early and long politically opposed, to you, who nobly forgetting this difference of opinion, and who, rejecting every feeling of party spirit, thought of my distress and sped to succour and support me, how can I express my gratitude?'[39]

About the time that O'Connell succeeded in King's case, he was in grave danger of featuring in a public scandal, when an Ellen Courtenay, who accused him of having assaulted her and fathered her child, called on the Rev. Charles Boyton, the leading Irish Orange polemicist, and Remigius Sheehan, the editor of the leading Orange newspaper, the *Dublin Evening Mail*, to publicize her charges. Later she demanded that they report her threatened proceedings against O'Connell in the Dublin lord mayor's court. Both steadfastly refused to give Courtenay publicity. O'Connell was profoundly grateful. On 17 July 1832 he asked Fitzpatrick to call on Sheehan and

> express to him for himself and for Dr Boyton my hearty thanks as a private gentleman and quite independent of politics . . . it has enabled me to see the personal good qualities and high-mindedness of men who have been, and are upon principle, my very violent and most decided political enemies. It is pleasant to find that Irishmen are better than our passions and prejudices make us imagine.[40]

Boyton and Sheehan may well have been influenced by O'Connell's advocacy of their friend King's cause. But they may also have been obeying a sort of tacit code of honour which often mitigated the asperities of nineteenth-century Irish communal conflict, at least at the higher social levels. Perhaps in so small and interactive a middle and upper middle class as Dublin's it was only prudent that certain restraints should be observed.

Of course, O'Connell tended to inflate every manifestation of private kindliness or forbearance into a sign of coming union. He responded, for example, to the news of Boyton's and Sheehan's repudiation of Courtenay with, 'I trust . . . that the day is not distant when we will join our "little senates" [their respective political associations], and compose only one body concerting together for the good of Irishmen of every class and persuasion.'[41] It was true that Sheehan 'set great value' on O'Connell's compliments and spoke largely of the important changes which might ultimately be 'produced by the interchange of such kindly sentiments between parties hitherto so actively belligerent'.[42] It was also true that on particular – though rare – occasions or issues, the Irish political classes, Catholic and

Protestant, or portions of each, might temporarily coalesce. But to read into all this the promise of ultimate constitutional agreement was to miscalculate completely the determining forces in Irish society. From boyhood, however, O'Connell had, off and on, pursued this will o' the wisp; he would do so, off and on, until he died. Never did he pursue it more ardently or pertinaciously than in 1832.

IV

On 24 April 1832 O'Connell left Dublin to resume his seat in the House of Commons. As before, he made a leisurely journey to London, addressing meetings of reformers and radicals on the way. His primary purpose was, as before, to assist in carrying the English and Scottish reform bills, and to induce the government to recast the Irish bill on the same lines as the other two. In partial imitation of his Irish spring campaign, he spent almost as much energy in popular agitation in London as in supporting the 'Reform' ministry in parliament. He could count only on the backing of radicals such as Cobbett and of such organizations as the English National Union of the Working Classes when he demanded that Ireland be treated equally in parliamentary reform; the government merely strove to evade the issue of parity for all parts of the United Kingdom. The British bills were eventually carried; but so too was the Irish – with a solitary significant amendment. O'Connell had especially objected to the retention of the traditional Irish registration system which was conducted by assistant barristers, 'a totally irresponsible body – already encumbered with more business than they can well discharge and five-sixths of whom were appointed for their high and inveterate Tory principles'.[43] But Grey and Stanley absolutely rejected the proposal that Irish registration be placed upon the same basis as the English. O'Connell fared no better with his secondary parliamentary objective, the defeat of Stanley's Irish tithe bills. Both the tithes arrears bill, whereby the state took over, in part, responsibility for the collection of tithes overdue, and the tithe composition bill, which transferred the liability for tithes from tenants-at-will and yearly tenants to their landlords, were duly carried. The second especially was anathema to O'Connell, 'the most violent invasion of private property I ever read of'.[44] Not only did it leave tithes intact; it also, in effect, involved landlords (including O'Connell himself) in their collection. Small wonder that he was soon eager to leave London, 'this vile town'[45] – or that he should have abandoned the House of Commons well before the ending of the current session.

Even while O'Connell was in London, he attempted to sustain an Irish agitation. During May 1832 he issued three public letters for reproduction in the Dublin newspapers in order to signal his immediate political concerns. The first asked for a pledge in favour of full parliamentary reform, should the government be forced to call a general election; the second denounced the bias and ill-will of Anglesey's administration in Ireland; and the third repeated his call for an Irish reform bill fully equal to the English in all particulars. Through Fitzpatrick and Edward Dwyer, he kept up a mild flow of meetings and demonstrations in Dublin, and flagged his directions to the movement as a whole. With an eye to the next general election (whether or not it preceded the attainment of reform), he also maintained a correspondence with key men in various Irish constituencies. His fund of knowledge of local political circumstances and combinations throughout Leinster and Munster was expanding all the time. Fitzpatrick's rapidly swelling store of political information was also at his disposal.

It may have been just one such piece of information which led O'Connell to insist upon a Repeal pledge from 'his' candidates in the forthcoming general election. On 19 July 1832 Fitzpatrick reported that a '*good* authority assured me yesterday that no man will be returned by the county [Dublin] that refuses the pledge of *Repeal*. The same is averred of the city of Limerick with the addition that the "Representative Aspirant" must exhibit *your* introductory letter.'[46] After a month's political reading and rumination at Derrynane, O'Connell fell in with Fitzpatrick's proposal that he himself should run for Dublin city. The Repeal pledge was to be a *sine qua non* for the metropolis: 'no candidate should be tolerated but a Repealer'.[47] According to O'Connell's scheme, however, his running mate was to be a tory. Best of all would be the sitting conservative member, Frederick Shaw, if only he could be induced to take the pledge. In a letter of 29 August 1832, O'Connell declared a whig to be 'much worse' for Ireland than a conservative:

A Conservative has but one fault, which is indeed a *thumper*: he wants ascendancy – a thing impossible to be revived. But he is, after that, Irish, often very very Irish, and whilst in opposition he may be made more Irish than the Irish themselves. An *Angleseyite*, on the contrary, is a suffocating scoundrel who would crush every Irish effort lest it should disturb the repose of our English masters.[48]

But his scheme for Dublin city, probably chimerical from the outset, foundered when the National Political Union put forward E. S. Ruthven, a second Repealer, on 30 August. To make matters worse, O'Connell's 'beloved friend', Cornelius MacLoghlin, was later asked to stand for the city, presumably if O'Connell himself withdrew.

O'Connell was furious. 'Why,' he demanded of Fitzpatrick on 29 September,

> in the name of all that is absurd not wait until you know your strength before you talk of candidates, at least before you pledge yourself to them or make them pledge themselves to stand? The game *was* this. A Corporator [an 'Orange' member of Dublin Corporation] and an Agitator should have coalesced on the Repeal principle. The coalition should have preceded any declaration of any candidate. I believe it might have been well if I were the Agitator – well not for me, but for the cause. That plan, however, is knocked on the head by the premature starting of Ruthven . . . thereupon you go dreaming of another popular man to the total exclusion of a Corporator, and to the prevention of our taking the first great step to Repeal.
>
> I can hardly tell you how you annoy me.[49]

None the less, he still strove, up to November 1832, to find a conservative Repealer for Dublin, although in the end he had to stand with Ruthven against two tory anti-Repealers. O'Connell was practically alone in striving for an alliance with the Orange party upon the common platform of Repeal. Strangely enough perhaps, he could not understand his isolation. 'How shortsighted, how blind', he exclaimed on 7 November, 'must be the men who do not see the advantage of increasing their own forces by taking deserters from the enemy unless those deserters give themselves up tied hand and foot!'[50] This last referred to other causes, such as the abolition of tithes and church rates, additional radical measures of parliamentary reform and the overthrow of the grand jury system, which almost every Repealer (led indeed by O'Connell himself) was to advocate in the course of the campaign.

From an early stage, the Repeal pledge emerged as the startling novelty of the election. During 1828–9, demands on candidates for specific prior commitments arising out of the Catholic issue had been made, irregularly. But never before had subscription to a formula been systematically required in a general election. Now O'Connell determined to use the pledge to establish his (and his followers') complete independence of the whig-liberal party. He wrote, for example, of his close friend and fellow-counsel, Michael O'Loghlen,

I love him as my son and would trust him exactly in the same way . . . I would share my heart's blood with him. But I deal with him as I do with Maurice. If Maurice refused to give the Repeal test I would oppose him, decidedly oppose him, if I could get a *Repealer* in his place. I should bitterly lament to be in any species of hostility with O'Loghlen but 'Angleseyites' are now the bane of Ireland. Repealers are its only chance.[51]

O'Connell was not in fact so absolute in applying the Repeal formulary as this might suggest; and the ultra-democratic trades associations and political unions elaborated it into a catechism too particularized – and offensive to candidates – for his liking. But overall, through his organizations, his obedient newspapers and his personal influence, he pressed the pledge in almost every Irish constituency outside Ulster. Repeal had, therefore, a vital function in the general election of 1832. It was the instrument whereby O'Connell created the first prototype of the modern political party, with a distinct entity, a popular base, an agreed 'platform' and a universally acknowledged leader.

O'Connell's leap in the dark proved remarkably successful. Even when allowance is made for the later disqualifications, thirty-nine clear Repealers were returned. In only three constituencies, the close borough of Dungarvan and the counties of Limerick and Mayo, did a whig or liberal overcome a Repealer. O'Connell's principal difficulty was not defeating opponents but finding enough worthwhile candidates to run in Repeal colours; as he himself had put it earlier, 'Repeal appears to me to want nothing but sincere and uncompromising advocates'.[52] In nine counties, only a single O'Connellite stood (all successfully); a second would probably have been returned in each had there been another Repealer on offer. Similarly, seats almost certainly went begging in cos. Galway, Sligo, Wexford and Wicklow for want of Repeal candidatures. Thus, if fortune had consistently run O'Connell's way, and men with sufficient time, ambition, money and standing could have been found for every likely constituency, he would have captured at least half the total Irish representation in 1832. Even as things went, he had reason to feel complacent. To have built up quite a formidable Irish party, within six months and in the teeth of both government and the official opposition, was certainly a striking index of his power. The questions now were, how to keep this power intact until the next general election, and how to deploy it meanwhile in parliament, in so far as it could be maintained. Immediately, however, O'Connell could rejoice. Even before all the returns were in, he wrote on 20 December 1832, in the midst of successful electioneering in Tralee, to Fitzpatrick:

> Everything has – blessed be God! – hitherto passed in the most satisfactory manner. If Meath and Dublin county do as well [they did], why we shall be all triumph – and the best kind of triumph, that which furnishes hope and indeed appears to reduce hope into the certainty of being able to accomplish something for Ireland. My return for Dublin unsolicited, and even unavowed by me, is perhaps the greatest triumph my countrymen have ever given me.[53]

V

On 20 December O'Connell had written to his wife as well as to Fitzpatrick from Tralee. 'In short, darling, everything appears quite prosperous', he had reported.[54] It was of the general election that he spoke, but the phrase might serve as a motto for his fortunes generally during 1832. It certainly applied in its most commonplace sense, to money. Probably for the first time since boyhood, O'Connell was flush with funds, if not altogether free from debt. Fitzpatrick set out to raise £1000 per month for the O'Connell tribute for 1832, and easily exceeded his goal during the calendar year. O'Connell responded to the rising financial tide with his usual panache. His steward John Primrose may well have been astonished to receive, on 14 April 1832, not a demand for cash, but a declaration of O'Connell's intent to clear the *'principal money* of my Iveragh debts'. He announced that he was now

> in a hurry to get rid of all my debts all over the world. *I have £5000* lent on a mortgage of stock to keep by me. This I do not touch. I have settled that is paid off or deposited £2000 out of Betsey's fortune. Blessed *be the great God* I expect soon to be quite independent and not to have my income cut down by auditors [creditors]. Is there anybody that teazes you particularly for money [?]. If so, state it to me and we will, with the help of God, get rid of that auditor.[55]

His brother James was probably still more startled when O'Connell offered him, out of the blue, a loan of £5000 to purchase land for the benefit of James's younger children. With characteristic grimness – on the edge of irony – James rejected 'a purchase which I have no occasion for . . . if I should be able to save as much money as will provide for *my other children*, without leaving a heavy debt on my small landed property, it will in my humble judgment be the most prudent course . . . Borrowing money to purchase land has generally been found a most ruinous speculation.'[56] Undaunted, O'Connell proceeded, in the late spring and early summer of 1832, to deposit £3500 at the Hibernian Bank; lend (it would seem) £1000 to the parish priest of St James's, Dublin; pay off several Cork and Kerry debts; spend a little on his houses at Carhen (his birthplace) and Derrynane; distribute through Fitzpatrick small sums to various religious charities; and take his chaise and four to Liverpool to travel 'comfortably and sufficiently expeditiously' to London.[57] But perhaps the best index of all of O'Connell's unwonted 'prosperity' was the absence of any reference whatever to money in his extensive correspondence in the months preceding the general election of 1832, in which three of his sons, besides himself, were candidates.

In addition to the Tribute and his rents, O'Connell earned something at the bar in 1832; but it can only have been comparatively little. He joined the Munster spring circuit half-way through its course, but soon departed for his March-April political campaign. His notion of abandoning parliament for law was evidently evanescent. Despite very heavy pressure from Ireland he did not leave London in time to act for the accused in the very important Carrickshock tithe trial held at the Kilkenny assizes on 20 and 21 July. 'Your non-appearance caused great disappointment and dismay', Fitzpatrick told him[58] – although in fact acquittals were secured. But though he practised only occasionally, O'Connell's reputation as a counsel never shrank. Shrewdly Fitzpatrick attributed this to 'the *Caesaren vehis* feeling which induces the Irish people to rely so much not only upon your great powers but also on your *fortune*'.[59] Many much humbler persons agreed with Bonaparte that luck was the final virtue.

O'Connell suffered some illness, or at least depression, during his last three weeks in London in July 1832. He went so far as to seek a resident 'young physician or surgeon of sufficient skill'[60] for Derrynane while the family resided there from August to November – though this may have been principally for his wife's sake, as there are several references to her ill-health throughout the year. Possibly his concern for himself related to a rheumatic disorder – as well as to his everlasting battle against fatness – for his prescriptions seem always to have run along the lines of horseriding for exercise and regular hot baths. At a guess, his real trouble was the temporary over-taxing of his body; he was now fifty-seven years of age. Certainly, he did not suffer either before or after his summer sojourn in London. In the course of his arduous spring campaign in Ireland, he had written to Mary, 'I was not one bit fatigued by my exertions yesterday [29 March 1832], and never had a more refreshing sleep. I could rave of the scenes I have gone through';[61] six days later, he had reported that he 'never was better in health or spirits';[62] and these spirits appear to have stayed buoyant until he returned to Westminster in mid-April. They also revived almost as soon as he reached Kerry for his long vacation. He told Fitzpatrick on 11 August that his health was quite restored. 'I now enjoy my pristine elasticity of animal sensation. There never was so great a change in the tone of animal functions in any man within so short a period. I enjoy my mountain hunting on foot as much as ever I did and expect, with the help of God, to be quite prepared for as vigorous a winter campaign as ever I carried on.'[63] Though the winter campaign was vigorous indeed, O'Connell never complained of illness or even weariness throughout its length. His habitual 'elasticity of animal sensation' seems to have been re-enthroned in the last five months of 1832.

The glow of O'Connell's family feeling can be glimpsed only occasionally in his correspondence for 1832. During the year he was rarely parted from his wife, the principal recipient of his private hopes and fears. But he did report to her – *couleur de rose*, of course – the well-being of all her children who remained in Ireland when she went to London in the spring. On his visit of 1–2 April to his 'own Betsey' and his 'darling Kate', who was staying with her in co. Roscommon, he found 'Betsey thin but looking well . . . Catty [Kate] is perfectly well. So are Morgan [his son] and Ffrench [Betsey's husband].' Morgan was indeed 'as stout as a lion'.[64] O'Connell also called at Clongowes to see after his youngest son Daniel, who was still a pupil there, and then told Mary, 'Banish all kind of uneasiness on his account. It is not possible for him to be better . . . They [the Jesuits] praise him to the skies.'[65] Finally, he journeyed to co. Wicklow to call upon his eldest daughter, Ellen. Meanwhile he heaped praise on Maurice who had stayed in London with Mary and was acting, currently, as O'Connell's 'voice' in the House of Commons. Knowing how Mary would warm to praise of her first-born, he ardently applauded Maurice's speech on the Irish tithe bill on 27 March 1832, and told her, a few days later, that the priests at Clongowes 'are in raptures about Maurice – *so am I, sweetest*'.[66]

But no one, except presumably his bride, could have been enraptured by Maurice's elopement later in the year with Mary Frances Bindon Scott, the daughter of a tory Protestant landowner in co. Clare. It was certainly a romantic escapade. Maurice sailed his yacht into Cahircon, close to the Scotts' home, bore off Mary Frances across the

Shannon estuary, and then descended to Tralee where the pair were married, at a Catholic ceremony, on 29 September, and to Kenmare, where they married two days later according to the rites of the Church of Ireland. Subsequently, O'Connell said that he had agreed to Maurice's making proposals to Bindon Scott, but not of course to his marrying his daughter without Scott's consent or even knowledge. It is hard to believe that O'Connell liked the match, quite apart from the impropriety of its execution. Mary Frances's fortune, £6000–7000, was rather larger than those of his own daughters. But O'Connell and his wife had had much higher hopes for Maurice, and, in any case, Mary Frances was – immediately – a penniless acquisition, for her father at first disowned her. Worst of all perhaps was the fact that the Catholic champion's heir had married out of his own church, with the possibility that the female children of the union, at least, would be lost to the faith. But whatever his immediate reaction to the news of the runaway wedding, O'Connell soon drew Mary Frances into the family cocoon. 'Darling little Mary', he wrote to his wife from Tralee (where he was electioneering on behalf of Maurice) on 26 December 1832, 'has a sore throat and she stayed in bed all day nursing it. I have determined that she and Maurice should travel more slowly [than himself] to Dublin . . . so as to dine with us on . . . New Year's Day . . . Maurice and little Mary write in love to you.'[67] All that remained, it seemed, was to secure the new Mrs O'Connell's fortune and paternal pardon. The little domestic cloud had been driven off – for the time being – by O'Connell's resolute pursuit of family felicity.

VI

As we have seen, a much more threatening cloud had hung over O'Connell's own reputation at the beginning of the year. On 25 November 1831 the radical Henry Hunt had forwarded to him a letter from Ellen Courtenay accusing O'Connell of having raped her some fourteen years earlier and of being the father of her illegitimate son, born in November 1818: Hunt claimed that Courtenay had sent him this in 'applying to me for pecuniary relief'.[68] Courtenay's (or perhaps we should say Hunt's?) move was the first step in an attempted blackmail. Blackmailing public men for sexual misconduct (real or invented) was then a common practice, and even guiltless victims sometimes paid for silence in order to avoid a scandal. O'Connell denied all knowledge of Courtenay – and the evidence would seem to establish his complete innocence. But early in January 1832 his friend

Grove Jones warned him of 'the calumnies that were in circulation against him' in London.[69] O'Connell, widely feared, disliked and already classified as 'ruffian' rather than 'gentleman' (a 'gentleman' would, of course, according to the code, support his bastards), was extraordinarily vulnerable to hostile gossip among the political classes. None the less, he refused to buy off or have any truck with Courtenay.

Her next ploy was to issue from the debtors' prison in which she was detained a pamphlet setting out her charges against O'Connell in full horrid detail. Still, he held to his line of ignoring the accusations while endeavouring to prevent their coming to wider public notice. Thus, he wrote to his young relative, Walter Baldwin, in London on 29 April 1832:

> you must not publish anything about *my fair friend*. What she wants most is to have a controversy raised and I am sure that no friend of mine who appreciates her attack at its just value will indulge her in a controversy. You therefore, let me say it, *must* not indulge you *cacoethes scribendi* on this subject as I am sure that my request which is very unequivocal will decide you not to publish one line upon the subject. Nothing could annoy me on this subject but a publication purporting to come from a friend.[70]

Courtenay's final – and futile – fling in 1832 was, as we have seen, to ask the Irish tory press to print her story, and – this failing – to enjoin the editors to send reporters to the Dublin mayoral court when she would make an application before it. O'Connell's reputation may have suffered, to some small extent, from the whispering which must have accompanied the 'scandal', particularly as it was uncountered by open denial. But the brave course of defying Courtenay, and maintaining silence, was probably the wisest, too. No one took up or even made public reference to Courtenay's cause, despite all her efforts. O'Connell had come through practically unscathed: 1832 was indeed his prosperous year.

CHAPTER 4

The Uses of Repeal

1833–4

I

During 1832 O'Connell's politics had been, in one particular sense, built upon Repeal. But he was using Repeal as a political instrument rather than pursuing it as a goal. He employed it to justify his associations, to launch his agitations, to frighten the whigs into concessionary measures or appointments, to lead into 'Justice for Ireland' demands, to demonstrate good faith to British politicians when he shelved it, or to mark off a distinct political grouping of his own when he slapped it down upon the counter once again. But Repeal also lived on quite another plane; in fact, its natural habitat was the ideal. The young Michael Doheny, destined to become an insurrectionist in 1848 and the author of the famous fiery *Felon's Track*, wrote to 'the Liberator of our country' on 27 November 1832 from Clonmel gaol (where he was incarcerated for his part in resisting tithes):

> These are decisive times. The next few weeks will be teeming with events important to Ireland and much will depend on the energy of the people during that brief period. What a glorious object the people have to struggle for! How magnificent is even the hope of national liberation! As all bitter feelings against petty injustice and local tyranny are merged in the nation's predominant aversion to the Union, so all the mind and the might of the people should be directed to its *Repeal*.[1]

Had O'Connell, after the wear and tear of nearly thirty years of daily politics, lost his hold upon this visionary dimension of Repeal? No, by no means altogether: but his attitude was by now most complex. It deserves a full analysis, at the point at which he emerged, in January 1833, as the leader of a considerable parliamentary party committed to that single, but ramifying, principle.

Let us start by asking, what did O'Connell mean when he called for the repeal of the Act of Union? No one should have known better than he that his frequent demand for the 'simple repeal' of the British statute passed in 1800 contradicted the entire trend of his political activity since that date. Literally interpreted, it was nonsensical. He could not have meant to propose the re-constitution of the eighteenth-century Irish constituencies, controlled, as almost all had been, by crown, patrons, proprietors or bribes. Nor could he have accepted the re-imposition of those Roman Catholic disabilities which had been removed statutorily since 1800. Yet both of these 'safeguards' had been pre-conditions of 'independence' for the great majority of Irish Protestants before 1800. In fact, the Union had come about, so far as they were concerned, because they had come to feel that even these defences were too flimsy for the maintenance of the Protestant Ascendancy, or even Protestant security or possessions. On the one hand, the events of the 1820s in Ireland – in particular, the loss or potential loss of control in many of the parliamentary constituencies and the proven power of Irish popular agitation – had further weakened Protestant 'securities'. On the other, O'Connell could scarcely have contemplated reversing a series of changes which he himself had done most to bring about. Further, as the Repeal movement developed in the early 1830s it was closely linked, by and through O'Connell, to the full radical reform programme – manhood suffrage, vote by ballot, equal electoral districts, triennial parliaments, and the abolition of the property qualifications for MPs. Isaac Butt was surely right to contend later on that 'Repeal was a revolution . . . the proposition was not to return to any state of things that previously existed in Ireland – not to adopt the constitution of any European state, but to enter on an untried and wild system of democracy.'[2]

Thus, O'Connell could certainly not have intended what he often formally proposed, the turning back of the constitutional clock to 1799. Why, then, did he present the issue in such terms? Various types of answer may be proffered. First, Repeal appeared to evidence extraordinary political consistency, given the great length and variety of O'Connell's public appearance. Throughout his long campaign for Catholic civil rights, he had lost no opportunity of emphasizing its secondary nature: religious liberation, he always said, was ultimately meaningful only in the context of Repeal. Even his abatement of Ireland's claims, during the course of his first parliamentary flirtation with the whigs in 1831, was presented as contingent, and was in fact apparent rather than real. When, therefore, towards the close of 1832 he committed himself, at last, to a direct and total assault upon the Union, the mature man of fifty-seven may have looked back in imagination to the young man of twenty-five, and told himself that in his beginning was his end. The very Act which he had opposed in 1800 he still opposed in 1832; all that he had ever sought was the restoration of the status quo. Thus, Repeal gave unity to O'Connell's long career. He could present himself, even to himself, as changeless from first to last, tacking perhaps to contrary winds, but unvarying in his destination, a Fabius among national liberators. This may have been important. Demagogues may live through a temporary failing in applause, but hardly disbelieving in themselves.

Secondly, O'Connell was not only an Irish nationalist but also a leading British radical, in certain senses the leading British radical of his day. In radicalism, he could reconcile his personal ambitions and his early grounding in the ideology of the Enlightenment. Resentment of, and refusal to acquiesce in, the condition of inferiority into which, as an Irish Catholic, he had been born, were the steady urges in his life. His consequent passion for parity could be readily articulated in terms of civil equality. That O'Connell was the complete egalitarian, in the formal and legal senses in which contemporaries understood the word, there could be no reasonable doubt. One could find no measure of civil rights which came within his sphere of action or comment which he did not earnestly support. Thus, he could honestly present his drive for formal political equality for Irishmen and Catholics within the United Kingdom as a particular manifestation of a general and absolute principle. Repeal fitted with equal neatness into his universalist radicalism. The demand for legislative independence could be paraded as the apotheosis of egalitarianism, while serving, at the same time, as a burning glass for all the bitterness which racial and religious discrimination had engendered.

There was, however, another level at which O'Connell's radicalism helps to explain his emphasis on the repeal of a particular statute. As a political technique, as distinct from a body of ideas, British radicalism for the first two-thirds of the nineteenth century centred on the removal of clearly specified abuses or restraints. The classic form of campaign, beginning with the anti-slavery movement, was to institute an agitation for the abolition of a particular evil by parliamentary action. Each campaign was a separate undertaking with a separate target; happiest of all if the target were a specific Act of parliament. To present the constitutional rearrangement of the British Isles in the same sort of terms as the abolition of the slave trade, or church disestablishment, or the repeal of the corn laws, was therefore a natural action for O'Connell. His long and successful campaign for

Catholic Emancipation had taken precisely this form, down to casting the objective in terms of, to use the official phraseology, the removal of the statutory 'Disabilities ... imposed on the Roman Catholic Subjects of His Majesty'.[3] Focusing on a single repealing measure had, moreover, for the purposes of mass agitation, the solid advantages of limpid simplicity and the clear identification of a visible enemy. That this enemy was a comparatively recent Act of parliament, and one besides of so large a sweep that almost every contemporary misfortune could be plausibly ascribed to it, were further significant advantages for a popular movement. Thus, both the nature and the art of contemporary mass politics suggested the wisdom of a campaign for 'simple repeal'.

Thirdly, it should never be forgotten that O'Connell had to work in and through the political system of the United Kingdom. He had to move British opinion, a British ministry and a predominantly British House of Commons – and behind all these, requiring a still greater force to overcome, the British crown and House of Lords. He could use threats, blandishments, demonstrations, dangers and discomfort – but violence was disavowed. In the best of circumstances, it was a daunting journey. But had O'Connell announced in so many words that his objective was to advance to a novel state of things which, whatever its constitutional form, implied mass democracy, tenant right and disestablishment of the Church of Ireland, it would have been pointless for him to have ever put one foot before the other.

Instead, the chosen issue was well designed to counter the British 'great fears' – of revolution, of popery and of separation. The choice of 'simple repeal', with its implicit as well as explicit invocations of '1782', could scarcely have been bettered as a device for allaying the *furor Britannicus*. 'Simple repeal' was meant to convey the ideas of restoration and of Protestant security, if not of actual Protestant domination. The repeated use of 'Grattan's Parliament' and 'College Green' in O'Connell's Repeal oratory suggested mere moderate colonial nationalism and even perhaps the acceptance of renewed Ascendancy leadership, if freed of its former sectarian oppression. The backward references also commonly included the comforting incantation of 'king, lords and commons'; and fervent expressions of adherence to the crown were from first to last a leading feature of each O'Connellite campaign. O'Connell inscribed 'Loyal' on his banners with all the purposive ostentation of an Orange Lodge; he called incessantly for cheers for His Majesty with all the sentimental hyperbole of a two-bottle parson. On the surface, it was difficult to assail any of this as unconstitutional. Thus, Repeal constituted, in O'Connell's view, the safest means of exerting mass, extra-parliamentary pressure and represented the highest opening bid which an Irish agitation of the 1830s could safely make.

Fourthly, as this last point suggests, the truth would seem to be that O'Connell did not intend to put forward a specific proposition or make a specific demand in launching his movement for Repeal. It was, in lawyer's language, an invitation to treat rather than a firm offer. What he probably intended in 1830–2 was to elicit a proposition from the British government. Repeal was only apparently a demand. Its true counterpart was not so much Catholic Emancipation, tithe abolition or Irish church disestablishment as Parnell's 'Home Rule'. Like O'Connell, Parnell avoided, so far as possible, specification of his objective. Like O'Connell's, Parnell's pressure appears to have been designed to force out a counter-offer, which might be accepted, rejected as insufficient, or used as a start for bargaining. The essential similarity of O'Connell's situation and leadership to Parnell's is apparent in this extraordinary passage towards the close of the great Mansion House debate of 1843 upon the desirability of Repeal:

> a Parliament inferior to the English Parliament I would accept as an instalment if I found the people ready to go with me, and if it were offered me by competent authority. It must first be offered me – mark that – I will never seek it. By this declaration I am bound thus far, that if the period should come when I am called upon practically to act upon it, I will do so; but I will not give up my exertions for the independent legislation until from some substantial quarter that offer is made . . .
>
> Upon this subject I must not be mistaken, I never will ask for or look for any other, save an independent legislature, but if others offer me a subordinate parliament, I will close with any such authorized offer and accept that offer.[4]

Despite the initial hedges of 'an instalment' and 'the people ready', O'Connell was showing more of his hand that Parnell would ever do. Still, he worked within the same ambience. Each man sought to force a declaration from a British party, and to make none himself. Some apparently specific goal had to be announced; otherwise a movement could never have been set afoot. Parnell's devices were silence and an ambiguous and amorphous name and programme, 'Home Rule'; O'Connell's, garrulity, inconsistency and an impossible ostensible object, 'Repeal'. But this was a mere difference of mode and style. They were at one in being 'comparative separatists', who recognized that the *degree* of separateness would be determined ultimately in

Great Britain, and who committed themselves to no abstraction or ideal form of state.

O'Connell came nearest, perhaps, to particularizing his conception of the relations between Great Britain and Ireland after the Union was repealed in a speech delivered to the reformers of Bath in May 1832. It was an occasion for minimizing the degree of autonomy which the rupture would entail. O'Connell was anxious to lead British radicals on from making common cause on parliamentary reform to making common cause on the constitutional rearrangement of the government of the British Isles. He was reported as saying:

> The Irish have been accused of wishing to have a separate Legislature, and to be divided entirely from England. Nothing can, however, be more untrue than this. We are too acute not to be aware of the advantages which result particularly to ourselves from our union with this country. We only want a Parliament to do our private business, leaving the national business to a national assembly; for it is well known to all who are acquainted with the subject that the private business of the House of Commons, if properly attended to, is quite enough to occupy its entire consideration. Each of the twenty-four States of North America has its separate Legislature for the dispatch of local business, while the general business is confined to a national assembly, and why should not this example hold good in the case of Ireland?[5]

He was immediately assailed in Ireland for having abandoned the Repeal cause. His use of the phrase 'our union with this country' was seized on as the very ensign of surrender. O'Connell may well have spoken loosely or inadvertently of 'union', but the context makes it clear that in no sense was he arguing for the maintenance of the Act of 1801. In any event, as commonly happened, he claimed to have been misreported and that the word which he had employed was not 'union', but 'connexion'. He went on, in his public letter of explanation to 'the People of Ireland', to make it clear that he saw Repeal as issuing in a federal system for Great Britain and Ireland. He proposed that a domestic legislature, consisting only of a House of Commons, should be created for each country. These legislatures should meet in the last quarter of each year, and deal with such issues as law and order, agriculture and commerce within their respective territories. Then in the following January or February, an imperial parliament should meet in London to determine matters of common concern to Ireland and Great Britain, war and peace and imperial and foreign relations.

Despite the lack of detail and the impracticality of the machinery in

O'Connell's proposal, it is deeply interesting. At first sight, his domestic legislature might appear a meagre objective, especially when he employed the direct analogy of the states of the American union. It seemed to fall far short of parliamentary independence. But the independence of 'Grattan's parliament', the holy grail of the Repeal movement, had been largely illusory. The British cabinet, through its control of the crown, the Irish executive and, normally, the majority of votes in both the Irish houses of parliament, had been the ultimate authority in Ireland throughout 1782–1800. O'Connell's domestic legislature was meant to be *exclusively* effective in the areas which concerned him most, the economy, the civil service, local government, and the legal and police systems. Secondly – and perhaps still more important to O'Connell – his proposal reduced Great Britain to the same constitutional level as his own country. The British domestic legislature would have no greater range of business, no larger powers, than its Irish counterpart. The equal footing of the two was driven home by the further proposal of a joint imperial parliament to deal with external and colonial relations, and everything that bore on these, such as the armed forces and the foreign service. It is true that the imperial parliament would be dominated by its British members – to say nothing of its embracing the current House of Lords. None the less its very character, composition and duties would imply that Ireland was no less a mother-country, no less a nation, than Britain herself. No less than the domestic assemblies, it would serve as a symbol of political equality.

All this probably expressed O'Connell's fundamental purposes throughout his Repeal agitations. His notion of 'internal' affairs may have been ill-defined and certainly failed to come to grips with the inherent problem of how economic policy and the levels of taxation and public expenditure should be determined. But his general division was clear enough. Ireland should govern itself in what concerned itself alone; and so should Britain. In matters which concerned the outside world – physically speaking – he was prepared to allow Britain the substantial power, provided that Ireland was *formally* accepted as an equal partner. Parity was the key to all his thinking on Repeal, no less than to all his thinking on Emancipation. The great driving force of his politics from first to last was his revolt against inferiority of condition. But he was ever a pragmatist; and while the accidents of his Bath speech and its aftermath may have drawn from him a comparatively specific avowal of his ideal settlement, he never again allowed himself the indulgence of detailed speculation, but rather used Repeal *sans phrase* as a popular rallying-cry, a mode of intimidating governments and a hoped-for bargaining counter.

II

The general election of 1832 had scarcely ended before O'Connell attempted to broaden the base of his support in the House of Commons beyond the Repeal MPs. He seized upon Richard Barrett's proposal of 30 December (conceivably inspired by himself) that a 'national council' of all Irish MPs and representative peers be called to consider the state of the country. Immediately, O'Connell summoned a meeting of the 'council' in Dublin, before the beginning of the new parliamentary session. By publishing the responses to his 'invitation' in the newspapers, he exerted the utmost pressure on the freshly elected Repeal members and even on liberals returned for 'open' county constituencies, to present themselves before him. Similarly, when on 10 January 1833, he still considered it possible that his son-in-law's brother Nicholas Fitz-Simon, MP for King's Co., might not appear, he saw to it that Fitz-Simon received this message: 'Let him not listen to base advisers. He is ruined for ever if he shrinks from the people at this juncture.'[6] In fact, all the Repeal MPs either attended the 'council' or provided good reasons for not doing so. Dr Macintyre has described the outcome succinctly:

> of the 30 to 35 MPs who attended the Council's two sessions in a hotel opposite the old Irish Parliament on College Green, only three were not Repealers. The Council heard a report on Irish revenue, taxes and funded debts from Michael Staunton, the editor of the *Morning Register*; it discussed the soap and paper trades, grand jury reform, the abolition of tithes and various measures of franchise reform, but there was no discussion of Repeal itself, and in general the results of the Council disappointed those like Henry Grattan and John O'Connell who hoped that it would lead to unity of purpose and action and that it would act as the working model of an Irish legislature.[7]

There is no evidence that O'Connell ever thought of the council (which never met again) as a dry run for a future Irish House of Commons. It is much more likely that in gathering together whatever parliamentarians he could, he hoped to establish more firmly, and to expand, an independent Irish pressure group at Westminster. Clearly, Repeal had served its purpose for the moment. It was not to be pressed further immediately. Instead, O'Connell brought to the foreground the Irish issues of common concern, doubtless to draw some non-Repeal liberals into the fold. Another of his purposes in promoting the council may well have been the confirmation of his personal authority and leadership.

All the same, O'Connell hedged his bets. On the one hand, he prepared the way for another sustained agitation at home. On 3 January 1833, he replaced the National Political Union by a 'Society of Irish Volunteers for the Repeal of the Union'. The precedent of 1782 was not only deliberately invoked but even declared to be the model for the sort of action called for now that parliamentary reform had been achieved. On the other hand, he put what pressure he could upon the new whig government to appoint a more sympathetic and amenable Irish administration. 'You are the only person connected with power', he told Duncannon on 14 January, while the national council was meeting,

> to whom I could write what I know and what I believe and indeed I should not feel at rest if I did not tell you that the Government cannot appreciate the exact state of this country. Stanley has had considerable success in enforcing the Tithes. He has overawed many, very many parishes, and there was an adequate force for that purpose but the result is just what those who know Ireland foresaw – the spirit which is curbed by day walks abroad by night. Whiteboyism is substituted for open meetings. *There is almost universal organisation going on.* It is not confined to one or two counties. It is, I repeat, *almost universal.* I do not believe there is any man in the rank of a comfortable farmer engaged, not one man probably entitled to vote. But all the poverty of our counties is being organised. There never yet was, as I believe, so general a disposition for that species of insurrectionary outrages . . .
>
> I know you will excuse me for my cause in troubling you at this length. But, indeed you who are acquainted with the history of Irish affairs, must have been prepared for this result. The insanity of delivering this country to so weak a man as Lord Anglesey and so obstinate a maniac as Stanley, is unequalled even in our annals.[8]

O'Connell had thus devised a multiple strategy at high speed, in the three weeks between the conclusion of the general election and his departure for London on 23 or 24 January 1833. He was trying, simultaneously, to produce a disciplined parliamentary party, a national support organization, and a shift in the Irish policy of Grey's re-elected ministry. As all this filtered through to the liberals at Westminster, it seemed that it was 'evidently the game of O'Connell to keep the Repeal question out of Parliament, but to agitate and stir up Ireland from its foundations with the question; to embody the whole population of Ireland as unarmed Volunteers, [and] to make Repeal of the Union the prevailing sentiment of that body'.[9] These were three-quarters truths at least. Throughout the session, O'Connell made only one considerable speech on the Union; and until the 'Society' was suppressed by proclamation on 10 April, he strove, so far as was practicable from a distance, to breathe life into his re-created Volunteers. Moreover, with Fitzpatrick as his channel of communication, he renewed his efforts to entice the Orange party into the Repeal camp. Hoping to build upon a common hostility to the whigs, he went to the limit to render Repeal palatable to a wounded and resentful Ascendancy. On 21 February, through his faithful intermediary, he offered these generous terms to Boyton, the Dublin Protestant champion:

My plan is to restore the Irish parliament with the full assent of Protestants and Presbyterians as well as Catholics. I desire no social revolution, no social change. The nobility to possess lands, titles and legislative privileges as before the Union. The Clergy, *for their lives*, their full incomes – to decrease as Protestantism may allow that decrease. The Landed Gentry to enjoy their present state, *being residents*.

Every man to be considered a resident who has *an establishment* in Ireland.

In short, salutary restoration without revolution, an Irish parliament, British connection, one King, two legislatures.[10]

A month later, he asked (again through Fitzpatrick) 'Would *they* [the Irish tories] take up *the Repeal* as founded on the basis of a local parliament for *local objects* merely and the present 105 members to come over to the Imperial Parliament for all *general* purposes, as at present? In short, see what we can do to satisfy him [Sheehan, the Dublin Orange leader] and his.'[11]

But all this was a secondary theme. O'Connell was perforce not active but reactive once he got to parliament. He was immediately confronted with a king's speech which, at Stanley's direction, threatened throughgoing repression in Ireland. He was moreover pitched at once into the old hand-to-hand combat with Stanley himself. As Le Marchant described the opening night's debate on 5–6 February 1833,

O'Connell's speech, artful and persuasive in a very high degree, made a deep impression. It required a very skilful answer, and certainly did not receive it from Stanley. His invective upon O'Connell, though pointed and forcible, did more injury to himself than to his opponent. It was not accompanied by a proper confutation of O'Connell's changes, so it looked like invective alone, and the evening ended by O'Connell standing in a much higher position than in the last Parliament. The new members thought he had much right on his side.

Luckily for ministers O'Connell was not satisfied with this moderate success. He must needs shew his strength, or perhaps shew the Repealers in Ireland that they had not sent so many representatives to the House in vain. One after another these Hibernian orators rose to repeat in lengthy and declamatory harangues their complaints of the wrongs of their country and their accusations against the ministry. Their coarse manners, fierce deportment and baseless assertions, at length heartily wearied the House . . . It cannot be denied that many of the facts stated in his [O'Connell's] speech were far from being satisfactorily answered. Still his injudicious tactics produced the same effect as if they had been.[12]

The familiar diastole and systole, the alternate dilation and contraction in O'Connell's relations with the whig government, also re-emerged. Initially, he was softened by the Irish Church temporalities bill introduced by Althorp in the Commons on 12 February. The bill proposed to substitute a tax on clerical incomes for church cess (which Irish Catholics as well as Irish Protestants had to pay), the abolition of nearly half the Church of Ireland bishoprics and archbishoprics, and – by the so-called 'appropriation' clause – the sale of episcopal estates to build up a surplus fund which might possibly be drawn on, inter alia, for the support of the Catholic clergy. Though O'Connell regarded this as 'very short of what it ought to be in point of extinction of burden', he was, overall, delighted with the measure. 'It establishes valuable principles', he told Fitzpatrick, ' – first, that Parliament is to *cut down* the magnitude of the *establishment* (admitting, by way of parenthesis, that the establishment is too large) to a reasonable extent. It establishes, also, the parliamentary right to manage *that* species of property.'[13] O'Connell was at one with Pusey in seeing in the appropriation clause the beginning of the end for the traditional Anglican pretensions.

He was equally pleased with the setting up on 14 February 1833 of a select committee, with himself among its members, to inquire into the workings of the municipal corporations: it seemed to him a heaven-sent opportunity 'to prove the entire System of Dublin Corporation abuses'. Next night, however, the whigs showed him their other face when Grey introduced the government's Irish coercion bill in the Lords. Even the tories were amazed at its severity, Ellenborough describing it as 'a compound of the Proclamation Act, the Insurrection

Act, the Gagging Bill, the Suspension of the Habeas Corpus Act, & Martial Law'.[14] Grey justified the harsh measure as called for by O'Connell's mastery of Ireland. The truth was that the cabinet had swallowed lock, stock and barrel the wild account of the Irish situation which Anglesey had sent them on 6 January: 'We have to deal with a widespread conspiracy ... I apprehend the greatest possible danger must result, from allowing the People of Ireland to labour under the delusion that the Repeal of the Union, is an object which it is within *their* power . . . to accomplish.'[15]

O'Connell was outraged at Grey's 'project of Ministerial despotism . . . the Irish [MPs], of course, will fight it inch by inch'. Lest, however, the ardour of some might cool, he told Fitzpatrick on 17 February, 'There is nothing so necessary as to pour the vial of popular indignation on all the Irish members who are liable to popular influence and yet desert their colours on this vital occasion.'[16] This was seriously meant, and executed. A fortnight later, for example, the Athlone Trades Political Union publicly condemned their liberal member for failing to support O'Connell in a division, and resolved 'to displace him if he does not reverse his conduct'.[17]

According to the general judgment, O'Connell was worsted in the initial – by now almost ritualistic – bout with Stanley when the coercion bill, having sailed effortlessly through the Lords, was introduced in the lower House on 22 February. Even the moderate liberal, E. J. Littleton, who was comparatively well-disposed towards O'Connell, reported that Stanley

> made one of the most masterly and effective appeals to the House ever heard ... O'Connell was quite subdued, and could hardly falter out a shuffling explanation of his conduct at a city meeting a day or two before, where he had spoken of the House of Commons as 'six hundred scoundrels'. The Mob King seemed completely humiliated.[18]

But in the long run O'Connell redeemed his promise to '*emasculate* the act at the very worst'.[19] Although a meeting of nearly sixty Irish MPs which met at Palace Yard rejected his formal proposal that the coercion bill be systematically obstructed in the Commons, in practice he achieved this end. At every stage in the bill's progress, he used delaying tactics, constantly insisting upon divisions, extending both the length and scope of the debates on particular clauses, and using the various forms of the House to hold up business. Once again, O'Connell, at bay, proved a remarkable political innovator. His coercion bill campaign of the spring of 1833 foreshadowed, decidedly if crudely, the celebrated disruptive tactics pursued by Parnell's party in the opening parliamentary session of 1881. Moreover, O'Connell had to work with much less reliable tools and in less favourable circumstances. It was uphill toil for him to mobilize even the Repeal MPs, and several 'popular' Irish liberals actually supported the government's measure in the end. 'I am afflicted beyond measure', he wrote on 11 March 1833, 'at the conduct of many of the Irish members: Lambert of Wexford – atrocious; Keane of Waterford County – trecherous [sic] to the last degree; Evans [MP for co. Dublin] – very, very bad.'[20]

None the less by 21 March he had secured so many important amendments (such as the abandonment of retrospectivity and the exemption of the press from the new courts martial clause) that he could claim, with much justice, that it was 'now more a foolish than an infernal bill. To be sure it tramples on great principles, masking the rascality of those who bring it forward but it contains little that is formidable in its powers.'[21] Moreover, his guerilla warfare held back the passage of the bill until 2 April, and left a considerable number of the English liberal MPs disenchanted with their masters. The government had been shown up as both repressive and vacillating, and gibbetted by O'Connell as a mere bundle of whig men and tory measures.

III

As the session proceeded, O'Connell's emnity towards the whigs deepened. His sourness intensified with each exercise of obstruction; he was making no progress towards his cherished objective of reforming Dublin Corporation; and when the ministry dropped the appropriation clause from the Irish Church bill, he became contemptuous of the remaining concessions and rounded fiercely on the entire measure. 'I have no doubt', he wrote on 27 April at a moment when Grey's government seemed tottering, 'that the scoundrel . . . Whigs are out, and I have done my best to give them the last kick. The base hypocrites, with Liberty in their mouths and tyranny of the worst kind in their hearts!'[22] Yet already the pendulum was swinging again in the opposite direction. Indeed, in one sense, the worse O'Connell's relations with the whigs, the more he expected some junction with them. As he himself put it, 'To be respected by them they must feel one to be a formidable enemy. They have always courted their enemies. I look to success *with* them only from attacking them with virulence until they believe me formidable.'[23] But also his sky was lightened when, on 29 March 1833, Stanley exchanged the Irish chief secretary-ship for the colonial office; for three years Stanley had stood as the greatest single obstacle to O'Connell's political designs, as well as his most effective opponent in the House of Commons. Stanley's immediate successor, J. C. Hobhouse (whom O'Connell soon dismissed as 'only milk and water'),[24] served a mere seven weeks; and Littleton, who replaced him as chief secretary on 17 May, was quite amenable to negotiation with the Repeal contingent. The second factor which opened the way to some degree of rapprochement with the whigs was a protracted governmental crisis. From late April, when it suffered a temporary defeat in the Commons on its proposed malt tax, until mid-July, when it secured the Commons' re-endorsement of its Irish Church bill, the ministry's fate hung in the balance. Its dependence upon O'Connell's support grew evident. As early as 6 June, he saved Grey's government when it was threatened in a vote of confidence on its foreign policy. As he noted next day,

> I joined [with] the Whig ministry last night and contributed perhaps a good deal to the extent and satisfactory nature of their victory. I have helped them at this crisis which, however, is not yet over . . .
> My speech and vote last night gave me a *proper introduction* to Mr Littleton. If anything can be done it is now. I am, I think so at least, formidable as an enemy. I have shown an act of unmerited friendship. We shall see whether anything can be done. Littleton will be in town this day.[25]

The imminent prospect of the tories returning to power had had its usual effect upon O'Connell; but he had two further reasons for moderating or intermitting his opposition to Grey's government. First, on 6 April 1833, before Littleton took over the chief secretaryship, the Irish executive instituted a prosecution of Barrett for having published in the *Pilot* an allegedly seditious letter from O'Connell to 'the People of Ireland'. Dublin Castle's immediate purpose was to force O'Connell to accept responsibility for the publication or, if this failed, to show him up as a poltroon who hid behind editors and printers, and thereby intimidate 'his' press. Probably correctly, O'Connell dis-cerned the more general object to be an attempt 'to suppress the agitation of the Repeal of the Union. It [the charge] states it to be *seditious* to bring the Union into what the law terms *contempt*.'[26]

He had no intention of proffering himself as a victim in Barrett's place. He had warned Barrett beforehand of 'the fact that every letter I ever published *could* be declared a libel . . . you knew the risk and accepted it'. But when it looked as if Barrett (under the influence of another editor, Staunton of the *Morning Register*) might throw him to the Castle wolves, O'Connell truly feared imprisonment. On 7 June, he appealed to Barrett,

> there never yet was a moment of my political life in which it was so essential to the interests of Ireland that I should be *at large*. My power of locomotion in England as well as in Ireland is, I think, essentially necessary, for the sake of Ireland, to be preserved at this critical juncture. To be sure, I may be mistaken; I may be deceiving myself; but I would not have published one line in Ireland if I thought such publication would put me in a situation to be withheld from action for *three years*, a period which the Court of King's Bench would readily inflict on me.[27]

In fact, Barrett was to remain true to O'Connell, who guaranteed him complete indemnification – so far as money could indemnify him – should he be convicted. None the less, until the trial took place O'Connell could not feel altogether safe. Nor could he, as tribal chieftain, relish the possible exposure of his inability to protect a follower who was about to suffer grievously for his fidelity. With all this, good relations with the whigs became suddenly desirable. Should it seem worth their while, the government could drop or (as in the case of O'Connell himself in 1831) deliberately mismanage the prosecution. They had the power to lift, more or less at will, the financial, political and moral burden from his shoulders.

O'Connell's second reason for coming to terms, if possible, with the whigs was that such an accommodation would stave off, for another term, the raising of the Repeal issue in parliament. Anxious to postpone the humiliating defeat which awaited any motion in favour of Repeal in the House of Commons, he had omitted the subject entirely from the agenda of his national council, when it had met in Dublin in January 1833. Down to the passage of the coercion bill on 2 April, he could argue that the struggle against this odious measure must take priority. But thereafter pressure mounted in Ireland for him to test the water at Westminster by bringing Repeal forward to debate. Several young Turks, chief among them the newly elected MP for co. Cork, Feargus O'Connor, openly denounced his procrastination (O'Connor doubtless saw this as the first step in a challenge to O'Connell's leadership); and partly through their agitation, though partly independently, demands for immediate action on Repeal began to be heard in various parts of Ireland during May. All this helps to explain the olive branch implicitly offered to the government by

O'Connell when he saved them from defeat in the House of Commons on 6 July. A whig effort to conciliate Ireland would be his best security against the importunate rashness of his would-be rivals.

O'Connor, however, threatened to press a Repeal motion on his own, and O'Connell was forced to summon two meetings of the Repeal MPs at Westminster in order to hold him back. O'Connell carried the day, but only barely. At the meeting of 10 June 1833 his motion opposing the raising of Repeal during the current parliamentary session was carried by a mere 12 votes to 10, with 10 abstentions; even two of his own relatives, his cousin Herbert Baldwin and his brother-in-law W. F. Finn, voted with his opponents. After O'Connor had challenged this vote, the decision was confirmed a few days later; but again the number voting and the margin of O'Connell's victory (17 to 7) were far from reassuring. Meanwhile, Fitzpatrick had warned O'Connell that the pressure for a Repeal motion was growing so rapidly in Dublin that it would be dangerous to run athwart it. Even had O'Connell received this warning before the first meeting of the MPs, he would have ignored it. 'I am bound in candour', he replied,

to tell you that the advice of my friends in Dublin would not induce *me* to consent to bring it on this session because I know that any rational discussion upon it is impossible in this advanced and complicated state of the public business. We should have been either deprived of a house by members going away or we should be treated with contempt and ridicule by men who are now thinking of nothing else save *escaping* from London and getting rid of the session. You have no idea of the effect which must be produced in this country as well as in Ireland by the total and ludicrous failure of the attempt to debate it *now*. It would literally be equal only to the plan of 'privateering after the war' . . .

One great reason why I would not bring on the Repeal this session is, that it would give a fictitious patriotism to men who have been voting badly through three fourths of the session; and indeed it is just such men who in general are for forcing it on at present . . . *working up* their popularity by giving a vote for Repeal just at the moment when no rational result could ensue . . .[28]

None the less, O'Connell was still on the defensive. A number of influential ill-wishers – chief among them, the alienated editor of the *Freeman's Journal*, Patrick Lavelle, and the Dublin radicals, Thomas Reynolds, vice-president of the National Trades Political Union, and Patrick O'Higgins, a warm friend of O'Connor, who was later to be called 'The Irish Chartist' – maintained the campaign against him. On 19 June 1833 they carried a motion at a parish meeting of St Audeon's,

Dublin, deprecating the decision to postpone raising the Repeal issue in the House of Commons. O'Connell felt this repudiation deeply. From London he reproached the faithful Fitzpatrick on 22 June; 'how is it possible that you should not in all that parish have been able to procure fifteen more friends of mine to turn the scale?' He grieved to learn that the merchant Thomas O'Connor on whom he could normally rely was

> arrayed in the adverse ranks. I thought he knew me better than to believe that anything but the impossibility of doing good and the certainty of doing harm would have induced me to postpone a discussion. It does, I confess, mortify me especially after your representations on the subject.

O'Connell proceeded to list for Fitzpatrick's (and presumably, through him, for others') benefit the current parliamentary issues in which he was playing a vital part, whether in opposition or support. These included the church temporalities, anti-slavery, Bank of England charter and East India government bills, and O'Connell concluded, in pique, 'I repeat this thing to you because I feel dissatisfied and disgusted with the triumph that has been had over me by Reynolds and O'Higgins and beings of that description'.[29] This coda is revealing. It brings out not only O'Connell's vision of himself as a Gulliver in Lilliput but also the chasm between Westminster and Dublin politics.

None of this was likely to allay the Irish resentment of his backsliding on Repeal. Yet O'Connell could play the kingmaker in the Commons only by reason, ultimately, of his Dublin political base, and it was he himself who, by making Repeal the touchstone in the general election of 1832, had forged the very weapon which his domestic enemies were now brandishing in his face. Moreover, Feargus O'Connor was emboldened (and perhaps also manipulated) by the opposition at home into declaring that – the adverse votes of the 'party' in London notwithstanding – he would introduce a resolution in favour of Repeal before the conclusion of the current parliamentary session. Without even apprising O'Connell beforehand, he put down his motion for 16 July 1833. Lavelle saw to it that this was duly publicized, and lauded, in the *Freeman's Journal*.

O'Connell was now in a still more awkward fix. His wife, who was with him in London, declared herself 'strongly against [his] taking any part'. He himself thought that he should 'merely stand by' and do no more than reply to some speaker towards the close of the debate. 'It is cruel to have my plan deranged by this interloper [O'Connor]', he fretted, 'His debate can do nothing but mischief.'[30] Whether or not O'Connor had been bluffing or whether he was sobered by O'Connell's threat virtually to disavow him, O'Connor in the end withdrew his motion, though only on the very day set down for it to be debated. But meanwhile O'Connell had been trapped. Earlier he had promised his own parliamentary 'party' that he would himself propose a motion in favour of Repeal when parliament re-assembled in 1834. In giving the undertaking (to which he was driven by fear of defeat in one or other of the meetings held earlier in June), he had argued that the delay was necessary in order to prepare the ground by petitions and to ensure full and fair reportage in the press. Even if this was not altogether disingenuous, O'Connell's dominant objective was postponement *per se* – much in the spirit of St Augustine's prayer, 'Lord, give me chastity, but do not give it yet.'

He may well have hoped, originally, to evade his commitment for the next parliamentary session: he had, after all, proved himself to be the Houdini of Irish Political Promises over many years. But the maintenance of the campaign for the immediate discussion of Repeal by O'Connor, Reynolds and Lavelle rendered escape virtually impossible. O'Connell bowed – temporarily, at least – to the inevitable, and began to prepare 'the People of Ireland' for an offensive by a series of public letters. 'There is', noted the young Dublin physician, William Stokes, in his journal on 27 June 1833, 'a bawling fellow under the window just now crying, "Counsellor O'Connell's most important letter to the People of Ireland to *terrify* them to have the Parliament in Ireland, for the small charge of one halfpenny." This *is* a most comical country!'[31] In a mood of gloomy resignation, O'Connell told Fitzpatrick on 5 July, 'I will now begin in earnest to prepare myself for the contest. All my fame, alas, as an orator and statesman depends on *this* exertion.' So low had his spirit sunk that he went on to instruct Fitzpatrick, who was about to set forth from Dublin on a tour of Ireland to raise money for the O'Connell Tribute, 'Wait a few days before you begin *your circuit*. Let the *discussion* question be at rest first.'[32]

Perhaps O'Connell did not despair altogether of putting off Repeal beyond even 1834. He certainly cultivated Littleton (who fully realized that he was the target of 'O'Connell's coaxing' and himself hoped to tempt O'Connell out of politics by offering him the Irish Mastership of the Rolls) during the remainder of 1833. As early as 24 July, Littleton recorded that

O'Connell today thanked me privately in the House of Commons for having muzzled in some degree the Irish newspapers, as far as personal abuse of him went; and told me that I was the only Irish Secretary who had ever evinced a disposition to afford publicity and enquiry into Irish abuses – which I really believe to be true.[33]

In wooing Littleton, O'Connell may well have hoped to gain enough concessions from the whigs to warrant his launching a 'Justice for Ireland' experiment. Not the least merit of such a move, in his eyes, would be that Repeal could be held in abeyance until it was apparent that the 'experiment' had failed. It was probably with some such objective in view that, on 20 October 1833, O'Connell sounded his Cork 'manager', William Fagan, about arranging a meeting which he might address. He was uncharacteristically tentative. 'Let the matter drop', he told Fagan, 'if there be any indisposition to put it on its *right legs* again.' Obviously in the hope of winning back O'Connor, he asked that the county members be invited: 'O'Connor may be a little self-willed occasionally, but he is calculated to be a useful man.'[34] This proved a gross mistake. When at the public dinner held in his honour in the Cork Chamber of Commerce on 4 November, O'Connell invited the government to undermine Repeal by introducing generous remedial measures, O'Connor challenged him repeatedly with contemptuous interjections. When it came to his turn to speak, O'Connor called on all Irishmen to fight for 'repeal, the whole repeal and nothing but repeal',[35] and with fatal aptness described O'Connell's attitude to Repeal as akin to Frankenstein's towards his monster. This finally turned the key upon O'Connell. To be shown up before the 250 leading nationalists of the leading nationalist city in the country was unendurable. Now there really was nothing for it but to face the music in the House of Commons.

IV

'The year 1834', wrote O'Neill Daunt much later, 'was rendered remarkable by the introduction of the Repeal question into the House of Commons. O'Connell told me he was forced to take this step, bitterly against his will. "I felt", said he, "like a man who was going to jump into a cold bath, but I was obliged to take the plunge." '[36] Despite his announcement in June 1833 that he would 'bring them [notices of his motion] on the next thing after the King's Speech is dismissed',[37] O'Connell selected a comparatively late date in the session, 22 April 1834, for the commencement of the debate. He seems to have put off his preparations as long as possible; but by early April he could delay no longer. He soon felt himself to have been all too well justified in his earlier foreboding. 'I never felt *so nervous* about anything', he told Staunton on 9 April,

> as I do about my Repeal effort. It will be my worst. I sink beneath the load. My materials are confused and totally without arrangement. I wish you *could* come here and bring MacCabe [the chief reporter on the *Morning Register*]. I would readily be at the entire expense; but you should come without delay. In fact it is at the last moment I venture to write to you on this subject. I say venture, because I am convinced there will be nothing in my speech deserving recollection or any extraordinary exertion, by my friends. It is quite true that I have often desponded before a public exertion and afterwards succeeded, but this cannot now be the case. I feel for the first time *overpowered*. Well, can you come to me? Can you bring MacCabe? If I had in the Galleries here such a reporter as he is of my speeches, sinking the weak points and mending the best, I would stand high among orators. But it is in vain to dwell on minor points.[38]

He showered Fitzpatrick with requests for reference books and other materials for his address, and oscillated wildly between hope and dejection. In successive sentences, he planned to turn his speech into a pamphlet, if MacCabe would help him; observed, 'But, after all, I can make but little, miserably little, of my subject. Would to God it were in abler hands!'; and resolved to reorganize the Repeal agitation radically the 'moment we are defeated'![39]

O'Connell's speech introducing his motion for a select committee to inquire into the effects of the Act of Union reads flatly. The 'case' he stated was exclusively legal and utilitarian. For five hours he trawled through Irish history since 1246 for evidence that Ireland had been constitutionally wronged and economically sacrificed by her more powerful neighbour. The fact that he was interrupted only once – and that after his first few sentences – probably tells its own story. 'O'Connell', one sympathetic listener noted, 'was encouraged by the cheers of the Irish voices alone, and, as far as any symptoms of the perception of his argument by any of the English members present was concerned, his orations might as well have been bestowed upon the inmates of a deaf and dumb asylum.'[40] O'Connell was mildly boastful once it was over. 'I never felt more buoyant in spirits . . .', he told Fitzpatrick, 'When an accurate report of my speech appears, as it will without delay, from the notes of Mr McCabe, with the documentary illustrations, I *do* think it will make an impression in Ireland.'[41] But this may have been nothing more than the ordinary light-headed reaction to the end of a long-dreaded ordeal. While he was delivering his speech, he could not but have felt that he was undergoing a prescribed, mechanical, and ultimately unmeaning exercise.

After O'Connell's speech had been countered by a still lengthier address from Spring Rice (now chancellor of the exchequer), the hostile majority became increasingly impatient as the 'debate' meandered over three more nights. A personal attack on O'Connell by Henry Lambert, a Catholic liberal MP for co. Wexford whom O'Connell had denounced for his tergiversation on the Irish coercion bill, provided their solitary interval of glee. Lambert declared that the Tribute which

> once was a voluntary effusion, now became an exaction of contrivance and a management of tact and business; and when he reflected, that places of public worship were desecrated, and made scenes of dissension and turbulence, for the sake of collecting this rent from the impoverished peasantry, he felt it his duty to . . . express his feelings to the House . . . his family were obliged to abstain from a place of worship, merely to avoid Mr O'Connell's jackalls [sic], who, during the whole Sunday were enforcing the tribute.[42]

Lambert was to pay dearly for his half-hour of British glory; O'Connell saw to it that he never sat again for Wexford or any other seat. His own Repealers remained steadfast; all but one supported him in the lobbies − even if rumour had it that some bewailed their commitment privately. But he secured no other vote except that of an eccentric English opponent of Repeal who none the less approved of an inquiry into the workings of the Act of Union. On 29 April 1834 the motion was defeated by an immense majority, 523 to 38.

Now O'Connell truly was released. Superficially, he had been humiliated, his weakness nakedly exposed. How could he hope to gain thirty British votes in the House of Commons, let alone the three hundred he would need to carry Repeal through even the first stage of its journey towards enactment. He had stirred English nationalism, and it had rent him, politically, limb from limb. Yet it was not with false jauntiness but with a genuine ease and renewal of confidence that he wrote to Fitzpatrick ten days after his defeat, 'Now I laugh at the chuckling triumph of our silly and mercenary Irish Unionists. Poor creatures! they are like the Indian savages who occasionally in dark nights fear that the sun is extinguished for ever and will never rise again. Naboclish!!*[43] O'Connell's happy recoil is far from incompre-

---

*A corruption of the Gaelic 'Ná bac leis', meaning 'Never mind'.

hensible. It was only on the surface that O'Connell's own politics in 1833–4 (or 1830–2, for that matter) appeared to be 'manic-depressive' in type, with rapid swings from enthusiasm to revulsion. Such an impression obscures their steady trend. Beneath the incessant public gyrations we can discern a persistent endeavour to reach an understanding with the whigs. It was, in O'Connell's eyes, the strategy that promised most advantage at least cost. He had no desire to campaign squarely for Repeal or to launch another mass agitation if he could make significant political progress otherwise. Each was useful, even necessary, as a threat. But both seemed, at this juncture, distasteful, unpromising, and dangerous as actualities. Thus, the defeated motion – and not least the scale of the defeat – was far from an unmitigated loss. It freed O'Connell to deploy a hopeful strategy which the campaign to bring Repeal before the House of Commons had long immobilized.

The essence of the strategy was to exploit the disagreements in the whig cabinet and party on the issue of Irish tithes. It was clear by 1834 that the Grey-Stanley faction would swallow a degree of internal reform of the Church of Ireland, but insist on its retaining its revenues intact lest this bulwark of British control in Ireland be undermined. Conversely, Russell, Althorp and their followers regarded the 'surplus' of these revenues as a sort of stake-money which might be drawn on to buy some relief from the Irish pressures in the House of Commons; to them, moreover, the Irish established church constituted the least defensible of all the anomalies in the machinery of British rule. Only three days after the defeat of the Repeal motion, O'Connell's friend, David Roche, MP for Limerick city, proposed a resolution for reducing the tithes *in toto* by 20 per cent, and their burden upon the occupiers by 60 per cent. O'Connell himself renewed this proposal on 6 May, with the additional object of procuring 'a share of the fund for Hospitals, Infirmaries, Dispensaries and [Catholic] Glebes'.[44] Although the government refused to endorse the scheme, O'Connell's principal purpose in promoting it was secured when Lord John Russell (without informing any of the colleagues) announced – in effect – that he accepted the principle of appropriating Irish ecclesiastical surpluses for secular ends. In little more than a week the wheel had come full circle. It was now O'Connell's turn to capitalize, if he could, upon the embarrassment of his antagonists.

He proceeded to play out the rubber with great skill. Through Sir Francis Burdett he let the government know that 'he would answer for quieting' Ireland should his tithe plan be adopted;[45] meanwhile all agitation would be suspended and Repeal lie dormant. But how was such a programme of inaction to be sold to the faithful at home, who smarted under the brutal rebuff of 29 April? As Reynolds had already set in train the calling of major protest meetings in Dublin and perhaps elsewhere, O'Connell ordered Fitzpatrick on 7 May 1834 to call upon the firebrand immediately and

> beg of him not to agitate for a Repeal meeting for the present. This is a critical moment and I am endeavouring to make the most of it for Ireland. Either the Ministry will concede to me the Tithe question or they will not. If ... no concession is made, then I will be able to recommence the Repeal agitation with tenfold force after having given this fair and fortunate trial to the British Parliament.
>
> You must not suppose that there is the least relaxation in my opinions on the subject of the Repeal. My conviction on that subject is really unalterable, but I will get *what I can* and use the Repeal *in terrorem* merely until it is wise and necessary to recommence the agitation. It is quite discreet not to give the Ministry any excuse for further coercive measures or for continuing any part of the Coercion Bill.[46]

Next day he followed this up with a still more desperate appeal to beard

> my friend Reynolds as speedily as possible, and give him in strict confidence my most anxious advice not to call any meeting *directly* or *indirectly* on the subject of the Repeal for some weeks. He is not a man to yield to mere authority although I do believe he has some confidence in me, but he will yield to a just and sound reason. Now that reason is, that the parliament are ready to enact any law, however atrocious, to meet Repeal agitation. My game therefore is, and it ought to be that of every sound Repealer, to suspend any demonstration on our part until the session shall be so far advanced as not to leave time for any other Coercion Bill ... If, while I take this line on the one hand and Ireland is silent on the other, any further coercive attempt is made, see on what strong grounds I shall be able to oppose it, and what a Repeal reawaking speech I shall be able to make in that opposition! Put this view before Reynolds and other honest Repealers and I think they will be likely to concur with me in a short postponement of any meeting. I am working the Tithe question *well* ... Implore, then, of Reynolds and of the other honest Repealers to allow my experiment its full development. He may depend on it that the cause of Repeal will not, and *shall not*, suffer by a short postponement of *direct* agitation.[47]

But O'Connell's initial letter had sufficed to stop the Dublin radicals in their tracks. As Fitzpatrick later recalled, its arrival 'prevented the publication of a formidable requisition for a meeting to renew the Repeal agitation. The requisition was actually in type, but the subscribers deferred at once to O'Connell's recommendation.'[48]

The policy of 'lying-doggo' paid its first dividend on 27 May 1834. In the absence of Irish pressures which might have re-cemented their unity, the whig ministry split on the appropriation issue; Stanley, Sir James Graham and two other ministers resigned from the cabinet. O'Connell was disappointed in the replacements – 'There never was a mountain in labour [which] produced a more ridiculous mouse' – although he was pleased that Stanley, 'the worst of the bad in everything which relates to Ireland', was gone, and that in the general reshuffle his Irish liberal friend, Richard More O'Ferrall, became a lord of the treasury: 'it is a brain blow to [the] Orange party ... in Ireland'.[49] But he confidently expected that the reconstituted ministry would at least allow the Irish Coercion Act, due shortly for renewal, to lapse. Accordingly, his fury was unbounded when he learned, from Althorp's statement in the Commons on 16 June, that 'this mean, dastard, rascally administration have determined to renew the Coercion Bill! The scoundrels!!!' At once, he told Fitzpatrick to announce to Ireland that his Repeal speech was being prepared for publication, as the first shot in a new campaign.

> I will set about preparing it without delay. I have begun and will proceed with 'the Repeal'. My experiment has been perfectly successful. I have shown that the most energetic anxiety to conciliate the British Government and British Parliament is totally useless. We humbly ask for bread; they give us a stone. Well, can there be one wretch so base found as to consent to wait longer before he becomes a Repealer?[50]

The threat had immediate effect. As Macintyre observes, 'the section of the Cabinet anxious to conciliate O'Connell were prepared to go to any lengths' to prevent his being driven into hostility again.[51] After hurried internal negotiations with other ministers, Littleton, with Althorp's approval, met O'Connell privately and left him with the distinct impression that the key clause to which O'Connell objected, the ban on public meetings, would be dropped. In fact, the prime minister, Grey, in terror that this would open the door to a fresh Repeal agitation, insisted upon its retention. Of course, this second 'betrayal' relit O'Connell's rage, and he proceeded to reveal to the House of Commons his version of Littleton's approach to him on 20 June, and the subsequent parleying *sub rosa*. Though Littleton disputed this account, O'Connell's exposé precipitated yet another cabinet crisis, which this time ended in Grey's resignation. Melbourne succeeded him as prime minister.

Generally speaking, O'Connell was justified when he laid claim, about 11 July 1834, to the role of arbiter in the current parliamentary circumstances.

> It was I, in fact, that turned out the Administration. I get this credit from everybody; and if the next be not better we will turn that out also. From the moment Littleton told me that Lord Wellesley [the Irish viceroy] and he himself were adverse to the Coercion Bill, the game was in my hands if I did not throw it away . . . My victory is therefore admitted by everybody to be complete, and its ultimate results will, I think, be eminently useful to Ireland. We are on the way from a half Whig, half Tory Government to one half Radical, half Whig, without the slightest admixture of Toryism. The moment such a Ministry is formed there will be a famous *turning off* in Ireland. The Attorney-General will certainly be dismissed, and the entire Orange clique will go with him.[52]

Less than three weeks later O'Connell proved his power when on 30 July he proposed and carried two vital amendments to the government's Irish tithes bill. Under the revised bill, all tithe arrears were to be forgone, and the tithe burden on occupiers was to be reduced by 40 per cent, half of the shortfall to be met by the state and half to be absorbed by the Church of Ireland itself. This concluded neatly the counter-attack launched by O'Connell on 6 May. He had gained (so far as victory in the Commons could do so) the substance of his original proposal which had meanwhile served to re-shape the cabinet to his liking.

It was a masterly recovery from the débâcle of the Repeal motion. Yet we should not forget that for more than a year and a half, ever since the general election of 1832 was first bruited, Repeal had been O'Connell's broadsword in working towards a transformation of the whig government and preparing the way for some lasting compact with them. It was of course ironic that the issue of Repeal was of most use to O'Connell when he undertook finally not to use it! But this was in the nature of the game to which he was committed, and did not necessarily imply a cynical indifference to constitutional ends. There remained a level at which O'Connell saw himself as still pursuing Ireland's legislative independence. No rock-climber (he might have said) would attempt to ascend directly to the summit, or even to ascend continuously; Odysseus did not despair of ultimately gaining the Ithacan shore because he was continually diverted.

CHAPTER 5

St Martin's Summer

1834–6

I

Ａnd we'll plant a laurel tree,
And we'll call it 'Victory',
Said the Shan Van Vocht,

so O'Connell exulted in a letter of 31 July 1834 to Fitzpatrick.[1] He
was cheering his own achievement in securing the amendments to the
Irish tithe bill in the House of Commons, the repudiation of all claims
to arrears and the reduction of future tithe payments by 40 per cent.
These were, he continued, ' "pour commencer," as they say at Paris
. . . I see no reason why more of the same dose may not be useful for the
next *draft*.'[2] This struck the note of political joyousness which
O'Connell was to sustain, with scarcely a break, throughout the long
campaign to consolidate his initial victory. Immediately he met
disappointments. His amendments, together with the Irish tithe bill as
a whole, were thrown out by 'the scoundrel Lords' on 11 August;[3] and
his first trial of his influence with the new ministry – a ferocious
attempt to get the serving 'Orange' attorney-general, Blackburne,
removed from office – failed completely. But he was quite undaunted,
and looked to the next parliamentary session for another assault not
only on tithes but also on the Irish municipal corporations. What
sustained him was the shift in the power centre of the whig-liberal
party. Melbourne himself was scarcely less reactionary, or disdainful
of O'Connell and his tail, than Grey; and he also spoke for such
ministers as Lords Lansdowne and Palmerston, to say nothing of the
king. But leading liberals in and out of the new cabinet, in particular,
Duncannon, now home secretary, Edward Ellice, the party manager,
Littleton and the 'advanced' Henry Warburton, were reconciled to the
necessity, and perhaps even desirability, of Irish reform and of frank
and open dealing with O'Connell. Between August 1834 and April

1835, O'Connell's primary objective was to secure the dominance of this element within a whig ministry which depended on Irish votes for its survival.

O'Connell returned to Derrynane by way of Waterford ('the state of cholera in that town [Dublin] . . .', he wrote, 'makes me unwilling to go there'[4]) on 18 August 1834, and remained in Kerry for almost three months. Although he threw himself into hare-hunting and the entertainment of his numerous visitors with his accustomed gusto, much of this time was spent in managing politics, from a distance. His first care was to play down Repeal and direct popular pressure into more profitable channels. As Fitzpatrick advised him on 20 August, when a revival of the Dublin Trades Political Union threatened, 'your most judicious course would be to address the *quondam* Trades at once exhorting them not to give a chance to their enemies . . . by renewing a description of agitation inapplicable to the crisis and the objects of the country'.[5] This particular danger was averted. 'The Repealers will, I hope,' O'Connell laid down, 'see the propriety of allowing the Tithe question to take precedence.'[6] In a series of public letters, he declared that he had at last abandoned his attempt to conciliate the Orange faction as hopeless: 'I am now – and for ever – convinced that Orangeism must be put down.'[7] Practically, his new policy implied a concentrated attack on the privileges of the established church and the municipal corporations, which in turn implied cooperation with the ministry. The government had foreshadowed reforms on both these fronts in the king's speech closing parliament. On 27 August O'Connell told Fitzpatrick that

> the impulse should be given by the establishment of County Liberal clubs and Liberal clubs in every town. Parochial meetings to get up petitions for the abolition of tithes should also be held as speedily and as numerously as possible. It is of vital importance that a great stir should be made as soon as possible to show the determination of the people universally to get rid of the blood-stained impost of tithes. I am greatly inclined to confine the agitation as much as can be to the tithe question. If we could but get an universal expression of detestation of tithes, it would secure our victory in the next session.
>
> The Corporate Reform will be the first measure of that session. The present Ministry *must* carry that measure; and what a blow it will be to the late ascendant party![8]

No formidable anti-tithe campaign was developed during the autumn of 1834; still less was the scheme for a universal Irish network of Liberal Clubs realized. None the less O'Connell's general strategy succeeded. Repeal was quietly and rancourlessly withdrawn from the public's attention – apart from an occasional healthy reminder to the whigs that it might readily be wheeled on-stage again. Meanwhile, the declaration of war upon the Irish tories enabled O'Connell both to press harder for changes in the personnel of the Irish administration and to forge further links with the forward section of the liberal party. It also enabled him to demonstrate to the government that he could 'deliver' his Irish support, as well as restrain the violence and disorder of the masses. As he made the point delicately to Duncannon on 2 October 1834, 'I had no notion that I could so long keep down active agitation by the popular party. But I perceive that there is more of tact in the public than I could have believed. They see, as I do, that our business is to allow the Orange faction to display its hostility.'[9]

While keeping the chosen Irish issues at a comfortable simmer until parliament reassembled in November, O'Connell focused his energy on securing more congenial Irish appointments. Law offices took pride of place: he believed that these largely determined the character of executive action. Accordingly, he renewed his importunities to seize the chance of a vacant judgeship to remove Blackburne from the attorney-generalship, stipulating that it was of equal importance that he be not replaced by the solicitor-general, another anti-O'Connellite, Crampton. On 2 September he even sent Duncannon a list of 'the liberal barristers fit for that office [the Irish attorney-generalship]' – Holmes, Michael O'Loghlen, Perrin, Richards, Keatinge and 'Mr Pigot, a young man but of great, very great legal knowledge . . . Would be, I trust will be one day, an ornament to the Bench'. O'Loghlen and Pigot were Catholics, and O'Connell added the significant rider, 'if emancipation is not to continue to be a dead letter, you will not pass over Sergeant O'Loghlen'.[10] He followed up his pressure on Duncannon, which also took the form of four public letters published between 5 September and 11 October 1834, by similar appeal-menaces directed to Ellice and another sympathetic and influential liberal, James Abercromby.

As things fell out, it was Crampton who was raised to the judiciary; Blackburne remained attorney-general and O'Loghlen filled Crampton's place. O'Connell was furious. Yet, had it not been for accidents of personality, Blackburne would have ended on the bench, with Perrin, the third of O'Connell's nominees, attorney-general. This is what the government had attempted to achieve. Such men as Duncannon, Ellice and Abercromby were already anxious that O'Connell should be satisfied, so far as practicable. In fact, in several ways the episode foreshadows his later dealings with the whigs in power. Often he did not gain immediately the appointment for which he pressed. If he had 'friends' in the upper ranges of Melbourne's administration, so also had he enemies or ill-wishers – Melbourne himself and his coterie, and chief of all William IV. Equally, however, 'O'Connell's men' rarely failed to get their preferment in the end. Four of the Irish attornies-general appointed during Melbourne's second government (1835–41) were drawn from O'Connell's original list of six. Of course, it does not follow that the credit for this belongs – sole and entire – to O'Connell. Some were obvious choices for the liberals. None the less the desire, or supposed necessity, to appease him was a major consideration in every such decision.

Although it was still early days, with the high whig repugnance to O'Connell as yet scarcely tempered by experience, his applications during the autumn of 1834 extended well beyond the range of legal offices and were answered with extraordinary compliancy by his governmental allies. Despite O'Connell's bitter words in private and calculated public *exposés*, Duncannon kept on terms, insisting that he sincerely welcomed and would do his best to adopt O'Connell's 'suggestions' for preferment, even though 'I must now repeat to you that I should be acting unfairly by them – those with whom I am particularly connected – if I made promises or gave assurances that it did not depend on me to perform'.[11] Ellice pleaded the difficulties of making sudden and sweeping changes, and of dealing with the vested interests of incumbents. 'In saying this however', he went on,

> I do not mean to express an opinion in favour of the employment of adverse or unwilling instruments in the direction and execution of liberal measures. On this point I have long entertained sentiments not dissimilar from those you express and Ireland is not the only country, or the administration of her affairs the only department in which the Whig Government have suffered serious inconvenience and injury from a policy for which too much respect for the feelings and interests of individuals and an accession to power after fifty years' exclusion are the best excuse.

As an earnest of goodwill, Ellice acceded to O'Connell's request to take up the case of the widow of his cousin, Darby Mahony, formerly an officer in the 16th Foot: she sought an army pension. 'Although in principle ... an economist', Ellice assured O'Connell, 'I am no advocate for saving public money at the expense of meritorious officers.'[12] While we may discount a little for judicious flattery, there is no reason to believe that the leaders of the liberal *avant garde* were

substantially disingenuous in dealing with O'Connell. Their fundamental interest marched side by side with his – for the stretch of road
now coming into sight, at least. They were deeply anxious to check a
tory revival – above all a tory return to power – and to increase their
own influence and share of offices within the whig-liberal complex;
they were also sincere advocates of a radical reform of the finances of
the Church of Ireland. Obviously, O'Connell held the key to even the
partial realization of their hopes.

O'Connell's immediate gains in September and October 1834 may
have been small, but the very fact that he had begun to make inroads
on the exclusive system of local Irish power was enough for present
jubilation. When Melbourne assumed office in July 1834, no Catholic
had yet been appointed a judge or a law officer or a stipendiary
magistrate. None had ever been an O'Connellite supporter, scarcely
any, even an active liberal. It was this which made the first shoot or
two, with the promise of a much greater crop to come, seem so
significant in the later months of 1834. On 22 October, *The Times*,
which still backed the right-wing whigs, expressed its and their
outrage at 'the monster's' pretension. His public letters, it declared,

> all said in plain, though not the most civil or modest, language – I,
> O'Connell, am 'the people of Ireland;' and if you don't put the
> Government of the country into the hands of the *'people of Ireland,'* you
> shall be d—— everlastingly ... To that Moloch [the Repeal cause] he
> would sacrifice not merely all the freedom and discretionary power of the
> King's advisers in their present and future nominations to office, but, to
> multiply the victims of his ferocious idol, he would, without a shadow of
> equity, decency, or apology, dismiss from his situation every man who has
> not been baptized in the waters of bitterness and hatred against the existing
> Constitution, and against the connexion of Ireland with Great Britain ...

This was the cry of a raging wounded animal, of a caste whose
monopoly was being breached. Conversely, O'Connell himself was
blithe as air. 'My own opinion of politics', he told Fitzpatrick on 11
November, 'is to the last degree favourable to Ireland. I do think we
are approaching a great national triumph.'[13]

II

Meanwhile O'Connell believed that he was about to breach another
monopoly of the ruling caste, and to approach another national
triumph, during the second half of 1834. He founded a bank. At first
sight this may seem bizarre. O'Connell had lived most of his adult life

on the edge of financial ruin, and for years his time had been engrossed by the most strenuous politics of every kind. But, although a marplot in handling his own affairs, he was otherwise a first-rate man of business, with serious, if sometimes eccentric, views on current fiscal and economic issues. Correspondingly, his incursion into Irish banking was, primarily, politics by other means. He may have hoped to increase his capital and London dignity thereby. But his principal purpose was to reduce the domination of the Ascendancy in Ireland, and strengthen instead the nationalist-liberal-Repeal interest.

On 13 June 1834 O'Connell told another would-be entrepreneur that 'the "Irish National Bank" . . . is about to be formed under my auspices . . . The more banks in Ireland the better, provided they be founded on a sound banking principle, and not merely got up by schemers or over-speculative persons.'[14] Three weeks later he and his committee, which included his son Maurice and several others of his personal following in the House of Commons, issued the prospectus of what he now termed the 'National Bank of Ireland'. This stressed its anticipated commercial superiority to the Bank of Ireland and Provincial Bank, which then largely monopolized Irish banking but lacked, the prospectus continued, 'the ability, from the nature of the principles on which they are founded, to confer any decided advantages, on Ireland'.[15] The Bank of Ireland was still primarily a central and metropolitan bank, with a statutorily established monopoly of branch banking within a radius of some sixty miles of Dublin. The Provincial, despite its name, had set up a mere 21 branches in its nine years of operation. The prospectus allowed that the Provincial could boast some remarkable achievements, but discerned two fundamental weaknesses in its development, over-centralization and the failure to 'unite itself with a body in Ireland, with whom to share its profits, as well as to fortify itself on a principle'.[16] 'O'Connell's Bank' would remedy the first by devolution – subsidiary local banks owned half locally and half by a London parent company – and the second by extending Irish banking facilities much more widely geographically and much deeper socially. Under the first head at least, the National lived up to its word. After a year's operation – its doors first opened for business at Carrick-on-Suir on 28 January 1835 – it was running twenty-seven branches, and several of these in places without any existing bank. In O'Connell's own county, Kerry, for example, it was already serving not only Tralee but also Cahirciveen, Listowel, Killarney and Killorglin. From the start the National set out to attract small capital as well as large, by paying interest on current accounts, by preferential interest on deposit accounts below £30, by offering extra-banking financial services for a small commission and – significantly – by waiving all charges for religious and charitable institutions. By the beginning of 1836, it had already more share-holders than the Provincial (773 to 644).

The prospectus failed, however, to mention O'Connell's leading reason for launching a new financial institution. The 'new bank . . .', he wrote confidentially to Fitzpatrick on 8 July 1834, 'has been for a great while a subject of anxious speculation with me. I have sensibly felt the want of a counter-check to the rascality of the Bank of Ireland and of the Provincial Bank. You know that they play into the hands of the Anti-Irish party. I want a *mutual friend* at the other side.'[17] With some justice, O'Connell regarded the Bank of Ireland as a bulwark of the Anglo-Irish (and in particular the Dublin mercantile) establish-ment; and although the Provincial was less tory in complexion as well as governance (Spring-Rice was one of its leading spirits), it was certainly no friend to nationalists. In O'Connell's estimation, the major Irish banks had long denied his camp both capital and credit. He therefore had no scruples about making them (together with local Munster savings banks), the targets of 'runs for gold' in 1830, 1831 and 1833, in order to bring pressure on governments in various crises. None of the runs proved especially damaging financially. But O'Connell had undoubtedly added a small weapon to his political armoury. It was costly and laborious to carry and distribute sufficient quantities of gold to meet these sudden demands. At the least, he could preen himself on causing trouble and creating expense for his Irish enemies.

As usual, sectarianism intertwined with politics. O'Connell, like many others of his class and kind, believed that the Bank of Ireland and Provincial were deeply inimical to Catholic as well as nationalist interests, although – business being business – they of course included some Catholics among their customers. In response to the conviction that they were discriminated against, a group of Catholic merchants in Dublin had established their own bank, the Hibernian, in 1825, in which O'Connell himself took a small amount of stock. But the Hibernian was discriminated against in turn. Unlike the politically influential Provincial, it was confined to Dublin and denied the right to issue notes which, in contemporary circumstances, doomed it to operate on a very small scale. Thus, while secure enough in its Dublin Catholic mercantile base, the Hibernian was no answer to what O'Connell thought of as the pressing need, a bank for Catholics and

Repealers upon a national scale. 'We want a bank of our own', he declared in Dublin on 5 December, in which customers would be neither rejected nor disadvantaged because of their 'politics and religion'.[18]

In the title of his bank, 'National' was really meant in two senses. It set out to provide both a comprehensive network for the whole island and a financial organization for Repealers. As well as eight of the originating committee being Repeal MPs, four of the first directors were O'Connell himself (as Governor), his son, Maurice, and his son-in-law, Fitz-Simon, and Cornelius O'Brien who sat for co. Clare. Indeed, the whole venture depended on O'Connell's Irish fame. Two of the resolutions passed unanimously at a meeting of the Bank's organizing committee held on 15 October 1834 read, 'That it would be of very great importance to the welfare of the Bank that the Bust of Mr O'Connell should appear upon all the notes of each Branch' and 'That Mr Reynolds shall be desired to consult with Mr O'Connell as to holding meetings and establishing Committees in three or four additional influential [Irish] Towns, without delay.'[19]

At the same time, the founding committee included some City MPs and the first board some London moneymen, among them, T. Lamie Murray, an able disciple of the great banking reformer, Thomas Joplin. Thus, despite its Irish nationalism, the National had access from the start to London capital and expertise, and these must have contributed something to its early success. Moreover, the prospectus notwithstanding, it rapidly moved back to an 'over-centralization' as marked as the Provincial's. Indeed, it was always more centralized than its launching rhetoric would suggest, for the London parent company retained 'supreme control' of lending as well as a veto over all proposed new subsidiaries and local directorates. As O'Connell had written at the outset, when – but only when – 'a sum large enough to establish a branch bank in any locality is subscribed, the London managers will double the amount'.[20] In any event, as early as 1837 the subsidiary company system had proved so cumbersome that all these companies except two (Clonmel and Carrick-on-Suir) were amalgamated with the London parent; and within two decades even the two survivors were swallowed up.

Thus the whole enterprise was paradoxical in a way that reflected a dualism in O'Connell's own situation and disposition. On the one hand, the National was the most cosmopolitan and sophisticated of Irish banks. It alone was asked to join – at that at a comparatively early stage – the profoundly influential London Clearing House; it alone had a London headquarters and close and continuous connections with the City. On the other hand, initially at least, it reached lower and spread wider in Irish society than either of its major rivals. It drew even the middle class of farmer and shopkeeper into its clientele; it tapped even the very small depositors; above all, it was the natural resource of the ordinary Catholic customer, and especially of the Catholic Church in its rapidly developing need of financial services. It does not seem extravagant to see all this as mirroring O'Connell's double-sidedness, as, on the one hand, an extra-Irish giant, the very symbol of European liberal Catholicism and secular British radicalism, and, on the other, the great Irish ethnogogue – to use Gladstone's telling word. At the second level, the National Bank promised jobs – to say nothing of jobbing – for O'Connell's particular circle and class. He told Fitzpatrick shortly before the bank's foundation, 'it is [a matter] of course that if we succeed it will be my anxious study that you, your brother [Hugh] and brother-in-law [J. C. Ayre], should participate in that success'.[21] In practice, O'Connell must have often come, in later years, to curse the power and patronage which was assumed to reside in him as Governor. He was to be subject to endless embarrassing appeals, from influential priests and other key Irish supporters, to intervene in Bank appointments or promotions, or take sides in local wrangles. None the less, the National was, in its own particular and circumscribed fashion, an exercise in self-government – at any rate, in O'Connell's estimation.

Viewed in certain lights, therefore, O'Connell's establishment of the National Bank might appear to have been a form of alternative or parallel institution, to provide a vital service for an alienated and frustrated element in society. Although his own financial, as well as other sorts of, ecumenism was genuine, the National was widely regarded, in its early years, as essentially confessional in character, essentially the bank of Irish Catholics and the Catholic Church. O'Connell's earlier venture into the most dynamic field of Dublin manufacture, porter-brewing, already dominated by the Protestant firm of Guinness, might be similarly represented. Unlike the formation of the Bank, the purchase of Madder's – re-named O'Connell's – Brewery in 1831 proved a failure. He himself lauded its product as 'the very best Irish porter I ever tasted . . . It is really superlative';[22] but too few of the public shared his taste. For all that, O'Connell's essay into a 'Protestant' business, and in particular his entrusting the management of the brewery to his son Daniel, Fitzpatrick and other Catholics, might perhaps also be regarded as an attempt to set up a rival structure in Ireland to match the island's underlying duality.

None the less, these appearances are probably deceptive. O'Connell would never countenance an open division in Irish society or national exclusiveness in any of his undertakings. Herein lay an as-yet hidden difference between him and the coming generation of Irish nationalists. One of the first manifestations of this divergence was Fagan's critique of O'Connell's rejection in 1838 of a proposal by a body of Cork merchants to institute a run on gold in protest against the House of Lords' rejection of an Irish municipal reform bill.

O'CONNELL's reason for . . . connecting himself with the Banking system of the country was because of the monopoly – the religious monopoly – carried out in the management of the Bank of Ireland, and because of the political influence exercised by that establishment. These were undoubtedly good reasons for getting up such a Company as the National Bank of Ireland, provided always that it was an Irish Bank . . . But be that as it may . . . we assert, as a truism, that a political agitator leading on millions, in a peaceful course, to obtain from a reluctant legislature their rights, should be unwholly unshackled and freed from a monetary system, the great principle of which is to leave things as they are, not to risk ruffling the surface of society, and to bear existing ills sooner than encounter unknown evils. In the ordinary affairs of life, these maxims may do well; but when a nation is struggling for justice, its leader should have no connexion with such a system. We therefore, always, since 1836, felt that there was an inconsistency in O'CONNELL's position as Governor of a Bank.[23]

But whether or not he was influenced by private or occupational interest in the particular case which Fagan criticized, O'Connell's was generally the larger and the wider view. He found no difficulty in inhabiting both an English and an Irish world. He saw no incompatibility between the flattering appearance of City man with access to the *arcana* of international money, and the uncomfortable realities of an agitator whose finances depended upon the pennies and threepences of the poor. London and Dublin were simply different fields of combat; the struggle itself was everywhere the same. Of nothing was this more true than politics proper, and never did these seem to open into more interesting possibilities than in the phase in which he set the National Bank afoot.

III

British politics were transformed by the death of Earl Spencer on 10 November 1834, which removed his heir Lord Althorp to the House of Lords, leaving behind the problem of who should succeed him as leader of the Commons. The obvious choice, Lord John Russell, was too close in views to the Duncannon group for Melbourne's comfort. William IV abruptly solved the whigs' conundrum for them by using the prime minister's difficulties as a pretext for replacing them in office by the tories. O'Connell's immediate reaction was one of contemptuous irritation. 'I have just heard of the change of Ministry . . .', he wrote, 'It is well that we are rid of the humbuggers.'[24] But this was merely the reflex response of disappointment. As soon as it was clear that the tories, although a minority in the Commons, would form a cabinet – it was not yet certain that Peel, then on vacation in Italy, would take over the premiership – O'Connell swung back immediately to his set position. '*We* are out. The Whigs are out', he wrote to his wife on 18 November 1834 from Cork, where he had just been fêted at a banquet in his honour,

> Peel is on the Continent and cannot be heard of for some weeks. In the meantime it is likely that the Radicals of Great Britain will rally and recommence political unions and all manner of agitation. We, Repealers, must take a dignified station. I believe I will be able to give the proper tone, at least I think so. I am on the whole exceedingly pleased. I do believe that you never were so near being the wife of a Minister of State as you are. But God's will be done. Whether it be so or not, if Wellington does not succeed in forming a Ministry or if he be turned out, our time will come in either case.
>
> The dinner here went off splendidly, nothing could be better, your husband the cock of the walk as usual.[25]

Although speaking specifically as a 'Repealer', he had leapt forward in imagination to taking up station himself in the next liberal administration or even cabinet!

Three days later, he summoned a meeting in Dublin of all 'sincere friends of Reform . . . to consider the best means of combining all the friends of Political amelioration, in opposition to the supporters of oligarchy and monopoly in Church and State'.[26] A number of Irish and two English MPs who happened to be in Dublin (one of them William Cobbett with whom O'Connell was currently on the warmest terms of friendship) attended: 'a great meeting', O'Connell rejoiced to Mary, 'where I . . . got them unanimously to agree to postpone the agitation of the Repeal until we drive Wellington from the ministry. I was greatly cheered.'[27] A Dublin tory journalist confirmed O'Connell's account in reporting to Wellington 'the presence of a good many of the Whig lawyerlings. Conway, the editor of the [*Dublin Evening*] *Post*, the government organ, appeared and made his peace with O'Connell – so that your Grace may be prepared for an *unprincipled* agitation'.[28] O'Connell had tested the water and felt its temperature to be right; and he proceeded on 24 November to launch his Anti-Tory Association, open to all Irish whigs, liberals, radicals and Repealers. O'Connell threw himself into the work. 'The new Association is going on swimmingly', he told Mary next day, 'We have already 110 [fully-subscribed] members, more in fact than we had after a year of the Catholic Association. We are preparing everywhere for battle.'[29] According to Fagan, O'Connell remained the Association's 'moving spirit'. It met three times a week, and 'At every meeting he delivered a long and effective speech. It has often been a subject of amazement, how even his fertile mind could thus day after day pour forth on the same topic a stream of uninterrupted eloquence and each day in a different form ... as a working speaker, untiring and practical, no man ever approached near him.'[30]

Many of the Irish liberals both resented and feared O'Connell's assumption of control over, and driving management of, the general election campaign. Even his 'protégés', Perrin and O'Loghlen, attempted – unsuccessfully – to set up an independent organization in Dublin. Perrin, in particular, believed that O'Connell was endeavouring to establish the 'principle that no liberal person shall come into parliament [for an Irish constituency] who shall not be bound hand and foot by him'.[31] But O'Connell had undercut the ground of Irish liberal 'independence'. 'This is a peculiar election', he told Mary on 3 December 1834, 'at which we [the Repealers] are ready to allow every or almost every anti-Tory in possession to continue so.'[32] In fact, with the sole exception of Lambert (whom O'Connell had earlier sworn would never again represent co. Wexford), all sitting Irish whig and liberal MPs were guaranteed O'Connellite support. This was much too tempting a prospect for any of them to run athwart him in the end, however great their initial anger at the demagogue's exorbitance. Even Perrin tried eventually to bargain with him on Lambert's case. The Repealers also swallowed what was for some a very bitter draught. Thus, Fr John Sheehan wrote from Waterford about the incumbents for the city:

To secure unanimity here I have made up my mind to support Barron and Wyse at the election . . . But I assure you that in doing so, I make a very great sacrifice of feeling. For Wyse's sense I have the poorest possible opinion. No man but a fool could in times like the present have a contempt for the people such as he has manifested. In Barron's honesty I have very little confidence . . . However as the cause of reform requires that we should take them I am satisfied to do so.[33]

A Killarney Repealer wrote in the same vein that although the 'conduct in private life [of Mullins, sitting member for co. Kerry] exceeds in turpitude his political recreancy . . . I have no doubt but the liberal men of Kerry would agree with you that for the purpose of defeating the enemy it is advisable to support' him.[34] Conversely, O'Connell exercised prudent restraint where necessary. His son John stood for Youghal not as a Repealer or even specifically as his father's supporter but as 'a reformer': this enabled the whig Duke of Devonshire's agent to let him run unopposed.

Once the Irish polling dates had been set for 9–27 January 1835, O'Connell threw himself tempestuously into electioneering. He remained in Dublin until late December, arranging candidate adoptions, funds and tactics in constituencies throughout the south and east. He seemed to touch everything, to be in touch with everyone; he practically forced himself into acceptance as a sort of national commander of the 'anti-tories'. Generally, he continued in tearing high spirits, sending cheerful news or predictions almost every day to Mary. 'Have you a mind to be Lady O'Connell, my own heart's darling love?', he asked her, on one occasion, 'Tomorrow you shall know more. Now I can only say I expect that this change [Melbourne's dismissal] will have the most fortunate results.'[35] His sole worry was his 'family party': three of his sons, his son-in-law Fitz-Simon and his nephew Morgan John O'Connell were also candidates. He fretted that Maurice's lackadaisical behaviour might lose him Tralee – 'I hope Maurice has not left Tralee too soon. It would be better for him to be there more frequently',[36] he told Mary on 5 December – and towards the end he began to fret lest he himself should fail in Dublin city: he feared that many of his freeholders would be disqualified because of their rates arrears or perjure themselves by falsely claiming to have paid them up to date. In the event, his entire family 'tail' was returned successfully, although his apprehension for himself was eventually justified when on 16 May 1836 Ruthven (his running-mate) and he were unseated for Dublin on petition.

Although the 'anti-tories' lost nine Irish seats in all, they remained in a large majority in Ireland, 65 to 40. With justice O'Connell claimed that he controlled at least 60 of the Irish 'liberal' members; 34 of these might even have been classified as Repealers, though of varying degrees of fervour. Given this result, was he to attempt again to constitute an independent Irish party? From the day that the whigs lost office, he had endeavoured to make common cause with them and the English radicals. This was not necessarily a permanent commitment. Obviously, his course after the general election depended on its final outcome, even if his own preference would be to continue the alliance which he himself had done so much to initiate and sustain. As things turned out, his parliamentary contingent held, theoretically speaking, the balance of power in the House of Commons. While precision in allocating members to parties was impossible in 1835, it looked, after the general election, as if the tories might muster up to 300 votes, the whig-liberals up to 200, and the assorted radicals 90 or so between them. It seemed, on paper, the ideal 'Parnellite' situation in which an Irish 'brigade' of members could make and unmake British governments.

But this appearance was misleading. O'Connell in the 1830s could not conceivably have played the part of a Parnell in the 1880s. First, political allegiance was much looser in the earlier phase. In 1834-5, it seemed quite on the cards that, given over-pressure by O'Connell, a considerably body of the whigs might coalesce with the Peelite tories to form a secure centre party. Secondly, O'Connell's control over his 'tail' fell far short of Parnell's iron command of a ferociously disciplined party; in particular, a fair number of the O'Connellites were prepared, not to say eager, to be lured, by place or office, to the official benches. Thirdly, O'Connell (unlike Parnell) was still deeply enmeshed in the Catholic question; the fight to *realize* Emancipation, even for the superior classes, was still in its beginning stage. Some share in state power seemed vital if any of the discriminatory system were to be dismantled and replaced; and in 1835 – as against, say, 1845 – there was no hope that the tories would enter any bargain with the Catholic clergy which might diminish the strength of their Irish 'garrison'. Finally, it must be stressed again that O'Connell was the pathfinder in popular-parliamentary politics. Parnell had all the maps deriving from O'Connell's explorations at his disposal, but almost every journey undertaken in the 1830s was a journey into the political unknown. Fifty years later the ground then being traversed was thoroughly familiar to conservatives, liberals and nationalists alike. They, too, were in their own way pioneers but not in the sense of

O'Connell's absolute originality. Nor should we forget, when all is said and done, that Parnellite 'independence' ended in a still closer and more 'fatal' liberal alliance than O'Connell's. An alliance was, after all, the logical conclusion to the accumulation of parliamentary treasure: sooner or later it must be spent in a commitment, or it would rust.

At any rate, O'Connell never wavered in course after the general election of 1835 was concluded. It was the high whigs who tacked backwards and forwards. The key question was whether or not they would pay the price of partial dependence on O'Connell in order to regain office; and the central figure in this decision was Lord John Russell. Ultimately, Russell was prepared to pay the price; his own reward would be leadership of the House of Commons and a decisive role in cabinet. But it was necessary for him to work through at least one layer – and possibly two layers – of intermediaries in reaching an understanding with O'Connell. He had to conceal any such dealing from Melbourne, initially, and, in the long run, from the world at large. It was also in O'Connell's interest that there should be no overt agreement – provided that the tacit bargain was firm and unambiguous.

The issue on which to challenge Peel's government was chosen carefully. Whigs, radicals and Irish of every hue would, it was hoped, rally behind the nomination of James Abercromby for the speakership. It was Warburton who, in respectful and even deferential letters to O'Connell, recruited him to the cause. On 20 January 1835 he wrote to O'Connell 'to enquire . . . (and I shall report your answer to the Whigs) whom you feel disposed to support as Speaker. All on this side of the water agree in thinking Abercromby the fit man . . . But in case he would not consent, whom would your friends agree to support? Spring Rice, Cutlar Ferguson, Bernal, Sir James Graham? or whom?'[37] But Abercromby proved complaisant – as of course did O'Connell in proffering his support; and, with Russell's implicit connivance, Warburton took the decisive step of sending O'Connell a bundle of printed invitations from Russell to attend the pre-sessional meeting of liberal MPs on 18 February at Lichfield House, Westminster. Duncannon probably acted as a secondary channel of whig communication with O'Connell at some stage in the business of his enlistment.

O'Connell responded eagerly to the invitation, writing directly to Russell on 13 February 1835 that he could count on the 62 or 'at the very lowest' 60 Irish MPs at O'Connell's disposal. Using the pretext of averting civil war in Ireland now that Peel had set loose 'the sanguinary Orange gang', O'Connell went on to

> promise that the Irish members of the popular party will avoid all topics on which they may differ with you [Russell] and your friends, *until the Tories are routed*, and that you will find us perfectly ready to cooperate in any plan which your friends may deem most advisable to effect that purpose. In short, we *will be* steady allies without any mutiny in your camp.[38]

Russell replied cautiously and coolly. His letter would have been still more frigid had not Duncannon (who said from the start that the election results 'had imparted an almost sovereign sway to O'Connell'[39]) told Russell boldly that the whigs might as well throw up the game if they began by 'trembling at shadows' and 'quaking' at the prospect of Irish and radical support.[40] O'Connell, however, continued serenely upon the path of cordial collaboration, attending faithfully all the liberal party meetings held in 'the dusty unfurnished drawing-rooms of that dingy-fronted mansion [Lichfield House]' during the spring,[41] and ardently supporting Russell in each of the seven defeats which he inflicted on Peel in the House of Commons between 17 February and 7 May 1835. O'Connell cheered every liberal triumph like a schoolboy. 'Victory! I write on my knee in a crowded room. Victory, victory!', he crowed to Fitzpatrick after Abercromby's election to the Speakership.[42] A later success was greeted with, 'The scoundrels [Peel's ministry] are, I believe, in point of fact, *out certainly* . . . Blessed be the great God for this prospect! . . . It is joyful to think that the iron rule of Orangeism is so nearly at an end . . . I would give a pound for an attested copy of Shaw's [Shaw was tory MP for Dublin University] visage as he went just now into the House. I cannot describe my delight.'[43] By the end of March O'Connell had openly accepted the whigs' leadership; and on the night of 18 April, in a historic scene, O'Connell and his followers joined the mass crossing from the opposition to the ministerial benches, as the government changed hands. But he had already stipulated his 'terms of support'. On 26 February he had declared in the Commons,

> If I am asked if I give up the repeal of the Legislative Union, my answer is, that I suspend it. But for what? To give time for carrying into full operation the three measures I have described [Irish tithe, parliamentary and municipal reform]; to give them a fair trial, to see if they will amend the condition of Ireland, and if they fail, then again to resort to repeal; but if they succeed, then to give it up for ever.[44]

All this represented the essence of the notorious 'Lichfield House compact' between O'Connell and the whigs, whose very existence both parties to the supposed bargain consistently denied. Still, as even Russell himself allowed in later years, 'an alliance on honourable terms of mutual co-operation undoubtedly existed'.[45] The understanding with O'Connell was no less a contract for being unwritten and in part implicit. Tacitly, O'Connell promised the whigs support in the House of Commons except when their government was not at risk *and* so long as they gave him a considerable degree of influence over Irish measures and appointments. Tacitly, they promised him, not necessarily his full demands, but at least ten shillings in the pound. As he himself saw it, O'Connell had at last advanced significantly in his post-Emancipation or second grand campaign. The prospect of sharing power, and enjoying an equal standing in their native land was finally unfolding before Irish Catholics – of the middle class, at least. It seemed a decisive stage in the process of turning the emancipists into the truly emancipated.

IV

O'Connell, as we have seen, had repeatedly written to his wife in the preceding months as if he expected to benefit himself, and handsomely, from the coming change in government. When in mid-April 1835 Melbourne made his first attempt to form a ministry, O'Connell wrote confidently to Fitzpatrick, 'You may be convinced that I will not accept offers of any kind without distinct pledges. Nor is there any office I should accept save [Irish] Attorney-General or Secretary for Ireland.'[46] We may well take this with a grain of salt. O'Connell must surely have known that no British government, however well-disposed or necessitous, would contemplate placing him in either of the two controlling positions in their Irish administration. In fact, he virtually indicated as much when he added, to Fitzpatrick, 'there may be objections in the prejudices of the King against me which may render it unwise to have me named to any situation. The result, however, will be that the less of personal advantage I acquire the more of national benefit shall I stipulate for.'[47] Moreover, on the very same day he pressed Ellice to have O'Loghlen rather than Perrin succeed to the attorney-generalship. O'Connell's benignity was undisturbed when it finally became clear that neither William IV nor Melbourne (to say nothing of other influential whigs) would agree to his being offered any post whatever. Russell, as in honour bound, informed O'Connell that he would not participate in the new government should O'Connell feel seriously aggrieved at his exclusion. But not only was O'Connell unoffended, he may even have been relieved to have escaped an awkward choice: it is noteworthy that for all his apparent preliminary hesitations he was invariably to end by rejecting invitations to take office. There can be little doubt that he was consulted about – or at least informed beforehand of – the whigs' proposed appointments to the major Irish posts. It was he who on 13 April 1835 passed on to the Repeal newspapers in Dublin the correct predictions that Lord Mulgrave would be the new lord lieutenant, Lord Morpeth the new chief secretary, and Blackburne removed from the attorney-generalship. It would be absurd to conclude from this that O'Connell virtually nominated the new Irish administration. Despite his urging, Perrin was preferred to O'Loghlen for the senior legal office, although it is true that both had been among O'Connell's original nominations. On the other hand, he left the whigs in no doubt that 'the Corporation and Orange factions' must go – 'Delenda est Carthago is my device as opposed to *that* horde'[48] – and we can be sure that the incoming ministry at least heeded this, and was extremely careful to appoint nobody in Ireland of whom O'Connell disapproved.

That the composition of the new Irish administration was the most urgent of all questions in his eyes was clear from his first speech on returning to Dublin after Melbourne's second administration had been formed. Then, he set out for his audience the price of his support: 'That the power and malevolence of the vile Orange faction must instantly cease . . . That the country will cease to be governed by its unrelenting enemies . . . [and] that the administration in Ireland will be purified.'[49] He said nothing about legislative programmes. O'Connell had no qualms in laying his implicit concordat with the whigs, and the consequent shelving of Repeal, before his Irish public. Fitzpatrick had supposed that he would be chary of openly admitting the *entente*. For once the diligent student misread his master. On his way back from London, on 22 April 1835, O'Connell briskly replied:

You seem to wish that I should shrink from public meetings or exhibitions. I totally disagree with you. I have no apprehension of unruly Repealers. I should desire to give them a public opportunity of discussing their views in contrast with mine. I am as much a Repealer as ever I was but I see the absolute necessity of confuting those who say we prevented the Union from having a fair trial in the hands of a friendly Ministry, and also of giving a decisive check to Orangeism . . . I have two objects – to overthrow the Orange system and to convince the most sceptical that nothing but a domestic parliament will do Ireland justice. With these views of the present aspect of affairs, the sooner I come before the Irish public the better. I know the magic of being right. I never saw that which was founded on common-sense defeated at a public meeting. Commonsense sanctions and directs my present course – the experiment I am making to confound the Orange party and to give a fair trial to the measures of those who declare themselves our friends. I will therefore attend every public meeting and every public dinner I possibly can.[50]

Of course, O'Connell was justified by the event. He could always, as Lecky observed, 'play on an Irish popular audience like a great musician on his instrument, eliciting what tone and what response he pleased'.[51] Instinctively he understood the interior rhythms of Irish agitation; now he could exploit what Moore once described as the characteristic national mood, 'a burst of turbulence dying away into softness'.[52] Moreover, like the prudent advocate, O'Connell had multiplied his defences. He could place his emphasis on either Irish government or Irish legislation, as he willed; he always could fall back upon Repeal; he could demand good works from the Union while yet denying faith in its durability.

O'Connell needed all the ebullience he was displaying. As it became clear that he was the pivot on which the change of government in Britain and the control of Irish patronage would turn, he became the direct target of malign toryism. He felt this first in purse. Although almost half the Irish seats were uncontested in the general election, opponents were found for all six of those in which the members of O'Connell's 'family party' stood. His three sons and his nephew and himself were later subject to more or less expensive petitions against their returns. 'The Orange party hate me with a most malignant hatred', O'Connell wrote to J. D. Mullen on 11 March 1835, 'They have involved me in the expenses of four [recte five] petitions';[53] and six days later he continued in the same despondent vein:

> Even my health and strength are leaving me. The whole burden of the city of Dublin petition in all its arrangements, the whole expense of that and four other petitions are thrown upon me after having sustained the expenses of five contested elections. The Orangemen are determined to crush me and only think the subscription in Dublin to sustain the election is not sufficient to pay the local expenses there – that is – the expenses of clerks, attornies, porters, printing and stationery . . . For the first time in my life I am disposed to feel heartbroken but God's holy will be done.[54]

By 25 March, however, he was his old dauntless self, telling Fitzpatrick that he had overcome his 'mental agony respecting the elections and these petitions . . . intended certainly, to ruin me . . . my mind has, thank God recovered its tone and energy'.[55] None the less, more than a year of electoral troubles and expenditure still lay ahead, and the final cost to O'Connell of the 1835 general election and its aftermath may well have reached as high as £15,000. Small wonder that in a later moment of dejection, he confessed to his 'comforter', Fitzpatrick, 'Really, I sometimes almost despair. I must, I think, mortgage perhaps all my family property [to meet petition expenses] but do not breathe a word of this to anyone.'[56]

Secondly, in 1835 as never before, O'Connell aroused a species of national rage in Britain, deriving from intense distaste for his vulgarity and still more intense fear of his supposed, as against his declared, intentions. In celebrated doggerel, *The Times*, which had swung over to the conservatives largely because of the whigs' junction with O'Connell, expressed on 26 November 1835 the personal detestation and congeries of prejudice which had kept up tory (and Greyite whig) hatred of him throughout the year:

> Scum condensed of Irish bog!
> Ruffian – coward – demagogue!
> Boundless liar – base detractor!
> Nurse of murders – treason's factor!
> Of Pope and priest the crouching slave,
> While thy lips of freedom rave;
> Of England's fame the vip'rous hater,
> Yet wanting courage for a traitor.
> Ireland's peasants feed thy purse,
> Still thou art her bane and curse . . .
> Safe from challenge – safe from law –
> What can curb thy callous jaw?
> Who would sue a convict liar?
> On a poltroon who would fire?

As the last jibe in particular showed, the spearhead of the attack was social: a man who insulted others without affording 'satisfaction' was beyond the pale. This was the point made by Lord Alvanley in challenging – or more precisely not challenging – O'Connell on 21 April 1835, 'I can hardly hope that you will make an exception in my favour, by doing what any other gentleman would do.'[57] O'Connell who had, after some provocation, given offence by rounding on Alvanley as a 'bloated buffoon' in the House of Commons,[58] responded with the expected denunciation of duelling. 'I treat it', he told Alvanley through George Damer, Alvanley's 'second', on 1 May, 'with the most sovereign contempt, as a practice inconsistent with common sense, but, above all, as a violation, plain and palpable, of the divine law.'[59] Thereupon Alvanley set in train a motion to have O'Connell expelled from the whig club, Brooks's, for, in effect, conduct unbecoming an individual with pretensions to gentility: it is impossible to say whether or not Alvanley had intended such a move from the beginning. Surprisingly, several even of the whig oligarchs rallied to O'Connell's defence and the managers of Brooks's, led by Ellice and Duncannon, saw to it that the motion for O'Connell's expulsion was declared inappropriate for the club to consider. The new political bonds between O'Connell and his English allies had taken the strain with ease.

In turn, the Brooks's rejection did lead to a duel – but between Alvanley and Morgan, O'Connell's second son, who sought satisfaction for Alvanley's attempted social degradation of his father. Hard on the heels of this affair (which ended in the harmless exchange of shots) came a challenge to Morgan from Disraeli. Disraeli, now a young tory on the make, had abused O'Connell at the general election as an 'incendiary and traitor' of 'bloody hand'. Of course, his victim replied with interest, out-O'Connelling even himself with, 'England is degraded in tolerating, or having upon the face of her society a miscreant of his abominable, foul, and atrocious nature.'[60] Disraeli purported to believe that Morgan had set himself up as his father's duelling *alter ego*, and, when Morgan sensibly refused to take up the endless work of shooting in defence of O'Connell's vituperation, promised a later vengeance in the House of Commons. With characteristic floridity, he told O'Connell, 'We shall meet at Phillipi.'[61] Six months later Sir Francis Burdett (a recent convert, like Disraeli, from radicalism to conservatism) again proposed that O'Connell be driven out from Brooks's, now because of the low tone and scurrility of his public speeches. Once more, Ellice and Duncannon held the fort. This time, however, it was at the cost of some 100 resignations from the club, though many of these had, like Burdett, already passed over from the liberals. Unquestionably, O'Connell was damaged by the sustained barrage. But though Melbourne himself fully shared the general aristocratic disdain of O'Connell's 'ruffianism' – 'Why, you know', he remarked, having encountered O'Connell at dinner, 'after one has had O'Connell, one may have anybody!'[62] – the whigs *en bloc* refused to throw him over. The bonds of political interest still held. In fact, the practice of mutuality had rendered them more secure.

V

It would be a mistake to attribute the solidarity between O'Connell and the government, which developed steadily during 1835, solely to the self-interest of the parties. We should also recognize, as Dr Ó Tuathaigh has done, that there was 'warmth and . . . genuine loyalty and respect . . . [on] both sides of this alliance'.[63] The foundation for mutual sympathy was the character of the new Irish executive. From O'Connell's standpoint, it could scarcely have been bettered. He would have preferred O'Loghlen to have been attorney – rather than solicitor-general, but both Perrin and O'Loghlen strove for impartiality (tempered, if anything, by a leaning towards the 'Catholic' side) in the administration of the law. Lords Mulgrave and Morpeth, lord lieutenant and chief secretary respectively, were able and sincere liberals, Mulgrave excelling in affability and the common touch, Morpeth in depth of knowledge and practical efficiency. Equally important was the replacement in July 1835 of the tory under-secretary, Gosset, by Thomas Drummond, generally adjudged the greatest Irish public servant of the nineteenth century. Drummond was high-principled, fearless, torrential in his energy and acutely intelligent; above all, he both knew Ireland well (having spent 1825–30 in its countryside working for the Ordnance Survey) and loved it as his adopted country. Finally, the entire executive was extraordinarily harmonious, aiming at agreed objectives by agreed means. Small wonder that the regime has been described as 'a St Martin's summer in the long winter of the Union'.[64]

This is not to say that O'Connell was wholly satisfied by the new government of Ireland. It was impossible that he should have been. It would have taken much more time and ruthlessness than Melbourne's administration was granted or possessed for the entire structure of Irish rule to have fallen into liberal and nationalist hands. At the beginning of 1835, Irish government was, practically speaking, an exclusive tory preserve. Six years later, at a rough estimate, about one third of the Irish judges, magistrates, sheriffs, assistant barristers and other important officers of national management belonged to the 'anti-tory' camp. At a still rougher estimate, some 30–40 per cent of the new appointments were of Catholics.

O'Connell may have complained repeatedly at the slow pace of the substitution, Dublin Castle's over-caution and the ministry's timidity in the face of a House of Lords ever-ready to charge it with favouring papists and subversives. But this should not disguise his steady joy at what seemed to him a marvellous transformation, not least in the incorporation of Catholics in the national system of power. He spoke of the Relief Act of 1829 as 'one portion of Catholic emancipation . . . that Act was but a part of the justice we looked for'.[65] The benign rule of Mulgrave, Morpeth and Drummond was the next instalment. It mattered little that the majority of the replacements of office-holders were moderate or liberal Protestants. As yet, comparatively few Catholics possessed the necessary property or formal qualifications for the posts or functions; indeed, a modest degree of positive discrimination was exercised on their behalf. What counted was the parity implicit in recruiting them at all. Hence the notes of pride and confidence struck by O'Connell in writing to Fitzpatrick on 4 September 1835 of O'Loghlen's promotion to attorney-general:

> I know of my own personal knowledge that the Government . . . are resolved to discountenance the Orange faction everywhere and in every respect. We have for the first time in near two centuries a Catholic Attorney-General . . . His ears will be open to the complaints of the Catholic Clergy as well as of the Catholic laity upon every act of oppression and tyranny practised against the poorest of the people. Every care will be taken to give the Commission of the Peace to every liberal man qualified for it. The Attorney-General will not allow jurors to be packed against the people. And if the Orangemen or police commit any more murders, they will be prosecuted seriously . . .[66]

Hence, too, the note struck by the O'Connellite *Pilot* when it reported in 1840 the swearing in of David Pigot, the *fourth* Catholic Irish attorney-general to be appointed by the Melbourne government. The newspaper noted that both the officers concerned, the acting chancellor and the clerk of the hanaper, were also Catholics, 'a situation unthinkable a decade before'.[67] It might have added that two of the three were close friends of O'Connell, and the third his son-in-law.

The advancement of what was coming to be called (to avoid former, now-embarrassing names) the 'popular party' was one side of the equation. The other was curbing the power of the Ascendancy. The whig government, heavy with proprietorial interests, would never countenance – nor would O'Connell have welcomed – a direct attack on Irish landlordism. The Grand Jury Act of 1836, which introduced some central surveillance and eradicated the very worst of the old corruption but left the gentry still in command of major county expenditure, represented their utmost boundary of reform in this regard. But 'Orangeism', by which O'Connell meant not merely the

Order itself but also Protestant supremacism in general, was quite another matter. Here he confidently called on Mulgrave to help in cutting back the most galling manifestations of Ascendancy; and luck played into his hands when in July 1835 a select committee of the House of Commons reported on the operation of Orange lodges in the army, thereby causing a public revulsion against their clandestine and occasionally sinister activity.

O'Connell lost no time in pressing the government to counteract Orange dominance in Ireland. Skilfully, he presented this as the precipitant of mass disorders. 'The restoration', he reported confidentially to Ellice on 11 May 1835, 'to power of the Orange faction under the late Peel administration was followed by such a virulent display and practical *exertion* of the worst and most sanguinary passions of the Orange faction that the country from one end to the other felt as if handed over to the most vexatious and insulting oppression.' The natural and inevitable consequence was the rapid revival of the conspiratorial, terrorist Catholic counterforce, the Ribbon Societies.

> Since the new ministry was formed there is a sensible decline in this faction. The Catholic clergy are beginning to be listened to by many of the Ribbonmen and if the Orange party continues to be discountenanced by the Government, we shall be able *once again* to put down the spread and strength of Ribbonism without any legislative interference or much public display if any.[68]

Throughout the remainder of 1835 O'Connell maintained his pressure on the government: the Orange peril was the constant theme of his correspondence. In his last surviving letters of the year to Mulgrave (4 and 8 December) he concentrated upon the forthcoming nomination of the county sheriffs, who among other things, controlled the jury panels.

> We have party judges, we have still party sheriffs and of necessary consequence we must have partisan jurors. It really is the only thing to be wondered at, that the people are *so* patient, for really I have beheld scenes in our courts that would drive the most apathetic mad . . . you have before you the great game – the all-important selection . . . What must the condition of the people be if the judges, instead of being checked by juries, find that they have sheriffs to aid them by giving juries who, instead of resisting, will favour party spirit, give party verdicts and enable the judges to distribute vengeance not to administer justice. The state of Ireland requires a firm hand of power to stem the torrent of oppression legal as well as practical.[69]

O'Connell added a particular plea that Samuel Hickson, a local enemy of the O'Connells and 'of the Catholic clergy', should not be appointed sheriff of co. Kerry.[70] Mulgrave proved responsive. Not only was Hickson passed over but also the Irish government eventually took the audacious and much-denounced step of departing altogether from the customary judges' lists of prospective sheriffs whenever these lists would 'force' an outrageous Orange or gross supremacist appointment upon the lord lieutenant. This was in line with the settled policy of the new Irish government. By the threat, and effective deployment of adequate force, it had ensured that The Twelfth (12 July) in 1835 would not be marked by the usual violence or provocations; and two months later the privy council actually disallowed the election of a mayor of Cork because he was an avowed member of the Orange order. There can be no doubt that O'Connell saw the clipping of the 'faction's' wings as critically important to Irish reform. As he wrote to Fitzpatrick on 4 September 1835, 'when the Orange faction ceases to have political existence there is *nothing* Ireland cannot command',[71] and, a week later, 'if the Orange faction were put down, the combination [of the ministry and himself] in Ireland would be too strong to permit any misgovernment. Indeed, indeed, I do anticipate better days.'[72] Whether disingenuously or not, he even justified the shelving of Repeal in terms of the struggle against Protestant supremacism: 'the cry for the Repeal would only give increased strength to the vile Orange faction, who are violent anti-Repealers, that they may have the appearance of being devoted to British connection. We must not strengthen their bonds.'[73]

All this was hard political business for O'Connell, but no business could have been more delightful. It was with real gusto that he threw himself into the importuning of Dublin Castle for favours or appointments for his friends and connexions. Equally satisfying was the baulking of his enemies, with its superadded pleasurable sensation that the world of Irish patronage had turned upside down. While there is no evidence that he was greedy on his own account, O'Connell's natural expansiveness was deeply gratified by feeling that the good things of office were, to some extent at least, at his disposal. In promising his daughter, Betsey Ffrench, for instance, to put her husband forward for a commissionship of the projected Shannon improvement authority, he wrote joyously on 23 June 1835, 'We are a great support to the Ministry so that I am as able I think, as I know I am willing, to be of use to him [Ffrench] . . . Never did father love a daughter better than I do, my own Betty.'[74] Well in the spirit of the

1830s, O'Connell was more concerned with the securing of a place than with which place was secured. A characteristic letter – to J. D. Mullen, currently his main support in the fight to retain his seat for Dublin against petition – ran:

> I need not tell you that I made every exertion to succeed in procuring the nomination for you of the tide surveyorship. I got my final answer only yesterday. It is unfavourable. 'The appointment belongs to the Board of Customs. It goes by seniority amongst the officers of that Department. A new man cannot be brought in.'
>
> I do believe, if the thing were possible, you would at this hour be the man. But there is as good fish in the sea as ever was caught. We will have a remodelling of the paving board and of the police magistracy within six months, and assuredly you shall be *one* if I live . . . *Rely on me*.[75]

It must not be supposed, however, that O'Connell attempted to aggrandize on behalf of his own family to any considerable extent or that he spent his influence chiefly in the pursuit of personal favours. The bulk of his applications were more generally political in objective, such as the securing of favourable (and the frustration of inimical) assistant barristers – who oversaw the registration of parliamentary voters in the counties – or the counterbalancing of 'Orange' by 'popular' magistrates. Whichever form of request he made, O'Connell was met with courtesy and, quite commonly, compliance. This was as true of Russell in London as of Mulgrave in Dublin Castle. Small wonder that O'Connell maintained his air of jubilee and elation throughout the year. Even if only at second hand he was tasting a little of the sweets of power. When 1835 had all but run its course, he summed it all up for Fitzpatrick,

> Tomorrow [1 January 1836] I begin agitation afresh. The last, after all, was a glorious year! One other such and the faction is down for ever. I am, blessed by God, in the best health and the highest spirits.
>
> Goodnight, God bless you![76]

VI

O'Connell's satisfaction owed nothing to Irish remedial legislation, for none was passed during 1835. On assuming leadership of the House of Commons in April, Russell had confirmed, in general terms, the new government's willingness to accept O'Connell's conditions for support and to propose Irish electoral, municipal and tithe reform bills. Electoral reform proved difficult, but on 26 June 1835 Lord

Morpeth introduced in the House of Commons an Irish tithes bill, which fixed a rent charge of 68.5 per cent in lieu of tithes and appropriated £58,000 'surplus' revenue of the Church of Ireland for other purposes. As this approximated closely to O'Connell's own proposal of the preceding year, he welcomed it warmly and supported it pertinaciously; in fact, it was the votes of his 'tail' which provided the necessary majorities to carry it through the lower House.

The tithe issue had never been especially close to O'Connell's heart. We might describe it as a passion of his supporters rather than himself. It was far otherwise with the next whig measure, the Irish municipal corporations bill introduced by Perrin on 31 July, for this held the keys to various treasuries of local power. Accordingly, O'Connell greeted the proposal with 'infinite pleasure and delight'. It would, he declared in the House of Commons, 'For the first time . . . identify the people of Ireland with the British Constitution'.[77] This was a flamboyant acknowledgement that his original demand that Irish municipalities be placed under popular — that is, middle-class and artisan — control had been met. The whig government would have conceded less had it not been for their English municipal corporation reform bill, currently embattled in the House of Lords. As Spring Rice, the chancellor of the exchequer, wrote privately, 'we were bound by English Bill analogies . . . If we depopularized the Irish Bill by a measure of less extensive reform than was conceded to [England] and Scotland we gave an immediate countenance to the cry of Repeal'[78] — a confession which vindicated most remarkably O'Connell's strategy. Perrin's bill rendered Irish municipal government fully elective, with householder qualification (£10 in places above 20,000 in population and £5 in those below) for the franchise, and a large measure of corporation control of the formerly autonomous commissions for such urban matters as lighting, paving and sanitation. It was less democratic than its English counterpart. £10 and £5 minima were, effectively, much more restrictive qualifications in Ireland than in England; the largely Protestant freeman vote was retained intact; and the Irish lord lieutenant was given powers over the appointment of borough magistrates and – later – sheriffs which had no equivalent across the Irish Sea. But to O'Connell all these mattered little in the light of the massive shift in urban management which the bill promised even as it stood.

This was, however, the limit of success in 1835. The House of Lords rejected the appropriation clauses of the tithe bill by a majority of more than 3 to 1; and since this was the issue which had originally fused whigs, radicals and O'Connellites, the government dropped the entire measure for the present. The Irish municipal corporations bill passed the House of Commons on 17 August 1835 without a division but only because, as one tory observed, the House of Lords could be depended on to defeat it. They were not required to do so. The government was in difficulty enough with English municipal reform – which it was forced eventually to lop and crop in order to ensure its passage – and accepted the plea that it was too late in the session for the upper House to proceed beyond the first reading of the Irish bill. Thus O'Connell left Westminster empty-handed. But by no means did he consider his comparatively long sojourn in London – he spent more time on parliamentary business in 1835 than in any other year – a failure. The House of Commons had endorsed two of his three major legislative demands, in forms which he could accept wholeheartedly, and the remaining obstacle to their enactment now stood clear and naked before the world. It was evident from the character of its opposition to the English municipal corporations bill that the House of Lords was bent upon systematic obstruction of the whig measures of domestic reform. It was clearly their hope to force a general election in which the impetus of the tories' revival (already manifest in the January polls) would carry the party forward into power. The logic of the situation, as O'Connell saw it, was to campaign against the upper House itself, and so far as practicable to mobilize British radical and liberal opinion in a cause similar to that carried to so triumphant a conclusion in the Reform Act of 1832.

O'Connell used an invitation to address the Manchester liberals to launch what he called a 'Mission to the people of England and Scotland'. Although brief, extending only from 11 to 21 September, it included mass meetings and public dinners in four of the great northern cities, Newcastle-upon-Tyne, Edinburgh and Glasgow, as well as Manchester. O'Connell shot at a single target, the

> impediments now thrown in the way of all amelioration of our institutions by a factious majority of the House of Lords . . . Liberty is an empty name and constitutional rights are vile delusions if any two hundred men, no matter by what titles or denominations styled, can prevent every improvement in the social system and continue every abuse.[79]

Instead, he proposed an upper house of 150 popularly elected peers. O'Connell chose this theme in order to maximize the appeal to British reformers while striking at the main citadel of resistance to his 'Justice for Ireland' programme. He himself was delighted at his reception. As he wrote excitedly to Fitzpatrick after the conclusion of the Manchester dinner, there never was anything more enthusiastic than my reception here. The procession of the trades, notwithstanding the wetness of the day, exceeded thirty thousand. I made ten or twelve thousand hear me in a spurt of about an hour . . . I never was so well received in Ireland [as at the dinner]. It is a strong measure to say so and yet it is true . . . You may imagine that I must have been encouraged by applause of an enthusiastic nature to go on or I would have sooner terminated. Indeed, it is impossible to give you in the compass of a letter any idea of the sensation I made . . . The prospects for Ireland brighten. I am beginning to think that I shall be a Cabinet Minister next session, with the rule of matters in Ireland officially committed to me.[80]

Throughout the 'Mission', O'Connell employed the techniques of demagogic denigration and self-projection so well tested before Irish mass-audiences. The House of Lords was dismissed as 'the soaped pigs of Society', Wellington as 'a stunted corporal' and Lord Lyndhurst as 'a contumelious cur'; and he arrayed himself (according to the *Caledonian Mercury* of Edinburgh) in 'a green surtout vest, and pantaloons, with a green travelling cap, encircled by a gold band . . . The people crowded round his carriage in their eagerness to get a near view of him, and he replied to their salutations with the greatest affability and good humour.'[81] Despite much mobbing of this kind, O'Connell was painfully adrift when he declared that it 'is only now that the people of England are beginning to understand me'.[82] The hostile British press pounced with glee upon his gutter language; the *Annual Register* for 1835 pronounced it a mere intoxicant for 'the ignorant rabble . . . instead of being fitted to convince and convert the rational and sober-minded, it only excited disgust and some degree of alarm'.[83] This was a partisan view; many 'respectable' British radicals closed their ears to the Billingsgate and simply enjoyed the novel spectacle of the haughty being pulled along the mire. It was true, however, that O'Connell made only a superficial and temporary impression on English and Scottish opinion: he was sowing on very stony ground, and though the seed sprouted fast, it died as quickly. But this was to be hidden from O'Connell until well into 1836. Meanwhile he carried his euphoria with him into his winter, or more exactly his autumn, quarters at Derrynane.

O'Connell spent an extraordinarily lengthy 'vacation' at Derrynane, from late October 1835 to mid-January 1836, and, on the evidence of his surviving correspondence, devoted much less of it than usual to politics. One letter, for example, explored the early history of Calvinism; another rehearsed, in delightful counterpoint, two of his cherished enthusiasms, Irish spirituality in the sixth and seventh centuries AD and the modern progress of personal rights.

> I rely on the fragment of Gildus and on Bede for my notions of Ireland in the Dark Ages. That there was *all* the learning of the times, a high spirit of religious devotion, much ascetism, is perfectly true but what must be the state of civil policy when the lands were held not by individuals but by the clan, when the succession to the chief power and property was governed by no rule of descent but belonged to the nearest relation who was also the *bravest* man. That ingredient in the right had all its natural effects.[84]

Apart from laying in materials for the demolition of Peel when parliament re-assembled, and striving to keep Mulgrave up to the mark, O'Connell's only significant political venture, while at Derrynane, was an attempt to launch an 'Irish Reform Society' which would draw in the few Irish liberal peers and landed magnates. 'I regret to see', he told Lord Cloncurry on 14 December 1835, 'that all my efforts appear insufficient to excite to the formation of a "government party" of rank and fortune in Ireland [although] the odious Orange party rally at once round a Tory party.'[85] This is a significant indication of the way in which O'Connell's mind was moving during his Kerry break. He was to 'plunge' more heavily than ever before upon the whig alliance.

That he was ready to raise and re-raise his stake with seeming recklessness became apparent during the series of public meetings (at Tralee, Tuam, Stradbally in Queen's county, Dublin and Liverpool) which marked his slow progress to Westminster in the second half of January 1836. At each Irish meeting, he took the supreme gamble of asking his audiences to release him from his commitment to Repeal should Britain provide Ireland with true justice. As he himself fairly described the outcome at the Liverpool meeting of 27 January,

> I have very lately been entertained in Kerry I said to my countrymen there, 'if we get justice will you give up repeal?' What was their reply? 'Get us justice and give up repeal' (hear). At the great Connaught meeting in Tuam ... I have said to 50,000 of my countrymen, 'If I get justice will you give up repeal?' – and one and all replied 'get us justice, and give up repeal' (hear, hear). I have put this question in various other places and have received the very same reply. On Monday last [25 January] I put it to my constituents in Dublin. If any men could have an inducement to seek a resident parliament, it was the tradesmen of Dublin. They would all be fully and well employed, and would have opportunities of making their fortunes (hear). Well, I put the same question to them. I asked the Trades' Political Union, if they got justice would they give up repeal? I put this to them clearly and distinctly,

and what was their reply? 'Give us justice' (hear, hear, hear) . . . Now, here I am, authorized by my country to give up repeal at once and for ever, if England will barely do us justice; and what kind of people are those who would deny this to us (hear)?[86]

As Lecky observes, 'With any other public man, such a course would be dangerous in the extreme',[87] all the more so as O'Connell had, even in Ireland, pressed his language of prospective loyalism to the limit, with, for instance, 'The people of Ireland are ready to become a portion of the Empire . . . they are ready to become a kind of West Britons, if made so in benefits and justice; but if not we are Irishmen again'[88] or 'Ireland is now ready to amalgamate with the entire empire. We are prepared for full and perpetual conciliation.'[89] He seemed even to reduce his former Repeal demand to the level of a trick when he told his Liverpool audience that it was his 'flapper [cudgel]' to counter the 'flapper' of tory oppression in Ireland.

> I too have found it necessary to use a flapper; and the flapper I took up was of no ordinary size . . . I took up a cudgel, and that cudgel was the repeal (hear, hear). [I] was like the gun beggar in Gil Blas, who begged with a gun, and was the most successful beggar on the road (laughter). He looked at the gun occasionally, and pointed to it before travellers, but he always asked charity in the name of Heaven (laughter and cheers). That was the very nature of the political charity of those who had misgoverned Ireland (cheers).[90]

O'Connell banked successfully on being the nonpareil among politicians, the father of his country, the accepted expressor of the national will. In part, his strength lay in his capacity to convince himself, as the preliminary to convincing 'the Irish people', that he was their constant reflex. 'I am nothing', he had proclaimed the year before, 'but the straw rolling on the surface of the stream. I show by the manner in which I am carried along, the strength, the rapidity, and the course of the current.'[91] The most interesting question is not why his faithful listeners accepted all he told them without demur but why he now announced so plainly his apparent eagerness to be assimilated to, or absorbed in, a British imperial structure. The very words 'West Britons' – even if, patently, they did not carry for O'Connell their later vilely-perjorative connotations – suggested gross servility. Was Moore's terrible insinuation of 1834 –

> Say, is it that slavery sunk so deep in thy heart,
> That still the dark brand is there, tho' chainless thou art. . . ?[92]

all too well justified by the event?

There can be no question that by the canons of later nineteenth-century (and still more twentieth-century) Irish nationalist orthodoxy O'Connell stands condemned from his own mouth. But a higher court – on the daring assumption that such could exist! – might well reverse this judgment on appeal. The first explanation of O'Connell's extraordinary rhetoric of January 1836 is the tactical. He had already attempted to sap the enemy's main institutional defence-work, the House of Lords. Now, with the positive encouragement of the cabinet as channelled through Warburton, he was assailing the Lords' main support in English public opinion by stressing that he asked no more than the rest of the *soi-disant* United Kingdom had already won, and that as grievances disappeared so too would *inimical* differentiation. It was a carefully designed offensive directed at specific objects. Secondly, we should note that O'Connell was not really deviating from his settled 'justice' policy. He was merely drawing out more boldly, for persuasive ends, its ulterior implications. When he declared – as often in this set of speeches – that Ireland was now prepared to amalgamate completely with the empire, he invariably added some such proviso as 'But for this purpose equality – perfect equality of rights, laws and liberties – is essentially necessary'.[93] He did not add, as he had been wont to do and was to do again, that he did not expect his condition to be met. These were not the circumstances for expressing dubiety out loud. But doubtless he made due mental reservations. Thirdly, when he said, 'but if not we are Irishmen again',[94] he spoke only of political formalities. In O'Connell's pre-modern view of nationality, constitutional arrangements had little bearing on cultural identity. He lacked the new sense of organic historical development; shaped intellectually by older values and presuppositions, he would have found such concepts as 'anglicization' or 'mental colonialism', in the last analysis, incomprehensible. It would never have occurred to him that his offer – if seriously meant – to merge 'his' Ireland in the empire generally implied even a diminution of its *haecciatas* or inherent singularity. Finally, we may well question whether the offer *was* seriously meant. 'Justice for Ireland' was O'Connell's own coinage. He, and only he, could say when it had been attained. Perhaps instinctively rather than by deliberate design, he had given himself all the elasticity he might need. Even the best-disposed British government conceivable in the 1830s must fall far short of providing perfect equality for its Irish constituent; and well-disposed British governments were bound to be succeeded, sooner or later, by their opposites. The return of the tories to office would certainly be taken by O'Connell to presage the return of 'Injustice for Ireland'. Thus, not only need there not be but also there could not be any final commitment on his part. In short, we should see the apparent extravagance of January 1836 as another stage in O'Connell's eternal tacking. This audacious tack was probably as far rightward as he could safely go; the swollen sail must almost have touched the Irish water. It was certain, however, that, early or late, the time would come when he would put about and attempt to catch a wind blowing from the contrary direction.

Yet the very fact that O'Connell was stretching so intently to conciliate the British political classes is an index of his hopefulness of success. On the eve of parliament reassembling, on 4 February 1836, he looked forward confidently to the generation of sufficient public pressure to cow the Lords into substantial surrender on the forthcoming Irish tithe and municipal corporation bills. It was still a season of joy. Well might he have repeated – blithely indifferent of course to the irony of plundering a revolutionary anthem –

> And we'll plant a laurel tree,
> And we'll call it 'Victory',
> Said the Shan Van Vocht.[95]

CHAPTER 6

Liaisons

1836–8

I

If 1835 had seemed the best of years to O'Connell, 1836 might well have seemed the worst. Parliament had barely reassembled when on 11 February a backbencher, John Hardy, moved for an inquiry into the alleged sale by O'Connell of one of the co. Carlow seats at a contested by-election in June 1835. O'Connell offered no opposition but declared the inquiry to be necessary to clear his name. The charge was very grave and the implication that he had profited financially still more damaging.

The affair was complicated. In his eagerness to win co. Carlow for the anti-tories at the general election of January 1835, O'Connell had, at considerable cost to himself, put forward his own son Maurice and another 'Repealer', Michael Cahill. They were defeated by 33 and 34 votes respectively, but the successful conservatives were unseated on petition; meanwhile Maurice had been victorious at Tralee. When the new writs for co. Carlow were issued, O'Connell, desperate to increase his numbers when the whig government's regular majority was precarious, threw himself into the search for fresh candidates. In the end, he induced a London 'City man', the sheriff of Westminster, Alexander Raphael, as well as a local liberal, N. A. Vigors, to stand. 'Mr Raphael's principles are all that we can desire . . .', he told Vigors, 'His opinions on the Corporation Reform and Tithe system are those which you and I cherish.'[1] Perhaps Raphael's business habits were less to O'Connell's liking. O'Connell had to provide him, on 1 June 1835, with a written statement of the terms they had agreed on.

You [Raphael] having acceded to the terms proposed to you for the election of the County of Carlow, viz. you are to pay before nomination £1000 – say one thousand pounds – and a like sum after being returned, the first to be paid absolutely and entirely for being nominated, the second to be paid only in the event of your having been returned, I hereby undertake to guarantee and save you harmless from any and every other expense whatsoever, whether of agents, carriages, counsel, petition against the return, or of any other description. I make this guarantee in the fullest sense of the honourable engagement that you shall not possibly be required to pay one shilling more in any event or upon any contingency whatsoever.[2]

Although Raphael and Vigors were duly elected on 19 June 1835 by considerable majorities, a petition against their election was launched immediately; and while this was being heard, O'Connell pressed Raphael, in very peremptory terms, for the payment of the second £1000. Presumably Raphael's argument was that he had not yet been 'returned' – although he had in fact taken his seat – but on 28 July he reluctantly lodged the additional money, with a proposal that the difference of interpretation of the agreement should be arbitrated by some 'mutual friend'.[3] A week later (according to his own account) Raphael discovered that he was bearing the cost of defending the Carlow seats alone, and called upon O'Connell 'as an act of justice to me, to fulfill your engagement'.[4] Meanwhile, O'Connell had dangled the consolation prize of a baronetcy before him: 'Tell me, in the strictest confidence', he wrote, 'whether you have any wish to be a baronet. Of course I do not ask you without a sufficient reason'.[5]

Raphael and Vigors were unseated on 19 August 1835, and no baronetcy coming Raphael's way, he made public his belief that he had been swindled. Eventually, as we have seen, the entire business, complete with correspondence between the combatants, landed up before the Commons inquiry. O'Connell won through. On 11 March 1836, the inquiry exonerated him from all charges of corrupt practice, although it declared that his conduct in relation to the by-election had been intemperate.

> Your Committee cannot help observing, that the whole tone and tenor of this Letter [O'Connell to Raphael, 1 June 1835] were calculated to excite much suspicion and grave animadversion; but they must add, that, upon a very careful investigation . . . no charge of a pecuniary character can be attached to Mr O'Connell.[6]

Little he cared for such reproof. He had been cleared of the potentially disastrous accusations, explicit and implicit, of dishonest behaviour. He had been able to establish that he had paid over the £2000 (in fact, by his own error, £2015) to Vigors. This was the vital thing, for O'Connell had in his usual careless way mixed the 'political' with his private money. The innuendo that he had gained personally from the transaction had represented his gravest danger. After some digging for the necessary vouchers and receipts, he could also fairly claim that the money had gone to meet electoral expenses. 'Why', he declared,

> no usurer ever made so good a bargain as this man [Raphael] did. No man ever was subject to a worse bargain than that which, in his absence, I made for Mr Vigors, but which he at once adopted and ratified . . . Surely it is only necessary to say, that no man ever yet had a five days poll for a county who would not rejoice at having but £1000 to pay as his moeity of the expenses – sheriff, sub-sheriff, booths, poll-clerks, deputies, agents, inspectors, books, paper, printing, advertising, carriage of voters to the assize towns, and a tremendous train of et ceteras. If there should be no petition, I agreed, on the part of Mr Vigors, that the greater part of the second £1000, more than one-half of it – whatever might be the amount of the election expenses – should be applied to the formation of a fund to indemnify the voters, and their friends and relations, from that persecution which the Carlow landlords then threatened and have since exercised. This plan Raphael . . . approved . . .[7]

Members of the Commons in 1836 would have had little difficulty in crediting that £2000 or even £4000 might soon be swallowed up in any county contest; and voter indemnification funds had been common in Ireland since 1826. O'Connell may have been aided too by a feeling among MPs that Raphael's insistence upon highly restrictive conditions for his advance bordered on sharp practice; many of them would have been all too familiar with electoral accounts soaring beyond the original 'tenders' for expenses. Certainly, O'Connell was aided by the government, in whose interests, ultimately speaking, he had acted. When on 21 April 1836, Hardy attempted to have the report of the committee of inquiry set aside, Russell and other ministers came to O'Connell's rescue and, in a vote on substantially party lines, crushed the renewed assault.

Despite his 'acquittal', the episode damaged O'Connell – and by extension the ministry which supported him. Some mud always sticks, and plenty had been thrown. Moreover, O'Connell's correspondence with Raphael, now widely known, showed him in some unpleasing lights, alternately wheedling and threatening, trying to buy Raphael off and sliding over the apparent promise to see Raphael clear of petition expenses over and above those covered by his £2000. O'Connell tried to rebut the last charge by claiming that Raphael had

> admitted, that although, VIGORS was bound to pay all the expenses as long as he saw any prospect of a successful issue, he was not bound to continue the contest after expending the [second] £1000 and, that, when he had no adequate motive to expend more money, he was under no

obligation to go further. If RAPHAEL afterwards employed an agent, and counsel of his own, he did so upon the most explicit understanding, that he had no claim upon any person for his voluntarily choosing to do so.[8]

O'Connell also protested strongly 'against the treacherous practice of publishing letters, written in that careless and confidential way, which results from the belief that what one writes can never meet the public eye'.[9] But even these defences (let alone Raphael's counter-claims) were grist to the tories' mill; and their newspapers ground them gleefully to the last.

Meanwhile, more grist had arrived. Soon after O'Connell's return to London, Ellen Courtenay and a youth claiming to be O'Connell's son began to follow him each Sunday as he walked from his residence in Langham Place to mass at the Spanish chapel; on the way they importuned him for support. At last, on Sunday 13 March 1836, John O'Connell, who accompanied his father, strove to drive the boy away, in the end hitting him several times with his umbrella. Three days later, he found himself before the Bow Street magistrates, charged with assault. John was fined 20s., but the self-styled 'Henry O'Connell' gained no other satisfaction. The magistrates refused to listen to his claim and, in effect, instructed him to stop dogging O'Connell in the streets. O'Connell himself did not appear in Bow Street but John was supported by his brothers Maurice and Morgan and his brother-in-law Fitz-Simon in a brave show of family solidarity.

Apart from a brief but total denial of Ellen Courtenay's and 'Henry's' allegations, made through Fitz-Simon in court, O'Connell adopted the same tactic as in 1832; he maintained public silence. He should have been secure. As one of the magistrates told 'Henry', there were 'legal and proper modes of redress' open to him if he had any claim upon O'Connell,[10] and neither 'Henry' nor Ellen Courtenay appears ever to have pursued these. But with the hostile press, led by The Times, in full cry after O'Connell, and even English liberal newspapers bound to notice so rich a potential scandal, the affair was widely publicized. In an oblique attempt to counter the damaging gossip Mary O'Connell, despite her failing health, accompanied her husband on a brief midlands and northern tour (3–12 April 1836) to rouse the English radical reformers. It can scarcely have been a coincidence that 'the ladies of Nottingham' (where he spoke on 4 April) added to their gift to her of a locally-made lace veil 'a testimony of their estimation of her husband's services . . . and of admiration of the domestic support and zealous encouragement which she has always given him in his political career, especially in periods of the greatest trial, difficulty, and discouragement'.[11]

Inadvertently, O'Connell revived the 'scandal' when in a letter read to a meeting in Dublin on 25 August 1836 he threatened to 'bring, in all its proper bearings, before the public the hideous details' of Lord Lyndhurst's life:[12] Lyndhurst was his current *bête noire* for both his recent denigration of the Irish majority as 'alien in language, loyalties and religion'[13] and his close association with *The Times*. O'Connell appears to have had only Lyndhurst's political misdeeds in view, although he did refer, in an unspecific fashion, to a former 'partnership'. But *The Times* made itself an opening by warning the 'unredeemed and unredeemable scoundrel' of what he might expect should he attempt an *exposé* of Lyndhurst's intimate affairs. 'As surely', it 'thundered' on 29 August,

> as he dares to invade the privacy of the life of Lord Lyndhurst, or of any other man, woman, or child, that may happen by themselves or their relations to be opposed to him in politics, so surely will we carry the war into his own domiciles, at Darrynane and Dublin, and show up the whole brood of O'Connells, young and old.

The Times may have had O'Connell's son Maurice in its sights: Maurice fathered, writes Professor M. R. O'Connell, 'several illegitimate children'.[14] In turn, O'Connell 'hurl[ed] defiance' at those 'vile instruments', the editors, and their still 'more vile employers [the Walters]', on his family's as well as his own behalf. They were, he exclaimed, 'blessed be God! [as] unstained as they are cherished'.[15] To answer at all was probably unwise as every word from him fed rather than doused the controversy. Even the support of such liberal newspapers as the *Morning Chronicle* and *Examiner* merely gave new life to the war of words; and the tone of their tory counterparts may be gauged from this conclusion to a *Standard* editorial, 'no other combination of letters that can be put upon paper so comprehensively describes all that is vile, cruel, sordid, and false as the name "Daniel O'Connell" '.[16] Small wonder that O'Connell spoke of 'a political and personal meanness hitherto unknown'.[17] But of course he had only his own success, atop his own scurrility, to blame.

As the Raphael and Courtenay affairs developed during February and March 1836, O'Connell was also embattled on another front, as the committee hearing of the petitions against his and Ruthven's return for Dublin in 1835 at last got under way. Here he faced a host of difficulties. Initially, he was hopeful. After the committee ruled on 9

March 1836 that voters should not be disqualified for non-payment of paying taxes unless they were more than six months in arrears, he wrote, 'I believe this makes us safe'.[18] By 22 March, however, the inquiry had taken so unfavourable a turn that he confessed to Fitzpatrick that the 'expense and vexation are so great that I really am not competent to do any other business until this matter is closed. My own expectations are very gloomy.'[19] He had already solved his leading problem, where to find another constituency should he be unseated. Richard Sullivan, the Repeal MP for Kilkenny city, had given him a letter of resignation from the House for use at his discretion. Sullivan had also arranged for O'Connell to succeed him in the Kilkenny representation at a moment's notice. Well might O'Connell assure his loyal supporter, 'I never can and never will forget your kindness. You have paid me one of the greatest compliments that one man could to another.'[20] But what if the committee determined upon a new election in Dublin? In that case, O'Connell faced a further range of problems. First, Ruthven was at death's door (he died on 31 March) and it was proving most difficult to find another potential candidate; secondly, the tories would ensure that the second contest was at least as expensive as the first; and thirdly, if O'Connell stood again for Dublin, he could scarcely take up Sullivan's offer in the meantime, and would perforce be absent from the House during the most critical phases of the session. If, on the other hand, the committee seated O'Connell's conservative opponents, he wished to counter-petition against them on the ground of bribery. But the timing and form of such petitions were nice questions of tactics, as well as of comparative expense.

With all these hypothetical outcomes and expedients before him, O'Connell was pegged down by glum electoral calculations and precautions throughout the spring of 1836. The one unpalatable certainty was the ruinous expense. The original Dublin contest had cost O'Connell some £650 'exclusive of the sum subscribed in that town',[21] and he had to bear the entire cost of the committee hearing (over £7000) alone. He told Fitzpatrick on 13 May that he would find him

at the loss of full £8000 at the lowest calculation. It has cost the opposite party four or perhaps five times that sum but what comfort is *that* to me? . . . Why am I thus attacked? It is a compliment the Orange faction pay to my utility.

This may be glorious but it is very vexatious. You, therefore, will see at once that the expenses of my large family here – . But I am sick, heartily sick of thinking on this subject. There is nothing fictitious in the fury with which I am pursued and persecuted. The worst is that I have lost more than a year from active agitation. I felt, pending this petition, like a winged wild fowl.[22]

It may well have been a relief to O'Connell when, on 16 May 1836, the committee finally declared the conservative candidates to be elected, in place of Ruthven and himself, for Dublin city, and when, soon after, his own petitions against the substitution were rejected. O'Connell lost only one day's membership of the House, for, by Sullivan's skilful arrangement, he was returned for Kilkenny on 17 May. At least, he was clear of one morass, even if, as he said himself, 'with heavily encumbered fortune'.[23]

In fact, his long and costly struggle to retain his Dublin seat had won him some sympathy among English liberals and 'respectable' radicals; and after the adverse decision was made known, an 'English testimonial' was set up to compensate him for his losses. About £3000 was subscribed at the meeting to launch the appeal; the 'whole amount he received after deducting expenses, was £8489'.[24] So far so good: O'Connell more or less recouped his heavy Dublin costs, and, in the process, called forth public evidence of substantial English support.

But even this was not without alloy in his unhappy year. He had meanwhile fallen into another trouble. On 10 May 1836 he and his 'tail' voted for the second reading of a government factory regulation bill, although he had earlier assured Lord Ashley that he would back his alternative 'ten-hours' measure. The government bill, having been carried by a majority of only two, was then dropped; but O'Connell was widely denounced for both his tergiversation and his cruel indifference to the sufferings of the factory children, who would continue to work more than ten hours on certain days. It was soon rumoured that he had been bribed. The July number of *Blackwood's Magazine* reviled him for selling out 'the infant supplicants for mercy ... The sordid Judas of these days betrayed them for gold';[25] this typified the charges made freely in the tory and working-class press. They would seem unwarranted. The 'English testimonial' (which somehow served as the basis of the indictment) was not set afoot until well after the vote on the factory bill, and there is no evidence to suggest that it was inspired by any consideration other than the Dublin debt, which had been incurred as much on the government's behalf as on his own. Nor should O'Connell's claim that he had been persuaded to change his mind by the statistics and 'authorities' quoted in the debate be scouted out of hand. The matter was not (despite its popular presentation) a simple issue of right and wrong but rather 'nothing less than a deplorable contest in inhumanity'.[26] *The Times* was not far from the truth when it observed that the mill owners had 'found in Mr P. Thomson [the president of the board of trade, who introduced the bill] a ready tool of their cupidity, and the right hon. gentleman, on looking at his primer, found that "the less labour is interfered with the better" '.[27] But Ashley's bill was equally defective. It implied the raising of the weekly total of the children's hours from forty-eight to fifty-eight; by abandoning any attempt to provide checks on age, it opened the door wide to the employment of children under nine; and it totally ignored education, safety and welfare. A much more likely charge against O'Connell is that he switched his votes in order to stave off the government's defeat; this would have been in keeping with his general line of conduct in 1836–41. None the less, it was the charge of pecuniary corruption which dominated in the furore of mid-1836.

Fuel was added to this particular fire by a concurrent rumour that O'Connell had accepted a douceur of £5000, through the agency of Pierce Mahony, to carry a Dublin-Drogheda railway bill through the House of Commons. Certainly, O'Connell had chaired the meeting which recommended that such a bill be prepared, and he regarded the projected railway (later built) as 'a speculation of the utmost value if in nothing else in expending £400,000 in labour'.[28] But such railway schemes and acts were a commonplace of the time, and there was nothing in itself sinister in either O'Connell's conduct or his views. Mahony publicly repudiated the charge as a downright lie and challenged the anonymous 'slanderer' to declare himself, so that he might hale him before the courts for defamation. As to O'Connell, Mahony declared,

> he owed it to that most eminent man to state, that he did not believe there was one existing more above the suspicion of entering into so base an arrangement; and after a confidential intercourse of nearly 25 years, he did not hesitate to avow that, upon Mr O'CONNELL'S honour, he placed the most entire reliance . . .[29]

The shortlived 'scandal' was of small importance in itself, but undoubtedly significant as an index of the extent to which O'Connell's reputation for personal probity had by now been stained – at least, in the eyes of his innumerable British ill-wishers.

As if his cup of controversy were not already full, he was also assailed during the summer of 1836 for the Roman Church's supposed endorsement of intolerance and persecution, as revealed by one of its text-books of moral theology: the point was of course to establish the perils of handing over even municipal government – let alone an independent parliament – to a driven rabble of Irish papists. O'Connell was challenged to participate in a grand debate at Exeter Hall on 12 July (symbolic day!), the arrangements for which were to be drawn up by a body of MPs nominated in equal numbers by O'Connell and the British Protestant Association. Sensibly, O'Connell refused to be embroiled. In a public letter to the reverend secretary of the Association he mocked the proposed 'mummery' and good-humouredly bade the meeting to 'resolve away' to its heart's content.[30] This did not of course silence the rabid Protestants, who formed yet another corps in the army of O'Connell's denigrators.

As if he stood in a pillory, variegated tory missiles had flown at him from all directions throughout the parliamentary session of 1836. At the very least, they ate up his time and broke his concentration on his essential business. Kevin O'Higgins' depiction of his own plight in 1922 seems remarkably apropros O'Connell's in 1836 – 'standing amidst the ruins of one administration, with the foundations of another not yet built, with wild men screaming through the keyhole'.[31]

II

A still more grievous blow was to fall on O'Connell later in the same year: his wife died. It is impossible to fix in time the onset of Mary's final illness. As early as 13 September 1835 O'Connell wrote to her from England, 'how I do long to hear ... of your health being reestablished'.[32] But between this date and the end of January 1836 she appears to have journeyed from Derrynane to Dublin, back to Derrynane and thence eventually to London, which suggests, though not certainly, a considerable measure of recovery. As we have seen, she also accompanied O'Connell on his brief tour of English industrial cities in early April, but she was by then clearly an ill woman. Within four or five weeks she was in Tunbridge Wells, taking the waters, under the direction of O'Connell's friend, the Harley Street physician, John Elmore. On 30 May O'Connell expressed his relief at her report that this treatment was 'agreeing with' her, though he suspected that she might, out of a mistaken kindness, have misled him as to her improvement. In the usual sad and probably unmeant fashion, he begged to be told 'nothing but the truth'.[33]

In August 1836 the O'Connells returned to Derrynane. Possibly

Mary had stayed in Tunbridge until their departure from England. At any rate, her case was clearly hopeless by the time that she reached Kerry once again. In a 'Strictly confidential' letter of 4 September to Barrett, O'Connell struggled to come to terms with his impending loss:

> God help me! my ever beloved is in a state of much suffering and daily losing ground. I do most potently fear she cannot recover. She may linger weeks. One week may . . . Oh God help me. . . !
>
> The purest spirit that ever dwelt in a human breast. She did not believe in the existence of evil. I am incompetent or too womanish and too weak to do my public duty and this is what she would condemn. But I think I can rally.
>
> She would advise me to devote my energies, even in misery, to Ireland. I need not smile for that would resemble a crime; but what am I writing! Only, after all, my great consolation will be a dogged and determined activity in the cause of Ireland.[34]

In mid-September she was moved to John Primrose's house near Cahirciveen in the desperate hope that it might prove a healthier place. But she was soon returned to Derrynane to die. Throughout her decline, O'Connell made no mention of his affliction in his letters, except for those to close Irish political friends. Even to them he wrote with uncharacteristic restraint – to Pierce Mahony, 'This is a subject not to be obtruded on others. Its pressure is alas mine own';[35] to Richard Sullivan, 'my domestic prospects are not brightening';[36] and to Fitzpatrick, 'Hope, which comes to all, comes not to me.'[37]

O'Connell was suffering doubly for he feared that Maurice might also be on the way to death – apparently from tuberculosis. 'Maurice is in a very precarious state', he told Barrett, 'I will act upon your hint and send him to a warmer climate for the winter.'[38] Of Mary he despaired, but almost worse was the agony of doubt about his son's survival. On 9 September 1836, telling Fitzpatrick of his great alarm, he added, 'These afflictions impair my public ability, as well as tear to pieces my private affections.'[39] Maurice came through a very severe 'attack on the lungs' in mid-October, but O'Connell had been so frightened that he decided to leave Mary temporarily in order to

> take up [to Dublin] an exact statement of his case and . . . have a consultation of medical men – Crampton, Colles, and White – on my arrival . . . I must decide about Maurice. At his time of life it is the saddest of the sad but I *must* think of something else. If he is to go southward for the winter, there is no time to be lost.[40]

On 26 October, he wrote to Fitzpatrick: 'Expect me in Dublin on the 2nd of November . . . Mrs O'Connell is in that state that she will not perceive that I am away. She may linger on week after week with nothing but despair of amelioration. Alas, alas! I cannot describe to you my own *mental* state.'[41] He never reached Dublin, however; he had got no further on his way than Killarney when on 31 October word reached him that his wife had died. She was 58 years old.

Mary O'Connell was buried in the same tomb as Hunting Cap on the Abbey Island at Derrynane. There are obvious ironies in the old antagonists being gravemates and in Mary's coming finally to rest in a place from which she had striven so often to escape. But there are fitnesses as well. A single slab covers the two persons who did most to shape O'Connell's life; and they lie at the far extremity of that strip of land which O'Connell thought of as woven into his very being – within the broken monastery walls among the dunes and grasses of the wave-torn spit which runs from the house and pleasure ground of Derrynane into the sea.

O'Connell's private grief is necessarily beyond estimation. Part of his very being had been cut away, in a sort of surgery without anaesthetic. Even his 'public' loss was irreparable. For more than thirty years, Mary had received and responded independently to his inner political thoughts. In his first surviving letter after her death, he described her as 'the most right-thinking woman *I ever knew*', adding 'It is however passed, and I only remain to recollect.'[42] Three years before, on the crucial question of canvassing Repeal immediately in the House of Commons, he observed, 'My wife – who in almost all my political resolves has been, I believe, uniformly right – is strongly against my taking any part.'[43] It would be absurd to suppose that he followed her political dictation, or always sought or heeded her political advice. But, unquestionably, he believed her judgment to be sensitive and sound; it would always be frankly yet delicately delivered, and ever-coloured by a fierce regard for his reputation, especially his integrity and consistency. There could be no substitute for such a confidante. Even shrewd, loyal intimates such as Fitzpatrick and Barrett were far from privy to all O'Connell's mind; nor would they dare to open their own minds completely to one who so towered above them in name and station. Moreover, they could not provide the reflective sympathy which O'Connell, like most men, needed – or at least yearned for – to sustain his confidence in himself. On Christmas Day 1834, for instance, he had described in considerable detail to 'the most tender of wives, my own darling Mary!' his marvellous forensic triumph in *Hodgens* v. *Mahon*, which had just been decided. 'I was most vehemently cheered', he concluded, 'and even the judge did not intervene to prevent it, that is, the continued cheers. Darling, I indulge my vanity that you may share in it.'[44] Never again would there be anyone to whom he could write such words or say such things or look to for glowing comfort. The well that he had drawn on for a third of a century or more was now sealed and soundless.

III

O'Connell had entered 1836 confident (he asserted) of sweeping advances towards his declared legislative objectives, parliamentary, municipal and tithe reform. The first was much the least important because the cabinet would not entertain the proposals from which he might have gained significantly – an enlargement of the Irish electorate, an increase in the number of Irish seats, or an equalization of the Irish constituencies – but instead focused on the single issue of voter registration. Although O'Connell himself had taken a hand in the drawing up of the government's 1835 registration bill, which had been rejected by the Lords, it was far from certain that his party stood to profit from its passage; and when its successor, introduced on 10 March 1836, was later dropped, the O'Connellites were relieved rather than resentful.

The key measure of the year was of course the Irish municipal corporations bill. It was to counter this that the tories, with *The Times* and Lyndhurst in the van, unleashed their intensive and protracted campaign against O'Connell, both personally and as the main subversive. The animus of O'Connell's assailants sprang from their penny-dreadful fears that the Ascendancy's loss of control of the Irish municipalities would prove the first step towards surrendering the entire 'sister' island to the forces of priestcraft and revolution. O'Connell seemed to them to give some substance to this horrid vision, when, early in the debate on the 1836 bill, he announced that each reformed Irish corporation would constitute 'a Normal school for teaching the science of peaceful political agitation'.[45] In fact, the new bill was practically identical with that abandoned in 1835, when parliamentary time ran out. The only substantial change came in the committee stage when, to O'Connell's fury, the government conceded that the vital office of sheriff should no longer be partly elective but instead filled at the lord lieutenant's nomination. For internal conservative party ends, Peel eventually took up the counter-policy of the 'abolition of all [Irish] corporations without exception', with the corollary of 'direct rule' of the Irish municipalities by Dublin Castle.[46] This alternative fared badly in the House of Commons where the government secured resounding majorities of more than 60 in each of the critical divisions. Greville (prematurely) read these triumphs as a sign that the storm against O'Connell had blown itself out: 'the Tories . . . have overdone their attacks on him, and as it has been their sole *cheval de bataille*, they have ridden it till it has not a leg to stand upon'.[47]

The House of Lords, however, fastened on the simple 'solution' of abolishing the corporations and 'amended' the government's bill accordingly. Strangely, O'Connell's initial reaction was to acquiesce in this attempted *coup*. After all, spoiling the Egyptians was an inviting prospect. As he explained himself to Barrett on 16 May 1836,

> For my own part, I will candidly confess that my first impression was that the extinction of the present Corporations would be a substantial benefit. That they interfere with the administration of justice, and render it partial and corrupt, is now admitted by everybody. There cannot be found any man in either House to offer the least defence, or even palliation, of the conduct of our infamous Corporation[s]. Only think what an avowal by those who were hitherto the protectors of those very Corporations, that they were too bad to be allowed to exist longer, and yet Ireland has endured these now avowed evils! . . .
>
> I thought no sacrifice too great to get rid of such a system; but that is not now my opinion . . . We should be, I think, disgraced if we were to accept it, and we may trust that the people of England will assist us effectually to have 'justice done to Ireland.'[48]

O'Connell's conclusion gives us the key to his about-face. Lyndhurst had challenged his entire strategy for 1836 when he told his fellow peers on 9 May that to apply 'the same principle . . . to different places must produce dissimilar results, and could not lead to equal justice'.[49] Not merely did Lyndhurst imply that the Irish majority was unfit for even municipal 'liberty' but also he struck at the heart of O'Connell's 'Justice for Ireland' reasoning. Mulgrave appreciated what O'Connell had now at stake. 'I believe', he wrote to Russell from Dublin on 15 April,

> that there is no other question on which there is more general anxiety [in Ireland], not perhaps that they anticipate any very great actual advantages from it [municipal reform] except in the large towns but because they consider it as embodying the principle of *equal justice to Ireland* . . . the [Irish] Liberal Party will unite in counting the Municipal Bill as the last of

equal Rights on points not connected with the Church, and it would be very difficult to ensure continued confidence in the Government with our submitting to be beat upon such a point without an appeal to the people.[50]

Russell tried to save something from the wreck by proposing, as a *pis aller*, that only the eleven largest Irish municipalities should retain their corporations, the remaining towns to be directly administered by the crown. Most reluctantly, O'Connell fell into line, but, as he later told Pigot, was happily rescued from the consequences of this embarrassing surrender by the Lords' intransigence. 'The Corporate Reform Bill was *amended* by Lord John against my consent. I protested in private against the compromise but was driven in public to support *the party*; and it is now well I did so, as we have had the credit of moderation without being tied to any restrictive enactments.'[51] The Lords' second rejection was enough to stiffen the government's resolve. Russell went so far to appease O'Connell as to advise the creation of new peers to offset the tory majority in the upper House. Although there was no possibility that Melbourne would endorse such a step on any Irish issue, Russell's gesture of solidarity had its effect in re-binding O'Connell to the whigs. As he himself affirmed on 30 June, during the debate on the Lords' obstruction,

> I know the present Government are disposed to do all they possibly can in order to obtain justice for the people of Ireland. Let my support of them be misrepresented as it may, I shall support them because I know there is no alternative between a system of uncompromising despotism in Ireland, and the maintenance in power of the present Ministry.[52]

None the less, the cabinet support promised to O'Connell was a barren sort of satisfaction. The fact remained that Irish municipal reform, the leading prize of the parliamentary session, was lost for 1836. O'Connell would have to try again in 1837 to mount sufficient Irish and English popular pressure to force the Lords' hand. It was all ominously reminiscent of the fruitless successes of Catholic Emancipation in the House of Commons before 1829, and the grinding toil to be re-commenced with every failure. This might be balanced by consciousness of the eventual triumph; but no man in his sixties can afford to invest much in 'the long run'. Moreover, the fate of the new tithe bill seemed to form a gloomy precedent. The 1836 tithe measure was practically a copy of that defeated in the upper House in 1835, and it followed, with depressing fidelity, the sad course of its predecessor. Having passed its third reading in the Commons on 4 July 1836, it quickly foundered in the Lords, where the essential appropriation clauses were rejected. Was it not all too likely that the municipal corporations bill would fall similarly in 1837 at precisely the same obstacle as had brought it down in 1836?

O'Connell responded to his political repulses in his customary way. He proclaimed a new agitation and, with lightning speed, designed an organization to control it. Significantly, it was to MacHale, the leader among the sympathetic clergy, that he first announced his project. 'I intend . . .', he wrote to him on 2 July 1836,

> to propose the revival of the Catholic Association in a new name and somewhat broader basis. It will bear the name of 'The General Association of Ireland', to be dissolved so soon as full corporate reform and a satisfactory adjustment of the tithe are obtained by law.
>
> I intend to have the 'Irish rent' to replace the Catholic rent and to find a friend to indemnify *tithe victims* but this part of the arrangement will require discretion, tact, and some cautious management. You will see my plans fully developed in the *Pilot* of Wednesday [6 July].[53]

The great curiosity of this mass movement was its specific commitment to support the current government and preserve public order; and in fact it did serve the general liberal as well as Irish interests. But primarily it was meant, as its author clearly implied, to replicate the Catholic Association in machinery and fervour. As an agitator, O'Connell was nothing if not practical. 'The Government will *not* discountenance us', he assured Fitzpatrick, also on 2 July,

> Our organisation will be complete. Treasurers, Finance Committee, Committee for each Province, a person responsible for each county, Registry Committees *out* of Dublin . . .
>
> Every man who subscribes one shilling will have his name enrolled. Every man who subscribes a pound to be a member, being proposed and seconded. In short, all and more than the Catholic Association has done. This is the precious moment to set to England one example more. I am determined that nothing shall prevent me from working out my plan. One way or the other, we must succeed in obtaining justice for Ireland.
>
> I write to Barrett a letter, a short one for publication [in the *Pilot*]. This is private, that is, not for the newspapers. Can you get me ten names of men who will work? If I had but *ten* real *working* men it would be quite enough. Surely ten such men can be found. The day of meeting must be *Thursday*, to give the weekly papers time to send the debates to the country.[54]

In several respects, the General Association was one of the more successful of O'Connell's popular excursions, especially after Mary's death and Maurice's recovery released him for serious management and campaigning. He was fortunate in having a readymade enemy to rouse the necessary element of passion in his following. Irish tories had formed a Church Property Protection Association which, in the spring of 1836, resurrected an antique form of writ by which they successfully pursued tithe defaulters, even to the point of arrest and imprisonment – in the process compelling the reluctant Irish executive to employ the police and army to execute court orders. Nothing was better fitted to enflame tenant resistance and clerical indignation, and thereby fuel O'Connell's movement. The General Association could busy itself with counter-actions on behalf of the defaulters. These had, from O'Connell's standpoint, the sterling merits of both stirring up enthusiasm and belligerency and justifying the call for generous subscriptions. As always, 'Rent' was O'Connell's chief measure of an agitation's health, and by this criterion the Association flourished. As one of his faithful disciples put it in May 1837,

> see the silent and increasing influence the General Association is acquiring through the agency of Justice Rent. Observe the alarm of the lordly aristocrats of England. How well and surely does their experience enable them to calculate the result. Why is this? Not in consequence of the power money of itself bestows; but because it is a sure and steady index of the People's feelings – because it is the thermometer by which the warmth of those feelings can be best ascertained, and in proportion as the contributions increase or diminish in such proportion are the National sentiments indicated.[55]

None the less, O'Connell trod on delicate ground in basing much of his appeal upon the tithe issue. As early as 1 July 1836, Sharman Crawford, an independent and crochety Ulster liberal, challenged him in the Commons to revert to his original demand for the total abolition of Irish tithes. O'Connell dismissed Crawford as the sort of visionary who would invariably sacrifice an achievable good for an impossible ideal. Although a mere half-dozen O'Connellite MPs backed Crawford, it was irritating that a persistent dissentient voice should be raised in parliament on a matter deeply engaging the sympathies of the Catholic clergy and substantial tenant farmers. Worse still, Crawford also raised it again at meetings of the Association late in 1836, adding to his demand for complete eradication strong denunciations of O'Connell for sacrificing Irish to governmental interests. This did little to disturb O'Connell's mastery of his movement, but it certainly placed him on the defensive, in particular with the bolder spirits among the priests and bourgeoisie. A rift with MacHale began to open.

The *contretemps* was all the more unfortunate because it was clear to O'Connell by the end of 1836 that he would have to make more instead of less concessions on Irish tithes. A possible compromise was beginning to be mooted at Westminster whereby the House of Lords would allow the substance of the Irish corporations bill to pass in return for the abandonment of the appropriation clauses in the tithe bill. O'Connell succumbed privately to the temptation and confessed himself ready to yield up appropriation should need be. 'I wish with all my heart', he told the cabinet on 29 December 1836 through his usual intermediary, Warburton,

> the Ministry were decently freed from that *Dilemma*. If there were a proper deduction from the burden of the tithes, there would for the present be no surplus; and it is really too bad to risk *on such* a point a ministry who are for the first time in history conquering the 'Anti-Saxon' spirit of Ireland and adding eight million to the King's subjects.

As a *quid pro quo*, O'Connell sought the restoration of the clause in the corporations bill which left the shrievalty a primarily elective office. 'This plan', he justly pointed out, 'was abandoned as a concession to the Tories who made use of it as an argument against any new corporations in Ireland.'[56] But even if he were to gain his point, it would be but a miserable offset to his numerous large, yet fruitless, retreats on Irish bills throughout the year.

Thus O'Connell ended 1836 not only with no legislative trophy to display for all the labours and obloquy he had endured but also with the centrepiece of tithe reform virtually given up, Irish parliamentary reform virtually forgotten, and the battle for the municipal corporations unresolved. Even had he not lost Mary, it might still be counted as the worst of years.

IV

Was the crescendo of all O'Connell's strivings since July 1834 to be nothing more than an Irish municipal corporations bill in 1837? Apparently – but this should not be written off as necessarily negligible, by O'Connell's measurement, at least. First, he was faced by a large tory majority in the House of Lords bent on systematic obstruction. The degree of intransigence varied. Wellington was comparatively pliant, Lyndhurst, an ultra of ultras. But all were ready to use their blocking power to kill liberal Irish legislation, steeled in their resolve by widespread public support and the belief that the conservatives might well win the next general election. O'Connell's logical course, to campaign seriously for the abolition of emasculation of the House of Lords, was not really a practicable proposition in the 1830s. His best counter was to increase popular pressure; and, accordingly, during January and February 1837 he whipped up meetings and petititons of the General Association not only in favour of the Irish bills but also in support of such general radical reforms as the secret ballot; he also strenuously wooed the British non-conformists by throwing himself into their current campaign for the abolition of church rates. But his Irish agitation was respectable (in all senses) rather than a menacing concentration of the masses. Fagan, one of its principal managers, wrote afterwards, that although it

> had all the appearance of a political crisis it passed off like a dark but fleeting cloud. It was but a transitory exhibition of feeling . . . In fact, none, but those who complied with them can know how deep was the disappointment of the people, at the adjournment of the great question, for the success of which they felt an intense anxiety, and for which alone they have an inclination – the question of Repeal. O'Connell while in England, aided, by letters addressed to the people of Ireland, and to the National [i.e. General] Association, the agitation for Justice – and, like every act of his, it had its effect amongst the middle classes, but the people had but one all-absorbing interest – the attainment of Repeal, and, until he opened that bright prospect to their view, it was difficult to urge them into exertion.[57]

O'Connell's English meetings also failed to win a fiery response. His radical support in Britain had been both narrowed and weakened by the events of 1836.

Secondly, although the municipal corporations governed only one-tenth of the Irish population, their capture was a dear objective to O'Connell. Albeit with some over-simplification, we might specify this as the third of his major emancipationist goals – the first being the removal of Roman Catholic disabilities and the second a share in the exercise of Irish central power, a voice in the shaping of Irish policy and a hand in the filling of Irish offices. The corporations may have been generally impoverished and often futile. But any important constituent in the system of Irish Ascendancy was *per se* a prime target for O'Connell. He coveted moreover their hoards of petty patronage, rights of local legislation, magisterial courts and influence over parliamentary elections. Finally, they represented, on however small a scale, a form of the self-government for which O'Connell craved. Shaw once said of nationalist movements in general, that they were 'only the agonising symptom of a suppressed natural function';[58] the dictum applied fully to O'Connell's eagerness to control even a City

Hall. All this helps to explain the seeming extravagance of the price he was prepared to pay for municipal reform. Both practically and symbolically it appeared to him the next stage in a long and difficult advance.

Meanwhile, it looked as if the major parties were moving towards the sort of compromise on Irish legislation to which O'Connell had consented at the close of 1836. He prepared the way for it in Ireland by a carefully worded letter of 18 February 1837 to Fitzpatrick. In this, he considered Peel's likely terms, 'to allow the Irish Municipal Reform Bill to pass *both Houses*' in return for an appropriation-less tithe bill, with the commutation fixed at 70 per cent. 'Should they [the government] accede,' he continued,

> the Irish members will probably feel it their duty to protest against any compromise on the subject of the tithes and accept the deduction merely as an instalment . . . Certainly something would be gained by carrying into effect the bargain between Peel and the Ministry but none of the Irish popular members could commit themselves to the plan.[59]

Clearly O'Connell was ready, for the sake of his Irish public, to withhold support from the government on the major Irish issues, *provided* that it was safe to do so. If Russell and Peel came to an understanding, a favourable majority was assured in the House of Commons, and O'Connell could abstain, or even oppose, secure in the knowledge that the clause or measure in question would be carried none the less. He would not of course take any action which might actually endanger the corporations bill, all the more so as the ministry had yielded to his wishes on the election of sheriffs issue.

As the parliamentary session progressed, the conditions of a tacit settlement between the liberal and conservative leaderships gradually clarified. Peel insisted on the establishment of an Irish poor law – which the whigs already favoured – partly in the hope that a new rating system might do something to preserve tory interests in the municipalities. O'Connell reluctantly consented. For almost a decade he had fought against any such measure, even at the cost of endangering Bishop Doyle's support in earlier days. His reasons were a characteristic compound of traditionalism and 'modernity'. On the one hand, he argued that a poor law would obliterate Christian charity and compassion, and weaken the human interdependency which he idealized as the mark of his own sort of landed proprietorship. On the other, political economy told him that it was folly at the least to disturb the market forces; in particular, communal support of the able-bodied would be disastrous for themselves as well as the precarious Irish economy. Nor should we forget that O'Connell was himself a landlord, open to the usual landlord nightmare of Irish property sinking under the immeasurable weight of Irish pauperdom. Despite all this, O'Connell yielded to political necessity in 1837, and when on 13 February, Russell introduced an Irish poor relief bill modelled on the English workhouse form of 1834, he greeted it with assumed benignity, announcing that he 'cheerfully acced[ed] to the proposed plan'.[60] One other element in the legislative amalgam is worth noting. The government added a clause to the tithe bill imposing a tax of 10 per cent on the incomes of Church of Ireland ministers for general (and not merely Anglican) educational purposes. It was hoped that this would, inter alia, help O'Connell to justify his change of front at home.

O'Connell's position was now set. He would support the ministerial package of the three major Irish bills, with the proviso that he might formally oppose specific clauses where the government ran no risk of defeat. The grand scheme, however, foundered, more or less accidentally. Twice the House of Lords postponed consideration of the Irish municipal corporations bill (which had passed through the lower house unscathed) until it could legislate on tithes and poor relief. But on 20 June 1837, before either of these measures could be settled, William IV died. This meant a new general election and the ruin of the entire legislative programme of the session. O'Connell was – by his own view of things – badly out of luck. Despite Wellington's initial reluctance to follow Peel's line in accepting the trinity of measures, and Lyndhurst's inveterate opposition to them all, the three bills would probably have passed the House of Lords had the parliamentary process not been interrupted; and two of them, the corporations and tithe bills, were much more advantageous to O'Connell than the measures subsequently enacted. Besides, he had surrendered his position on the poor law without any counterbalancing gain, and uselessly given up considerable ground on tithes. Meanwhile, this last had precipitated a serious revolt in Ireland.

On 26 May 1837 MacHale sent O'Connell a petition from the clergy of the Tuam archdiocese protesting hotly against the concessions made in even the 1837 tithe bill. Pointedly, MacHale used O'Connell's own formula 'Justice for Ireland' as his frame of reference. 'The Tithe Bill', he concluded, 'they [the people] took on as the test of the justice which has been so long promised but of which the performance is, they complain, so long delayed. Wishing you many happy years to aid in the consummation of that justice which the country expects.'[61] Alarmed, O'Connell reported to Fitzpatrick, 'Dr MacHale's resolutions have made a considerable sensation . . . Unless he shall relax, the Connaught members will vote against us.'[62] He pleaded for reconsideration, or at least delay in presenting the petition. Attempting at once to frighten, flatter and feed the sectarian animus of the archbishop, he wrote on 31 May,

> I am, I own, timid and could have wished that this blow had not been given to the falling fabric of ministerial power. I do believe it will be decisive of their fate. But do not understand these as tones of reproach. I may be sorrowful but, in plain truth, I can have no elements in my mind which could create anger when, as in this instance, the wise and the good adopt a course too bold for my humbler temper. What I grieve at is simply that it should have been necessary for your Grace to have adopted that course at the moment of all others most critical to the continuance of the only bearable government Ireland ever experienced since the fatal day when the followers of the murderers of Becket polluted our shores.[63]

O'Connell went on, in labyrinthine self-justification, to argue that the 1837 tithe bill had surrendered comparatively little. But MacHale would have none of this. For him, it was enough that the 'enemy' was rejoicing. 'What confirms the distrust of the people . . .', he told O'Connell on 4 June, 'is that the bill is palatable to many of the parsons of the country and to the Tory landlords.'[64] MacHale had come to distrust both O'Connell's leadership and his judgment. The breach now opening up between the two was to last until 1840. In effect, O'Connell had lost his political control of the western province.

Immediately, however, he was absorbed in the forthcoming general election, to be fought out during August 1837. On 28 June, he instructed the General Association of Ireland to reconstitute itself 'The Friends of the Queen' for the purpose of conducting the electoral campaign. This purported to be, literally speaking, an ultra-loyal body: 'we must all', he wrote in his public letter to the Association, 'with one accord, rally round the throne of the Queen, and in support of her Majesty's government'.[65] In fact, O'Connell meant simply to revive the election strategy of 1835, whereby all Irish 'anti-tories' – whigs, liberals, radicals and Repealers – made common cause, refraining entirely from opposition to one another. The bonds would be all the stronger now that O'Connell could claim the Queen as a liberal sympathizer and point to the liberals' 'proven' Irish record while in office. With extraordinary fidelity, the pattern of the last general election was repeated. O'Connell was again the great energizer, accommodator, manipulator and dictator – as circumstances suggested – of the Irish campaign. Again he suffered all the anxieties of conniving the safe, and where possible cheap, return of his family connection. He even played once more the difficult game of arranging a fall-back position for himself in Kilkenny city, should he fail in Dublin; he was determined to win back the capital if he could, writing 'confidentially' to Fitzpatrick on 1 July, 'You know that I can be *compelled* to stand for Dublin.'[66] Similarly, Maurice proved as negligent as ever in his 'contest' of Tralee. Having learnt that his son intended soon to leave the county town for Derrynane, O'Connell wrote on 11 July to one of the local managers of the campaign, 'See him [Maurice] and tell him from me that I shall be utterly offended if he leaves Tralee without my express permission. Read this passage for him, and if you coincide with me in opinion, pray urge him to remain until after the assizes at least, nay, until I tell him he may go to Derrynane.'[67] In fact, O'Connell won Dublin city, and despite Maurice's temporary loss of Tralee (he was later seated on petition) could claim an Irish triumph overall. Whereas the liberals lost considerable ground in Britain, the Irish 'anti-tories' of 1837 carried 71 of the country's 105 seats as against 67 in 1835.

The Melbourne ministry now depended absolutely on O'Connell's Irish votes for its existence. Without them it would have been in a minority of at least 25 in the House of Commons on several of the main contested issues. Theoretically, then, O'Connell held the balance of power in the lower house and with it the capacity to make or destroy British governments *ad nauseam*. But, as has been said, such a mechanical model of the Commons bears little relation to the realities of the mid-1830s. Party discipline was still weak. Even O'Connell suffered from regular defections from his 'tail', as for example his injunction of 21 April 1837 to Barrett of the *Pilot* makes very clear:

> *write a paragraph* – observe, a paragraph IN LEADS, upon the Irish Members. Mention Mullins of Kerry, who has been *missing* ever since the recess. Mention the folly of pairing as to election petitions. Mention Smith O'Brien's refusal to vote on the late division respecting the Irish Legion . . . Take care that this should not appear to originate with me. Comment upon the absence of every other member who was absent but of course, treat the real friends lightly.[68]

About fifty of the British members still followed the old practice of normally supporting the government of the day, whatever its political complexion. Moreover, the idea of constituting a permanently independent Irish party, let alone an independent Irish opposition, was altogether foreign to O'Connell's concept of the contemporary political alignments in both Britain and Ireland. The liberal as against the reactionary cause was the essential divider everywhere. It would be equally anachronistic to visualize the conservative party of 1837 considering for a moment a junction with O'Connell for the sake of office. Part of their *raison d'être* was his defeat and if possible destruction, just as the very principle of their post-1886 successors was perpetual and absolute resistance to Home Rule.

In such conditions, the general election of 1837 should be regarded as greatly weakening instead of strengthening O'Connell's political position, all the more so because the liberal losses in Great Britain had been largely among radical MPs. This meant a serious diminution of his natural sympathizers in the House of Commons, and a consequent rightward swing in ministerial policy and conduct. O'Connell felt the change immediately, when the government put pressure on him to wind up the General Association. He yielded without a struggle, comforting himself with the reflection that he could recreate a national organization whenever suited. 'The Ministry', he wrote to Fitzpatrick from Derrynane on 4 September 1837, 'wish to dissolve the Association and I see no reason why we should not gratify them. It is easy to start another whenever necessary.'[69] When he announced his decision publicly in the following month, he presented it as a spontaneous avowal of faith in the Irish executive: 'I think we are arrived at a period when we should give this proof of our satisfaction at the improved state of the administration of the government in Ireland, and of our confidence in the good intentions of our gracious Sovereign, and in those of her Majesty's ministers.'[70] Although O'Connell retained his Dublin 'Registration Office', now under T. M. Ray, for the scrutiny of electoral qualifications, the dismantling of the Association symbolized a further contraction of his political independence.

A second blow fell when parliament re-assembled in November 1837, and Russell, capitalizing on the diminution of the radical numbers in the Commons, rejected out of hand their demands for the secret ballot, triennial parliaments and the extension of the franchise as 'nothing else, but a repeal of the Reform Act [of 1832]'.[71] This was deeply embarrassing for O'Connell. Only a short time before he had urged the English radicals to agitate strongly 'in favour of short parliaments, extended suffrage and the ballot ... The less the Ministers do, the more remains to be done by the reformers. Let each of us then bestir himself to do his share of the work. Ireland at least will support us.'[72] There could be no clearer identification of himself with the cause of further parliamentary reform or of Irish with British radicals. But once Russell had spoken, *salus imperii, suprema lex*: upholding the Melbourne ministry overrode all else. O'Connell's difficulty came to a head at a major rally in Birmingham on 14 December 1837 at which he was guest of honour. While he fully endorsed, of course, the entire reform programme, he pleaded with the meeting to continue to support the government, for Ireland's sake. The chairman, Joshua Scholefield, MP for Birmingham, rebuked him gently, 'You must however be guarded when you meet us again and say *rather less* in praise of the present Administration . . . The men of Birmingham claim you as one of their own kindred and are jealous that any preference should be given *by you* to Ireland over England!'[73] When, however, O'Connell, on reaching Dublin, declared that only a handful of the Birmingham audience of 7000 demurred at his appeal to keep the whigs in power, a young radical, P. H. Muntz, who had spoken at the meeting, left him in no doubt about the depth and bitterness of English radical opposition to his waiving parliamentary reform in the interest of maintaining a friendly government in Dublin. In the name of members of the Birmingham Political Union, Muntz wrote, on 1 January 1838, that

> they knew well that Lord Mulgrave was almost the sole boon the Whig government had given to Ireland; they knew that you had no guarantee for a continuance of that boon an hour longer than the Whig administration lasted; they knew that that administration as now composed could not exist many years if even many months . . . Their [the whigs'] object has been to lull the people of Ireland, under your auspices and with promises of future benefits, into security; to quiet them by poor laws and a constabulary force. . . . Ireland in chains, a coalition between Whig and Tory would take place and both would then laugh at you when you found yourself in the position you were in 20 years ago, and the power which might have saved your native country glided from your hands. . . . You pleaded for a government which had declared its deadly hostility to those reforms which the people demand, and then you quitted the meeting without giving any reason for what you asserted. Sir, the people of Birmingham . . . care little whether you call yourself Whig or Radical, they want deeds, not professions . . .[74]

V

O'Connell had meanwhile precipitated a conflict with other radicals – this time Irish and working-class. His return to Dublin from Derrynane at the beginning of November 1837 more or less coincided with the worst of a long series of trade union outrages. On 5 November 'an employer named Armstrong, in company with his wife, four children and another family, was attacked by thirty armed carpenters, while the police looked on'.[75] Next day at the Trades Political Union O'Connell denounced not only the brutal attack but also the associations themselves. They were both a-political (evidently an offence in O'Connell's eyes!) and committed to 'objects connected with the regulation of trade and wages, which they assume the control and management of'.[76] This was the opening shot of a brief but fierce engagement.

O'Connell's liaison with the Dublin artisans (some of whom were Protestants) had its basis in their common interest in Repeal. That the Act of Union had destroyed the city's prosperity was an article of faith among the tradesmen, and O'Connell was always ready to second this belief. Astonishingly, his comparatively good relations with the unions had survived his capture, in November 1831, of their new, independent organization, the Dublin Trades Political Union, and his turning it into an instrument of his own. It was otherwise with O'Connell's postponement of the Repeal issue in 1833, and again after the defeat of the Repeal motion in the House of Commons in 1834. This did arouse working-class hostility. But, as Dr D'Arcy observes, 'Working-class discontent with the shelving of repeal agitation could indeed only be expressed by implication since the artisans now lacked an organ of expression following the domination of the Trades' Political Union by non-artisan elements after 1831.'[77] Besides, O'Connell had endeared himself at the Dublin unions when at the end of 1833 he had refused to align himself with the city's employers in anathemizing a recent wave of labour violence. He told the employers, at their public meeting, that they 'should not have cast the imputation of crime upon the people and then shrunk from coming forward to substantiate their charges'.[78]

A sort of mutual forbearance kept O'Connell and the artisans more or less in harmony until his outburst of 6 November 1837. He ignored – publicly, at least – the trade union outrages which grew apace during 1836-7. They ignored – publicly, at least – the calls from British unions to repudiate him for his 'betrayal' of the factory children in

1836. But the Armstrong bloodshed proved to be one of those 'last straw' cases which bring a train of scandals to a head; and in the general Dublin furore it was only to be expected that O'Connell, then back in residence in the city, should give a lead. This was especially the case because most of the current industrial 'crimes' were conspiracies issuing in the savage use of armed force, precisely what O'Connell had persistently condemned in the agrarian secret societies. Moreover, his contretemps over factory legislation in the preceding year had led him to consider and declare himself on trade associations in general. His speech of 6 November made it clear that while he conscientiously supported the freedom to form such combinations, he considered that the refusal to admit apprentices, the closed shop and the minimum wage all offended the fundamental principles of political economy. Since the Dublin unions were striving to enforce all three, direct conflict was now inevitable.

At first the unions, after the usual fashion of reluctant rebels, blamed the king's evil advisers rather than the king himself. O'Connell was declared to have been deceived by the employers' misrepresentation of the case. The secretary of the stonecutters union, for example, announced that it would grieve him deeply 'should [it] be for a moment supposed that the trades of Dublin had any quarrel with Mr O'Connell. It was with those by whose false and calumnious communications Mr O'Connell had been misled that they contended.'[79] Such pious pretences were sustainable for a time because O'Connell was out of Dublin, in attendance at the House of Commons, for most of November and the first half of December 1837. But when, on his return, the unions memorialized for a chance to be heard by him in their own 'defence' at the Trades Political Union, 'the same place where the charges were made',[80] he left them in no doubt of his utter opposition to their three offensive practices. This led in turn to a mass meeting of the artisans on 26 December at which not only O'Connell's opinions but also his conduct and character were assailed. The chairman called on the meeting to 'make daggers of their tongues and use them against that man who attempted to lower them in the scale of civilized society';[81] one stab was sneers at O'Connell's shuffling on Repeal.

It had always been a merit and mainstay of O'Connell's popular leadership that he answered challenges to his authority immediately and decisively. On 8 January 1838, virtually single-handed, he confronted the artisans in a pre-arranged public disputation in the Corn Exchange rooms. During his three and a half hour opening harangue, he re-traversed his original objections to the unions' restrictive and dictatorial practices, with lengthy excursions on the law of molestation and intimidation and the economics of pricing labour. But he also threw aside, on this occasion, all Queensberry rules of debate and verbally gouged and rabbit-punched his opponents (and especially the artisan's leader, Patrick O'Brien) like a street fighter. He insinuated repeatedly that they were the dupes of his tory enemies and that some at least of the unions were deeply implicated in the trade burning, beatings and murders of the past two years. He played not only the sectarian, but even the spiritual card. Those who refused apprenticeships, he said, denied their own and other children the right to work.

> I, therefore, turn upon you, and tell you, the tradesmen of Dublin, that you are doing that which is unjust and illegal – that which is contrary to religion. There are many of you who frequent your religious duties, and of you I ask do you think that when this speech is read by the Catholic clergy, and the question brought in its true and real light before them, that they can, in the just fulfilment of their duty, give the sacraments to any Catholic who belongs to this system (hear, hear, and confusion).[82]

To the taunts that he had betrayed Repeal, O'Connell responded with a blend of braggadocio and personal denigration:

> But should I fail in attaining that justice [for Ireland], Irishmen, do you imagine, I despair (no)?
>
> > 'Hereditary bondsmen, know ye not,
> > Who would be free, themselves must strike the blow!'
>
> If I fail, I will come back to repeal, if the tradesmen of Dublin do not allow any portion of the faction or any blockhead which may be placed at the head of you to divide you and me (hear, and cheers). As to that Paddy O'Brien, I pity him. I remember once saying of a great squire in the country, that he had a great deal of hair outside his face and nothing at all inside of it (laughter). He was a great man – poor Paddy O'Brien was a great man the day he was at the head of the trades; but I do implore the tradesmen of Dublin to fling away from them any man who attempts to sever the friend of Ireland from the objects of his patriotism (hear, and cheers).[83]

He ended with a well-calculated personal appeal, which also conjured away the 'factory children' charges:

> The calumny of the Manchester children is among the most grievous of those charges, and when I hear it repeated without any ground, and the charge made by the tradesmen of Dublin, I cannot help exclaiming – who,

after me, would serve his country (tremendous cheers, followed by uproar)? Am I not to be treated with even ordinary respect? Am I not old or venerable enough? Am I to be told that that is Irish respect; or have I no tradesmen of Dublin to stand round me (cries of plenty, and cheers – a voice in the crowd exclaimed that it was Orangemen, and none but Orangemen, who produced the confusion). I require that that man hold his tongue; now I put it to every honest Irishman whether he could stand by that man, Mr O'Brien, (cries of no, no,) by him who has calumniated me – the only person who has never deserted the cause of Ireland (loud cheers) – who am doing a painful duty – a duty more to you than to myself. . . . I call on all trades to witness that this man has made use of the subject of the Manchester children as a calumny against me (cheers).[84]

It was a cruel and unscrupulous use of oratorial power. As one of the unionists exclaimed, 'As well might the lion be let loose on the lamb as Mr O'Connell attack such a one as Mr O'Brien, so unable to defend himself against a powerful antagonist like him'.[85] On the other hand, O'Connell was fighting for his political life. The Dublin artisans were an important constituent of his power base. He was also fighting against much initial hostility and continual challenges and interruptions; it seems clear that he was at times in danger of physical assault. Archbishop Whately later speculated – perhaps in hope! – that it might all end in O'Connell's assassination. 'What a curious Acteon-like fate would it be if O'Connell were to be murdered by a mob!. . . In his speeches on Poor-laws, and much more against the combinators, he has shown his usual skill, but a courage which he certainly never displayed before.'[86] Moreover, O'Connell's claims and counter-charges were far from baseless. Before the Corn Exchange meeting, he had gathered evidence from artisans of the violent courses being urged on the Dublin trades committee, of prohibitions on apprenticeships and of successful competition from outside. 'I have also to state', one tradesman testified, 'that in the stone cutting a man can procure a chimney piece 30 per cent cheaper in Glasgow, Belfast or Armagh than in Dublin, taking all charges into calculation. All other manufactures in proportion.'[87] As early as 24 December 1837, O'Connell had concluded that he could show the Commons select committee into combinations, which he intended to propose, 'that in Dublin these combinations have had the most important and unhappy effects on wages and employment'.[88]

The really extraordinary feature of the meeting of 8 January 1838 was O'Connell's crushing and unalloyed success against the odds. Even before it closed, he had cut off the trade union leadership from the mass of their followers, and indeed O'Brien from the remainder of the leaders. When he again met the unions, at a public meeting which they organized some three weeks later, his triumph was complete. There was no counter to his demonstration of the illegality of the critical union practices. It was, however, far from a mere matter of silencing a sullen opposition; O'Connell appears also to have converted the Dublin labour movement *en bloc* to his own creed of using 'public opinion and the press' instead of 'the bludgeon or the "knobstick" ' to achieve its ends.[89] While a simple *post hoc propter hoc* explanation of this extraordinary charge may be unwarranted, the fact remains that, from the day of the Corn Exchange confrontation until after O'Connell's death, Dublin labour disputes were virtually free of violence and even of much that we should now regard as legitimate coercion. Undoubtedly, O'Connell's return to the serious agitation of Repeal in the 1840s enlarged the ground for common action with the trades. But the rapprochement was quite as much methodological as political. He had, it seems, convinced the unions of the superior utility of peaceful agitation and systematic propaganda. When, for example, the journeyman bakers were fighting for better working conditions in 1842, they declared that they might 'have effected the object they had now in view by means of combination, but they had learned a lesson from O'Connell, and thought with that great man that there was no social or political advantage that could not be most easily and most advantageously acquired by means of moral force, and the irresistible impulse of public opinion'.[90]

O'Connell's handling of the Dublin crisis of November 1837–January 1838 was a remarkable exhibition of political virtuosity. It is true that he possessed an immense store of accumulated prestige so that there was a bordering of *lèse majesté* in any challenge to his Olympian command. Even before the meeting at the Corn Exchange, six of the Dublin unions had dissociated themselves from all personal criticism of O'Connell, and a seventh proclaimed its fealty to him when the proceedings opened. None the less, he showed consummate resource and skill in winning back, slowly but surely, a body of angry men who had already thrown over his authority and 'freed' themselves from their habitual respect. To induce others to adopt opinions directly opposite to those with which they started is surely the final achievement in the art of public persuasion. However unscrupulous the means – and O'Connell drew on his full demagogic repertoire of ridicule, mob-humour, vituperation, pathos, particularity, sensitivity and cunning misdirection in his crucial speech – it was the performance of a master.

Yet, however much we distinguish the different elements, or admire the skill, we cannot wholly explain, or exactly appreciate, such works of politics as O'Connell's coups of 1831 and 1838 *vis-à-vis* the aberrant Dublin tradesmen. As well as all else, some strange, irrecoverable chemistry of the relations between man and man must have worked its spell. Nothing less could account for his success. But it is one thing to assert as much, another to know what actually happened. The cramped and smeared columns of the contemporary press may pile up detail after detail of the events; but they still leave us ignorant – we can only infer even the necessary existence – of the final factor. What is to be said when the limit of re-creating the dead reality has been reached?

> I am satisfied with that,
> Satisfied if a troubled mirror show it . . .
> An image of its state. . . ?[91]

CHAPTER 7

Declinations

1838–41

I

When parliament re-assembled after the general election of 1837, O'Connell's first and most anxious concern remained the survival of the liberals in power; but he was bound also to hold them so far as possible to their Irish legislative programme. Peel, now strengthened in the House of Commons, would no longer consider the threefold compromise, and although on 5 December 1837 Russell re-introduced the Irish municipal corporations bill, practically unchanged, there was little hope that it would pass the Lords. On 10 February 1838, O'Connell told Fitzpatrick that, despite the ministry's powerlessness to press the bill in the upper house, 'I do believe that there will be a yielding on the part of Wellington's party sufficient to carry it through. My own opinion is that it will be law this session.'[1] But this was rank wishful thinking; O'Connell had no ground whatever for his 'opinion'.

He was now free to oppose the Irish poor law bill, also re-introduced in December 1837. It would no longer serve as a *quid pro quo* for favourable municipal and tithe reform. With the whigs and tories vying in the bill's support, there was no danger to the ministry in O'Connell's opposition, and he could securely recant his earlier acquiescence, even to the point of confessing publicly that it sprang from his own want of 'moral courage'.[2] On 18 December 1837 he denounced the poor law bill as proposing 'a species of social revolution in Ireland [which] will necessarily create a new and heavy charge on property'.[3] His principal fear was for the 'responsible' landlords who would carry much of the burden properly belonging to their evicting and absentee brethren. But he also pleaded on behalf of the future paupers who, denied outdoor relief, faced nothing but 'imprisonment in a workhouse'.[4] As a gesture towards conventional Irish values and apprehensions, O'Connell actually moved the rejection of the bill on 9 February 1838. He must have anticipated a miserable defeat, even if not by the actual ignominious margin of 277 votes to 25. 'Never was cant more conspicuous', he mourned to Fitzpatrick next day, 'than in the cry of some of our Poor Law mongers. Others imagine that, because they point out distress and destitution, they make a case for a Poor Law. Yes, they forget that Poor Law affords less relief than it inflicts injury, but the delusion will end in greater misery and more dissatisfaction. I have done my duty.' Characteristically, however, he ended this letter with the postscript, 'The Ministers are quite safe. All right with the queen.'[5] There could be no doubting his priority.

Tithe was the third major Irish issue left hanging when William IV's death had precipitated a parliamentary dissolution. By then, it had driven a wedge between O'Connell and MacHale, as well as certain of the other Catholic clergy; and in an attempt to recover this lost ground, he proposed on 9 November 1837 an entirely new approach whereby the state (through the Consolidated Fund) would take over responsibility for a commuted tithe in return for the cost of the new Irish Constabulary being borne by a local tax. Thus, while achieving a not dissimilar result, O'Connell ingeniously avoided the contentious and hitherto fatal issue of direct appropriation of the Church of Ireland 'surplus' for general purposes. Even MacHale was coaxed at first into part-approval. He told O'Connell on 27 February 1838 that 'to have the payment of the Protestant clergy charged on the Consolidated Fund . . . [would be] an excellent instalment since we could securely calculate on the cooperation of England and Scotland in finally doing justice as far as regarded the Protestant Establishment.'[6] The scheme had also some attraction for a government caught between the devil of commitment to the principle of appropriation and the deep sea of a House of Lords committed in the opposite direction. Russell's proposals for a new tithe bill, revealed at last in March 1838, generally resembled O'Connell's outline. The main addition was a rent-charge, fixed at 70 per cent of the tithe composition of 1832, which was to finance the Irish Constabulary and some other 'secular' expenditures. O'Connell was so gratified by a plan close to his suggested *via media* that he promised publicly to meet his own tithe debts, to pay '*all* my parsons' the accumulated arrears of several years.[7] His euphoria was short-lived. Conservative pressure in both houses soon transformed the bill. The quasi-appropriation and state funding clauses were dropped and the rent-charge raised from 70 to 75 per cent of tithe composition. The consequent tithe act of 1838 was a meagre return for almost a decade of agitation. Yet O'Connell, who had declared only a year before that they 'might sell the very bed from under him but he would never consent to pay a single fathing for tithes',[8] backed the final measure, even at the cost of dividing his supporters in the House of Commons. This endorsement is difficult to explain other than as a recognition of the *force majeure* represented by the tory majority in the upper house. O'Connell had lost not only a grievance which had helped his movements throughout the 1830s but also an important target for popular indignation. With tithes now absorbed in rents, the Church of Ireland was removed from the direct line of O'Connell's fire. By the same token, his capacity to mobilize the Catholic clergy as his auxiliaries was diminished. MacHale had written to O'Connell condemning even Russell's initial proposal as falling

> far short of what the Ministry was pledged to and the people of Ireland expected. It has no appropriation clause. It does not reduce one of the supernumary parsons even where a single Protestant is not found. Nor does it, out of the proposed reduction of thirty per cent., . . . give any advantage to the occupying tenantry.[9]

The cabinet's subsequent pusillanimity, and what the archbishop regarded as the ultimate triumph of the parsons, did nothing to endear O'Connell to him.

II

On 15 February 1838 O'Connell had written excitedly to Fitzpatrick that the queen desired him to attend the next *levée*, in order, he believed, to discuss the conciliation of Ireland. The wish must have been father to the thought. There is no evidence that the queen so much as mentioned Ireland to him when, six days later, he and his sons were presented to her at St James's Palace. None the less, it is interesting to observe that the 'great objects' which he had intended to lay before her were still 'the final settlement of the Tithe question, [and] the completion of the corporate reform and of the electoral franchise in cities and counties'.[10] The tithe question was, as we have seen, finally, though humiliatingly, settled later in the session. But municipal reform suffered, first, from backsliding by the ministry in their anxiety to come to terms with Peel, and subsequently from so many and such drastic amendments in the House of Lords as to be no longer worth pursuing. As to the Irish parliamentary franchise,

O'Connell would very shortly find himself on the defensive, as the conservatives launched a powerful campaign to have its conditions altered in their favour.

Thus by mid-1838 even O'Connell would have had to own that the liberal alliance had failed to produce worthwhile legislative fruit. 'Justice for Ireland' seemed as far off as ever, and hope so repeatedly deferred had sickened the heart of Irish agitation. To many, O'Connell seemed to have reduced himself and his parliamentary faction to a mere governmental instrument. He had dismantled even the innocuous General Association to placate Dublin Castle. The Paris newspapers *Courier Français* saw this last as a marvellous instance of a demagogue's dominion.

> The work of difficulty was, not to set in movement these mighty masses, and make every impulse obedient to his will, but when in the conscious possession of power, and within view of the great object of their contest, thus to induce the voluntary surrender of their matured organization, and implicitly confide in the Government, of which they had so long experienced the oppression, is a source of astonishment and admiration, and evidence of the highest moral influence which man can exercise over his fellow man.[11]

But the complete indifference which greeted the Association's dissolution was also a sure indicator of the current apathy.

For O'Connell, however, the very occupation of the government benches by so 'well-disposed' a ministry as Melbourne's more than compensated for its legislatory weakness and double-dealing. After all, each month brought its trickling increment of change in the composition of the Irish administrative system. It was O'Connell's habit to speculate gleefully on the effects of each gain in time, as the successive parliamentary crises were surmounted. For instance, on 4 May 1838, he wrote confidentially to Fitzpatrick,

> I am delighted to tell you the Ministry is *safe*. I was yesterday in great alarm . . . You may therefore reckon with certainty that the present ministry will have all the coronation [June, 1838] patronage, and without any difficulty another year of office. This, after all, is cheering for Ireland, as it leaves with us Lord Mulgrave and gives us another winter *to kill* our worthless judges. They will stick fast as long as they can, the vagabonds!![12]

It was his unshakable conviction that the Irish tory judges hung on in office, in the hope of surviving long enough to have their successors appointed by a conservative administration! There was moreover a steady stream of offices appearing on the 'market', in which to place his political creditors and friends. Within one fortnight, between 18 September and 1 October 1837, he applied to either Drummond or Morpeth for a stipendiary magistracy for J. D. Mullen, a filizarship (a legal appointment on the chancery side) for Patrick Costello and the clerkship of the rules for his attorney, William Woodlock. Even when, as sometimes happened, O'Connell failed in applications such as these, the successful candidates were usually men of his own party or inclination, so that his strategic end of 'popularizing' the Irish public service was still being met. This was especially important with the many posts to be filled in the new constabulary. One parish priest pressed O'Connell to secure regular recruitment on the basis of religion: 'Could not a rule be made . . . that at least one half of those that are added to the Police should be Catholics[?]'.[13] Even well short of this, a considerable number of Catholics (including Archbishop Slattery's brother) did become officers of the new force.

The greatest single gain, in O'Connell's eyes, from the continuance of the liberals in office was the widespread changes wrought by the Morpeth administration in the Irish magistracy in the spring of 1838. O'Connell was very early in cheering on what he regarded as potentially a 'brain-blow' to Orangeism in Ireland. 'Will you be so good', he wrote to Drummond from Derrynane on 25 September 1837,

> as to let me know all that is *tellable* about the forthcoming revision or restriction of the commission of the peace. There are some very improper persons in the Commission in this county [Kerry] but as they are Protestants – that most uncandid thing in the world – the affectation of over candour will I fear prevent Lord Kenmare [the deputy-lieutenant] from striking them out or concurring in that measure. Besides we are literally *inundated* in this quarter with parsons as *justices*. I wish much to know what precautions you think will be taken to purify these nuisances.[14]

It was just as important that Dublin Castle should remain viligant against 'Orange' excesses among the surviving JPs, and Drummond's later strong and well-publicized interventions against a handful of grossly 'unreconstructed' magistrates brought equal joy to O'Connell's heart. The abasement of his hereditary Irish enemies struck a chord at least as deep as that set singing by the advancement of his Irish friends. A few years before, a fellow-barrister had caught well – in fun yet seriously – the expression, even in his very gait, of O'Connell's ferocious hatred of the inferiority imposed upon him by Irish circumstances:

As he marches along through the [Dublin] streets to court, he . . . flings out one factious foot before the other, as if he had already burst his bonds, and was kicking the Protestant ascendancy before him; while ever and anon, a democratic, broad-shouldered roll of the upper man is manifestly an indignant effort to shuffle off 'the oppression of seven hundred years'.[15]

When it came to social and religious 'liberation', the heart had the same reasons as the reason, and was much the more powerful engine. Of course, O'Connell was too reflective and acute a politician to miss the fact that the centralizing and expansionist tendency of the Morpeth administration could be used later by a conservative government for the advantage of *its* Irish partisans. But he also knew that the 'popular' layer being gradually inserted into the Irish forces of law, order and local authority could never be totally eradicated, and that the precedents of comparative impartiality in the running of the country could never totally dismissed. Besides, he was already old: sufficient unto the day . . .

Yet even the warming sense of governmental favour and of influence over the distribution of patronage no longer afforded O'Connell its original satisfaction. For one thing, he was worn down by the multiplicity of applications. Even, or perhaps particularly, those issuing from the ranks of his Irish opponents meant inroads on his time and energy. These ranged from the unknown daughter of the 'late Dep. Judge Advocate of Ireland' begging his support in a pension claim to a co. Limerick parson soliciting his 'good word' in applying for the deanery of Dromore. He often grieved that he was exhausting his credit with government by the great number of his requests, although his inbred courtesy and politician's wariness forbade him to reject any suitor for grants or offices out of hand. He also protested, with some justice, that his very power in Ireland held the administration back from over-indulging him with favours lest it be paraded as his mere marionette in the inimical British press. 'It is also strictly true', he told one of his Kerry relatives in 1837, 'that instead of a readiness to comply with my request there is a jealousy in certain quarters of being supposed to be dictated to by me which dispossesses me of my share of patronage.'[16] Worse still, failure to secure an objective led to resentment in supporters. When O'Connell failed to stave off the appointment of an enemy of the formidable Fr Sheehan of Waterford as JP, Sheehan wrote to him in anger: 'Dr Jones has been sworn in a magistrate. There never was a more unworthy appointment. It is calculated to bring Lord Mulgrave's administration into contempt.'[17] One of O'Connell's bursts of counter-irritation, in a letter to Richard

Barrett, serves to show how grievous a burden all this place- and prize-dealing might become:

> Really private, I did what I could for Mr [James] Birch [an Irish journalist]. There is this cruel treatment which I receive from everybody – that when I do not succeed for any applicant, which is the case in 99 instances out of every 100, I am blamed for want of zeal or sincerity. 'ONE WORD' – how I hate that 'one word!' – from him would have done it!! In future I ought to say no, bluntly, to every application. I feel that I ultimately get the same displeasure and have all my trouble for nothing. I must say Mr Birch has treated me badly in complaining to you. I explained to him, as far as I could, without mentioning names, what I had attempted on his behalf and the nature of the obstacles in the way of having his wishes complied with, whereupon he *disavowed* the present Administration and left me without as much as one expression of thanks for the effort I made. I wish I were in opposition again but I must say you and Birch treat me most unjustly.[18]

By a final irony O'Connell was practically debarred from using his influence on his own behalf. He was tempted most sorely of all in June 1838, with his fortunes, pecuniary and political, at almost their lowest ebb, by the offer of a baronship of the exchequer or alternatively the Mastership of the Rolls. But, as he told Fitzpatrick on 15 June, 'my friends may (but most confidentially) know that I do not intend to accept any office whilst Ireland is so totally unredressed. I nail my colours to my country's mast.'[19] Although we may detect in this a hint of leaving the door not completely closed, three days later he confirmed his rejection of the offer. 'The die is cast. *I have refused office* . . . You know that, if I took anything, it would be the Rolls. But I could not bring myself to accept it. My heart is heavy but *I have made this sacrifice*.'[20]

In doing so he referred back to Mary. 'If SHE was alive I should have my reward and my consolation, but *her* memory casts a protection about me which will prevent me from abandoning my struggles for Ireland save with my life.'[21] The recollection of his dead wife deepened the wound but also helped him to cauterize it by a revived feeling that he was true to his chosen track. Ireland was to consume him always.

III

When parliament rose on 9 August 1838, O'Connell found himself in a most complex political position. He was immensely relieved that the whig ministry still held office. 'Blessed be Heaven', he told Fitzpatrick on 11 August, 'that the Session is over and that we have a respite from the enemy and good government for another year!'[22] On the other hand, the cabinet had by then given way on two critical Irish issues. It had surrendered the appropriation clause of the tithe bill (the original cause of Melbourne's accession to power) and agreed to the substitution of a £8 for a £5 valuation as the basis for the municipal franchise in its forthcoming Irish municipal corporations bill. O'Connell had had to stomach the first as the price of the continuation of whig government; and while denouncing the second as 'only going over to the enemy . . . It will almost annihilate the franchise in Dublin and at £8 render it quite exclusive',[23] and predicting (correctly) that this first 'compromise' would lead in time to a second, raising the qualification to £10, he had no intention of breaking with the ministry on that account. But worse than his own dissatisfactions were the dangers, first, that the government would throw in its hand as hopeless, and, second, that it would be repudiated by many Irish nationalists and, in particular, by many of the Catholic bishops and priests. Russell's refusal to consider any further measure of parliamentary reform had driven the British radicals into semi-revolt; a sufficient number of them might well move on to a full insurrection, which would cost the government its bare working majority in the House of Commons. Correspondingly, the whig failure (increasingly read as a failure of will or of desire) to carry its Irish legislative programme had alienated considerable bodies of O'Connell's supporters. His control of the popular movement seemed under threat.

To this intricate problem, O'Connell responded intricately. On 18 August 1838, immediately after his return to Dublin, he launched the Precursor Society of Ireland at a meeting of his constituents. Its declared objective was the mobilization of 'the national will . . . [in] a last attempt to procure from the British legislature full justice to Ireland' before instituting a Repeal association.[24] O'Connell set the time limit as the end of the parliamentary session of 1839, and once more listed as the principal items of 'full justice' the total abolition of tithes and complete parity with Great Britain in parliamentary and municipal reform. O'Connell sought to speak with many voices. To MacHale, he argued that with 'steady and universal exertion [the Precursor Society] would free us from the incubus of the State-paid Church and obtain for us all we desire besides'. Lest MacHale should suppose that he had abandoned Repeal, he added, implausibly, that this achievement would render 'ninety-nine out of every hundred of the Irish of every persuasion friendly to a domestic Parliament'.[25] He tried to persuade a liberal editor that the '*agitation*' raised by the

Society would help 'to show the Tories that they cannot possibly hold office'.[26] He told Pigot (for transmission to the Irish administration) that

> we have no hope from the Ministry in England. I solemnly assure you that, in dealing with them on the Irish bills, I found the same repulsive coldness last session that I experienced in Lord Grey's time. In the Irish phrase, they 'neither love us nor like us.'
>
> We must act for ourselves, we must raise the cry again all over Ireland. It is the only mode to obtain anything for the country. I believe it to be the only mode of fencing the Ministry in office but at all events we must rely on ourselves. We have nothing else to rely on.
>
> As to the 'Precursor', instead of its being a Repeal society it is directly the reverse. It is a society to prevent the necessity of seeking Repeal. I have called on enemies to Repeal to join us in order to consolidate the Union.[27]

Finally, he handed down to Fitzpatrick, for the benefit of a recalcitrant supporter, the oracular pronouncement that the Society 'may precede justice to Ireland from the United parliament and the consequent dispensing with Repeal agitation. It may precede Repeal agitation – and will, shall, and must precede Repeal agitation if justice be refused'.[28]

Despite this fan-spread of appeals, the Precursor Society was coolly received. MacHale stayed aloof, and some priests continued to assail O'Connell for his tergiversion on the tithe issue. O'Connell was careful to cultivate friendly bishops, and obtain their approval, or at least consent, before holding a Precursor rally in their dioceses. 'I am bound', he assured Archbishop Slattery on 7 October 1838, 'to struggle for the religion and liberties of Ireland but I am deeply convinced that these struggles to be useful must merit the sanction or at least avoid drawing down any censure from the high dignitaries of the Catholic Church in Ireland.'[29] As to agitation, O'Connell set up the usual sort of headquarters at the Corn Exchange and, from Derrynane, on 15 September promised ' "a progress" on my way to Dublin in November'.[30] This aroused small enthusiasm. Nearly six weeks later, O'Connell confessed to Fitzpatrick that he had 'as yet received only four invitations' to hold meetings.[31] In the end, he managed to agitate decorously (his own phrase) at public dinners in co's Kerry, Cork (where there were three venues, Kanturk, Youghal and Cork itself), Tipperary, Waterford, Limerick and Galway, in an adequate but unexciting circuit. One reason for O'Connell's rather *piano* performance was Dublin Castle's strong disapprobation of the Precursor Society, which was conveyed to him in letters from Pigot.

O'Connell was apparently undisturbed when Pigot told him that the Society was in breach of the Convention Act of 1793, thereby rendering its leaders liable to imprisonment. Even if Pigot were right in law, it was most improbable that the Irish executive would prosecute those who were still its best Irish friends. But when Pigot followed this up by the threat that supplies, in the form of further patronage, would be cut off ('the Government, I am convinced, would find themselves unable to advance to public office any individual . . . pledged' to adopt Repeal if the Precursor programme were not achieved 'within *one year*')[32] the blow appears to have struck home. Although O'Connell did not respond to this immediately, within a month of his return to Dublin from Derrynane he dissolved the Society and reconstituted it in what he hoped would be an inoffensive form. 'Every reference to the Union has been omitted', he told the new viceroy, Lord Ebrington, 'and its purposes are now quite consistent with the *objects* avowed by the Irish government.'[33]

This signalled, not the end of the Precursor, but a fresh understanding with the whigs. In general, O'Connell used both brake and accelerator in directing the Society. When a tory government threatened, he held back in the interests of maintaining the liberals in power; but when the liberals seemed secure in power, he attempted to increase the pressure on them. But he also braked when it seemed that his influence over Irish appointments was falling off. In deleting Repeal from the Precursor programme at the end of 1838, he was moved in part by fears that Melbourne's cabinet was losing its appetite for office and that Irish intimidation might, in consequence, prove counter-productive, but mostly by his intense desire to have a say in filling the vital legal position of lord chancellor, which he then believed would soon be vacant. He pressed Ebrington on 3 January 1839 to support 'the popular cause with the Irish Bar, with whom *we* are but too weak already . . . I owe it to you in candour to state that the Irish Government have no small occasion to take a leaf out of the Tory book wherein it is written, "Oppose your enemies, back your friends".' As a sweetener, he added, 'if the Radicals [Chartists] in England give you any trouble you can withdraw from Ireland by a few arrangements *all* the regiments now here'.[34] Conversely, when the supposed crisis was over, and the whigs had settled back, in apparent security, in power, O'Connell changed tack. 'With respect to Ireland', he wrote to Fitzpatrick from London on 6 February 1839,

there is a thorough indifference in both parties. In the Whigs, coldness and apathy; in the Tories, suspended hostility. They equally desire to keep Ireland out of sight and to let her people continue in, I may call it, hopeless servitude. I am thoroughly convinced that my plan of going back [to Dublin] once a fortnight [to address Precursor Society meetings] is of the utmost importance.[35]

In fact, O'Connell did return for meetings of the Society in Dublin several times during the parliamentary session; he also maintained his siege on MacHale, imploring him to countenance the spread of the Precursor into Connacht. Thus, he constantly changed emphasis according to immediate circumstances. During one 'braking' phase, he told MacHale, 'There was never anything more hopeless than to attempt to bully them [the liberal ministry]. *I know it from experience.*'[36] But an earlier letter had run, 'I have been written to menacingly ... but their menaces, I need not tell your Grace, I despise.'[37] It was quite true that O'Connell had been and would be 'menaced'. But the Precursor Society was itself a 'menace'. In short, in the half-cock agitation of 1838–9, each side attempted to exert pressure on the other while yet avoiding conflict.

IV

O'Connell's serene assumption that the ministry was safe at least for the current session died suddenly on 7 May 1839 when, on the issue of the Jamaican constitution, the government's majority fell to five; Melbourne resigned next day. Some radicals, alienated by the whigs' resistance to further parliamentary reform, had opposed the ministry, and much to O'Connell's chagrin, two of his Irish 'supporters' failed to appear in the division lobbies. He was still more infuriated by the defection of William Smith O'Brien, liberal MP for co. Limerick, who voted with the tories. 'He is an exceedingly weak man', O'Connell exclaimed soon after, 'proud and self-conceited ... You cannot be sure of him for half an hour.'[38] But abusing the renegades brought small comfort in the crisis. 'I do not know when I felt so uneasy and unhappy', he told his ministerial friend, More O'Ferrall, on 7 May, and implored him to do all in his power to persuade the cabinet to hold on to office and 'preserve Ireland from the [Orange] faction as long as they possibly can'.[39] Next day, in a public letter to 'the People of Ireland', he proposed, not an intensification of activity by the Precursor Society, but the formation of a new Irish reform association to bring together all anti-tories. O'Connell probably believed that a general election was imminent. At any rate, the resignation of

Melbourne's government brought home to him how greatly his current political position depended on its continuance.

Then, fortune came to the rescue. In the so-called Bedchamber crisis, Queen Victoria refused to accept Peel's nominations for her ladies of the household; Peel thereupon refused to assume office; and, the old cabinet having conciliated the recalcitrant English radical reformers, Melbourne returned to power. Meanwhile, Russell had tried to make the whigs' assurance of O'Connell doubly sure by writing to him on 9 May,

> It is a pleasure which I cannot refuse myself to acknowlege the constant and disinterested support which you have given to the Ministry in which I held a department chiefly connected with the affairs of Ireland.
>
> I am glad to see that [in the public letter of 8 May] you exhort your countrymen to abstain from acts of violence and I feel little or no doubt that, although you differ from me with respect to several measures relating to Ireland, you will persevere in refraining to press for Repeal while there is any prospect of equal justice to be obtained by other means.[40]

But O'Connell's support was never in doubt. 'Hurrah for the darling little Queen! Peel is out; Melbourne is in again', he wrote excitedly to Fitzpatrick on 10 May 1839,[41] and, next day, 'The queen has behaved nobly. To her we are indebted for our safety.'[42] He proceeded to arrange a form of political *Te Deum*, held in Dublin on 23 May – 'an Irish demonstration',[43] to use his own terms – at which a solemn address of gratitude to Victoria was drawn up.

For a considerable time, O'Connell was happy enough to report to Fitzpatrick merely that Melbourne's government was surviving. But of course he expected some reward (over and above a finger in the disposition of Irish patronage) for his fidelity. The Dublin demonstration of 23 May had called once more on the government to equalize Irish and British municipal and franchise reform; and, at a lower level, O'Connell also pressed for an Irish railways bill and amending legislation sought by two influential Irish lobbies, the vintners and the grocers. By the end of June 1839 it was clear that he had failed at every point. The ministry had blocked his parliamentary efforts to achieve his lesser ends; and although the Irish municipal corporations bill was still before the Commons its voting qualification had been set at £8, and even this would probably be rejected by the Lords. 'Nothing will be done for Ireland', he now cried, 'and, in fact, Ireland has nothing for it but the REPEAL.'[44] It was, however, a vapid, unmeant threat. O'Connell was not yet nearly desperate enough to break with or even endanger the ministry. This became painfully apparent when the

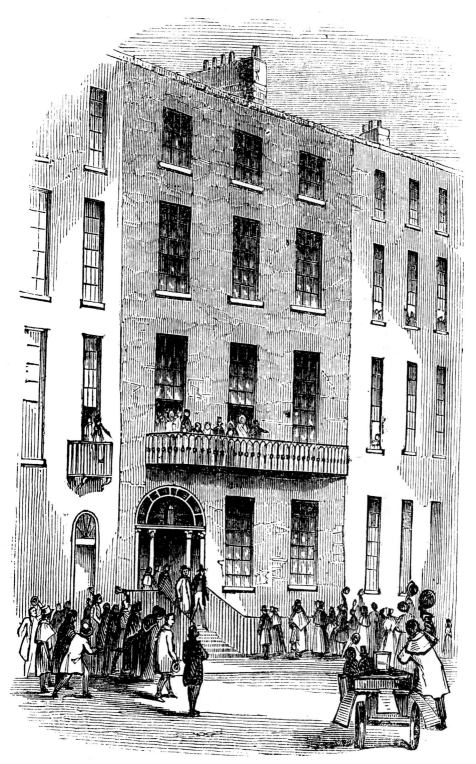

MR. O'CONNELL'S RESIDENCE, MERRION SQUARE, DUBLIN.

O'Connell's house, 1843

The House of Commons in 1833

O'Connell in 1834 painted by George Hayter

O'Connell's supposed attempt to continue raising the Repeal Rent after the onset of the Irish famine in 1845

"RINT" v. POTATOES.—THE IRISH JEREMY DIDDLER.

"You haven't got such a thing as Twelve-pence about you ?—A Farthing a week—a Penny a month—a Shilling a year ?"

A contemporary sketch of O'Connell by an unknown artist

In August 1838 O'Connell spent a week's spiritual retreat at the Cistercian Monastery of Mount Melleray, co. Waterford. He was accompanied by O'Neill Daunt

This meeting, which took place in July 1844, was one of the last to be held in the Corn Exchange before the Association moved to Conciliation Hall

WEEKLY MEETING OF THE REPEAL ASSOCIATION, CORN EXCHANGE, DUBLIN.

Thomas Davis (1814–45) drawn by Sir
Frederick W. Burton

(*Right*) John MacHale, Archbishop of
Tuam (1791–1881) painted by
Alessandro Capalti

O'Connell by Sir David Wilkie

Derrynane House

MR. O'CONNELL, IN HIS TRIUMPHAL CAR.

The scene at College Green in the course of the triumphal procession following O'Connell's release from Richmond Penitentiary, September 1844

THE O'CONNELL PROCESSION.

A procession held in
Dublin on 30 May 1845 as
part of the celebration of
the anniversary of
O'Connell's imprisonment

O'Connell by G. F.
Mulvaney

The statue of the Emancipist in O'Connell Street, Dublin

A statue of O'Connell appears in a niche in O'Meara's Irish House in Dublin. Eire occupies another. Both are beneath the motto 'Erin Go Bragh'

House of Lords so altered the municipal corporations bill as to win back ground for the almost entirely Protestant freeman voters and raise the property qualification for the rest from £8 to £10. O'Connell was outraged, at first. The mangled measure, he exclaimed when he learned of the lords' amendments on 5 August, was 'impossible to take . . . I cannot sacrifice my conscientious convictions'.[45] But almost immediately he began to yield ground, and within three days surrendered unconditionally. When, in a letter dated 6 August, Ebrington pressed O'Connell to accept the changes, arguing that even the lopped bill was better than none at all, and that there was no 'reasonable prospect of obtaining better terms by further delay',[46] O'Connell fell into line with distressing alacrity and parade. 'I do therefore yield', he replied,

> any doubts I may have had to your superior judgment, and although I am bound – but this is consistent with your advice – to protest very strongly against considering this a full or adequate measure of corporate reform yet you have convinced me that I ought not to risk any opposition to the bill and of course I will not do so, being indeed well pleased to have this opportunity though small in itself, to testify how entirely your Excellency's Government of Ireland commands and obtains my entire and respectful confidence.[47]

Thus the £10 franchise and the other tory limitations on the reform of the Irish muncipalities, against which O'Connell had struggled for so long, became law at last virtually without resistance from him.

Perhaps in self-disgust at what he must have believed to be a necessary abasement, perhaps because he feared that the latest humiliation would finally destroy his support in Ireland, O'Connell sank into a rare despair. 'I am, I confess, very unhappy', he wrote to Fitzpatrick 'in the most strict secrecy' on 7 August 1839, 'I do not believe I will long survive the blow I apprehend from the desertion of me by the country at large. It weighs upon my heart.'[48] Expecting that the Tribute for 1839 would fail, he continued next day,

> God help me! What shall I do? I think of giving up my income, save an annuity of a small sum to myself and my two sons, and going, if I am received, to Clongowes, and to spend the rest of my life there. I want a period of retreat to think of nothing but eternity. I sigh when I look at the present agitated aspect of affairs, foreign and domestic, and vainly think that if Ireland thought fit to support me I might still be useful; but it is plain I have worn out my claim on the people. You are aware that Connaught [i.e. MacHale] is, of course, estranged from me . . . Still I do not regret that I gave up my profession and refused office.[49]

As usual Fitzpatrick steadied and cheered him, and by 21 August his natural resilience had done the rest. While claiming – improbably – that if left to his own wishes he would 'retire altogether from political life' because of the 'disgusts' he had received, he launched into schemes for fresh agitation in both England and Ireland, ending with the aim of 'animating' the Irish 'quietly and cautiously' for the Repeal.[50] He was an indomitable and incorrigible politician.

He was, however, far from ready to go wholeheartedly for Repeal as yet. On 2 September 1839, almost immediately after he returned to Dublin, he dissolved the Precursor Society, replacing it by a Reform Registry Association in which Irish whigs and liberals could participate. The grand emphasis was now on rousing 'all Ireland for the Queen and Constitution',[51] the particular, on the registration of voters against the next general election. O'Connell could never formally forgo Repeal. But he reduced its current function to that of a far-off prospect. Ebrington reported on 8 September, after a confidential meeting with O'Connell,

> though he said he could not dissolve the Precursor without holding out Repeal in the distance as his remedy for the political grievances of his countrymen, he assured me that he would agitate as little as he could, & would not be a party in forming any Society except that which he had announced for revising the Registration.[52]

The Irish government meanwhile attempted to cut off any retreat on O'Connell's part by announcing that Repealers would not be considered in future for official appointments.

In setting up the Reform Registry Association, O'Connell soon found the Irish whigs to be, as usual, slothful and devious allies. Despite his assurance that only a little money was needed 'to secure Ireland to the Melbourne Cabinet', they failed to fulfil their original engagement to pay £1000 into the new organization. 'If I had kept on foot any *agitating* body', he wrote angrily from Derrynane to More O'Ferrall on 29 November 1839, 'we should have friends in abundance, but because I have dissolved my poor Precursors I am left on the strand with the tide out.'[53] Off and on, O'Connell considered schemes for refloating himself as a popular leader during the last months of 1839. In particular, he toyed with raising the tithe issue in another form, that is, to applying the tithe rent-charge either to offset the new poor rate or for general public purposes. This was not promising material for a national campaign, but at least it was aimed at what O'Connell saw as the essential problem at this stage, how to re-engage the Catholic Church in Irish politics. One difficulty was the continued estrangement of MacHale, and O'Connell sought – though vainly – to ensnare him by a blatant appeal to his fierce religious partisanship. 'The time is come', he wrote to MacHale on 23 December 1839,

> when all Catholic Ireland should rally – should form a strong and universal combination.
>
> The Tories are united. You perceive that they are daily becoming less careful to conceal their intentions. They avow their bitter hostility to the religion and to the people of Ireland.
>
> The furious and most sincere of the British Tories avow their intention to re-enact the Penal Code, whilst the more wily declare their designs not to go farther than to render the emancipation act a mere dead letter . . .
>
> We want protection for the Catholic against all parties, Ministerial as well as Tories. My object would be once again to organise all Catholic Ireland in an effort of resistance to all our enemies.[54]

A second stumbling-block for O'Connell was the bitter and persistent conflict between MacHale and his ecclesiastical province and Archbishop Murray and the majority of the other Irish bishops over acceptance of the national education system. Whatever one prelatal party might support was likely to be opposed by its rival. Perhaps O'Connell's most hopeful sign was the rapid spread of Fr Theobald Mathew's new temperance movement in the last months of 1839. Mathew himself had no wish to be linked with O'Connell or nationalist politics in any form; this might hinder, perhaps even destroy, his work. But his recruits were largely those whom O'Connell had recruited earlier in his political mobilizations: Mathew's emphasis in order, discipline, respect for institutions and, of course, sobriety was identical with O'Connell's ground-plan for all his agitations; and, in the early days at least, even the forms of the temperance rallies – their banners, procession songs and slogans – were those developed in the O'Connellite agitations. Significantly, O'Connell declared at a public banquet in Bandon on 5 December 1839 that he was watching the influence of the temperance societies before unfurling the banner of Repeal. If they succeeded, there was *ipso facto* material for him to work with. So indeed it was eventually to prove.

Meanwhile, O'Connell placed at least as much emphasis on English as on Irish agitation. He considered that the English middle-class radicals, especially the advanced parliamentary reformers and the anti-corn law men, offered the best prospect of vivifying and securing the liberal ministry. Before he left for Ireland at the end of the parliamentary session of 1839 he chaired, on 18 August, a London meeting from which a Precursor of Reform Society, committed to household, artisan and even some lodger franchise, emerged; and he had of course long been a principal advocate of the leading reform issue of the year, the secret ballot. Correspondingly, O'Connell cooperated warmly with Richard Cobden (who disliked and distrusted but also needed and flattered him) in promoting the Anti-Corn Law League. He assured Cobden that Ireland, presumably under *his* direction, was safe for the cause, and on 13 December 1839 accepted Cobden's invitation to 'star' at the great League dinner to be held at Manchester in the following month. O'Connell proposed that a 'meeting of Operative Reformers to organise for a struggle to obtain an *effectual* extension of the suffrage and to put down the physical force Tories' be also held at Manchester on the following night.[55] Cobden having given him a *carte blanche*, he intended, he said, to include a defence of the Irish government's promotion of Catholics to office in his banquet speech.

'The meetings [on 13 and 14 January 1840] in Manchester', O'Connell told Fitzpatrick as soon as he reached London, 'were most glorious. It was utterly impossible to be received better than I was.'[56] He had assailed not only the corn laws but also the Chartists, and warned the workers of Manchester against being tempted into violence. This set the tone for the first quarter of 1840. Up to the end of March, O'Connell was the complete ministerialist, largely taken up with British issues and the local manoeuvrings at Westminster, and exulting in every repulse of a tory assault on Melbourne's government. His first accounts to Fitzpatrick from London were uniformly complacent and almost proprietorial in terms of the exercise of power: 'I have pleasure to tell you that the political prospects are daily becoming more bright';[57] 'Be joyful and rejoice and thank God for the Tories are completely discomfited. They are in absolute despair of gaining office';[58] and 'we are now soberly engaged in enjoying our triumph, and the certainty of the Ministers remaining in office'.[59] Correspondingly, Dublin Castle conveniently ignored its own resolution against placing or promoting Repealers in office – at least, when it came to the O'Connells. At the beginning of 1840, O'Connell's second son, Morgan, was appointed assistant registrar of deeds, and O'Connell's appeal for a stipendiary magistracy for his son-in-law, Charles O'Connell (who had, he said, 'like so many other Irish gentlemen "outbuilt" himself'[60]) was met most sympathetically by Ebrington. 'I have delayed', the lord lieutenant wrote to O'Connell on 22 February, answering your letter of the 18th because I could not bring myself to give the denial which I fear I must at least for the present, to the touching appeal returned herewith though it almost brought tears into my eyes when I read it. You do me justice in believing that that appeal does not lose its force in my estimation from its coming from a member of your family, backed by a recommendation from yourself. I have never hesitated to express to you my strong disapprobation of those parts of your conduct in which I thought you liable to blame, and I have with equal readiness and greater satisfaction done you full justice for those where I considered you entitled to praise and particularly for your late most essential service to the cause of social peace and tranquillity by the exertion of your influence in keeping away Chartism from these shores. If, therefore, I consulted only my own wishes and feelings, they would very much incline me to comply with your wishes but I am greatly pressed at present for the next two or three appointments of stipendiary magistrates whenever the vacancies may occur, besides which I must candidly confess my apprehension that it would not be advantageous either to the Government or yourself that so near a relation and a namesake of yours should be put into the place of a stipendiary magistrate so soon after the late appointment of your son, Mr Morgan.[61]

None the less, Charles eventually got his stipendiary magistracy.

V

The days of security ended abruptly on 26 March 1840 when Lord Stanley carried the second reading of his registration of voters (Ireland) bill in the House of Commons by 250 to 234. This essentially tory measure aimed, by its clauses enjoining annual registration and the withdrawal of registration certificates, at restricting the Irish franchise, greatly to O'Connell's detriment. O'Connell was cast into despondency. He genuinely feared that the measure would be carried (it did in fact reach the committee stage despite the government's opposition) and the ministry was, concurrently, also in danger of defeat on a motion condemning its conduct of the 'opium war' with China. In these straits, he sounded MacHale once more on 'making a *great* popular movement or a movement which I hope to be *great* . . . a "Justice or Repeal" association'.[62] Pride of place was to be given to attacking the privileges of the Church of Ireland; the remainder of the programme consisted of the usual demands for parity in Irish and British parliamentary and municipal reform.

O'Connell attempted to undercut the principal cause of MacHale's coldness.

You were in your former letters pleased to labour with me to use my influence with the present Ministry to adopt a more liberal course of legislation in Ireland or, I should say, *for* Ireland; and you conveyed the idea to my mind that I ought to obtain from the government that adoption by menacing to desert them at their need and to allow the Tories to put them out. It was in vain that I assured your Grace that the leading men of the present Ministry and, especially, Lord John Russell desire and anxiously desire an honourable opportunity of giving up power.

They do not cling to it, *believe me*. I do beg of you to believe me, for I know the fact, they do not cling to office with that tenacity that would make such a menace of the slightest avail. Now do, my dear and most revered Lord, believe me that this is the simple fact. Nay, they menace me to resign unless I satisfy them in my conduct.[63]

If O'Connell was disingenuous in promising a new campaign against the established church in Ireland, he was truthful in saying that it was the ministers who were threatening him with resignation rather than his threatening them with the withdrawal of his support. By now this must have been apparent even to MacHale, for he immediately blessed O'Connell's undertaking. 'Whilst the franchise remained', he replied on 11 April, 'there was yet hope for a peaceful assertion of our rights – take that away and the people are left without any arms in their hands . . . Come, then, among us as early as you can find it convenient and you will have a *céad míle fáilte*.'[64] In turn, O'Connell acted quickly. Four days later, he launched the 'National Association for full and prompt Justice or Repeal' in Dublin;[65] as with the Precursor Society, he promised to adopt Repeal if 'justice' were not attained during the parliamentary session. Although O'Connell's address from the Association to 'the People of Ireland' on 21 April 1840 emphasized Repeal and called for the collection of a Repeal Rent, he maintained his old pursuit of the liberal alliance in parliament. Characteristic was his use of the plural in reporting to Fitzpatrick on 30 May: 'We lose a Welsh county and, they say, the County of Monaghan. Ireland is in foolish apathy. May God help us!'[66] Correspondingly, he expressed deep relief when at last, on 30 June, it looked as if Melbourne's ministry would endure into 1841. Once more the queen had come to the rescue. After a government setback during the committee stage on Stanley's bill, O'Connell , as he wrote,

did much apprehend that the ministers would . . . throw up the game in despair . . . I confess my heart sank within me at the dismal prospect that resignation would open for Ireland, especially as there are so many base and sluggish amongst our own people and, in particular, amongst the wealthy classes, to countenance any government that condescended to play the hypocrite ever so little. The restoration to power of the Orange faction would be accompanied with such horrible vexation as to render it impossible to calculate how long we should be able to preserve the peace. But I need not for the present dwell on these things because one of the men in power told me they were determined that nothing should induce them to resign until after the birth of the Queen's child . . . Thus we are sure of remaining in our present position until next February. In the meantime many a card may turn up a trump.[67]

It was all a curious beginning to a movement which was to culminate in 1843 in much the greatest and most menacing demonstration of Irish popular strength during O'Connell's lifetime!

On 13 July 1840, on a brief visit to Dublin, O'Connell transformed his Justice or Repeal Association into the 'Loyal National Repeal Association', dedicated simply to the achievement of Repeal. This may seem a strange response to the prolongation of the life of Melbourne's government. But O'Connell was convinced that Stanley's bill had been only scotched, not killed; the struggle would be renewed next session. All the arguments in favour of an Irish agitation stood, and experience had shown that the complex and contingent objective, or pseudo-objective, of 'Justice or Repeal' roused no one outside the circle of his own particular acolytes. Repeal *per se*, he now declared, was 'the only topic that can animate the entire mass of the population'.[68] The further involvement of MacHale, who would respond eagerly to the more extreme demand and was the bellwether of the more 'advanced' prelates, may well have been a secondary reason for the change. O'Connell was obsessed by the supposed need to start serious campaigning in Connacht; and, practically, this depended on MacHale's yea or nay.

The archbishop proved gracious, and O'Connell immediately enlisted his aid in getting up a requisition to hold a Connacht provincial Repeal meeting at Tuam on 13 August 1840, and in ensuring some respectable attendance. 'Excuse me being thus tediously particular', O'Connell ended, 'but I am most thoroughly convinced that the Repeal alone can keep secure the religion and the liberties of the Irish people.'[69] The Tuam meeting was moderately satisfactory, the attendance being reported at 10,000; and O'Connell, having spent the month of September at Derrynane, undertook a series of rallies throughout Munster, as well as a Leinster provincial meeting at Kilkenny, during October 1840. It was not an impressive tour. Of course, O'Connell drew respectful crowds and could call out some influential supporters in every town and city in the south and west. But it seems clear that the initial response to 'pure' Repeal was unenthusiastic, perhaps even apathetic. Joseph Hayes, a shrewd Cork merchant and O'Connellite, in the ungrateful role of candid friend, provided O'Connell with a devastating analysis of his current problems. It is worth quoting at considerable length.

There is no imaginable *phasis* which hatred or hostility to English domination, legislative or social, can assume, which shall not have my best wishes ... To agitate such a subject as Repeal, however, requires more than such individual feeling. It requires capability in the individuals undertaking it, willingness in the public mind to receive the impulsion, and that the question shall have some practicable shape as well as practicable result in view. On the former occasion that the Repeal was agitated here, the public crowded the ranks, regarding the agitation as auxiliary to the carrying of the elections then in progress. Many who allowed themselves to be ranked as Repealers laughed at the agitation and at themselves, so soon as the fever subsided and may I be allowed to say to you that the swappings and changes in the nature and character of the associations, which followed, have not tended to alter their feelings in relation to it. At present, then, I may say that there is great indisposition on the part of the people, who may be called of the middle classes, to join in agitation for the Repeal. This is chiefly grounded on the conviction that its attainment is impracticable and hereon, I must be candid to say, for myself, that I firmly believe England would war to the knife before she would legislatively concede the question. That to win it and wear it we must fight for it, and before we pursue such a course we must be prepared to say we have a rational chance of success. Have we that chance? If we have, we are justified in the hazard or is such a speculation nonsense?

'To die for treason is a common evil
To hang for nonsense is the very Devil.'

Thus is it reasoned among the people with whom I talk politics and I would feel altogether at a loss where to point for the material of an effective agitation. We have no lawyer now among us who will speak one word on the subject. There are offices for public prosecution, clerkships of the Peace and of the Crown to be occasionally given away, and a Repealer solicitor, nay a solicitor attending political meetings distinct from elections, will be as far from filling one of them as Yorick's head was from fitting a mitre. And writing of mitres, how are the clergy affected? Almost to a man withdrawn from Repeal, at least the secular order of that body. The Trades are no longer in any force here ... Some few of them of the best capacity for business have obtained situations ... and of course they are *hors de combat*. In fact a process of corruption has been going on through the instrumentality of place giving and, wherever a member of a family has been started a candidate for public employ, the whole division of kindred deem it necessary to eschew Repeal, lest of its embarrassing the speculation.[70]

The substantial truth of Hayes' critique was borne out by the difficulty O'Connell experienced in finding local leaders prepared to sign the requisition for the Leinster provincial meeting and by the ill-tempered wrangling in both Limerick and Waterford as to who should arrange his visits. Meanwhile, Ebrington had further depressed the prospects of professional and middle-class (and even ambitious tradesman) participation in the new Repeal movement. In a speech of 30 September 1840, he identified Repeal with separation and the destruction of the empire, and laid down that 'whatever favour or patronage the government were wont to bestow on its supporters, for those who take part in this agitation, whatever other claims they may have to consideration no application will on any account be attended to'.[71]

In one important regard, O'Connell himself began to hedge even before he undertook his autumn tour in Munster. He overrode every objection to drawing on the Repeal Rent to pay for work on the Dublin register of parliamentary voters, although all past experience had shown that this served the general liberal rather than any specific Repeal interest. He became still more ambivalent in the last two months of 1840. By-elections in cos Carlow and Mayo brought him back to his basic principle of striving to defeat the tories on every front. He was piqued when his offer to help in the Carlow campaign was rejected by the local liberals. 'Alas!', he grieved to Fitzpatrick, 'that they [would] not join in the Repeal cry'.[72] On 21 November 1840, he attempted to insert his son John into the canvassing, instructing him

> to volunteer your services at the Carlow election and at the preceding agitation. Write down to Arthur French or to Mr Fitzgerald who acts as secretary – [T. M.] Ray will give you his address – and offer any aid in your power to the success of Mr Ponsonby's [the liberal candidate's] election. Say that you will go about agitating or working in any other way in which you could be useful.
>
> Let these offers come as emanating from yourself and not at all as suggested by me.[73]

But John was not asked to join in the campaign. O'Connell was better placed in co. Mayo (MacHale was a power in that constituency) and tried to take a hand in the election. In an address to the electors of

Mayo, published on 7 December, he assailed the tories and warmly endorsed the choice of the Mayo Liberal Club, Mark Blake; his address ignored the issue of Repeal. He also offered 'my presence in Mayo . . . or my son John would go *agitating* there, if you [MacHale] thought that advisable'.[74] No invitation came for either, even though O'Connell proposed 'to assist *privately* the Mayo men'[75] (apparently from the Repeal Association's funds), and also made it known to Dublin Castle, through Fitzpatrick and some hidden intermediary, that he was ready to serve as a secret channel for any money the government might wish to spend on Blake's behalf. Again, he was rebuffed – although politely. Nothing could have been more galling to O'Connell than to have been treated as irrelevant in an Irish by-election – and one in which the liberals triumphed, into the bargain! What else could he expect, however, when he strove to hunt with the hounds of government while still running with the hare of his Association?

Thus O'Connell ended 1840 in a strange balance between political independence and collaboration. He drew, as he put it, a 'melancholy consolation' from the defeat of the liberal candidate in co. Carlow on 5 December: 'It proves that the Whigs cannot prosper without the Repealers.'[76] But he had no stomach for antagonism in this case. He refused to denounce publicly an Ulster Constitutional Association set up by liberals in Belfast to counter the Repeal movement; and when, at the beginning of December 1840, his liberal friend, Pierce Mahony, proposed a general meeting of Irish reformers, O'Connell seized the apparent opening for joint action with alacrity. 'I highly approve', he wrote to John from Derrynane on 4 December, 'of Pierce Mahony's Requisition [for the meeting]. It does not imply any dereliction of Repeal, and that I will *practically* prove . . . put my name and Maurice's to that Requisition. Tell Mahony . . . that I approve of and sign his Requisition.'[77]

At the same time, O'Connell maintained the regular organization of the Repeal Association, with its weekly meetings at the Corn Exchange and steady if small returns of Rent. During the last four months of 1840 he largely delegated the chairmanship of the Dublin meetings to John, whom he was 'educating' politically by a series of minute instructions such as 'I send an address on the subject of the registries. . . . Go and read it before the meeting so that you may read it *at* the meeting *legibly* . . . Move 1st. The admission of Dr Cantwell, the Bishop of Meath . . . 2nd. Move the admission of Dr Blake, the Bishop of Dromore . . . Read his letter, move its insertion on the minutes, and that I be requested to send him a suitable reply';[78] or 'Determine on *making* topics to speak upon. You will delight me by *doing* business.'[79] Ray (whom at this stage O'Connell described to John as 'just the best man in his station I have ever met with, beyond any comparison the best'[80]) managed – and helped to manufacture – the Association's ordinary proceedings. Barrett's *Pilot* served more or less as its official organ. Thus, for all his anxiety that Melbourne's government should remain in office and for all his readiness to work wholeheartedly with the liberals in Ireland to this end, O'Connell had no intention of dismantling once again the basic structure for an agitation. Stanley's registration bill would certainly be revived in the coming parliamentary session; meanwhile the whigs' ennui and purposelessness in office were growing month by month. In the midst of these dangers, the Repeal Association was (O'Connell hoped) a form of reinsurance, a mode of laying off his main political bet. Possibly it might not be needed – for the present – for anything more than marking time and disturbing Dublin Castle. But at least it constituted a reserve. The fact that Repeal had not caught on at first would not have daunted O'Connell overmuch. Thirty years of mass politics had taught him that a great deal of dreary labour had to precede the blaze of a crusade – and indeed that it was often more profitable to preach and prepare for one than to set out, in true earnest, for a Holy Land.

VI

O'Connell's *prime* objective was still to keep the whig government in power. This was tacitly recognized by Russell when he 'whipped' O'Connell (though courteously and tactfully) to appear in the Commons when parliament re-assembled on 26 January 1841. It was also noisily assumed by various English radicals who strove for O'Connell's attendance, as a leading lion at public demonstrations in favour of parliamentary reform, when he made his way southwards from Liverpool to London. He remained convinced that the greatest political evil of all would be the tories' return to government; and his current agitation of Repeal, no less than Reform, appears to have been directed specifically to preventing this. As he told Fitzpatrick, on his arrival in London,

> It is believed they [the whig government] will hold out another session, and
> if the Repeal agitation becomes imposing in Ireland, and a new Reform

agitation takes place, as I believe it will in England, the Tories may be kept out for ever. But their exclusion can be effected by nothing else unless the Repeal agitation becomes formidable.

How I wish that our friends in Ireland would all see this matter in its true light by first considering what will become of Ireland if the Repeal be not agitated. It is certain, in that case, that the Tories will come into power. It may be said that the Repeal will not prevent them but is it not clear that there is nothing else that will? Are they not on the very verge of being in office?[81]

O'Connell had several reasons for wishing the whigs to cling to power. First, 'with France arming, America threatening, the East unsettled, war in India, war in China, distress and Chartism in England',[82] conditions – all of a sudden – seemed unusually favourable for the application of Irish pressure. Secondly, he was ill-prepared to face a general election. The unreadiness ranged from the neglect of the voting registers and the decay of local organization to a marked paucity of likely candidates; but he was most worried by the lack of clerical enthusiasm for or commitment to his cause. 'If *all* our clergy aided the Repealers', he complained, 'we might make a noble demonstration, but, alas, the Whigs while in office will allure many.'[83] It was ominous that even so warm a friend as Archbishop Slattery of Cashel should have remonstrated with O'Connell, on 16 January 1841, for declaring publicly that he and his clergy had promised to become Repealers should Stanley's Irish registration bill be carried. (O'Connell was driven, lamely, to plead that he had been misreported and that 'Such a line of conduct would be . . . consistent with the patriotism and good sense evinced by your Grace upon all occasions'[84]). Given the tepid temperature of Irish politics, episcopal support was indispensable if the priests were to be enlisted in great numbers in the forthcoming campaign; and O'Connell tried his best to attract at least some of the bishops by presenting Repeal as the principal safeguard of the Catholic gains of the past decade. On 10 April he told the sympathetic O'Higgins of Ardagh, doubtless in the hope that it would be spread among the hierarchy,

I hold the prelacy of Ireland collectively and individually in too much respect to dare to do anything but bitterly regret that they are not all Repealers. I regret it the more because of my thorough conviction that we Catholics cannot hold what we have got without the Repeal and *a fortiore* that we cannot get anything that Ireland wants without an Irish parliament. The Orangist party will – it is manifest – be soon again in power, and the Irish people will have to feel all the active and unceasing virulence of that truculent party. I could weep tears of blood at seeing that the opportunity of now making a great and powerful rally for Catholic Ireland is lost owing to the unworthy selfishness of some of our influential laymen and also owing to the mistakes of some of our otherwise most deservedly respected clergy. God help us. It is indeed heartrending to see that the opposition to the Repeal is not left to the congenial spirit of Orangism but has alas mixed up with it some of our most excellent prelates. It is the first time that the people and any part of the Irish hierarchy were divided.[85]

Four weeks later, O'Connell sounded Fitzpatrick on the chances of discreet lobbying, 'Could you privately convey to Catholic dignitaries the propriety of assisting to agitate?'[86]

The third reason why O'Connell strove to maintain the whigs in government for as long as possible was, of course, the access to influence which had accompanied their rule. He regarded the corporation elections, due to be held in the autumn of 1841 under the new Irish Municipal Reform Act, as of special significance: if the tories were in command at Dublin Castle, the whole might of the administration would be thrown against Repeal, liberal and Catholic candidates. There was, moreover, the usual slow but cumulative effect of having a voice in appointments and awards to be considered. In replying to a letter of 27 April from O'Connell, at a time when it still seemed possible that the whigs might hold out until 1842, Fitzpatrick reiterated these arguments:

The intrusion of the faction previous to the new municipal organisation could not fail to have a calamitous effect upon the construction of the different bodies. This gives an additional and important reason for *keeping them* [the tories] *out* if it can continue to be done. Another year's blockade too can scarcely fail to reduce some part at least of the stubborn Bench.[87]

A final depressing prospect was that O'Connell might have to meet the costs of several contests in the course of a general election. 'For my part', he observed dejectedly to Fitzpatrick on 19 February 1841, 'I will have to sustain four elections [his own candidature and those of his sons Maurice, John and Daniel]. Where shall I get money? The tribute has not been successful this year.'[88] He even caught a black glimpse of himself as a finished man, with the work, which only he could do, undone.

It comes across my mind that my career will terminate just at the moment that Ireland ceases to have friends. I am, you perceive, disposed to be gloomy ... I do believe that Ireland is capable of being made once more and thoroughly a nation and that her hour is arriving but my vanity or self-reliance makes me think that I am wanting for the completion of a bloodless and not illegal change. Pardon me, my good friend.[89]

The government held on throughout the spring of 1841, despite a net loss of four seats in a round of English by-elections and the defeat of a major official measure, Morpeth's Irish registration bill, which O'Connell had warmly supported. By the end of April, however, it was apparent that its budget would be rejected. A general election would then become inevitable. This, wrote O'Connell sadly on 4 May, would certainly be 'destructive to me. I know not what I shall do . . . It will be a triumph of the enemies of Ireland if I am driven from the field.'[90] Still, he struggled to postpone the evil day, and to persuade the ministry to fight on to the last. 'I object', he told Morpeth on 7 May,

> to the present Ministry's resigning the management of her Majesty's counsels so long as they can *possibly* hold their station at the head of public affairs. They are placed as a kind of moral promontory between the people of Ireland and that furious and fanatical party, who have so often driven a kindly and naturally faithful people to the very verge of actual rebellion and into the gulf of agrarian crimes and of local but sanguinary outrages.[91]

But even more important to O'Connell than spinning out the time in office was the government's using, eventually, its power to dissolve and fight a general election, rather than resign. Otherwise, the tories would be entrenched in Ireland at polling time and 'the Orangists no longer restrained by superior power will come armed to each hustings, the command of the police and of the army will be in their hands'.[92] A tory-dominated Dublin Castle would mean both bloodshed and the loss of perhaps as many as ten seats. In his anxiety to avoid such an outcome, O'Connell virtually promised to offer no opposition to official candidates and to require no pledge whatever from his own.

> I do not want to promote my own peculiar opinions. I am quite certain that no supporter of her Majesty's Government would at any Irish election be embarrassed by being asked for any pledge beyond the unequivocal support of this Ministry or of opinions as, for example, respecting the Ballot which some more or less of that Ministry have avowed.[93]

For once the whigs did not disappoint O'Connell. They held on to office until Peel's motion of no-confidence in their administration, carried by a single vote on 6 June 1841, forced them to surrender; and even then Melbourne did not resign but used his single remaining power to dissolve parliament instead. Even more, the issuing of writs for the Irish elections was, at O'Connell's insistence, held back to the very last.

None the less, O'Connell had been in no doubt since the beginning of May that he would soon have to face the polls. His own seat was his first concern. He was unlucky in being a sitting member for Dublin city, for the tory strength in freemen votes in the capital meant that the issue would always be doubtful and the contest costly. He had a double hand to play. It was, he believed, important that he avoid having another Repealer as his running mate, for this would lessen his own chance of success. But better still if he could escape to another constituency without loss of face. He gained the first objective in the end: the other sitting member, Robert Hutton, a liberal who would not support Repeal, was re-endorsed *faute de mieux*. But the second failed: O'Connell's best hope here was that the young whig Lord Kildare (the heir of the Duke of Leinster) would also accept nomination, but Kildare refused to run, leaving O'Connell no choice but to go forward. Next came his family. O'Connell managed to save some money by substituting his son John for himself (whom the electoral committee wanted) as candidate for Kilkenny city. Athlone, for which John had sat in the preceding parliament, needed cash spent on it; Kilkenny was practically free. Nor would Maurice's return prove expensive. 'Tralee', O'Connell predicted correctly on 9 June, 'will cost from £100 to £150, not more.'[94] His nephew, Morgan John, could look after himself in co. Kerry. O'Connell also expected – wrongly as things turned out – that Carlow, where his son Daniel was put up with a whig, Ashton Yates, to wrest the country from the tories, would cost *him* nothing.

He had been talked into contesting Carlow against his better judgment. Fitzpatrick had told him on 17 May that 'it is understood that Carlow will be positively recovered from [Col. Henry] Bruen',[95] and his son-in-law Fitz-Simon made an equally confident prediction eight days later, adding 'it being understood Yates should bear the expense'.[96] On 28 May O'Connell gloomily acquiesced. 'If they can get no other candidate to stand along with Ashton Yates', he wrote to his son John,

I suppose I must give them your brother Daniel though it will be very hard on me to have to bear the expense of so many elections. I will of course go down to Carlow at once when wanted and go from parish to parish *agitating*. I will write off for Dan at once and meanwhile hold myself in readiness to go down at call and work for him. But those who are urging me to this trouble, risk and expense must recollect that protection for the tenantry by some species of an indemnity fund will be absolutely necessary as there will assuredly be plenty of evictions after the struggle. My accounts from Carlow say that under the circumstances I mention we should succeed, *viz.* ultimate protection for the tenantry, immediate and extensive agitation, and a son of mine.[97]

Once he had yielded to the pressure, however, O'Connell threw himself into the Carlow contest, declaring that 'My great object is to make Carlow the Clare of Repeal'[98] and setting about snaring the local bishop (Haly, an anti-Repealer), at least to the extent of exhibiting benevolent neutrality.

O'Connell's first general problem, how to run both a Repeal and a pro-government campaign, was comparatively easily solved. The advanced nationalists like Thomas Davis were told privately that 'the want of funds is a decisive reason for not urging the Repeal . . . This is really the secret of our weakness.'[99] Where need be, as in co. Tipperary, O'Connell intervened openly to restrain the rash and zealous from opposing liberals whom he wished to see returned. Meanwhile, he brought the nationalist press into line, ensuring that it was (as Fitzpatrick put it)

> . . . to their [the whigs'] faults a little blind
> And to their virtues *very* kind . . .[100]

The 'People of Ireland' were instructed in an open letter of 19 May to return Repealers in preference to radicals, radicals in preference to whigs, but any of them in preference to a tory: the essential order was to 'Oppose the Tories everywhere, and in everything'.[101] This blessed formula enabled O'Connell to have the best of both worlds, for Repealers, radicals and whigs did not stand against each other but only against conservatives.

Finding tolerably good anti-tory candidates – in some cases finding an anti-tory candidate at all – was a much greater problem. In Ireland as well as Britain, liberal politics had gone slack after ten years of almost unbroken whig rule. O'Connell still had useful lieutenants in some constituencies; generally the local political bosses were leading priests. Fitzpatrick and to a lesser extent Ray could provide other political intelligence, particularly for Dublin. Fitz-Simon and Richard More O'Ferrall, both in office, were further sources of political information, as well as go-betweens with constituency organizations or potential candidates in particular cases. O'Connell also regarded Fitz-Simon 'as a safe and discreet channel of communication with the government',[102] and used him in his efforts to secure government money for the Carlow contest, and to obtain final favours for friends or clients while the whigs were still in office. His son John, whom he had despatched to Ireland in mid-May, served, more than any other, as his confidential agent. 'I think', O'Connell wrote to him on 21 May, 'I *must* go to Dublin next week [he did not do so until 11 June] but in the meantime act for me as if I was *not* to go over – cautiously but *firmly.*'[103] All this provided national political machinery of a sort. But it was a ramshackle and defective form of management, supported by woefully inadequate resources. As O'Connell told Fitzpatrick at the outset of the campaign, 'these are disastrous times to me in my pecuniary prospects ... how ought my heart to sink at these contingencies, coupled with what I fear will be a failing fund! My heard is indeed sore but, I would hope, submissive.'[104]

Given these adverse circumstances, O'Connell fared remarkably well. The tories gained only six Irish seats in the end (leaving them with 38 out of the 105), and twenty of the successful anti-tories were Repealers. But Dublin city and co. Carlow were among the tory victories. O'Connell appears to have expected defeat in Dublin. From the outset, he considered alternative constituencies and was in fact elected for two, co. Cork and co. Meath (he chose to sit for Cork); and he took no part himself in the Dublin election. Instead he spent almost the entire election time, from mid-June to mid-July 1841, canvassing, cajoling and speechifying on behalf of Daniel in co. Carlow. It seems to have been a remarkably pietistic bout of electioneering. One of the Sisters of Mercy at St Leo's, Carlow, wrote later,

> He remained a month in town, and every evening from a raised platform in front of his hotel, he addressed his crowded audience, and having done speaking he would retire as if to take a short rest, but really to beg God's blessing on his labours; Father [James] Maher [O'Connell's Carlow 'manager'] told us, that those moments were always employed by the grand old patriot, in saying his beads. On Sundays he went to Confession in our Sacristy or rather in the screened off portion of our chapel, when his fervent act of contrition could be distinctly heard by all outside, then heard Mass and received Communion most devoutly. He also breakfasted here on these occasions together with His Lordship and some of the priests.[105]

At first, O'Connell was quite hopeful. Soon after he arrived in the constituency, he reported, 'We have glorious prospects here if we could but work them out. The people are rousing, and the Catholic clergy are, for the first time for years, taking their station.'[106] But his final assessment, during polling, was more realistic. 'We are fighting a good fight', he reported to Fitzpatrick on 13 July 1841, 'I hope we shall succeed though, you know, I am apt to despond.'[107] When the count ended next day, Daniel and Yates were trailing their opponents by eight and seven votes respectively in a total poll of 1401. O'Connell bore the blow with all his usual resilience and good-humour. 'Grieving is a folly', he exclaimed on 19 July, 'Hurrah for the next move-ment.'[108] None the less, it was most curious that the 'national' leader should have spent the entire campaign in a single doubtful constitu-ency. It cost him dearly, in the literal sense at least. Although the government appears to have contributed, under cover, a considerable sum towards the expenses, he probably paid £500 or more out of his own pocket – as well as about £1000 from the Repeal Association's funds, in protecting tenants who had supported Daniel and Yates from landlord reprisals. It was nonsense for O'Connell to speak of co. Carlow as 'the Clare of Repeal'. Repeal was not an issue in the campaign, and O'Connell was neither flanked by perfervid orators nor swept forward by hordes of directed enthusiasts. The decision to spend the critical electoral month in a modest provincial town and the second smallest county in the land is very difficult to explain. When we have said that it gave O'Connell a sort of political vacation, and removed him from the clangours and disappointments of the metropolitan struggle, we seem to have exhausted the benefits which his curious excursion may have conferred upon him.

Ultimately, however, neither his comparatively respectable showing in Ireland as a whole nor the narrowness of his defeat in Carlow mattered much. The tories were resoundingly successful in Great Britain and emerged from the general election with an overall majority of more than eighty. In defeat, the whig leader, Russell, determined to repudiate O'Connell; he and his party were by now thoroughly sickened of the alliance. It would be, it seemed, a long, hard winter at Westminster for the Irish cause.

CHAPTER 8

Divagations

1841–2

I

With the tories in secure control of the lower as well as the upper house of parliament after the general election in 1841, O'Connell saw no alternative to making Ireland the field of operations once again. On the morrow of the polls, he informed Fitzpatrick that there was now nothing for it but unwavering systematic opposition under the banner of Repeal.

> Repeal is the sole basis which the people will accept . . . We attempted half measures – registry franchise associations – and failed although we had the patronage of Government. A cobweb association of that kind may be attempted with a colour of success while the Whigs are in but it would be at best an abortion and should be flung away as a delusion, worthless and disagreeable, so soon as the Tory power begins. No, the Repeal and the Repeal alone is and must be the grand basis of all future operations, hit or miss, win or lose. The people will take nothing short of that and I bitterly regret to tell you that the popular excitement is of so exasperated a character that they will rush into insurrection unless my influence checks and controls them, and that cannot exist or operate unless I take the highest tone and make the most constant exertions in favour of Repeal . . . I say there can be no other basis of association save the Repeal, the glorious Repeal.[1]

Fifteen months, however, were to pass before O'Connell acted, with either determination or consistency, on his own resolution. The Irish Municipal Reform Act was shortly to be put into effect; its implications and immediate consequences were to engross him down to the end of October 1842.

The Act had deprived Irish civic authorities of several functions which even their reformed English counterparts retained. But it had at least opened up patches of local government and prestige to an elective process. Even with the new Irish municipal electorate reduced, proportionately, to little more than one-third of its English counter-part, O'Connell calculated that all the corporations outside Ulster could be captured by his supporters. The most crucial was of course Dublin, which he would contest himself. Winning and running the capital were to consume his energies for a considerable time. It was a welcome diversion in what otherwise promised to be his leanest season in nineteen years.

Meanwhile, comparatively speaking, Peel's government enjoyed a respite from Irish pressures. According to the usual pattern of British administrations in these conditions, it exercised a sort of negative opportunism – that is, it seized the opportunity to do nothing beyond satisfying, so far as practicable, the claims of the rival factions within its own ranks. The first two years of Peel's ministry were characterized by a sort of dualism, or even schizophrenia, in the response of Dublin Castle to O'Connell. In part (mainly, the executive part), the Irish administration reverted to the traditional tory 'Protestant' policy; in part (mainly, the legislative or parliamentary part), it toyed with continuing the whig policy of moving gradually towards parity between conflicting Irish interests and religions. The dichotomy was epitomized by the appointment in 1841 of Earl De Grey, a right-wing tory with Irish Protestant connections, as lord lieutenant, and of Lord Eliot, a liberal conservative, as chief secretary. O'Connell might well have thought himself back in the 1820s when the tory ministries of Liverpool, Canning and Goderich regularly 'balanced' their Irish administrations by alternate 'pro-' and 'anti-Catholic' viceroys and chief secretaries.

Certainly, during 1841–3 the new Dublin regime closely resembled those of the earlier epoch. De Grey, backed by O'Connell's old political enemies Sugden and Blackburne (now, respectively, Irish lord chancellor and attorney-general), attempted to turn the clock back in his appointments. Within the Church of Ireland, he advanced only those who were known to be opponents of the national education system, and, within the police force, only Protestants. He restored Orange magistrates who had been dismissed by his whig predecessor, and eagerly encouraged prosecutions of the press for 'libels' on his administration. This was precisely the form of British indirect rule which O'Connell had always resented most deeply, and ceaselessly assailed. Conversely, Eliot favoured the whig type of minimal, 'judicious' concession to Irish pressure. He defended the 'democratic' franchise of 1832, the Irish poor law of 1838 and the national board of education: he beat off an Irish tory campaign for state support for the

Church of Ireland schools. He also pressed for occasional Catholic legal appointments and a modest programme of legislative reform. The cabinet rejected his proposals for an increase in the Maynooth grant and an extension of the Irish franchise, and the Irish tory opposition secured the defeat of bills which he introduced in 1842 to reform Irish medical charities and the grand jury system.

Eliot succeeded occasionally in minor matters, but it was De Grey who generally carried the day in 1841–3. This is ultimately explicable only in terms of the cabinet's absorption, during these years, in extra-Irish matters – economic distress and social disaffection in Great Britain, troubles in India and dangerously deteriorating relations with the United States and France. For there was no shortage of Irish experience in the upper ranks. Almost half of Peel's cabinet consisted of ex-viceroys and ex-chief secretaries of Ireland; and Peel himself and the colonial secretary, Stanley, had developed during their secretary-ships particularly clear and elaborate views of the proper government of Ireland. Peel's in particular should have opened the way to ambitious 'remedial' measures. He was to write, on 19 October 1843:

> mere force, however necessary the application of it, will do nothing as a permanent remedy for the social evils of Ireland. We must look beyond the present, must bear in mind that the day may come – and come suddenly and unexpectedly – when this country may be involved in serious disputes or actual wars with other Powers, and when it may be of the first importance that the foundations of a better state of things in Ireland should have been laid.[2]

Perhaps Peel and his cabinet, their foreign and domestic preoccupations notwithstanding, would have followed and developed Eliot's line during 1841–3 had O'Connell not been correspondingly diverted from applying any serious pressure on them either in Ireland or elsewhere. But on the parliamentary front – with a secure majority in both Houses, O'Connell generally absent and most of his followers idle, feeble or inept – the tories had practically nothing to fear. So far as Irish agitation went, the government for long dismissed O'Connell's current Repeal movement as a gigantic sham – 'a failing concern' was Peel's contemptuous judgment;[3] and there was no increase in Irish violence or disorder during 1841 or 1842. Thus Peel did not feel himself impelled to work out any coherent Irish policy beyond alternate checks to the exuberance of Eliot and De Grey – for he and Graham made sure to rein-in not only the conciliators but also the ultra-tory party whenever it threatened to bolt too far back along the road of learning nothing and forgetting nothing. This *far niente* policy proved a costly error. O'Connell had been written off much too soon. In the event, he succeeded in turning his enforced holiday from agitation into the basis for a much more formidable agitation in the future. He returned from it like a giant refreshed.

II

O'Connell's lord mayoralty of Dublin (1 November 1841–31 October 1842) has been, in all senses, badly noticed. Contemporary British mockery of his peacocking in the robes of office and glee in the title 'Lordship' (Thackeray squeezed these 'jokes' dry in his *Irish Sketch Book*) has been occasionally recalled. But generally historians have dismissed his year in the Dublin Mansion House as an aimless interlude, interesting only in so far as it emblemized a further significant decline in the domestic sway of the Irish – and in particular the metropolitan mercantile – Ascendancy.

This is a serious misjudgment. O'Connell did glory, child-like, in the lord mayoral parade and fritteries; he did exult, on the morrow of his victory, that his enemies

> have no longer the power to hurt us. To be sure, there never was such a corrupt, bigotted, jobbing, robbing corporation (laughter), but now they are gone, and there's an end to them . . . and we will put for an inscription over them – 'Here lies the Rotten Corporation of Dublin; it did no good when living, and it is a burden to the earth when dead' (shouts of laughter).[4]

But O'Connell's vision of his office soared high above its trappings or the novelty of the Repealers' triumph. He saw it as offering a first trial in self-government. Dublin Corporation was not exactly College Green *in parvo*. But, in O'Connell's eyes, its management presented him with the chance to show the world at large that the 'mere Irish' could order their affairs with impeccable propriety, probity and dispatch. He justified his own aspiration

> to the dignity of Lord Mayor . . . [by] his habit of business and his familiarity with the rules of debate [which] conferred upon him advantages which might not, perhaps, be easily found in another person, and which he conceived might be of great service in ensuring the maintenance of strict order, regularity and decorum in the proceeding of a new corporation.[5]

A la Johnson and Thrale's brewery, O'Connell saw in the lord mayoralty the potentiality of political riches beyond the dreams of avarice, rather than a parcel of boilers and vats!

It was, of course, extraordinarily convenient for O'Connell to find another arena for activity just as his prospects in parliament were dimmed. It was also convenient that the Irish corporation elections were scheduled for 25 October 1841, only eight weeks after the whigs were at last forced from office; this minimized the tories' capacity to manipulate the local electoral system to their advantage. O'Connell had to sacrifice his beloved Kerry vacation to the cause. 'It is a cruel disappointment to all here', wrote his son John from Derrynane, 'There was quite a *scene* upon the mountain yesterday when Denis McCrohan told the huntsmen that you could not come. Two or three of them, led by Cormac, fairly sat down and cried.'[6] But the Dublin municipal election required the rapid construction of a new political machine. The first essential was revision of the electoral roll, and this was frantically pursued almost up to the election day itself. Beyond the grind of roll-scrutiny, O'Connell based his campaign upon parish clubs which were to select the candidates for the fifteen city wards. Their lists constituted what he termed 'the whole ticket', which he repeatedly instructed the burgesses (or local electorate) to support *en bloc*. A week before the polling date, he was confident of carrying thirteen of the fifteen wards, provided that the burgesses troubled themselves to vote, and obeyed the order to 'stand true to the whole ticket . . . If any man breaks through the ticket, we are lost; if any man does not vote for the whole ticket, he is not for Ireland.'[7] To drive these points home, O'Connell secured (and publicized) a resolution from the Repeal Association, 'That any burgess enrolled on the Liberal interest who does not vote for the whole ticket at the ensuing municipal election is an enemy to the principle of civil and religious liberty, injures the cause of the depressed Irish manufacturers, and is a foe to the Repeal of the Union.'[8] All fell out more or less as O'Connell planned. If he did not make quite a clean sweep in the thirteen 'popular' wards, he carried 'the whole ticket' in eleven, and more than three-quarters of all seats in the new corporation (47 out of 60). He also headed the poll himself in two wards – thereby securing an ordinary vote as well as that which he would possess as chairman. His political genius had not failed; he had conjured up, almost on the instant, a set of tactics and cadre of lieutenants to deal with the novel circumstance.

Doubtless John O'Connell mirrored his father's view of his elevation when he boasted that the capture of Dublin corporation was second only 'to that glorious and *certain* event', the restoration of the Irish parliament. 'You have', John continued,

> a legally recognized *lordship* from *the people*, utterly unconnected with court favour or aristocratic usage . . . We rejoice, my dear Father, that Dublin has paid you such a tribute of respect as to take you for its first freely chosen chief magistrate, but still more that you should thus have opened to you one additional and most available means of advancing that great measure which will be the compensation for all your labours and sufferings, as it is and has been the great object of your life, the raising Ireland to her proper condition as a nation.[9]

But though O'Connell had succeeded by a ruthless, though brilliantly executed, exercise in street politics, grounded in his Repeal organization and appeal, he at once declared that he would eschew both party and partisanship during his lord mayoralty. Of course, such olympianism would help him to display his remarkable executive powers; it was the nearest he would ever get to membership of a government. But, much more important, supra-factional rule would tend to verify his life-long assertion that Irishmen of all creeds and antecedents could work together in their own country for the common good. In postponing Repeal as an immediate issue, he hoped, he said, to persuade Irish tories that they had nothing to fear from their compatriots.

Even had he wished to do so – which was, of course, far from being the case – O'Connell could not have buried the triumphal fact that he was the first Catholic lord mayor of Dublin since 1688, or have fled mob adulation on every public occasion. But he certainly cultivated the image of selfless political impartiality. Inevitably his term of office began with a taste or two of the spoils system. The replacements for certain of the corporation officers had evidently been decided well before the municipal election. John O'Connell told his father on 4 November that he had informed an applicant for patronage 'that whatever might be at the disposal of the Corporation had been long ago bespoken'.[10] But thereafter O'Connell seems to have striven earnestly both to reduce the number of corporation officials, and to prevent jobbery, even in the Repeal interest. On 8 December 1841 he hotly resisted a motion of Councillor Callaghan and Alderman Purcell, both Repealers, that all officers should be elected by ballot as the 'best means' of ensuring the council's independence (Callaghan wished his own son to be appointed junior counsel to the corporation, and despaired of his succeeding in open voting). O'Connell threatened immediate resignation.

He had, he perceived, sat too long in that chair (loud cries of no, no, no, and great confusion) . . . and he had, therefore, prepared a notice which he would give into the hands of the Town Clerks, for the election of a new Lord Mayor (loud cries of no, no, and great sensation). It was of too much importance that even the quantity of influence which he possessed in Ireland – should be preserved by him chaste and undefiled (cheers) . . . in point of law he was bound to say that publicity was the principle of the new corporations, and any thing which went to prevent that would not only make him leave the chair, but the assembly also.[11]

The 'rebels' instantly surrendered, and a counter-motion begging O'Connell to withdraw his impending resignation was carried with acclamation.

> O! it is excellent
> To have a giant's strength; but it is tyrannous
> To use it like a giant.[12]

Unquestionably, O'Connell had acted, in effect, the bully. But the original motion was a direct challenge to his political as well as his civic authority.

The only open deviation from his vaunted neutrality as chairman came in response to tory provocation. On 23 December 1841 the 'Orange' councillors proposed that the corporation congratulate De Grey on his appointment as lord lieutenant. 'The notion of the reformed corporation of Dublin consenting to such a proposition', O'Connell broke out, 'could not be entertained by any man.' De Grey governed for a party that

seemed to despise the opinion of the people, and who assisted in restraining their [the corporation's] own powers by giving them a corporation bill far inferior to what had been granted to any of the towns in England (hear) . . .

[De Grey] has no public character but that which he ought to be ashamed to hear – that of making professions of impartiality and liberality, while he is doing the work of the partizan.

Of course, the vote, which went on party lines, favoured O'Connell. He himself, however, by no means considered his stance political. His concluding outburst revealed his inward thought – or perhaps unconscious assumption – that *he* was the embodiment of *national* will, and the opposition a mere nexus of *frondeurs*. 'The [O'Connel-lite] party referred to', he declared, 'consisted of the people, who were not a party, but who were opposed by a section of the country, that might properly be termed a party.'[13]

In this vein, O'Connell, while pouring fishwives' abuse upon Peel and De Grey at weekly meetings of the Repeal Association, treated their supporters with a sort of elephantine forbearance when acting or speaking as lord mayor. He ordered the statue of William III in College Green to be painted 'bronze' so that the Dublin Orangemen (having a colour near enough to their hearts presumably) need no longer try to deck it with garlands on their celebratory days, and thereby provoke sectarian disturbances. He cast off his official regalia at the doors of the Catholic Pro-Cathedral on New Year's Day, 1842, with the aside (for the benefit of the surrounding mob) that although the lord mayor was a Catholic, his robes were Protestant. He abandoned the traditional lord mayor's proclamation calling for the solemn observance of Good Friday. 'It was a rule with Roman Catholics, and they all knew he was one', he told the corporation on 23 March 1842, 'to leave these things with their clergy . . . He was disposed to pay the same respect to the clergymen of every other religious domination.' When this decision was generally applauded, O'Connell allowed himself a single flick of asperity. 'Such a feeling was certainly to be commended . . . the more particularly when it was recollected, that in the room in which they them met the most rigorous exclusion on account of religion was perseveringly adhered to.'[14] His momentary lapse from magnanimity was trifling, however, compared with the undying bitterness of some of his Orange opponents. Councillor Mackay, for example, decried the O'Connellites in the corporation as 'men who had neither principle, honour or character – the dupes and slaves of the greatest tyrant who ever lived . . . and amongst them, he was sorry to say, there were a great many Protestants, who attached a degree of respectability to the contemptible set'.[15] But O'Connell was finally rewarded for his laborious supra-sectarianism. On the day that he retired from office, he was eulogized in the corporation (to general cheers) as a tyrant who enslaved by the heart and not the hand. A motion 'expressing our . . . approbation of the impartial manner with which Alderman Daniel O'Connell discharged the duties of Lord Mayor' was also carried, unanimously.[16]

Some of O'Connell's gestures – the bronzing of William III's statue or the abandonment of his robes and chain at the church door – were comical enough. He also paraded, and was paraded, as Mob King. Immediately after his election, he appeared at the open window of the council chamber and asked the delighted crowd whether they knew him still in his new finery, and whether his cocked hat became him. For weeks after, as he rode about in the civic coach, flanked by footmen in a livery of green and yellow, his tattermadalion followers called 'Hats off!' to all spectators, tearing away the headgear of the reluctant. But it must be allowed that, as popular politician, O'Connell was more or less a licensed public performer. His role as lord mayor resembled his professional 'part' of barrister. Both occupations were akin to acting in being replete with rituals and costume, and in the prescribed emotional reactions, cultivation of rapport with audiences, and dispensation (for the time being) from many of the conventions governing ordinary life. All this was second nature to O'Connell – as well as first artifice.

Once in the council room, O'Connell was a very different being. His executive efficiency was at least as striking as his 'impartiality'. Early in his term, he set up finance, law, property and water committees, each under his own chairmanship – forgoing at the same time that portion of the lord mayor's allowance which was a charge on the impoverished pipe-water estate. Characteristically, he drew up, unaided, a complete pipe-water bill in twenty-four hours in order to give it the necessary notice to be considered in the next session of parliament. Equally characteristic was his flamboyant offer of his professional services free of cost to the corporation during a wrangle over the expense of employing legal officers. O'Connell was punctilious in his weekly attendance at the lord mayor's court and (if the absence of any charges to the contrary is conclusive) in adhering to his original undertaking to deal with litigants only in open court, and to see none in the Mansion House. A petition presented in the Commons on 6 May 1842 complained of his inactivity in admitting freemen to the franchise; but, in reply, he claimed to have missed only one admission day, and that through illness. It is true – as tory councillors kept pointing out – that he was absent from Dublin for considerable periods. He spent some eighteen weeks in attendance at the House of Commons; he also holidayed in Derrynane in September, although for less than half his usual time. Even O'Connell (when it suited him) allowed that his opponents had ground for dissatisfaction in this regard. In declining an invitation to stand a second time for the lord mayoralty, he told the corporation on 16 August 1842 that he 'was obliged to be absent more frequently that he would wish, which was an exceedingly wrong principle'.[17] Less grandly, he vowed a month later that he 'would not consent for any offer to forfeit my prospect of being here [Derrynane] all October in the ensuing year'.[18]

None the less, Dublin must have gained much more from his intelligent and decisive management for seven months of the year than it lost from having to suffer a *locum tenens* for the remaining five. It was not flummery when O'Connell was lauded for his 'distinguished ability [and] unwearied assiduity' in the corporation immediately after his retirement.[19] He had applied himself with his customary zeal. 'I never was worried out of my existence', he wrote on 4 December 1841, 'until after I became a great *City* Lord.'[20] So it remained to the concluding weeks of his term of office. Between 2 and 16 October 1842 (the fortnight allotted by law) he completed the revision of the burgess roll, labouring nine hours a day up to the 16th, when he worked almost until midnight. He also pushed through a reform of the weighmaster system at Smithfield market during the week that he retired. It is true that much of the substance of municipal government, as we see it, was ignored during O'Connell's no less than earlier regimes. He had nothing to say on sanitation, arterial drainage, housing, roads, gas lighting and similar matters, critical to the comfort and even tolerability of urban life, although these were the subjects of rapid change in both theory and practice in contemporary Europe. The omission was important. People dwell, wash, walk, play, live noisomely or not, live in light or dark, die young or old, as well as brandish tokens and struggle for vicarious power. But the fault lay at least as much with the politically-inspired limitations of the Irish Municipal Reform Act as with O'Connell himself, and in fact he can scarcely be blamed for not seeing the city which had been his chief home for nearly half a century – wrapping him round like an old familiar garment – with fresh eyes. By all the customary criteria of Dublin civic government, he was a remarkably efficient, even an imaginative, lord mayor.

The effectiveness of O'Connell's administration was the more remarkable because the new corporation was encumbered by the accumulated debts (over £300,000) and ill-kept financial records of the old. His first action as lord mayor was to institute an investigation into the accounts of the late treasurer, Sir John Kingston James. Eight and a half months later, James had still failed to produce detailed accounts. On 16 August 1842, O'Connell reported to the corporation that 'not a single date when any payment was made could be found. The entire affair looked as much like a fraud as anything he had ever seen.'[21] By the end of September 1842, James still having failed to divulge even the dates on which debentures and the interest on them had been issued, O'Connell moved from the chair that he receive no compensation or back salary. Meanwhile, the corporation had been in desperate financial plights. On 2 April 1842 seven of its wealthiest O'Connellite members had had to subscribe £500 each in order to procure the release of its estate from chancery.

Significantly, O'Connell himself was not among the subscribers. The reason was simple: his own finances were by then in little better state than the corporation's. The lord mayor's allowances under the new Act did not meet the outgoings which O'Connell (ever lavish) deemed indispensable, and his suspension of party politics, even if only when acting in his official role, dried up the contributions to his Tribute and the Rent. On 25 July 1842, he wrote to Fitzpatrick 'overwhelmed with affliction. It almost drives me mad . . . [Edmond] Smithwick's bill for £420, due on Wednesday week, *comes upon me*. I write again to him today in great anxiety.'[22] He did indeed write anxiously to Smithwick, one of his most loyal and necessary supporters:

> Unhappily I have this month made payments to the extent of some thousands of pounds, and next month is also heavy though comparatively light. I did not however foresee or make provision for your bill, foolishly thinking it impossible that I should not get it renewed. It makes me quite unhappy lest it should go back on you for want of my being ready to take it up . . . I really cannot describe my anxiety. What am I to do? If the bill goes back on you under present circumstances I never can forgive myself.[23]

Once more, however, the indefatigable Fitzpatrick came to the rescue; he arranged for all O'Connell's bills to be accepted. 'May God bless you!', replied O'Connell in relief on 29 July, 'I was actually in despair'.[24]

III

O'Connell could have ill-afforded a second term as lord mayor. But it was not this that moved him to reject it; never in his life had he regulated his actions by what he could or could not afford. It was the cost to his public life which really mattered. He had already creamed the office of such *éclat*, and opportunity to display administrative talent, as it had to offer. Meanwhile, his failure to make headway with any of his main objectives during the second parliamentary session of 1842 appears to have clinched his determination to revert from the municipal arena to the national. On 6 August 1842 he announced to Ray from London that he proposed 'to proceed at once to the perfect organisation of the Repeal agitation', and instructed him to prepare immediately accurate returns of the Association's activities throughout Leinster since the preceding 25 March. 'The apathy', he went on,

> by which the spirit of patriotism is paralysed must soon give way to the conviction that Ireland has nothing to depend on but her own exertions . . .
>
> But shall we despair? I will try the thrilling trumpet that has often before caused despair to hope and torpor to be roused into energy. I do not despair, nor does the chill of an ungenial Legislature diminish the glow of hope which I derive from the subdued but reviving flame of genuine Irish patriotism. The People of Ireland are true to the heart's core. The Clergy of the People are as sincere in their love of fatherland as they are eminent in Christian zeal and fervent piety. I do not despair . . .
>
> Have, I repeat it, prepared a list of all the parishes in Leinster, with the names of the clergy of each parish and of every layman therein, who shall have taken at any bygone time an active part in the Repeal agitation. It is by detailed and persevering exertions that public opinion will recover its tone and energy in Ireland.[25]

We should note the prominent role which O'Connell evidently envisaged for the Church. For some time, he had been steadily cultivating the hierarchy, acting more or less as their agent in various pieces of legislation which touched ecclesiastical interests; and on 9 May 1842 he had written to Paul Cullen, rector of the Irish College at Rome, on the multifarious benefits which would flow to Irish Catholicism from the repeal of the Act of Union. 'British!!!', he exclaimed in the course of his apologia, 'I am not British. You are not British. When the British north and south fell away and dissipated amongst the profligate and the renegades of Protestantism and of every species of infidelity, the inheritance of the Lord amidst the land, the Irish Nation and the Irish Church were the victims of and not the participators in these crimes.'[26] When on 9 September he ordered his personal secretary O'Neill Daunt to commence 'arrangments [sic] for opening the campaign of agitation', he also warned him to advance only with clerical concurrence. 'Be sure to have the approval of the Catholic clergy in every place you move to.'[27]

Well before his term of lord mayor ended, O'Connell set afoot what he called 'provincial agitation for the appointment of Repeal wardens in every parish'.[28] In mid-September 1842, the principal organizers of this preliminary work were dispatched to Munster, Connacht and Leinster. He himself was released from 'office' on 1 November, but the accumulation of business in arrears and the need to restore himself once more at Derrynane precluded him from wholehearted campaigning for a time. When the New Year began, however, he was ready for a full agitation. On 7 January 1843, he told Fitzpatrick, 'I intend to spend less time in London this Session than ever I did.'[29] In fact, he spent none. No skirmishing at Westminster could compare in significance with the onslaught which he rapidly succeeded in mounting at home. The lord mayoralty had served its purpose. O'Connell had played the part of sober and judicious statesman, in the utmost glare which the Lilliputian theatre of a city council could provide. Now it was time to take to the open air and use an entire country for his stage, and, by turns, Coriolanus, Brutus and Mark Antony for roles.

IV

A most striking feature of O'Connell's winning and wearing of the Dublin lord mayoralty was, as we have seen, his recovery of energy and spirit. The press of new work was nothing as against its accompanying colour and excitement. Rather, it was a break from care, from the anxious years of hand-to-mouth political existence, when the survival of the whigs in office – all-in-all to him – seemed practically forever at the hazard. Thus in late 1842 he came back to serious politics quite restored, with all 'the gloss of freshness'[30] once again.

His renewed exuberance and revitalization while in office were a remarkable testimony to O'Connell's power to subordinate the private to the public man, for, interiorly regarded, the early 1840s were not easy years. Central to everything which touched him individually was his religion, and O'Neill Daunt's record of his conversations with O'Connell during 1840–2 throws some light on this. O'Connell's belief tended to be grave and rigid. In a contention with Daunt (a convert to Catholicism) on 'whether errors in faith, or errors in morals, were the more dangerous to the soul and the more offensive to God', O'Connell argued strongly for the first:

Nothing short of a thorough and perfect sincerity – and, moreover, a cautious sincerity, – could acquit the holder of erroneous faith from the guilt of heresy. Of course, every person thus thoroughly and cautiously sincere, was free from heretical guilt; but those who belonged not to the Catholic church laboured under the grievous disadvantage of being deprived of true sacraments; or, in other words, they were deprived of those ordinary channels of grace and modes of reconciliation with God, of which *all* stand in need, inasmuch as *all* have at one time or another sinned mortally. Even though a Catholic should have sinned more grievously than a person without the pale of the church, yet the position of the former was in *one* respect better – namely, that he stood a better chance of obtaining the grace of true repentance.[31]

Even when he spoke of the astonishing rise in the number of 'male communicants' over the past quarter-century or so, O'Connell took it at its lowest computation – as an indication of greater earnestness in religion, and not necessarily of spiritual progress: 'Every Sunday you will see many more than you then saw at Easter or Christmas; and this is, at all events, an evidence that the persons who communicate, *intend*, at least, that they will not live in sin.'[32] It seems significant that one of O'Connell's two favourite Latin hymns, which he was accustomed to recite aloud when travelling, was that generally heard by Catholics on Good Friday only, when the Way of the Cross was being commemorated.

> *Stabat Mater Dolorosa,*
> *Juxta crucem lachrymosa*
> *Dum pendebat filius.*[*33]

Although he continued to deplore the temporal power, possessions and pretensions of the pope, and to assert that 'In fact, the democratic spirit is more favourable to the cause of morality and religion, than the monarchical', he took an absolutist view of papal authority in the field of faith and doctrine.[34] He wrote on 9 September 1841, for instance, that

> the spiritual authority in all its effulgence [is] the Apostolic See, the centre of unity, the safeguard of the Church. That authority is assailed in our day by the spirit of absolutism in many Catholic and other sovereigns, who not content with Caesar's portion claim what belongs to God. It is also assailed by the restless genius of false liberalism which whilst it affects to seek liberty principally desires to uproot religion.[35]

He cherished Dryden's lines exalting the inerrancy of the papacy,

> But Gracious God! how well thou dost provide
> For erring judgments an unerring guide . . .
> O, teach me to believe thee thus concealed
> Nor further search than what thyself revealed

---

*The sorrowing mother stands
In tears next to the cross
While her son hangs from it.

But her alone for my director take
Whom thou has promised never to forsake.[36]

It is silly as well as arrogant to believe that one can make windows into people's souls. But, for what they are worth, the outward signs suggest that O'Connell was an ultra-conscientious, fearful, straitened type of Catholic, almost morbidly observant. There appears to have been little or nothing in him of the spiritual joyousness and easy resilience which one might have predicted from his public bearing. He may even have been a victim – to a small degree – of a form of religious neurosis. Certainly, he had a thorough knowledge of the textbook responses to scrupulosity. During all this period, and indeed after he had died, his youngest daughter, Betsey Ffrench, was (intermittently, at least) in deep religious distress, though the specific subject of her 'scruples' is unknown. When O'Connell first learnt of her condition, in June 1839, he prescribed the set ecclesiastical remedy of utter submission to direction:

> It is quite true that you are in a state with which it is the inscrutable will of God to try the souls of His elect – a state of great danger if the spirit of pride, of self-esteem, or of self-will is mixed with it, so as to make the sufferer fall into the snare of *despair*. Despair is your danger, your only danger. Oh, generous God, protect my child from despair! If you by humility, submission, humble submission, to the church in the person of your spiritual director – if you give up every thought and throw yourself into the arms of God by OBEDIENCE and submission, you will soon be at peace and be so for life, and in an eternity of bliss . . . If your scruple be such as you cannot communicate to your father, go at once and consult Dr MacHale about it. Determine, before you go in the presence of God, to submit to whatever the Archbishop shall say to you.[37]

When Betsey's reply revealed her to be still caught in her maze of fears, O'Connell repeated the orthodox instruction:

> There is one remedy, and *only one*. That is, absolute, unqualified submission to your director – unreasoning submission. Do not argue with anybody. Let nobody reason with you, but *submit*. Do exactly what your director requires. In your case your director may – and, I think, should, compel you to go to communion without going to confession at all. Many persons in your condition have been perfectly cured by perfect submission.[38]

Had O'Connell himself been among the 'cured'? Certainly, he occasionally manifested something like obsession in seeking to make reparation for some past real or imagined wrong. He, whose Lenten mortification was often awesome, grieved over some self-exemptions from fasting in earlier days. He even worried – in his rare flushes of affluence – about distant, doubtful debts. He once wrote to his former steward, for instance,

> I cannot express to you how uneasy I feel about the money I received out of Segerson's lands after his death. I must satisfy my mind to the last shilling. I have an impression I received £72. I will pay it all over again if I [one word illegible] and if I should not recollect it, *it must be paid* . . . Where are the Brennans I put out of Bahaghs? It was for putting them out I made some compensation. There was a balance due to them of a bond debt by Segerson . . . Really this subject is troubling my mind and conscience.[39]

Ten days later, he followed up this *cri de coeur* with, 'I also earnestly request you will *at once* find out all particulars of the Brennans of Bahaghs . . . I cannot, my dear John, bear delay in this matter.'[40] All this may signify no more than bouts of extraordinary conscientiousness. But there seems little doubt that O'Connell's religion was very serious, in both the general and the contemporary evangelical senses. An acute awareness of (to use his own words) 'the evil of sin in its offending God and subjecting us to deserve punishment hereafter'[41] did not conduce to private comfort – not that O'Connell would have spoken of his spiritual pains, whatever they might have been, as anything other than part of the Christian dispensation, of the purifying design of (his own words again) 'a loving God who, in the excess of his love, died on a cross' for him.[42] 'Alas, alas,' he once asked O'Neill Daunt, '. . . of what use will future fame be to me when I am dead and judged?'[43] This rings authentic.

Despite the docility of his family, O'Connell's path as a father was steep and broken. Although the eldest was 39 years old in 1841 and the youngest 22, none of his children had really thrown off their early dependence on him, nor had he lost his old fearful solicitude or sense of responsibility for their affairs. One or other or even several of them, and their families, stayed with him, often for weeks at a time, at Derrynane or Merrion Square or in London. For all his control of the domestic timetables, this must have eaten into his working-time and concentration, as well as money. As with all his family cares, the loss of Mary told on him here. She (according to her daughter Ellen) had known that it

> was necessary for the success of affairs both of law and politics . . . that he should never be troubled with household affairs; and she therefore, while regulating his family with the great exactness, took care never to harass

him with her domestic troubles ... On the contrary ... [even] when engaging a governess, she was wont to stipulate that no chidings of the children should ever take place in their father's presence, but should be reserved for the schoolroom.[44]

Mary was no longer there to screen him as best she could from all that was disagreeable in a household.

To be pressed in by the business of his family was far from simply troublesome to O'Connell. He slipped naturally into, and revelled in, the part of patriarch; he enjoyed crowded tables and a domestic audience. He also doted on his grandchildren, calling them by the usual sort of childish names (Fanny Fan-Fan or Duck-a-day), and full of the usual foolish wonder at their infant talk; he remained almost cloyingly affectionate towards his own daughters and younger sons. But, as we have seen, a heavy tax was paid on such emotional commitment. The death of his favourite grandson struck O'Connell to the heart, and there is no doubting the reality of his anguish when he first learned of Betsey's sad condition: 'Represent to yourself your darling boy in mental agony and then you will read my feelings of utter misery at your state of mind. This, I own, is the severest blow that ever I experienced, to have you, my angel daughter, consuming your heart and intellect on vain, idle, and unprofitable scruples';[45] or again, 'I write to you by your pet name, to recall to your own tenderness your fond father's affection. I see your case clearly, and it breaks my heart to think of it.'[46]

Another blow was the break-up of Maurice's long-troubled marriage early in 1841. Evidently, Mary Frances deserted her husband, for Maurice wrote to O'Connell on 20 March, 'It has struck me that *her* family may set up insanity as a defence and I think that this ought to be considered.'[47] At first it looked as if some 'quiet arrangement' might be reached, but on 18 May 1841, through her brother, Mary Frances told her solicitor that 'she would listen to no terms under £300 a year [roughly, the income which her dowry would have earned], that she would not appear in Dublin and that she had been served with her citation'.[48] O'Connell was privy to the negotiations, and although his comments have not survived there can be no doubt that the marital scandal would have hit him hard. Such affairs generated a family-wide, ill-differentiated air of disgrace in early Victorian Ireland; and besides O'Connell had now to provide further support, domestic and financial, to Maurice and the four children who had been left upon his hands. There are also some indications that O'Connell fretted lest his little grand-daughters be deprived of

Catholic education. At the time, it was common in 'mixed marriages' for daughters to be reared in their mother's religion, and sons in their father's. Probably O'Connell feared that what was cruelly but all too accurately described as a 'habeas animam' struggle might follow Mary Frances's departure. In fact, she appears never to have demanded more than the £300 per annum for her own maintenance. But O'Connell must have been sick with apprehension, and the shame of the whole business, for a while.

Whatever the final settlement with Mary Frances, ultimately he would have borne the additional expenses, for, Atlas-like, he still carried the majority of his family on his shoulders. Although Maurice had a small independent income, O'Connell appears to have given him, as heir, an allowance of £700 a year. It also seems that O'Connell had to underwrite (at an annual cost of £85 for a life assurance premium) that portion of Mary Frances's dowry which even yet remained effectively in the hands of the Scott family. His second son, Morgan, who had been appointed Irish assistant registrar of deeds in 1840 and married in the same year, was no longer a financial burden; in fact the roles may have been temporarily reversed in 1841 to judge from Fitzpatrick's request of 27 January to O'Connell (the first of three such notes) for 'a cheque for £750 to pay Morgan's acceptance for your accommodation due early next week'.[49] Similarly, O'Connell's eldest daughter, Ellen, was more or less independent, although in 1841 her husband was complaining to O'Connell of 'the present too small salaries' of Irish public servants: 'I boldly assert the salary of "Clerk of the Hanaper" [his own office] is already too low at £600 a year'.[50] O'Connell helped his other daughters, Kate and Betsey, with occasional small gifts of money; neither was well-off. But his other sons were major charges. Despite the injection of considerable outside capital and more skilled management, 'O'Connell's Brewery' had proved an unsuccessful venture, and was sold – to re-emerge, appropriately enough, as the Phoenix – in 1840. Thus Daniel was back again, more or less, on O'Connell's hands. John, for whose marriage settlement O'Connell had had to borrow £5000 in 1838, was also in some measure a dependant. 'Instead of money for agitating expeditions,' he wrote to O'Connell from Dublin on 9 December 1840,

I am obliged, my dear father, to ask you to let me place to your account one or two of my heaviest household bills (not wine) since you left town. I have no choice as the money I calculated upon has suddenly failed me. House property is so precarious that after getting £200 a year these 2 years as my third of Eliza's [his wife's] joint property, I now learn I am not to get more than what I have received this year, viz., £130 – deficit £70 *on one third alone*, making on the whole £210. This, with the £70 Eliza's illness cost me, renders me a beggar for the rest of this year but *it shall be the last time.* I have had to raise money to meet Eliza's illness which will give some idea of my condition.[51]

The basis of O'Connell's financial troubles in the 1840s was probably expenditure, past and current, on his family. Such crises as the failure to meet Smithwick's bill in July 1842 had their roots in his chronic indebtedness, which in turn derived, to a considerable degree, from earlier spending on his children. At the very least, O'Connell had laid out £20,000 in financing their marriages, and their yearly drain upon him must have meant further borrowing. Early in 1842, the Board of the National Bank was so concerned about his rising overdraft, which by then totalled almost £30,500, that it set up a special committee to tackle the problem of its Governor's affairs. The minutes of their committee reveal something of the awkwardness of the extraordinary situation:

When [on 27 February 1842] the chairman presented to his Lordship [O'Connell] their Report, and in proposing to read the same he said it was unnecessary as he would read it over, himself, his Lordship then entered into some verbal explanations, when the Committee intimated that they would prefer having a reply in writing and which his Lordship promised to furnish, on the following Tuesday, the 1st of March.

In consequence of no reply being received from his Lordship on the 19th of March the Chairman with the concurrence of the other Members of the Committee, addressed the following Letter to his Lordship, the The Rt Honble Daniel O'Connell MP

My Lord,   19 March 1842
Not having had the pleasure of meeting your Lordship at the Court [Board meeting] this day, and, in consequence of the inquiries which have been made respecting the result of the Report now in your Lordship's possession, I have as Chairman of the Special Committee, and in accordance with the wishes of my Colleagues to solicit the favor of your furnishing us with the written communications as agreed upon when we first had the honor of an interview with your Lordship.[52]

When on 27 March 1842 O'Connell at last tendered his written submission, it was clear that the bulk of his security consisted of assurance policies on various lives, his own included. It was also evident that several of the policies had been entered into in order to secure capital sums, or underwrite commitments, for Maurice, John and perhaps other of his children. The premiums on the policies alone amounted to over £1250, and the overdraft interest to some £600, per annum. To these outgoings was soon to be added the obligation to reduce steadily his ill-secured overdraft at the bank. With it all, his younger sons at least remained in a precarious condition. Could O'Connell always keep out of mind the grim warning of his brother James, a few years earlier, 'a long experience of the cold heartedness of the world makes me fear these young men [in particular, "poor little Dan"] may, in the event of your being suddenly taken out of their life, be left without the means of existence'?[53]

In this way, O'Connell's public rebound of 1841–2, his outward gaiety, the renewal of his zest and sparkle, are to be set against his enveloping private cares. How did he keep such heart-sicknesses at bay, quite out of sight? Explain it as we will – by ferocity of ambition, by indomitability of nature, by matchless powers of recovery or the politician's innate sense of stage – it still seems a marvel of control. Whatever hidden weights he carried, he was, at the end of 1842, ready to spring, as lightly as ever, into the contest of his life.

CHAPTER 9

The Big Bang

1843

I

As we have seen, the new Repeal Association advanced little during its first two years in being. Yet, curiously enough, this slow progress was partly responsible for the development of something like a general programme for the movement. In his efforts to widen his appeal, O'Connell took aboard various popular demands, especially those attractive to the small tenant farmers. The abolition of tithes was one obvious example. Another was the replacement of the new Irish poor law by a quasi-charitable system financed by a tax on incomes of over £500 per annum, or better still by a state-aided scheme to succour the sick poor: the farmers were groaning loudly under the novel burden of the poor rate. But the most promising adoption was for fixity of tenure. This was rather a misnomer, as the Association's proposal amounted to little more than compensation for tenant improvements and a minimum of twenty-one years for leases. None the less, it was a radical demand in the climate of the early 1840s.

Similarly, O'Connell set up committees of the Association to sustain interest in, and manufacture business for, the weekly meetings. The committees (whose membership was identical and determined solely by O'Connell, the invariable chairman) investigated and reported on such subjects as the passage of the Act of Union, Ireland's financial relations with Great Britain, the progress of Repeal, and the restoration of the Irish House of Commons. The main consequence of these reports was to enlarge O'Connell's own oratorical armoury and to keep up the spirits of the faithful. Even the report on the progress of Repeal was much more an essay in propaganda than an attempt to remedy serious organizational failings. But the committees also led, almost accidentally, to the acquisition of policies at several points. By its very failure to take off politically, 'simple repeal' ended up with various shreds and patches of an extra-constitutional platform.

The critical change came in late 1842 when O'Connell's term as lord mayor ended and the inefficiency of the existing organization could at last come under serious attention. As a first step, the Dublin wardens were re-ordered. Next, inspectors of wardens, charged with the establishment and maintenance of a thorough-going system of propaganda, fund-collection and communciation with the centre, were appointed for the towns and groups of parishes, with chief inspectors for still larger regions. This was of course a harking back to models provided by the Catholic Association in 1827–8. O'Connell also began to emphasize much more strongly the importance of the wardens' work, and the need to recruit them widely. Leading members of the Association, notably W. J. O'Neill Daunt, Tom Steele and later Maurice O'Connell, were despatched on tours of the provinces to organize meetings, select officers and generally establish a network for agitation. Rapidly, the parishes were supplied with one, two, three or even four wardens. In turn, the wardens usually appointed collectors to gather in the Repeal Rent; and they themselves were subject to the control and direction, immediately of the inspectors, and ultimately of the Association headquarters at the Corn Exchange. As usual with O'Connell's movements, Munster led the way. But the enlistment extended rapidly, though in varying degrees of effectiveness, in every county south of, say, a line drawn from Sligo to Dundalk.

Thus well before the great Mansion House debate of 28 February 1843, when O'Connell virtually proclaimed a crusade for 'simple repeal', the foundations of the mass movement of that year were being laid. The new stress on organization was not without some ideological implications. Total community mobilization was being attempted. This meant extensions of the notions of internal policing and internal legal adjudication, which had been only intermittently applied or vaguely adumbrated during the Association's early years. Repeal police and a Repeal arbitration system for land disputes pointed in the direction of alternative government from below and the supersession, in part at least, of the official agencies of law and order. Again, the exigencies of agitation were adding new political dimensions to Repeal. When after large and enthusiastic popular meetings had been held in widely-dispersed places during November and December 1842, O'Connell was emboldened to declare that '1843 is and shall be the great Repeal year',[1] further developments were foreshadowed. The movement which he proclaimed was necessarily dynamic; it had to produce the impression of continuous growth, in both scale and intensity, if the strain on the British government were to be maximized. This implied in turn a climax to the season of agitation. An ultimate, apparently practicable, culmination to the campaign season had to be devised. At the dinner following one of the earliest monster meetings, held in Sligo on 4 May, O'Connell announced that once the first goal had been attained and three million members enrolled in the Association within three months – that is by early August 1843 – each 'district' in Ireland would express 'confidence' in particular persons who would meet 'spontaneously' in Dublin as the Council of Three Hundred. He added that the council would at once draw up 'Bill no. 1' to repeal the Act of Union, and 'Bill no. 2', to re-institute the Irish House of Commons.[2] It seemed to be implied that further parts of the Association programme would be taken up similarly, seriatim. Clearly, O'Connell was promising the unilateral establishment of a virtual parliament. But, equally, the 'expression of confidence' rather than polled votes, and the 'spontaneous' assemblage of individuals rather than the summoning of elected representatives, were meant to keep the Association within the boundaries of the law. There could be no doubt however that, under the pressure to formulate a climax, Repeal had taken a further massive step in the direction of something very different from its original character, that is, towards becoming a prototype Sinn Fein.

Secondly, the nature of the enterprise of 1843, with the need to marshal and inspirit many tens of thousands of people every week and to evoke and release sentiments of historic resentment and mass-attitudinizing, inevitably led the orators to the brink of the martial. As an English visitor described the meeting at Mullaghmast, co. Kildare, on 1 October 1843, 'The men yelled and danced with rage; the women screamed and clapped their hands. The vast multitude – I believe there were really 100,000 present – moved and moaned like a wild beast in agony.'[3] O'Connell guarded his language very carefully: bombast was one thing, words capable of being construed as seditious quite another. But in practice it was not possible to resist all military or minatory flights in the charged emotional exchange between demagogue and people. At the dinner following the Kilkenny monster meeting of 8 June, for example, O'Connell broke out,

> We stand at the head of a body of men that, if organized by military discipline, would be quite abundant for the conquest of Europe. Wellington had never such an army as we saw today. There was not at

Waterloo on both sides so many stout, active, energetic men as we saw here to-day . . . They would be as ready to obey their Repeal Wardens as if they were called sergeants and captains.[4]

Three days later, having been inflamed by a vast public meeting (reported as 400,000 strong!) at Mallow, O'Connell was led on by the thunders of applause and the presence of a ladies' gallery at the evening banquet to the fiery topic of Cromwell's massacre of women of Wexford.

300 of the grace, and beauty, and virtue of Wexford were slaughtered by the English ruffians. Sacred Heaven! (tremendous sensation, and cries of 'oh, oh'.) I am not at all imaginative when I talk of the possibility of such occurrences anew (hear, hear); but yet, I assert there is no danger of [sic] the women, for the men of Ireland would die to the last in their defence. (Here the entire company rose and cheered for several minutes.) We were a paltry remnant then; we are nine millions now.[5]

A short time earlier, he had cried out, in the celebrated 'Mallow Defiance', 'I say they may trample me; but it will be my dead body they will trample on, not the living man.'[6]

In short, the very scale and pace of the agitation of 1843 helped to reshape 'Repeal'; and the equivalent was of course true of the groups whom O'Connell had to recruit as sub-managers and local organizers. We have seen already how the programme was developed to appeal to the tenant farmers; attempts were also made to involve both shopkeepers and tradesmen by the establishment of Repeal boards of trade in Dublin and provincial cities such as Limerick. But much more important – indispensable, in fact – was active participation of the bulk of the Catholic clergy. The support, or at the very least neutralization, of the bishops was a pre-requisite, as they effectively controlled the lower clergy. This had been substantially secured by the beginning of 1843. As soon as O'Connell began serious campaigning, in 1840, Archbishop MacHale of Tuam and Bishops Browne of Galway, Blake of Dromore, Cantwell of Meath, O'Higgins of Ardagh, and Foran of Waterford and Lismore declared publicly for Repeal, and were ready to engage actively in the struggle as O'Connell's allies. Over the next two and a half years, eleven other members of the hierarchy committed themselves to Repeal. Slattery of Cashel was coaxed out of his non-combatancy, and Bishops MacLaughlin and Maginn of Derry, McNally of Clogher, Kennedy of Killaloe, Keatinge of Ferns, Feeny of Killala, Burke of Elphin, Coen of Clonfert, French of Kilmacduagh, and O'Donnell, Browne's successor in Galway, all became members of the Association, and most of them zealous partisans into the bargain. These adhesions accounted for a clear majority of the Irish episcopate, and in their dioceses the priests were active repealers almost to a man. Even in dioceses where their lordships were 'neutral' or covertly hostile, a large number of the clergy worked for the Repeal Association. This was important, for in the countryside at least it was the ordinary parish priests, and to a lesser extent their curates, who carried the movement on their shoulders.

When the Association was reconstructed in the winter of 1842–3, it was almost invariably the parish priest (as often as not O'Connell knew him personally) whom the organizers from Dublin first approached. He would arrange the initial meeting, nominate likely persons for wardenships, supervise the local Repeal rooms once they were established and largely plan the monster meeting if one were to be held later in the vicinity. A typical case was that of the Rev Mr McEvoy, parish priest of Kells. The Repeal organizer stayed with him on his first visit, and through him arranged the initial meeting. It was McEvoy who selected the Repeal wardens, and acted as general organizer of the later mass meeting of over 100,000 people which O'Connell addressed. He also served as host to O'Connell on the occasion, and from first to last was the channel of communication between Kells and the Association's headquarters. Many of the priests became Repeal wardens, though they by no means constituted a majority of the corps. Almost always, outside the cities and the larger towns, they filled the critical office of inspector. Even where they were not officially inspectors, most of the dealings with the wardens took place through them, and it was they who generally distributed the Association's circulars. The chief speakers at the monster meetings stayed at the local parochial houses; and clergy constituted a high percentage of the platform party at both the meetings and the evening banquets where one of the inevitable toasts was that drunk to 'The clergy of Ireland'.

This is not to say that the Repeal movement of 1843 was overtly or even substantially sectarian. Its difference in this regard from the Emancipation agitation of the 1820s was continually stressed in speeches and publications. Every Protestant recruit (especially if he were a clergyman) was fêted as a lost sheep found. None the less the Catholic priests and bishops were accorded the full deference which their indispensability to the organization and agitation deserved. After investigating one dispute at Waterford, O'Connell censured all 'language of a disrespectful nature' to the Catholic clergy, and threatened with expulsion any member of the Association who used such terms.[7] As it happened, no religious issue arose during 1843, and O'Connell was required to go no further in respecting clerical susceptibilities or in serving clerical interests than public flattery of the grossest kind.

Like the Catholic Association, the Repeal Association was overwhelmingly Catholic in membership, with a small number of eccentric or ultra-liberal Protestant adherents. But it had one unique component. The 1820s had produced no equivalent to the young intelligensia epitomized by their newspaper, the *Nation*, first published in October 1842. Its founders, Thomas Davis and John Blake Dillon, respectively Protestant and Catholic graduates of Trinity College Dublin, and Charles Gavan Duffy, an Ulster Catholic journalist, were archetypal of a new generation of Irish nationalists. Davis was indeed something more – their prophet, expositor and conscience, all in one. Significant differences of emphasis, and even of basic principle, between O'Connell and this Young Ireland group were eventually to emerge. Their anti-sectarianism passed far beyond his demand for parity among religions; it practically relegated religious belief to the sphere of the private and the personal, and proffered 'national consciousness' as a universal, overriding public creed. Moreover, the nationalism of the Young Irelanders derived – partly via Davis – from German Romanticism and the Prussian example, whereas O'Connell's was essentially a product of the eighteenth-century Enlightenment. This meant as has been said above that the Davisites stressed cultural rather than constitutional distinctiveness; group or collective rather than individual rights sympathies and antipathies rather than forms and institutions as the substance of political independence – and, of course, in the long run, on race and language, as in the Fatherland. At each of these points, O'Connell differed from the Young Irelanders fundamentally.

None of these differences, however, reached the surface before or even during 1843, and in the meantime the *Nation* and Young Ireland party strengthened O'Connell's hand and underpinned the Association in several ways. First, they generated enthusiasm and fervour of a different order from O'Connell's now-conventional, popular rapport. Secondly, they spoke for the young, and especially for the urban and educated or semi-educated young, from within a movement led by a man nearing seventy years of age whose primary appeal was to established respectability and the rural masses. Thirdly, they wrote

MAJOR REPEAL MEETINGS HELD IN IRELAND
DURING 1843

O'Connell himself attended (or in the case of Clontarf would have attended) the meetings held in those places printed in italic type. The map has been compiled from the newspaper reports of meetings in the *Freeman's Journal* and *Nation*.

and propagandized in the current idiom; they furnished the popular patriotic, often chauvinistic, literature on which not only the Repeal agitation of the 1840s but also all later nineteenth-century Irish nationalism could feed. They provided a much larger bank of sentiment, stances and rhetoric than O'Connell ever had before at his disposal – as well as a new bank of spirited speakers and activists. In their own way they were as indispensable to the great demonstrations of 1843 as the supporting Catholic bishops and their clergy.

II

The first public meetings of 1843 in Clare, Cork and Queen's County maintained the momentum of late 1842; but it was to his motion of 28 February 1843 before Dublin Corporation in favour of Repeal that O'Connell looked for the true launching of the new year's campaign. The subsequent three days' debate was closely followed and widely publicized, not only in Ireland but also in the British press. O'Connell triumphed. The motion was carried by 41 votes to 15; but much more important was the success of his own speech of more than four hours' duration. He did what he had invariably excelled in through his long professional career; he stated a case which he had had sufficient time and inclination to prepare thoroughly and to plan with forensic care. On this occasion he chose to pitch his oration in a conciliatory rather than a defiant tone, stressing his own respect for law, property and the social order, and the moderation of his objectives. He even made clear that, short of full Repeal, he was open to any reasonable offer. In repudiating violence, he was passionate and unbounded:

> Soon must I leave this fleeting scene. What is the world, and what are the world's glories, to me, that in order to grasp them for an instant I should imperil my immortal soul? Not for all the universe contains would I, in the struggle for what I conceive my country's cause, consent to the effusion of a single drop of human blood, except my own. Any other man's blood I dare not spill.[8]

O'Connell repeated his familiar formulae for agitation. Meetings were to be held for the sole purpose of petitioning parliament to repeal a statute: this was no more than the hallowed right of every British subject. These meetings must be orderly, no matter how large or how provoked. They must be peaceful, not only issuing in no disturbance but also offering no menace beyond that which the continued frustration of millions necessarily implied. They must ask for nothing more than equality, seeking no supremacy or favour, but only parity for all sects and parties.

It is not clear when or with what degree of premeditation the subsequent 'monster' Repeal meetings of 1843 were planned. The term 'monster' was an invention of *The Times* – although gladly adopted by the Association – and some of the earliest meetings after the great debate appear to have come about more by accident than purpose. One or two were, seemingly, casual appendages to public banquets held in O'Connell's honour. Moreover, his own initial scheme was that the other nationalist corporations should imitate Dublin in passing, amid popular acclaim, resolutions in favour of immediate Repeal. On the other hand, it was clear soon after the first post-debate mass meeting (held at Trim, co. Meath, on 16 March) that a larger project was quickly taking shape. On 24 March, O'Connell wrote to his friend and supporter, Charles Bianconi:

> And now, my good friend, is it not a crying shame that your noble county [Tipperary] should remain in such apathy and torpor when all the rest of Ireland is rousing itself into a combined effort for the Repeal? I want a Repeal meeting either at Clonmel or Cashel or Thurles. I want to see from 60,000 to 100,000 Tipperary boys meeting peacefully and returning home quietly, to adopt the petition [in favour of Repeal] and to organise the Repeal rent. Now you know you *must* get into motion, there's no use at all in hanging back any longer when you set about it. I know you will do the thing right well.[9]

Four days later the *Freeman's Journal* announced a series of meetings, at Sligo on 4 May, Cork on 7 May, Mullingar on 14 May, south Tipperary (Cashel was later nominated) on 23 May, and north Tipperary (Nenagh was lated nominated) on 25 May. This programme – with the subsequent addition of a meeting at Charleville, co. Cork, on 18 May and a meeting at Cork on 21 May after the one scheduled for 7 May had been transferred to the Curragh – was in fact faithfully fulfilled. The crowds at these assemblages were estimated at 300,000 or more in most cases. Thus, even if the 1843 campaign began as a renewal of the extra-metropolitan agitation of late 1842, it was turned almost at once into a deliberate and massive demonstration of numerical strength and organizational capacity.

Some forty of the outdoor rallies of 1843 might fairly be classified as 'monster meetings'. Between late March and late September, an average of nearly two a week were held, most of them on Sundays or church holidays, but also many in mid-week. Only two or three took place at 'historic sites'; the great majority were in strategically located country towns. We can safely infer that, from a comparatively early date at least, the places were chosen with a view to 'covering' almost the entire countryside, Ulster excepted. Contemporaries generally agreed that the meetings drew people from up to sixty miles away. But even if we halve this figure and use a radius of only thirty miles, we find that the meetings blanketed the provinces of Leinster, Munster and Connacht, apart from a few coastal extremities and the tips of elongated peninsulas. In addition, parts of cos Monaghan, Down, Armagh, Fermanagh, Tyrone and Donegal fell within the circles.

O'Connell was of course the very heart of the mighty movement. Not only did he dictate all the larger organizational work and manage the regular Dublin sessions and committees, but also he formed the centrepiece of no less than thirty-one of the monster meetings – a considerably higher degree of personal participation than in the equivalent Emancipation agitation of 1826–8. The 1843 campaign was O'Connell's Indian summer, his final blaze. Although he was sixty-eight years old before it was complete, he was tireless and exuberant to the end. The monster meetings he attended entailed over 5000 miles of travel in carriages or open cars, hours as the cynosure of every eye among multitudes of people, and open-air and banquet speeches, two or three times each week. It was a giant's theate, and virtually a year's long play. As the meetings settled into a pattern, their staging became ever more elaborate. For a day – or even two days – before a meeting, crowds began to converge from all directions, on foot, in carts or by horse, often in compact bodies carrying banners or green boughs, sometimes led by bands. Near the site, Repeal wardens, their hats inscribed 'O'Connell's Police', began to marshal them into sections. In the centre stood a huge wooden platform; on the outskirts, on every side, 'cavalry' and carriages eventually formed the perimeter. A German traveller, Jacob Venedey, thus reported O'Connell's arrival at the Athlone meeting of 15 June 1843:

> Now there arose a cry such as never before had greeted my ears; now all hats were raised in the air, and there burst forth the unanimous shouts: 'Hurrah! hurrah! hurrah! Long live O'Connell! Long live the Liberator!' A hundred thousand voices sent forth these salutations to the man whose magic power had circled them around him. He sat on the box-seat of a carriage drawn by four horses, and answered the salutation with head, hand, and cap. It was with the greatest difficulty that a passage could be forced from the carriage to the platform. How he made his way I do not even to this day comprehend, for there was not room for a person to fall, much less to walk. 'Make way for the Liberator!' was the charm word

which accomplished the wonder that otherwise had been an impossibility.[10]

Bulwer Lytton, present at another of the mass meetings, described in memorable verse O'Connell's undiminished power of voice and command of the reactions of a mass audience:

> Walled by wide air and roofed by boundless heaven;
> Beneath his feet the human ocean lay,
> And wave on wave flowed into space away.
> Methought no clarion could have sent its sound
> E'en to the centre of the hosts around.
> And, as I thought, rose a sonorous swell,
> As from some church tower swings the silvery bell;
> Aloft and clear from airy tide to tide,
> It glided easy as a bird may glide.
> To the last verge of that vast audience sent,
> It played with each wild passion as it went:
> Now stirred the uproar, now the murmurs stilled,
> And sobs or laughter answered as it willed.
> Then did I know what spell of infinite choice
> To rouse or lull has the sweet human voice.
> Then did I learn to seize the sudden clue
> To the grand troublous life – antique to view,
> Under the rock-stand of Demosthenes,
> Unstable Athens heave her noisy seas.[11]

In certain respects, the monster meeting was a people's festival, though one marked by sobriety and regimentation rather than licence. Perhaps the most striking, in terms of size and discipline at least, was the great demonstration on the Hill of Tara, co. Meath, on 'Lady Day', 15 August 1843. The lowest published computation of the numbers present was 800,000. Such a figure may seem to us necessarily – and perhaps also wildly – inflated, and it was of course in O'Connell's interest that his support be represented as immense. But even the Association's leading enemy *The Times* reported the crowds at Tara at approximately one million; and given the proximity of Dublin, the 'basin' – at least fifty miles in circumference – from which the attendance was drawn, and the regular organization of contingents, it certainly seems possible that over half a million persons were assembled. The fields for miles around the open sweep of country about the Hill were filled with vehicles; the mounted escort, told off in lines of four by the Repeal 'police', was generally estimated at 10,000 horsemen; it took O'Connell's open carriage two hours to complete the final stages of his journey through the throngs. Masses were said all morning at six altars scattered about the site; two bishops and thirty-five priests were among the hundreds of 'leaders' finally assembled on the 'Liberator's platform'; a vast dining pavilion was also erected on the Hill. Patently, all this constituted a spectacle, mass celebration and physical and emotional experience which would have impressed scores of thousands of people lastingly. What impressed – and alarmed – the opponents of the movement was the absence of disorder and the virtually mechanical obedience of so immense and diverse a body.

The audiences were far from passive receptacles of oratory. They shouted, groaned, laughed, scorned or exulted, according to their cues. The interaction was of course more concentrated and immediate at the public banquets which followed the monster meetings. At Mallow on 11 June, for instance, the dinner speeches were preceded by a singer rendering one of Moore's 'melodies'. When he reached the end of the verse,

> Oh, where's the slave so lowly,
> Condemned to chains unholy,
> Who, could he burst
> His bonds accursed,
> Would pine beneath them slowly?

O'Connell leaped to his feet and, raising his arms wide, exclaimed, 'I am not that slave!', and in a scene of passion all the room copied his very action, shouting over and over again, 'We are not those slaves! We are not those slaves!'[12] O'Connell the revivalist, the precipitator of something not unlike the conversion experience, was never more evident than in 1843.

The affairs were staged with care. At Tara, O'Connell's carriage was preceded by a car on which a harper sat enthroned playing Moore's 'Harp that once through Tara's Halls' – with its resonance of ancient coronations of the Irish high-kings upon the Hill. At the meeting at Mullaghmast (the scene, in popular belief at least, of the most notorious act of sixteenth-century English treachery), O'Connell wearing his alderman's red robes was 'crowned' by the sculptor, John Hogan. The 'crown', a green velvet cap edged with gold, was supposed to conform to the original Gaelic symbol of kingship. The sculptor, who had just completed his celebrated marble statue of O'Connell for Dublin's City Hall, was 'supported' by a painter and a graphic designer who had also worked on supplying 'art' for the agitation.

Hogan was a fine if conventional artist, but most of the visual expression, artefacts and decoration of O'Connell's movement would have been condemned three generations or so later as nationalist kitsch. The dominant motifs of everything from membership cards to Conciliation Hall (the Association's grand new assembly place in Dublin completed in October 1843) were wolfhounds, round towers and shamrocks, rendered with congruent sentimentality and convolution. Yet this was, after all, merely a variation of the Early Victorian mode, a fragment of a Europe-wide phenomenon. It also conformed to the general contemporary impulse to simplify and didacticize. Here it matched the design and conduct of the monster meetings. Their rhetoric, signals and responses were as bright, crude and singular as the paints in a child's first box. But if the art and interplay of the Repeal movement were naive, they were also direct, natural and, fundamentally, sincere. The unselfconscious gusto, crowd-warmth and delightful exitements and excesses of the monster meetings and the 'monster' banquets were of a piece with their accompanying pageantry and pictures. Richard Pares once wrote that men are 'in politics not only for party and for profit, but most of all for the due exercise of the talents God gave them, and for fun'.[13] With this in mind, let us remember that even the participating-listeners had some claim to being 'men in politics' in 1843.

If O'Connell was the distant, worshipful father-figure of millions, he was also the close, astute instructor for thousands, perhaps even tens of thousands of party helpers. The number undergoing education in political management, at various levels and with various specializations, was clearly very large. The Association's headquarters staff grew fivefold during 1843, to fifty clerks; but the proportional increase in active workers all through the country would have been greater still. Each of the later monster meetings required long and elaborate preparations, from the lowliest needs of crowd control to the planning of themes and the orchestration of popular indoctrination. Especially west of the Shannon, comparatively new ground for O'Connell, many fresh recruits to agitation had to be raised. The great upsurge in the Repeal Rent and in the public's resort to the Repeal arbitration system also drew in numerous political assistants. Everyone involved either had been, or was being, grounded in O'Connell's practised political methodology, for his writ ran and his hand stretched down to the humblest office-holder or occasional draftee. Many of his pupils were future emigrants. Seeds of the politics of the entire English-speaking world in the third quarter of the nineteenth century were being broadcast throughout Ireland in the course of the great campaign.

III

Dublin Castle showed no alarm at the continued growth of the Repeal movement during January and February 1843 or at the course or outcome of the Dublin Corporation debate. Even the development of the monster meeting in late March and the specific announcement on 6 April 1843 of a 'great tour' of Ireland to demonstrate the extent and peaceful character of the demand for Repeal were ignored. But with swelling audiences and ardour at the succession of meetings held in April, the Irish administration suddenly took fright. On 4 May the lord lieutenant, backed by the Irish law officers, asked Peel for emergency legislation to render the meetings illegal: he excused his earlier silence upon the dangers of O'Connell's latest move by claiming that until a few weeks before the agitation had been 'utterly undeserving of notice'.[14] Even at this point, De Grey was more concerned at O'Connell's growing middle-class and clerical support than at his extraordinary power to rouse the masses.

Peel would not be panicked by De Grey. O'Connell had chosen the right to petition parliament as his ground, and this was dangerous for any British minister to assail. He had also defended another flank by ensuring that his movement was strictly orderly: even Graham, the home secretary, had to admit as much in the House of Commons on 26 May. Moreover, any legislation directed against the Repeal Association would raise the question, 'Why is not the Anti-Corn Law League similarly suppressed?', for the League was essentially the same in organization, conduct and method as O'Connell's movement. Peel would certainly avoid, if he could, any direct junction of interest, let alone of action, between the two agitations. Instead, he attempted to compromise by a solemn statement on behalf of the government in the House of Commons on 9 May 1843 that the Union would be maintained at all costs and hazards: even civil war was preferable to the dismemberment of the empire. O'Connell saw at once that Peel had failed to find any illegality in the current Repeal campaign, and he proceeded, as Professor Nowlan puts it, to 'answer defiance with defiance'.[15] Before an Association meeting in Dublin on 18 May, he proclaimed, 'I will observe the spirit of the law – the letter of the law. I will, to be sure, shear it to its closest limits, but I will obey; and I set their blustering at defiance'.[16] Publicly at least, O'Connell made little

of Peel's extraordinary undertaking, in the name of the queen as well
as of the British people, to hold to the Act of Union to the death. Peel,
he declared, was the very man ultimately to concede Repeal. Patently
he meant his listeners to infer that because Peel had already 'betrayed'
the tory cause by supporting Catholic Emancipation in 1829 and by
acquiescing in parliamentary reform in 1833, he was likely to yield a
third time if sufficient pressure were applied. O'Connell proceeded to
increase the pressure through his monster meetings, to such effect that
– to take one obvious yardstick – the Repeal Rent which had risen to a
weekly average of £360 in March, and again to £600 per week in April,
leaped to £2000 per week in May.

O'Connell was aided by a false step taken by Peel to appease Dublin
Castle. In mid-May the government consented to the Irish executive's
long-pressed proposal to remove leading Repealers from the
magistracy. On 23 May Sugden, the Irish chancellor, withdrew the
commission of the peace from thirty-four members of the Association,
including Lord Ffrench, O'Connell himself and his son John, although
no warning had been issued, or justification of the 'punishment'
attempted. One predictable effect was to add impetus to the agitation.
In mild and painless fashion the movement had acquired nearly three
dozen martyrs headed by O'Connell himself. A less predictable but
more important consequence of Peel's *faux pas* – or, perhaps we
should say, sacrificed pawn – was the resignation, in protest, from the
magistracy, of a number of Irish whigs, led by Lord Cloncurry, Henry
Grattan and Smith O'Brien. It was not a costly gesture on their part,
and it helped to bridge the gap which had been rapidly opening up
between orthodox Irish liberals and Repealers.

None the less O'Connell was concerned that the government should
have conceded at all to Dublin Castle's cry for repression. He had
further cause for uneasiness at the beginning of June 1843. When
Edward Lucas, the Irish under-secretary, threatened to resign because
of Peel's and Graham's pusillanimity in dealing with O'Connell, he
was persuaded to remain in office by the government at the cost of a
further concession. Such yieldings seemed to give substance to the
recurrent rumours that legislation to suppress the monster meetings
was about to be introduced. All this helps to explain O'Connell's
'martial' speeches at Kilkenny and Mallow on 8 and 11 June: they
were oblique warnings of the sea of troubles on which the government
would launch itself should it attempt to abrogate the right to petition
for Repeal. Even at Mallow, when O'Connell was, to some extent,
carried away by the excitement of the moment, his careful briefing of

reporters before his evening speech makes it clear that he intended to raise the stakes in the game of menaces in which he was engaged with Peel and Graham. He soon came to fear, however, that he might have stepped beyond the limit of safety from prosecution or proclamation in speaking of laying down his life: his 'Defiance' at Mallow was to be the high-water mark of his disaffection. Eleven days later, at the monster meeting of Skibbereen, he signalled a change of course. 'I am not determined to die for Ireland', he now announced, 'I would rather live for her (cheering), for one living Repealer is worth a churchyard full of dead ones.'[17] This prudent retreat was matched – or perhaps we should say answered – by Graham's public withdrawal of his earlier refusal to consider any 'measures of further conciliation' in Ireland,[18] and by the government's assurance, at last, that the right to petition would not be suspended. The initiative was still O'Connell's.

Throughout June and July 1843 the monster meetings continued to grow in size. Attendances of half-a-million persons were regularly reported, and however we scale this down, indubitably the numbers were immense. Moreover, O'Connell was now opening up new territory systematically. By 31 July, meetings had been held in the majority of the counties of the three southern provinces, and considerable portions of the other counties were sufficiently close to the meeting places to supply further legions of attenders. The momentum of his movement was also gathering in more and more of the Catholic clergy. As early as 15 May, at the dinner after the Mullingar monster meeting, Bishop O'Higgins of Ardagh proclaimed

> that virtually you all have reason to believe that the bishops of Ireland were Repealers; but I have now again formally to announce to you that they have all declared themselves as such, and that from shore to shore we are now all Repealers (great cheering) . . . If they attempt, my friends, to rob us of the daylight, which is, I believe, common to us all, and prevent us from assembling in the open fields, we will retire to our chapels, and we will suspend all other instruction, in order to devote all our time to teaching the people to be Repealers in spite of them (cheers).[19]

This, as we have seen, exaggerated the degree of episcopal support for Repeal. Six of the bishops of the ecclesiastical provinces of Cashel, Tuam and Dublin still held back from joining the Association. But these constituted a small minority, and even they refrained from any overt opposition to O'Connell. Generally speaking, he could rely upon the Irish Catholic Church, and it was the clergy's deep commitment to his agitation which most alarmed the British government in the midsummer. 'It is a religious struggle', wrote Graham on 16 July, 'directed by the R. Catholic Hierarchy and Priesthood, on which we are about to enter; and I very much doubt whether any political considerations enter much into the causes or objects of this strife, which will lead to blood-shed and convulse the Empire.'[20]

No less significant than the mass enrolments and clerical enlistments was the impact of the campaign upon the Catholic, and even (albeit to a much lesser extent) the Protestant, upper and upper-middle class. In particular, the success of the monster meetings was forcing Irish whigs and liberals into a fresh series of positions. A minority actually declared themselves for Repeal. Doubtless, most of such converts were rich Christians, men who, in Palmerston's phrase, 'have of Course been compelled by Fear of Constituents to become Repealers pro Forma'.[21] But even these were scalps to be displayed on O'Connell's belt. Short of joining the Association, others, especially MPs from Irish 'popular' constituencies, were forced along the path of concession, or attempted concession, in the hope of countering O'Connell's influence. On 18 July a group of Irish whig members proposed that meetings be mounted in England to advertise the urgency of redressing Irish grievances. Although this was rejected by the English whigs, a larger body of Irish MPs later signed a collective protest against the government's failure to introduce reforms in Ireland. The list of areas marked out for reform is interesting: the church establishment, landlord-tenant relations, the parliamentary franchise, local government and the practical exclusion of Catholics from public office. O'Connell's list would have been identical: the MPs were asking, in effect, for what he had long termed 'Justice for Ireland'.

This raises the question of O'Connell's true purposes and anticipations in launching his campaign of 1843. He certainly could not have expected to achieve 'Repeal' in any substantial form within the year. No one knew better than a veteran of the long struggles to win Catholic Emancipation and parliamentary reform how slowly the entrenched interests yielded ground, even where (unlike the present case) powerful British parties supported the advance. On the other hand, he was already an old man; he could not afford to spend even half a decade in pursuit of an objective. Moreover, Britain's economic crisis of 1842, the resultant unrest and the rapid expansion of the Anti-Corn Law agitation all rendered the time propitious for the application of massive Irish pressure. Given these various considerations, O'Connell may possibly have hoped (and no more optimistic politician ever breathed) that the British government would offer some modified and circumscribed form of local assembly for Ireland before 1843 was out. In fact, as we have seen, he virtually angled for such an offer in his 'inaugural' speech to Dublin Corporation in February.

But even O'Connell must have acknowledged to himself that the odds against any quick accommodation were very long. Repeal had no extra-Irish support in the House of Commons. It was almost universally opposed in Britain at large. To most Irish, and to virtually all Ulster, Protestants, it was anathema: Wellington, in fact, was shortly to propose the arming of northern Unionists in order that they might crush Repeal by force. In such circumstances, it was far more likely that an attempt be made to undercut O'Connell's agitation by concessions on other fronts than that the Act of Union itself should be disturbed. O'Connell, for forty years a politician, must have understood this thoroughly. It is well to recall that his Association began its life in 1840 as a body dedicated to 'Full Justice or Repeal'. Such a formula permitted O'Connell to pursue simultaneously the goals of liberal reform and constitutional disruption. It could safely be assumed that no Irish reform programme adopted by a British party would exceed mere *partial* 'Justice': Repeal need never be abandoned except for some grand, final, negotiated settlement of the Anglo-Irish relationship. At the same time, Repeal could be held *in terrorem* over the heads of British politicians, and the more it was overwhelmingly and menacingly endorsed by the mass of the Irish population, the more the politicians would be driven to argue that the true source of Irish disaffection was not nationalism or separatism but economic, social or ecclesiastical ills, and to attempt accordingly to kill Repeal with kindness. Placed in this context, O'Connell's 1843 campaign seems rather to conform to than deviate from his customary tactics. If so, it was already bearing fruit when Irish whigs began to call for changes in land and church relations, the local representative system and the distribution of political spoils, and when even Peel's government began to consider what concessions might be made in these very fields. It is true that O'Connell had named 1843 'Repeal Year' and promised a climax to the monster meetings which would, in effect, challenge Dublin Castle's right to rule in Ireland. But he had never found it difficult to cover over a retreat while keeping his force intact, and he had no reason to suppose that, if need be, he could not safely re-order his priorities and re-arrange his timetables as the current season drew to its close.

IV

In fact, by September 1843 there were signs that O'Connell was extricating himself from his earlier commitments. On the 9th he manufactured an occasion for despatching a letter to Campbell, one of the whig law lords, in which he sought to bestir the opposition to take up an extensive programme of Irish reform as a 'counter' to Repeal.

> Allow me to say . . . that the Whig leaders do not behave well towards their supporters. Our Irish movement has at least this merit that it has roused the English nation from slumber. There can be no more dreams about Ireland. Our grievances are beginning to be admitted by all parties and by the press of all political opinions to be afflicting and not easily endured. I ask – of course without expecting an answer – why the Whig leaders are not up to the level of the times they live in? Why do they not propose a definite plan for redressing these grievances? Peel, while in opposition, used to enliven the recess by his state epistles, declaratory of his opinions and determination. Why does not Lord John [Russell] treat us to a magniloquent epistle declaratory of his determination to abate the Church nuisance in Ireland, to augment our popular franchise, to vivify our new Corporations, to mitigate the statute law as between landlord and tenant, to strike off a few more rotten boroughs in England, and to give the representatives to our great counties? In short, why does he not prove himself a high-minded, high-gifted statesman, capable of leading his friends into all the advantages to be derived from conciliating the Irish nation and strengthening the British empire?[22]

Simultaneously, O'Connell sought to inveigle Archbishop Murray (who had so far evaded joining the Association) into blessing his exertions for Repeal. He sought sanction for a novena of supplication, although – with matadorial skill – Murray successfully side-stepped the charge. 'I hasten to assure you', he told O'Connell, 'that the novena of prayers which you contemplate does not by any means require my sanction. The throne of Grace is all times open to those who seek to approach it through the merits of Christ for such purposes as you propose, namely, the promotion of the *honour and glory of God and the good of religion.*'[23]

Moreover, O'Connell had as yet prepared no plans for the summoning of the Council of Three Hundred, although a month before, at the Baltinglass monster meeting, he had promised that it would meet before Christmas. Possibly he knew or guessed that, currently, Graham was considering the use of armed force, if necessary, to prevent the Council from assembling. At any rate, on 17

September O'Connell told the 'Connemara' monster meeting, held at Clifden, co. Galway, that he might have to delay the sitting of the Council, and was quite prepared to brave the sneers with which his enemies would greet this news. A fortnight later at Mullaghmast he appeared to shift his emphasis decisively from Repeal to practical reforms, although, as usual, he swathed his message in gauzy generalities.

> I will see every man of you having a vote, and every man protected by the ballot from the agent or landlord. I will see labour protected and every title to possession recognised, when you are industrious and honest (loud cheers). I will see prosperity again throughout your land – the busy hum of the shuttle and the tinkling of the smithy shall be heard again. We shall see the nailer employed until even the middle of the night, and the carpenter covering himself with his chips (laughter). I will see prosperity in all its gradations spreading through a happy, contented, religious land. I will hear the hymn of a happy people go forth at sunrise to God in praise of his mercies – and I will see the evening sun set down amongst the uplifted hands of a religious and free population . . . Stand by me – join with me – I will say be obeyed by me, and Ireland shall be free.[24]

It was by now evident that the climax of the 1843 campaign would not be the constitution of an independent extra-legal legislature but merely the final monster meeting per se! This ultimate assemblage, scheduled to gather at Clontarf on the outskirts of Dublin on 8 October, was planned on a heroic scale. Not only the metropolis but also the surrounding counties and even the Irish communities on Merseyside and Clydeside were to be drawn upon to compose an immense audience and array. The size and fervour, and the stupendous pageantry, of the open-air demonstration at the close of a strenuous season would at least testify to O'Connell's continued power.

Meanwhile, throughout September 1843, the government's resolve was hardening. Fears that it would all end in violence grew rather than diminished. Additional troops were sent from Britain to strengthen the Irish garrisons; ammunition and provisions were accumulated in the Irish depots; and the number of warships at Irish stations and about the Irish coast was considerably increased. Graham took the decision to suppress the Council of Three Hundred by force should O'Connell summon it into existence, and became more and more impatient with what he regarded as the timorousness of the Irish law officers (and especially of the attorney-general, T. B. C. Smith) in not instituting proceedings against the Repeal press. Even Peel, who was less alarmist than Graham, and much less so than Wellington – he knew O'Connell better than either of them, after all – believed that there might well be outbreaks in Ireland before the year was out. But policy as well as fear seemed to demand a denouement with O'Connell. By the autumn of 1843, as Nowlan writes, 'the ministry was in agreement on the necessity of adopting new and more effective measures to tranquillize Ireland and to weaken the Irish opposition to the Government by winning some Catholic support. The repeal agitation and O'Connell's power stood in the way.'[25]

Unfortunately for himself, O'Connell's defence seemed to have slipped for a fatal moment when, on 24 August, he had injudiciously criticized the Queen's speech in opening parliament. At last the Irish law officers opined that his words laid him open to a charge of sedition. It is uncertain, however, whether this would in itself have led to any action in the end. The scale was tipped by the rash rhetoric of the Association's notice of the Clontarf monster meeting, which spoke of the assembly of 'Repeal cavalry' and lapsed unguardedly into other 'military' language. Forty years of legal fencing with the Irish Administration had rendered O'Connell acutely sensitive to danger, and as soon as he discovered the wording of the notice, on 2 October 1843, he repudiated it, publicly. But the damage had been done; the Irish executive had been steeled by the Association's indiscretion into a decision to proclaim the Clontarf meeting.

Dublin Castle's lingering faintheartedness led it to put off issuing the proclamation until 3.30 p.m. on 7 October, the day before the monster meeting was to take place. Peel later condemned this gross and dangerous tardiness, 'It is very fortunate that there was no collision at Clontarf. The shortness of the notice would have imposed a heavy Responsibility.'[26] In fact, the government was saved by the very efficiency, elaborate machinery and iron discipline of O'Connell's Association. The executive committee was in session on the afternoon of 7 October when a messenger arrived hotfoot from the Castle with a copy of the proclamation. Instantly, O'Connell decided on submission to the lord lieutenant's prohibition; not a person in the room demurred. There and then, he sat down to dictate to Ray an address to 'the Irish people', enjoining them to abide by the proclamation unswervingly. Within minutes, this was dispatched to the printers. Meanwhile the workmen were ordered to dismantle the great platform which had been erected already at Clontarf. Well-known members of the Association set out on each of the main roads leading to the capital to turn back the bands of people already converging on Dublin. By the morning of 8 October no one was moving towards the city any longer; and not only throughout Dublin but also in the towns and villages all about, O'Connell's announcement of the abandonment of the meeting, and appeal for calm and acquiescence, was posted up in the various public places. The 'Head Pacificator' himself, Thomas Steele, was pacing the ground at Clontarf, driving away the few who had assembled there, and leaving the field to detachments of the 60th Rifles and the 5th Dragoons, who possessed it in – literally – empty triumph. There was little heart in O'Connell's counter-move at the immense meeting of the Association held next day. Though he condemned the proclamation as 'the grossest violation of the law', he also condemned resistance to it until its illegality had been established.[27] Emboldened by the unexpected totality of its success, the Irish executive, two days later, arrested O'Connell, his son John, and seven other prominent Repealers (including two priests) upon the curious charge of conspiring to 'unlawful and seditious opposition and resistance to . . . [the] government and constitution'.[28]

Conventionally, O'Connell's spiritless submission to the proclamation of 7 October 1843 has been judged a crushing defeat. Even so indulgently sympathetic a biographer as Michael MacDonagh concluded sadly, 'O'Connell's game of bluff and make-believe had failed. He had mistaken the stuff of which Peel was made.'[29] This is much too crude an evaluation. First, the very suppression of O'Connell's last meeting, and his subsequent arrest, were in themselves an oblique testimony to his success. It was his earlier pressure which had forced Peel and his cabinet, at last, onto the path of concession in Ireland; and, once committed to that path, they saw the breaking of O'Connell's power as the necessary preliminary to a course of Irish reform. The fact that it was a tory and not a whig administration which intended to yield ground should not blind us (as it often blinded O'Connell) to the essential fact that it was a *British* government which would yield, in the face of an Irish agitation. O'Connell himself had repeatedly, if partly rhetorically, begged to be put out of business – the business of Repeal – by being outbid by 'Justice for Ireland'. Up to a point, this was precisely Peel's intention – to undercut O'Connell's movement by concessions. Secondly, the direct assault upon O'Connell and the Repeal Association was, in one sense, a confession of defeat by Peel and Graham. Throughout 1843, they had tried to hold the line that the agitation was no more than froth. Now they were committed to an about-face whereby they would have to argue that it threatened the constitutional stability of the United Kingdom. This meant moreover that O'Connell had gained the moral advantage. In effect, Peel's government had been driven to abandon 'the rule of law', for few who considered the matter dispassionately could truly believe that the Repeal Association was, in any sense, a proto-military organization, or that, in pressing for the repeal of a comparatively recent statute, O'Connell was preaching national subversion. Despite the show of legal issues, the fact remained that the government had been driven to resort to brute force, to act as if Ireland were a crown colony instead of an integral part of a united polity.

O'Connell's third gain was being rescued from impending political bathos. What remained after Clontarf but to retire, so to speak, to winter quarters? A popular agitation was, however, a far cry from an eighteenth-century army. It could not be easily re-assembled, let alone re-kindled, especially when the promise of victory within a single season had been the mainspring of the last campaign. Dublin Castle's intrusion rejuvenated the agitation. It provided the missing climax to the year's excitement, kept O'Connell in central focus and rendered him a likely martyr. In fact, the Association made striking immediate gains – in terms of public attention, Rent returns and even influential adherents. As a gesture of sympathy with O'Connell, several leading Irish liberals, such as William Smith O'Brien and Caleb Powell, soon threw their lot in with Repeal.

But it would be absurd to present the suppression of the Clontarf meeting and his own prosecution as, essentially, a victory for O'Connell. For one thing, they clearly exposed his limits as an agitator to the enemy's gaze. It was now certain that he would not resist direct repression, except in the arena of the law courts. Worse still, he had demonstrated only too well that his control of his followers was absolute, and that they would follow him blindly into non-resistance. In lightening ship, O'Connell had thrown a great deal of his minatory power overboard.

A second ill-consequence was the opening up of deep ideological divisions within the Association, though these took some time to reveal themselves fully. Initially, the young men of the *Nation* group acquiesced unreservedly in O'Connell's decision to call off the Clontarf demonstration. They rallied to him at once in his own troubles; in fact, Gavan Duffy himself was a 'traverser', to use the term generally employed for those charged and arrested on 11 October. But when O'Connell instinctively attempted to weave his way out of his new difficulties by presenting Repeal as a much more modest proposal than it had hitherto appeared, the *Nation* recoiled. On 13 November

1843, he announced that he was ready to settle for an 'Irish parliament [which] should have control within Ireland ... for all other administrative functions the British parliament would have the control'.[30] This was – doubtless deliberately – vague. It might have meant, more or less, the form of government foreshadowed in Gladstone's first home rule bill. But it might also have meant something still more circumscribed, a sort of magnified county council. Uneasily and implausibly, the *Nation* interpreted the new formula as 'all the power she [Ireland] possessed in 1783'.[31] Within a month, on 27 November, O'Connell withdrew his feeler altogether. By then it had greatly disquieted the advanced Repealers without attracting any of the Irish federalists whom he had hoped to tempt onto this new ground. Thus, open disagreement in the movement was avoided, for the time being. But the profound difference between O'Connell's mode of thought and style of politics and those of the *Nation* group had been already glimpsed. It was bound sooner or later to re-appear. O'Connell's authority had also been diminished. Just as he was no longer quite the frightening figure that he had seemed to the British public in the high summer of 1843, he was no longer quite the old titan of the agitation in the eyes of the increasingly confident and critical young men who had enrolled recently under his banner.

More important than all else perhaps was the stage in O'Connell's life at which he had received the decisive check. He was now in his sixty-ninth year. To have mounted and sustained a mass movement such as that of 1843 had been a marvel. Gladstone was little older when he conducted the celebrated Midlothian campaigns of 1879–80, which were far shorter in duration and made far fewer calls upon tongue, mind or body. Was it to be expected that O'Connell could ever again marshal the powers and endurance required for a national mobilization of such intensity, or over such a protracted stretch of time? His relief at the suspension of exertions, and welcome for at least an interval of passivity, were evident in his letter of 9 December 1843 to Fitzpatrick. He had at last escaped to Derrynane. 'We had a delightful journey down', he wrote,

> I have already been out hunting two days and am glad to tell you that, although the distemper killed some noble dogs of mine, yet I have a very fair pack remaining. I already feel the immense benefit of my native air and my delightful exercise. I am regaining strength and vigour to endure whatever my sentence may be ...
>
> All is peace and quiet in this county; although the people are as ardent

Repealers as any in the entire Kingdom it is understood to the most remote of the glens that there must be peace in order to succeed.[32]

The pieces tossed about by the upheaval of October 1843 may have fallen on either side of the advantage line for O'Connell. But had the player himself any longer the physical strength or hunger for mastery which the game demanded?

CHAPTER 10

The Fall Out

1844–5

I

O'Connell filled the Irish stage in 1844, but the play was now tragicomedy rather than heroic drama. Initially, he had feared that he might be indicted for high treason, and, oppressed by his memories of 1798, believed that he might very well be hanged. The actual charge, seditious conspiracy, came almost as a relief. Striking the anti-climactic note that was to be heard so often during the year, he told his son John, 'I do not think two years' imprisonment would kill me. I should keep constantly walking about, and take a bath every day.'[1]

The trial opened, so to speak, by being postponed. It did not formally commence until 14 January 1844, more than three months after O'Connell's arrest. It could not be denied that the special list from which the jurors would be chosen was badly out of date; and since Protestants outnumbered Catholics by about fifteen to one on the current list, and since it was assumed on all sides that the jurors would give their verdicts on strictly sectarian grounds, the first defence plea was, of course, for a revision. This could not be reasonably resisted. The new list increased the Catholic proportion, perhaps to as much as one in four. But while it was being drawn up, two pages of the names added to the list by the Recorder were mysteriously lost or abstracted; and the majority of those omitted were Catholics. Thus, even before the court sat, there were widespread allegations of foul play and claims that the wells had been poisoned in advance. The crown challenged all the eleven Catholic jurors who were eventually drawn by lot so that the jury consisted of twelve Protestants in the end.

In today's terms, it is difficult to see that O'Connell was being charged with more than conducting a massive political campaign: the 'crime' consisted of its success in mobilization and its objectives. As Thackeray, playing the plain blunt Englishman, later summarized the indictment and result, 'If you did not organise a conspiracy, and meditate a separation of this fair empire – if you did not create rage and hatred in the bosoms of your countrymen against us English – if *you* did not do, in a word, all that the Jury found you guilty of doing – I am a Dutchman.'[2] In British eyes, the real offence was, apparently, the very demand for Repeal (on the assumption that it would lead finally to imperial dissolution), and the very agitation which *faut de mieux* O'Connell was forced to mount in order to gain Britain's attention.

O'Connell defended himself (literally, for he acted as his own counsel) against different charges – those actually set out in the indictment. He strove to establish the altogether peaceable and constitutional character of his movement. Even the police evidence confirmed that no one had suffered the slightest physical injury; that no female had been 'exposed to the slightest indelicacy'; that not 'one shilling's worth of property' had been 'destroyed at any one of those meetings'.[3] O'Connell had, he claimed, merely repeated his proceedings in the Catholic Emancipation campaign – indeed, adhered to the principles that had governed his politics for more than forty years.

> From the day when first I entered the arena of politics until the present hour, I have never neglected an opportunity of impressing upon the minds of my fellow-countrymen the fact, that I was an apostle of that political sect who held that liberty was only to be attained under such agencies as were strictly consistent with the law and the constitution – that freedom was to be attained, not by the effusion of human blood, but by the constitutional combination of good and wise men; by perseverance in the courses of tranquillity and good order, and by an utter abhorrence of violence and bloodshed. It is my proudest boast, that throughout a long and eventful life, I have faithfully devoted myself to the promulgation of that principle, and, without vanity, I can assert, that I am the first public man who ever proclaimed it. Other politicians have said – 'Win your liberties by peaceable means if you can,' but there was *arrière pensée* in this admonition, and they always had in contemplation an appeal to physical force, in case other means should prove abortive. I am not one of these. I have preached under every contingency, and I have again and again declared my intention to abandon the cause of repeal if a single drop of human blood were shed by those who advocated the measure.[4]

In delivering his judgement later on, Mr Justice Burton made the extraordinary admission that O'Connell 'had that design [achieving the repeal of the Union without bloodshed] rooted in his mind, and that it was by the great influence which he possessed as a leader . . . that he kept the country, or part of the country where he resided, from the dreadful operation of civil war and the shedding of human blood'.[5] It seemed that the court itself believed, as O'Connell put it, that his only conspiracy was one to prevent a revolution!

None the less, on 10 February 1844, after a hearing of more than three weeks, O'Connell and his fellow-defendants were found guilty on several counts. The trial had an air of macabre carnival from the beginning. On the opening day, the 'traversers' were solemnly escorted to the Four Courts by the lord mayor and corporation of Dublin, in full regalia. O'Connell himself immediately donned, and continued to wear, his wig and gown. With each defendant separately represented, the prosecuting barristers correspondingly numerous, three judges on the bench and the court overflowing with the fashionable curious, it was the spectacle and sensation of the season. Even after the verdict was delivered, the affair continued in the same extraordinary strain. Sentence having been postponed, O'Connell crossed immediately to England where he was to receive continual sympathetic ovations. When he entered the House of Commons on 15 February – having passed through throngs of enthusiastic supporters in the Palace Yard – it was as if on cue: D. R. Ross, the liberal member for Belfast, was speaking in his defence. After the cheers from the opposition benches died away, Ross continued, 'Let the House judge by the reception which the head conspirator has just met, whether there be much cause for triumph. You may put that man in gaol – but what will you gain?'[6]

Next day O'Connell reported delightedly to Fitzpatrick that he had been 'admirably received in the House and outside the House, and my name was cheered to the echo at the [weekly anti-]Corn Law League meeting',[7] and, on 20 February, that he 'certainly did not expect anything half so generous or so kind'[8] as his popular reception in London. On 12 March about a thousand people, including several peers, a contingent of British MPs and his erstwhile antagonist, the doyen of 'old' English Catholicism, the Earl of Shrewsbury, attended a public banquet in O'Connell's honour at the Covent Garden Theatre: his treatment was denounced and his health drunk with equal fervour. One of the banquet organizers, W. Simpson, wrote to him later, 'when once aroused by a sense of injustice their [Englishmen's] determination and enthusiasm is unbounded, and I will venture to say that hearty cheer which reverberated through Convent [sic] Garden Theatre on Tuesday last has never had a parallel in any other country'.[9] No less was O'Connell fêted in Birmingham, Wolverhampton and Liverpool when, on invitation, he visited those towns. He was, however, chary of encouraging similar demonstrations in Ireland lest they be treated as an 'aggravation' of his offence when it came to sentencing. Instead, he tried to set in train in Dublin the 'appointment [of a] day of "humiliation and prayer". If universally adopted it would have a magnificent effect upon the enemy, besides being in its own nature most desirable.'[10]

II

When on 30 May 1844 O'Connell at last received his sentence – one year's imprisonment, considerably less than he had feared – he and his co-prisoners processed, in carriages, accompanied by thousands of well-wishers, to their place of incarceration, Richmond Penitentiary, almost in festival fashion. He was received with deference by the governor of Richmond, whose handsome residence was made over for his use and that of his son John. Again he was 'welcomed' as he crossed the threshold, this time by his daughters, Ellen and Betsey, and John's wife, who were alternately to act as his companions-cum-hostesses in the new ménage. It was martyrdom-de-luxe, not merely for O'Connell but also for the other prisoners who shared his comforts, in an appropriately lesser measure. Each had a suite of rooms, a servant or servants, and a resident wife if he were married. It was ultra-gregarious rather than solitary confinement. A few days after O'Connell's imprisonment began, the *Freeman's Journal* reported

> that the crowd of gentlemen pressing for admittance at the prison gate was greater than any we have ever seen blocking the doors of any place of public interest on occasions of the highest-wrought expectation. We saw gentlemen of the highest respectability content to take their places on the exterior of the crowd, and wait while numerous batches were admitted, until gradually they themselves approached the gate, and obtained the coveted entrance.[11]

Shortly afterwards, perhaps at O'Connell's instigation, specific visiting days and hours had to be set down. But Charles Gavan Duffy, who was a fellow inmate, later recalled that 'immediate political associates' still dined daily with the traversers. 'O'Connell', continued Duffy,

> was a genial and attentive host, full of anecdote and *badinage* while the ladies remained, and ready, when they withdrew, for serious political conference or the pleasant carte and tierce of friendly controversy. An artist's studio and a daguerrotypists camera were set up within the precincts to multiply likeness of the prisoners . . .[12]

O'Connell at Richmond was a sort of Lear inside-out. He was very careful to remain in health: like the ocean-liner passenger (and his imprisonment bore more than one resemblance to a protracted voyage in the first-class), he measured his daily perambulation around the interior perimeter so that it amounted to a three-mile walk. So far from being in ceaseless conflict with rejected or immoral daughters, he was cosseted by his. He was said to have sat often with his hands clasped in theirs. In fact, he seems to have developed a penchant for young female company and adulation. Clearly, he was on close terms with Margaret O'Mara, the half-sister of his eldest daughter's husband, even before he entered Richmond. On 23 May 1844 he had her escort him to a local convent, having written beforehand, 'My dear Margaret . . . I will go down without my breakfast so that unless you give me a cup of tea before ten I must starve till I return at one to the Association. If *your ladies* choose to come up with me I will have places kept for them.'[13] Less than a week later, he visited Margaret again, telling her later, 'I do not know when I spent so delightful a day.'[14]

The probable reason for his delight was that Rose McDowell was among Margaret's '*ladies*' at that time. Rose, on a lengthy visit to her close friend Margaret, was the daughter of the liberal Presbyterian, Robert McDowell, of Belfast, who had chaired the Repeal banquet held in the city in O'Connell's honour in January 1841. She was twenty-two or twenty-three years of age in 1844; later she was spoken of – with what justification it is impossible to say – in such conventionally-laudatory terms as 'charming', 'lively' and 'culti-vated'.[15] Certainly, she moved in the 'upper' Repeal circles while in Dublin. Possibly she was one of O'Connell's young devotees. At any rate, he fell victim to her attractions. Most accounts of the sequel derive from the reminiscences of Duffy, who was close at hand in Richmond:

> During the whole period of the imprisonment O'Connell was an unsuc-cessful wooer. He was labouring under the most distracting influence that can possess a man of his years – a passionate love for a gifted young girl, who might have been his grand-daughter. His family were naturally alarmed by this incident, and the more so doubtless that the lady whom he proposed to place at the head of their house differed from them in race and religion, and their feverish anxiety could not fail to react upon him. Their fears were allayed in the end by the lady's persistent refusal to become his wife, but this result was not calculated to restore the composure of O'Connell. In truth, it left him discontented and perturbed in a high degree.[16]

Duffy went on to assert that O'Connell was simultaneously suffering from the onset of 'softening of the brain'; and the conjunction has been widely read as implying that O'Connell's 'infatuation' sprang from 'senility'. It would have ill-become Duffy if this were what he meant to say or insinuate: he himself was sixty-five years old (only three years younger than O'Connell in Richmond) when he married and set about breeding a family for the third time. In fact, O'Connell's pursuit of Rose McDowell needs no pathological explanation. The last spurt of passion, the desperate urge to rise up against encroaching age, the cumulative loneliness of outliving others, are common enough, if wretched, experiences of the old; nor was O'Connell the first or last old man to succumb to a woman but a third his age. If, in fact, he did propose marriage, it was probably soon after he entered Richmond, for on 21 June 1844 he wrote to Margaret O'Mara,

> If Wednesday [26 June] about two o'clock suited yours and your dear mother's convenience I should take care to have you at once admitted. I need not tell you that I should be most gratified if Rose would condescend to accompany you *here*. She is indeed all you describe her and more both in head and heart. In fact she is *one* of the most superior women I ever met with intellect, sound judgment and facinating [sic] sweetness. Unless she comes with you I suppose I shall never see her again.[17]

This was, apparently, the pathetic end of the affair.

O'Connell put a brave face on the humiliation of being gaoled. The weekly bulletins on the traversers' condition at Richmond which he sent to be read to the Repeal Association meetings were generally ebullient, even jaunty, in tone. The most celebrated ran, 'The prisoners are all looking right well, and getting fat'![18] On 1 August 1844 he told his daughter Betsey that 'all enjoy excellent health and spirits. We are quite gay and cheerful as larks.'[19] He also professed to be gratified by his enforced suffering in the cause of Ireland. 'My imprisonment is not irksome to me', he told a visiting party of American sympathizers,

> for I feel and know that it will, under Providence, be the means of making our country a nation once again. I am glad I am in prison. There wanted but this to complete my political career. I have laboured for Ireland, refused office, honour, and emolument for Ireland. There was just one thing wanted – that I should be in jail for Ireland. That has now been added to the rest, thanks to our enemies, and I cordially rejoice at it.[20]

Underneath, however, he was embittered, and especially hostile towards the Irish liberals. When, soon after his imprisonment, Thomas Wyse moved in the Commons for a select committee to inquire into the composition of the special jury list at the state trial, O'Connell was contemptuously dismissive. 'I do not care a twopenny ticket for Wyse's motion. . . . All [it] will accomplish will be a knitting together once more the *disjecta membra* of the present party in power.'[21] He proceeded to round also upon his old ally Sheil, whom he now classified as another of the pusillanimous Irish whigs:

> Oh; plague take the shabby set! the Duke of Leinster – his name operates like a vomit – is getting up with Peter Purcell dinners for pig feeders and calf fatteners! Lord Miltown sent me a salmon – good for Friday – and Lord Cloncurry sent me his card. I am amused at condescending to have even the appearance of being angry with such beings. The Irish Orangemen are more friendly to Ireland than the Irish Whigs. But I have cheerfully done with them.[22]

Even when the Repeal Association took up Wyse's point, and insisted on making it the ground for an appeal to the House of Lords against the convictions, O'Connell remained sourly gloomy. He had, as he informed Betsey, 'no rational expectation of the writ of error being decided in our favour';[23] he told Fitzpatrick that there was 'not the smallest shadow' of a chance of his being set free.[24]

The more sensitive of O'Connell's supporters caught the sombre note to be heard beneath the surface jingle. Richard Dowden of Cork (to take one instance) was overcome by a profound sense of *lèse majesté* when he visited O'Connell at Richmond. He allowed that O'Connell's degradation served Ireland's cause. But even this scarcely outweighed his melancholy and anger. 'I own when I visited you *within the walls of a prison*', he wrote on 11 August, 'my sense of what you were working out forsook me, and I only saw in grief and indignation our country's true servant and eminent leader a prisoner because of his power and his virtue. I am not nor cannot get free of those feelings.'[25] Even O'Connell's political enemies, if they were sufficiently perceptive, felt the enormity of the 'king's' imprisonment. Macaulay, addressing the government benches, exclaimed,

> My belief is that, as regards the end that hon. Gentleman has lately been pursuing, it is not only mischievous but wholly unattainable. I regard with deep disapprobation some of the means pursued to obtain that end; and in saying this, I wish to speak with the respect that is due to eminence and misfortune; but with the respect that is due to truth. I must say too, that the position which Mr O'Connell holds in the eyes of his fellow-countrymen, is a position such as no popular leader in the whole history of mankind ever occupied.[26]

Some such feeling may have affected the outcome of the appeal in the House of Lords. Four of the judges appear to have voted on party lines, with the two decided whigs favouring the appeal. But the fifth, Lord Chief Justice Denman, although originally a whig, was widely regarded as non-partisan, and his support of the appellants may have been influenced by the consideration that justice should manifestly be seen to have been done in so portentous a prosecution. The deficiencies in the special jury list was the ground of his decision. At any rate, on 4 September 1844, the judgment on O'Connell and his co-prisoners was reversed by a majority of three to two.

Something of the original air of solemn farce-cum-fiesta was immediately restored to the affair. Desperate journeys (ending in a race of horsemen from the Westland Row railway terminus to the Richmond prison) were undertaken so that O'Connell might receive the good tidings as soon as possible, although, in fact, he did not believe them until confirmed by one of the traversers' solicitors. Upon his official release next day (6 September 1844), he remained in the penitentiary until evening, holding a sort of levee in the governor's garden, as thousands of admirers filed past him, shaking hands. After spending the night at home, he returned to Richmond with the other 'martyrs' for a formal, celebratory liberation. During the morning of 7 September, in a sort of royal gesture for the occasion, he procured the release of forty-two other prisoners.

> In his moment of triumph he remembered that within the same walls which had confined him and his fellow-martyrs there were other captives – captives more for human frailty than for depravity, who, guilty of assaults and other light offences, had been sentenced to pay fines, and being unable to discharge them were now languishing in gaol. Mr O'Connell . . . paid the fines of forty-two who had been sentenced in various amounts ranging from smaller sums up to sums of 5l and 6l. Thus, some of the poor prisoners of Richmond shared the happiness of the day, and the Liberator had the satisfaction of hearing that there was gladness in their hearts before he left the prison to enter on his own triumph.[27]

At 2 p.m. the prison gates were again thrown open and O'Connell re-emerged to mount his triumphal car. He climbed to the topmost level of this precarious equipage; on the middle platform sat an aged harper playing national airs; and beneath him, on the carriage floor, were ranged O'Connell's grandchildren, clad in green velvet tunics and white-feathered caps. The car, huge, ramshackle and splendidly decorated (it was draped in purple and gold and drawn by six dapple-grey horses), epitomized the celebration. The procession took more than two hours to pass each stage, and was headed by a chain of open carriages bearing the lesser traversers, their attornies, and, in an enormous volume, the indictment. The lord mayor and aldermen wore their scarlet robes; the Head Pacificator brandished a green bough aloft; the trades flourished successively their gorgeous banners; even 'the shipping on the river displayed their gayest bunting, floating in many colours from the mast heads'.[28] O'Connell's old showmanship had not gone to rust. When he reached College Green, he halted the cortege, tore off his Mullaghmast cap and pointed in silence to the former Irish houses of parliament, while he pivoted above the surrounding sea of faces. Nor had he cast aside any of his old shibboleths or catchcries. 'There must be no illumination this night,' he told the crowds beneath his balcony when he at last attained his house in Merrion Square,

> — tell that to everybody you meet, and say it is my advice – aye, and say it is my command (hear, and cheers) ... Conciliation is what we want – Protestants, Catholics, Dissenters, Irishmen of all classes, let us combine them all ... Yes; I am glad that I was permitted to suffer for Ireland (cheers). I rejoice that I was permitted to dwell in a prison for your sake. The Liberator wanted to be liberated himself for three long months (loud cheers and laughter) ... My course is a course of morality and peace. We have won much by it and by it we will achieve yet more (cheers). Ours is no sectarian cause.[29]

Two days later, O'Connell addressed the weekly meeting of the Repeal Association. Of course, this opened the door to another burst of popular rejoicing, and Conciliation Hall duly 'quaked and trembled with the applause'.[30] But the consuming interest was to discover O'Connell's future strategy. Even the most faithful of the faithful must have been disappointed in the result. He expended the majority of his rambling speech in a review of the twists and turns of the trial and appeal, ending with a startling recantation of his year-long denunciation of the whigs.

> And now I am going to make atonement to a public body – a class of men whom I often assailed ... Yes, we owe a debt of gratitude to the Whigs, and as I was never tardy in censuring them ... I am now equally eager to award them that meed of eulogy which it is their unquestionable right to receive ... I rejoice with an exceeding great joy at the escape we have had from the fangs of injustice – an escape for which we are, under Providence, indebted to the dignified impartiality by which the bench has been ornamented through the judicial appointments of the Whigs.[31]

His new programme (in so far as any emerged clearly from the address) followed much the same lines. He proposed the impeachment of the judges of the Queen's Bench, the Irish attorney-general and the British ministry! Around this fantastic scheme he laid a smokescreen of apparent violence and energy by scurrilous personal attacks upon the 'foul-mouthed letter-opener, Sir James Graham' and the 'monster liar of Parliament', Peel.[32] Not a word was uttered on the subject of a fresh agitation, other than a bombastic reference to a coming campaign *in England* to drum up support for the impeachment. Repeal itself was practically ignored. No one could doubt that O'Connell had yielded ground. By the time that he concluded, it was clear, even to his servile audience, that he had no intention of trying to revive or repeat the stirring demonstrations of 1843. Davis had been all too right when he observed, during the course of the Richmond incarceration, 'O'Connell will run no more risks . . . from the day of his release, the cause will be going back and going down'.[33]

III

Before the end of September 1844 O'Connell left Dublin for Derrynane. He travelled directly, being too worn out to halt for demonstrations on the way, although he promised to make good his omissions when he would return some two months later. Derrynane worked its usual magic on him. 'I found my pack in the high pride of beauty,' he told Fitzpatrick on 3 October, 'It would delight any strong being capable of delight to see them and hear them *trail*. I had a splendid hunt yesterday',[34] and, a few days later, 'I have had great hunting. My pack is splendid.'[35]

He had now the leisure and spirits to consider the political future carefully. The hare-brained impeachment scheme had served its immediate purpose – to help him through the difficult first meeting of the Association after his captivity – and could now be cast silently away. Since the autumn of 1842 he had virtually abandoned the House of Commons; since his emergence from Richmond – if not indeed since the Clontarf débâcle – he had virtually abandoned popular agitation; and the whigs totally ignored the oblique invitation to a new concordat which his address to the Repeal Association on 9 September had probably contained. So, with the avenues of parliamentary pressure, mass demonstrations, and inter-party confederacy closed, it was natural for O'Connell to explore the possibility of widening his national front at home.

With the sharp polarization of Repeal and unionism in Ireland in 1843, a body of 'moderates' seeking a way between the two 'extremes' gradually came together around the apparent compromise of federation. The federalists were never a coherent or organized body, nor was there ever an agreed definition (or even perhaps any clear concept) of political federation in the British Isles: in fact such notions as emerged suggested mild devolution for Ireland rather than a federation of states or peoples. The federalists were of mixed political origin: some of them Catholics, most Protestants, some of them whig-liberals, most liberal-radicals or liberals plain. It would be misleading to speak of federalist 'leaders', but some were at least prominent in the cause, in particular, Sharman Crawford and the Hon. Henry Caulfield in the north, and the businessmen, William Murphy and Robert Hutton, in Dublin. In fact, the movement had two 'capitals', Dublin and Belfast. Federalism had a special appeal for those Belfastmen who, although habituated to regarding themselves as radicals in politics, found separation from Great Britain repellent or frightening. Some years earlier, the *Northern Whig* had explained or rationalized the attitude of this group in economic terms: 'We are not devoid of national feeling as Irishmen, but as an industrious and enterprising people we are a thousand times more closely bound up with Liverpool and Glasgow, with Lanarkshire and Lancashire, than with all Munster put together.'[36]

Clearly, then, there were difficulties in O'Connell's coming to terms with a heterogeneous body that lacked both a formal organization and a mouthpiece among the newspapers. But he determined, apparently quite suddenly after his removal to Derrynane, to fish openly for an understanding with them. He had, he believed, stirred the Dublin federalists into activity before he left for Kerry. 'The first step', he wrote on 1 October to Smith O'Brien, who had formally headed the Repeal movement during his imprisonment and whom O'Connell now professed to treat as a species of co-leader,

> will be for the Federalists to display themselves. The second to appoint a committee of arrangement at which you and my son John should attend to secure us all from any compromise tending to render precarious the right of Ireland to 'legislative self-protection'. I do believe the men who are *about* to be prominent are sincere and inclined to go the full necessary length with us. Of course our duty is to avoid every delusion. And as to any compromise, *that* is not to be thought of.[37]

Despite this last assurance, O'Connell's essential purpose seems to have been to put additional pressure on the government to concede something tending towards 'home rule'. As he confided to Fitzpatrick, 'The truth is that a strong Federal display made by and with men hitherto non-Repealers would induce the Ministry to strike and to canvass the terms on which the Irish legislature should be re-established.'[38] But as the days slipped by without any public 'display' by the Dublin federalists, he began to fret. As early as 3 October he confessed to 'becoming very impatient to hear *authentically from "the Federalists"* '.[39]

A week later, O'Connell's patience snapped. The protracted fatal illness about this time of his eldest grandson, to whom he was deeply attached, may have increased the strain upon him; and on 12 October he mourned, in a letter to Fitzpatrick, 'the loss of my sweet boy, one of the noblest creatures that ever lived'.[40] On the same day he abruptly issued a manifesto from Derrynane announcing his own preference for a form of federalism over simple Repeal, and calling for a 'Declaration' from the federalists.

> I do at present feel a preference for the Federative plan, as tending more to the utility of Ireland and to the maintenance of the connection with England than the mode of simple Repeal. But I must either deliberately propose or deliberately adopt from some other person a plan of a Federative Union, before I bind myself to the opinion which I now entertain.[41]

This move did not perhaps represent so extensive a retreat as it has ever since been regarded. He himself does not appear to have seen the two objectives as clearly antithetical – to Smith O'Brien he had written of 'federative Repeal',[42] and to Pierce Mahony of 'the repeal Cause – federalist or otherwise'[43] – and it was altogether reasonable, even if politically unwise, for him to reject absolute distinctions. The federal system which O'Connell now sketched in outline consisted of a single imperial parliament with two subordinate legislatures for Great Britain and Ireland. This was essentially the same definition of the 'Repeal demand' that O'Connell had given at Bath in 1832 when under pressure to be specific. It reflected his own constitutional dualism, which embraced the notions of both national independence and participation in a worldwide empire. In certain respects, in particular, in placing Great Britain and Ireland on a level domestically, it was a more advanced demand than that of Home Rule in a later generation. Moreover, Davis himself was negotiating with the northern federalists at much the same time as O'Connell appealed to them from Derrynane, and, in part, for the same reason – that an infusion of new men and tactics might revive the national movement. None the less, O'Connell's ploy was presented to posterity as a surrender, and for this he had, if not himself directly, at least his fundamental strategy to blame. As he expressed this to Fitzpatrick on 8 October 1844, 'When you enter into details you give *handles* to your enemies to trace out difficulties and start objections.'[44] One of the major political uses of the Repeal slogan had been its deceptive simplicity and negativity. But the obverse of this agitatory merit was that any variation of the plain and specific demand seemed, to the general mind, a retreat.

Perhaps, in the absence of any formal federalist party, O'Connell's pronouncement had to be *urbi et orbi*. But it was carelessly made, with little preparatory private correspondence with either his lieutenants or the federalist leaders or influential critics in the Repeal movement. It was immediately repudiated by the *Nation* group on the grounds that the Repeal Association could not work against its own *raison d'être*, and that federation would perpetuate Ireland's cultural subordination to Great Britain. Even the faithful O'Neill Daunt was deeply embarrassed by O'Connell's apparent about-face. On 29 October 1844, he wrote to his 'dear Liberator':

> Do not think me factious, for I premise by saying I will either *act* or *not act* as you think best. I am not so unwise as not to know that *you* see farther than *I* do.
>
> I was desirous (subject to your approval) to speak in the Conciliation Hall to the effect that my own impressions gave a distinct preference to 'simple Repeal' as compared with Federalism, that having already given the reasons for such preference, which remained unaltered, I would not now repeat them but that, notwithstanding my unequivocal convictions on this head, I was not the less sensible of the wisdom of expanding the basis on which a struggle for local legislation could be made and that *this* was the policy of your recent letter on the subject. I meant to work out this last idea somewhat in detail. The utility of such a speech would in my mind consist in showing how an out-and-out 'simple Repealer' could yet consistently concur in the *policy* of your letter. It is on this head principally there are misconceptions aflow.
>
> Federalism is not new in the Association. But a *preference* for it on the part of our leader is new. For when I made the speech last winter sustaining the superiority of simple Repeal to Federalism, you then distinctly told me you thought I argued conclusively.
>
> I think you may trust my discretion in not doing mischief. At all events I shall be guided by your judgment.[45]

Even this political obeisance failed to save Daunt from bitter reproof, as his description of his next meeting with O'Connell makes clear.

> I rose to greet him on his entrance. His irritation at the public dissent from the policy of his recent experiment was visible in his manner.
>
> 'I am quite well,' said he, as he shook hands with me; 'that is to say, quite as well as a man can be who is opposed by one-half of his friends and deserted by the other half.'
>
> 'You cannot class me', said I, 'amongst either the opponents or the deserters.'
>
> 'Certainly not amongst my opponents,' said he, 'but as to the deserters – um! – I am not quite so sure.'[46]

The Ulster federalists simply failed to respond at all, despite a meeting held in Belfast on 26 October 1844, presumably to consider O'Connell's overture. From Dublin there came only (and even at that from an unspecified group) a timid devolutionary scheme that went no further than proposing that local taxation, the poor law, and industrial development should belong to an indigenous Irish assembly. There was nothing in this on which to build a new departure, and O'Connell hastily retreated. A second declaration from Derrynane, written on 8 November 1844, a month after the first, chided the federalists for their silence and the *Nation* group for its precipitate utterance, and wound up the whole business with a characteristic piece of compass-boxing – a gloss to the effect that O'Connell had never meant to accept for Ireland 'less' than she had enjoyed before 1801; as things had fallen out, it would be 'much better to limit our exertions to simple Repeal'.[47]

This exhausted O'Connell's resources. For the present, there was nothing left but thundering in Conciliation Hall, struggles to keep the Repeal organization in good repair, and his blessedly unfailing Micawberism. In June 1845 he was reduced to asking Smith O'Brien to decide for him whether his long absence from parliament should continue. 'Decide for me as well as for yourself . . . It will be no small sacrifice to give up my visit to my loved mountains but if you *continue* to think that sacrifice necessary I will readily make it.'[48] The sacrifice was made; but, as we shall see, quite in vain. What was there now to do at Westminster but to watch the skies for signs of another liberal dawning?

IV

Towards the end of 1843 the radical leader Charles Buller had canvassed O'Connell's ideas on Irish reform. In his response of 9 January 1844, O'Connell artfully eluded both the issue of the indispensability of Repeal and any clear commitment on his own part to the programme which he now proffered the British liberals.

> I am not telling you what would satisfy me personally but I will tell you what I know would deprive me of many of my present adherents. As for myself, you admit that the slightest shrinking from the Repeal is at the present moment impracticable. Even my usual doctrine of instalments would under existing circumstances have the appearance of cowardice or at least of paltry timidity. But as I have no notion of keeping up a party at the expense of sacrificing any measures useful to Ireland, I will candidly tell you what I think would mitigate the present ardent desire for Repeal.[49]

Pride of place went to the disestablishment of the Church of Ireland – significantly, on the ground of psychological rather than material satisfaction for Irish Catholics. 'If you reflect for one moment on the galling nature of the infliction of making one Hierarchy inferior and degraded, and making the other Hierarchy proud, inflated and exalted, you will not be surprised at this being the monster grievance which festers in the mind of the Catholic clergy'.[50] Secondly, O'Connell proposed two modest measures of land reform, the repeal of the several post-Union statutes which had, in various ways, strengthened the landlord's hand in destraining and evicting for non-payment of rent, and some form (unspecified) of fixity of tenure; he also suggested a heavy tax upon absentee landholders. His third antidote was movement towards political equality between Great Britain and Ireland. Practically, this meant a large extension of the Irish county franchise to end the scandalous disparity between the two countries in this regard; placing the Irish municipal corporations upon the same basis as English in terms of power and scope; and abolishing the Irish freeman suffrage – 'an ancient Protestant nuisance'[51] – to prevent the system being grossly distorted in favour of the Orange faction. As a parthian shot, O'Connell told Buller that he did not believe for a moment that the British people would make the necessary concessions to Ireland until, as in the case of America, too late. In particular, the whigs

> won't do it. The principal part of them will necessarily be under the control of Lord John Russell and he will never permit anything like justice to be

done to the Catholic people of this country. I know him well. He has a thorough, contemptuous, Whig hatred of the Irish. He has a strong and I believe a conscientious abhorrence of Popery everywhere but I believe particularly of Irish Popery.[52]

Greville, to whom Buller showed O'Connell's letter, responded in the privacy of his journal, 'There was nothing . . . to lay hold of; he passed over the real evils which weigh down the people, and their causes – poverty, hunger, nakedness, no employment, no capital flowing there to set them to work.'[53] But Greville was wrong in one particular. There was something to lay hold of in O'Connell's letter. In fact, Peel's design for the conciliation of Ireland followed the same track, in part. Peel and his main advisers on the Irish question, Graham, Stanley and Eliot, may not have appreciated the opportunities of splitting Irish nationalism which O'Connell's arrest and subsequent imprisonment afforded them. Here they sowed the seeds of division inadvertently. But they certainly aimed – as Peel had put it earlier – at detaching 'a considerable portion of the respectable and influential classes of the Roman Catholic population' from the Repeal movement.[54] Three of the five major proposals to emerge from the cabinet papers and deliberations of the winter of 1843–4 were directly religious. Whereas, however, O'Connell wished to draw down the Church of Ireland to a lower civil and social level, Peel planned to narrow the gap between the churches by a handful of judicious concessions to the Catholics.

The first Peelite measure, the charitable donations and bequests bill, damaged O'Connell badly. The bill, representing an attempt to remove one of the leading Catholic grievances – the difficulties in the way of the Church receiving gifts or legacies – set up a new donations and bequests board of thirteen, including five Catholics, three of whom were to be Catholic prelates. Property might be vested in the board in trust for the maintenance of Catholic clergy or churches. It was immediately denounced by O'Connell and MacHale as discriminatory against the religious orders, insulting in annulling bequests made less than three months before the testator's death, and dangerous in facilitating outside intervention in the domestic concerns of the Catholic episcopate. Despite the fact that only seven Irish MPs opposed the measure, O'Connell assailed it on 24 August 1844, from Richmond prison, in the most violent terms, as 'very dangerous', 'very pernicious' and 'untechnical'.[55] He did so as a professional lawyer, delivering an 'opinion'; and although O'Connell himself suspended his condemnation while he was parleying with the federalists, it was on the strength of his authority that MacHale and twelve other Irish bishops issued a 'Protest of the Hierarchy and Clergy of Ireland' on 9 October, and that Paul Cullen and other Irish ecclesiastics at Rome condemned it unreservedly. In fact, O'Connell had spoken rashly. He had made the elementary error of basing part of his argument on words in the bill which were deleted before enactment; and he had pronounced, 'layman though I be, nothing can, to my humble judgment, be more manifest than the uncanonical nature of this Commission jurisdiction',[56] although he was largely ignorant of canon law.

The true reason for his opposition was, doubtless, apprehension lest the issue would divide the Church and render a portion of it sympathetic to the tory ministry. It was the government's intention (as MacHale put it) to associate Catholics 'with the old and inveterate enemies of our faith, detached from their brethren, and acting against the interests of their religion; dependent on the crown, fearful of its displeasure, and fawning on its caresses'.[57] Unless three 'fawning' prelates could be found to join the board, however, the Act would be a dead letter, and the government correspondingly humiliated and rejected. Thus the matter became another trial of strength between Peel and O'Connell, with the Repealers, the Repeal press, and the Repeal bishops exerting the utmost pressure against any prelates who might be invited to take seats on the board. They failed. After some wavering and at least one defection, the archbishops of Armagh and Dublin, and Bishop Denvir of Down and Connor, were gazetted as members. Unquestionably O'Connell had suffered a moral and (with a breach now open between some leading churchmen and the Repeal Association) also a political defeat. Dublin Castle exulted: 'The "Roman Catholic party" as such has ceased to exist. O'Connell can no longer rely on the support of the church', wrote Eliot.[58] 'We have erected a barrier – a line of Churchmen – ', Heytesbury, the new lord lieutenant, added, 'behind which the well-thinking part of the Roman Catholic laity will conscientiously rally, and aid us in carrying out . . . measures of conciliation.'[59] While this exaggerated both the government's success and its significance, there could be no doubt that O'Connellism had been severely wounded.

Peel's and Graham's second proposal, to treble the annual grant to Maynooth (from £8,928 to £26,360) and to make it a permanent charge on the revenue, while providing a capital grant of £30,000 for the college buildings, struck at O'Connell in another way. Here the government batted on a plumb wicket. The bishops had privately requested assistance in 1841 and 1842, and could not but welcome the new offer, all the more so as Peel would have to brave a Protestant furore in Britain and confess to past illiberality in making it. Tacit acceptance was O'Connell's only course: though asked to do so, he did not speak when the Maynooth bill was at last debated in the Commons on 11 April 1845. It was all the more galling for him to know that the boon could be conferred only by a tory government; even had the whigs wished to grant it when in office, they would probably have been defeated in the House of Lords.

Most awkward of all for O'Connell was the government's declared intention to take up the Irish university question. This would certainly divide the Catholic hierarchy and educated laity. MacHale and his faction among the bishops would probably settle for nothing short of denominational tertiary (no less than primary) education. This faction more or less co-incided with the O'Connellite 'party' in the episcopate; and, reciprocally, O'Connell's stance on the university issue was substantially the same as theirs. He laid the ground of opposition carefully. As early as 2 December 1844 O'Connell stated at a meeting of the Repeal Association that 'in whatever college was made, every religion should be free', and that 'education in literature and religion should not be separated, but each persuasion should have the means of partaking of both';[60] and in the next month he sought, and secured, the endorsement of these principles by sympathetic bishops. Cantwell of Meath assured O'Connell of his 'unbounded confidence in your enlightened and *truly Catholic* views'; he added, 'I tremble at the very idea of the projected colleges and the *mixed system* of education which it is, I believe, intended to establish among the *middle* and *higher* classes.'[61]

But long before Graham introduced his academical institutions (Ireland) bill at the beginning of May 1845, it was apparent that a considerable proportion of 'the *middle* and *higher* classes' disagreed. Almost half the Irish bishops, almost all the Irish liberal and 'moderate' Repeal MPs and the bulk of the Young Ireland element in the Repeal movement were ready to accept it, at least as a *pis aller*, and to work within the new system. O'Connell saw the danger that his 'party of the sincere and practical [practising] Catholics' would be assailed 'as being supporters of narrow and bigoted doctrines'.[62] But though he carried the main body of Repealers with him, there was little he could do to counter such a representation of his support, all the more so as the exigencies of the campaign and the ardour of his clerical allies compelled him to play the card of denigrating Graham's proposed non-denominational colleges as 'godless' and 'infidel'.[63] Indeed, concessions made by Graham while the bill was in progress through the Commons drove O'Connell deeper into 'narrowness' and 'bigotry'. To Graham's amendment permitting separate denominational halls of residence, for instance, he could only respond, 'See what an advantage this gives to the Protestants who are rich over the Catholics who are poor!'[64] All this was but token resistance, its only value public show; and O'Connell left London before the bill passed through even the lower house. '*There is not the least use* in our staying here', he wrote dejectedly to Fitzpatrick on 27 June 1845, 'and we would incur some of the responsibility for the details, if we were to remain uselessly to battle upon the subject. The Ministry have a most overwhelming majority, especially in favour of any measure opposed by the old Irish.'[65] O'Connell's final words are most revealing. In common Irish usage, the 'Old Irish' signified the indigenous Gaelic and Catholic element in the population as against *all* the rest.

The remaining items of Peel's conciliatory initiative of 1844–5 did little damage to O'Connell. The further measures encroached directly on either Orange power or the interests of landed property and met a proportionately powerful conservative resistance. First, Peel and Graham considered steps towards rendering the Union more an association of equals and less an expression of British superiority and decided on a £5 freehold franchise for Ireland, which would do something to reduce the gross disparity between the voting qualification in the two countries. But they did not persist with the registration bill embodying this proposal beyond the second reading; it would almost certainly have cost the tories Irish county seats. Furthermore, they made no attempt to equalize English and Irish municipal corporations, perhaps the most scandalous and certainly the most recent instance of the double standard operated by British governments. It was, as O'Connell wrote on 25 April 1845, 'a bitter insult and a palpable injustice and a direct contradiction of anything deserving of being called a *Union* that the people of Ireland should not have the same corporate powers in point of law with the people of England and Scotland'.[66] Correspondingly, O'Connell's plea for substantial agrarian reform – 'it is the Repeal Association and the hopes it excites which prevent a rebellion . . . the mischief is most pressing, and a powerful remedy is alone applicable to the case', he informed the ministry through a private intermediary on 26 April 1845[67] – met with a timid response. At the beginning of June, Stanley introduced a meagre compensation for improvements bill in the

House of Lords, but encountered such fierce opposition that he abandoned it (together with all hopes of other ameliatorative agrarian measures) almost immediately.

Thus, Peel's counter-offensive, though conceived along O'Connellite 'Justice for Ireland' lines, in fact succeeded only in the religious field. But this single success was enough to render insecure, for the remainder of his life, O'Connell's major power base, the united 'national front'.

V

It was not only through its legislative campaign that the government pushed religion ever further towards the forefront of Irish politics from mid-1844 on. It also adopted the whig device of opening public offices to Catholics, thereby draining off a little more of O'Connell's middle-class support. Much worse, it attempted to use Rome to deprive him of all episcopal backing.

O'Connell's imprisonment had rallied, temporarily, even the most conservative prelates to his side. In fact, a national novena (nine days devotion) in petition for a favourable outcome of the House of Lords appeal, had been approved by the entire Irish episcopate; and Archbishop Murray himself had presided at the solemn *Te Deum* held in the pro-cathedral in Dublin on 8 September 1844 'in thanksgiving to Almighty God for the deliverance of the beloved Liberator to his country, and his fellow-martyrs from unjust captivity'.[68] Conversely, as we have seen, O'Connell desisted, for the time being, from his denunciation of the donations bill. Within a few weeks, however, the British government's pressure on Rome produced a fresh source of discord. Working directly through their agents in Italy and indirectly through Metternich, Peel and Graham induced the pope to reprove publicly all members of the Irish clergy who involved themselves in political agitation. Although the papal rescript of October 1844 was milder than Peel had hoped, it was none the less severe. A prohibitory injunction of 1839, it complained, had been ignored, to the discredit of the Holy See; and ecclesiastics were sternly reminded of their sacred duty to separate themselves from all secular concerns, and to dissipate popular excitements.

The O'Connellite bishops remained unmoved. Some took the line of Cantwell of Meath that it was 'conduct and language . . . unbecoming our sacred characters' and not participation in Repeal meetings or banquets which had been condemned.[69] Others, like O'Higgins of

Ardagh (who dismissed the rescript as 'very harmless') argued that 'being purely hypothetical, it leaves matters precisely as they stood before'.[70] MacHale and Browne of Galway went directly from the synodal meeting of 20 November 1844 which 'welcomed' the papal injunction to attend a Repeal dinner held in O'Connell's honour! None the less, O'Connell's cause was injured in two important ways. First, the new injunction emboldened the considerable minority of bishops who wished to distance themselves from O'Connell's politics to declare publicly their neutrality or even opposition. Secondly, it tended to deepen the division of the Irish hierarchy into two camps, and thereby paved the way for the emergence of a 'conciliatory' episcopal party, prepared to meet the government halfway. We have already seen some of the effects of this development, in producing significant episcopal support for such measures as the donations and colleges bills and rendering O'Connell himself half a prisoner of the MacHaleite faction, during the first half of 1845.

It was ironic that in his seventieth year O'Connell should have fallen foul of an important section of his native Church. His Continental reputation as Catholic champion was never higher. Only a year before, Montalembert, about to launch a fresh campaign against anti-religious education in France, had made a pilgrimage to receive his 'blessing' and encouragement in London. Correspondingly, O'Connell's personal piety (in the mechanical sense, at least) was even intensifying. He acquiesced in the attribution of his deliverance from Richmond to the intercession of the Blessed Virgin; and he maintained his own novena of petition to the end despite his release before the nine days were up. Early in 1845, he received a 'very great privilege' from Rome. This was, in the words of his intermediary, Rev F. J. Nicholson, 'a plenary indulgence *on every day* you may wish to obtain one, on compliance with the specified conditions. This indulgence, as you will perceive, is applicable by way of suffrage to the suffering souls in purgatory.'[71] Moreover, O'Connell continued to regard the papacy as the 'centre of unity', the safeguard of true religion.

> That authority is assailed in our day by the spirit of absolutism in many Catholic and other sovereigns, who not content with Caesar's portion claim what belongs to God. It is also assailed by the restless genius of false liberalism which whilst it affects to seek liberty principally desires to uproot religion.[72]

These two sentences reveal much of O'Connell's self-view as a Roman Catholic. He saw himself as balancing – but serenely – the claims of liberty and faith. For him, liberty was essentially the absence of privilege, compulsion or restraint. In terms of religion this implied that church and state were clear different spheres; that denominations should be both autonomous and publicly on a level; and that individual persons might choose, as they wished, amongst beliefs and spiritual practices.

For decades O'Connell had maintained this position without serious difficulties at home. But a concatenation of inimical forces formed quite suddenly in the early 1840s. First, the Young Ireland concept of nationality gave a new primacy to citizenship. Implicitly, it subordinated religion to the needs of national identity and unity, wherever (as in education) the two tended to conflict. Secondly, Irish Catholicism had rapidly become more confident, triumphalist and aggressive. By now, the MacHale school at least was prone to identify Catholic and Irish values, and sought to mould the new society –which they believed would soon succeed the old in Ireland – upon specifically Catholic lines. Thirdly, British Protestantism was likewise growing in confidence, triumphalism and aggression, while the main body of Irish Protestants (who participated fully in the general increase in zeal) were also deeply frightened by the prospect of even partial concession to Repeal. Finally, Thomas Davis, who was especially influential in shaping 'advanced' opinion within the Repeal movement and among the young intelligensia as a whole, was neurotically suspicious of popery and quick to detect schemes of priestly tyranny. This produced a series of flashpoints. Thus, O'Connell's world-picture, in particular his special ideas of 'the free church' and 'the free state', came to seem less and less apropos as the collective and the passionate began to replace the individual and the 'rational' as the master-notes of Irish political discourse.

VI

O'Connell was first awakened to some of the unpalatable consequences of his success in attracting Irish Protestants to Repeal when Smith O'Brien proposed to him that a reception in Cork which he had planned for Sunday, 7 April 1844, be brought forward to the preceding day lest offence be given to Church of Ireland and non-conformist members. O'Connell good-humouredly complied, 'I am quite sure you are right. The strictness of the Protestant practice . . . is the safer course.'[73] None the less, as Denis Gwynn observed, 'it must have seemed strange, after so many years of popular agitation which

O'Connell had habitually conducted after Mass on Sundays'.[74] As time went on, the temperamental discordance springing from the differences in religious background passed far beyond such specific issues as sabbatarianism. On 26 July 1845, Davis told his fellow-Protestant, O'Brien, 'between unaccounted funds, bigotry, billingsgate . . . [and] crude and contradictory dogmas . . . any cause and any system could be ruined'.[75] There may have been nothing specifically religious in finding scurrility in public speeches, or the mingling of public and private monies, or demagogic manoeuvring, disdainful. But Davis's charges certainly expressed the Irish Protestant's characteristic sense of superiority (reflected in the self-images of rectitude, candour, manliness and plain dealing) to the 'peasant' values by which he found himself surrounded. The crucial charge, however, was the directly sectarian, 'bigotry'.

Soon after O'Connell's release from Richmond, Davis's gathering fears of priestly domination of the national movement had broken out in a letter to John O'Connell, in which he denounced the censorship exercised in Catholic Italy, the attribution of the House of Lords decision to 'a miracle', the hooting and abuse in Cork of a convert to the Church of Ireland, and an article in the *Dublin Review* in which another Cork convert to the Church of Ireland, D. O. Madden, was dismissed as an untrustworthy witness on the character of the religion which he had abandoned. Evidently, Davis expected that his catalogue of grievances would be forwarded to O'Connell, whom he appears to have regarded as, in some sense, ultimately responsible for the excesses of his co-religionists. At any rate, O'Connell took up the challenge, replying to Davis at length on 30 October 1844. He granted that Davis and the *Nation* should enjoy the 'fullest liberty' to abuse Italian censorship and 'the State Trial miracle' (though Catholics had an equal liberty to credit it); and he repeated an earlier condemnation by himself of 'the Cork attack upon a Protestant proselyte'. On Madden, a bitter anti-O'Connellite, however, he would not yield ground. 'Would you not have a right', he asked Davis, 'if a person who from being a Protestant became a Catholic and abused the Protestant clergy, to state that his evidence against them ought to be considered as suspicious or even unworthy of belief?' O'Connell then staked his claim to be the true liberal in matters of religion, implicitly transferring the charge of 'bigotry'.

I really think you might have spared the insinuation that you and other Protestants were 'pioneering the way to power' for men who would establish any sort of Catholic ascendancy. I know this, and I declare it most solemnly, that in the forty years I have been labouring for the public I never heard one bigoted expression, not only in our public meetings but in our committees and private discussions, from a Catholic but I have often felt amongst *some* of the liberal Protestants I have met with that there was not the same *soundness* of generous liberality amongst them as amongst the Catholics.

I hate bigotry of every kind, Catholic, Protestant or Dissenter, but I do not think there is any room for my interfering by any public declaration at present. I cannot join in the exaltation of Presbyterian purity or brightness of faith. At the same time I assert for everybody a perfect right to praise both the one and the other, liable to be assailed in argument by those who choose to enter into the controversy at the other side . . . As to my using my influence to prevent this newspaper war [between the *Dublin Review* and the *Nation*] I have no such influence that I could bring to bear. You really can much better influence the continuance or termination of this bye-battle than I can.[76]

All this reveals a new polarization; fresh but deep cross-purposes are appearing. Davis no less than O'Connell prided himself upon his liberalism. His leading objective was to maintain the rights and standing of the minority in the new Ireland; and his natural response to the growing identification of 'Irish' and 'Catholic' was to attempt to impose a supra-sectarian view of social institutions and objectives. The logical conclusion was the secular state; Davis was foreshadowing the substance of what is generally regarded as 'liberalism' in contemporary Ireland. But O'Connell could also flaunt some modern 'liberal' credentials. He was the complete political democrat (where Smith O'Brien, for one, opposed the raising of such issues as household suffrage or the secret ballot), and, as we have seen, so thorough an opponent of slavery as to sacrifice in the end his American support–network to the cause (whereas Davis, for example, placed the forwarding of Repeal ahead of asserting the 'principle' of negro emancipation). Moreover, as his letter to Davis made clear, O'Connell saw himself and Irish Catholics in general as magnanimous, as well as correct, in claiming no advantage on account of their overwhelming preponderance in numbers. He could not (to be sure) be ever on his guard against a slip of tongue or pen which revealed his interior consciousness of the disparity. But he was satisfied that he allowed all practicable liberty of belief to every fellow-countryman and -woman. It was for him a very plain and simple matter of indefeasible individual right: such was the 'liberalism' which had been stamped indelibly on him in his early manhood.

The crux came when the nation and the state (in their modern senses) emerged upon the scene, for these implied, or might well be taken to imply, the 'privatization' of such matters as religious practice. To O'Connell, such a conclusion was illiberal: his liberalism regarded the indoctrination of the young as the concern of the responsible individual – and, by extension, of the individual's church – rather than a means of achieving social ends. Hence, with both claiming 'liberal' sanction, Davis could end by arguing for 'mixed' education, in the national interest, and O'Connell by standing on the individual's religious liberty, which perforce included the choice of his child's instruction. Looked at in one light, it was the 1840s challenging the 1790s; looked at in another, it was the opening skirmish in a campaign which grips Ireland still.

The issue was not, however, coolly classified in this fashion in the critical nine months from September 1844 to May 1845. Instead, Davis was driven to magnify a number of trivial incidents in his attempt to raise the alarm at the apparent Catholicizing of Repeal, while a clericalist faction, charging or insinuating that Davis and the *Nation* were anti-religious in tendency, began to form within the Association. From February 1845, when the government's colleges bill was announced, the sectarian antagonism between these extremities of the Repeal movement grew ever more embittered. O'Connell postponed formal discussion of the bill for as long as possible. Smith O'Brien tried to avoid expressing publicly his approval of the principle of 'mixed' education; he fully recognized, he told Davis, 'the importance of my maintaining sincere, unreserved and friendly co-operation with O'Connell'.[77] But the conflict was irrepressible; there was no hope that university education could be left an 'open' question in the Association.

When the bill was at last considered at a general meeting of the Association on 26 May 1845, it was Davis who precipitated a 'scene'. O'Connell may have irritated him initially by vigorously applauding M. G. Conway (a glib but disreputable young journalist who had jumped on the 'Catholic' bandwagon) when he lauded denominational university education to the skies. Davis followed immediately and immediately offended.

> I have not . . . more than a few words to say in reply to the useful, judicious, and spirited speech of my old college friend, my Catholic friend, my very Catholic friend, Mr Conway.
> Mr O'CONNELL: It is no crime to be a Catholic, I hope.
> Mr DAVIS: No, surely no, for –

Mr O'CONNELL: The sneer with which you used the word would lead to the inference.[78]

But Davis went on to further provocation, claiming, in a passage of perverse and contorted reasoning, that he and the Irish bishops were at one in their objections to the colleges bill. In fury, O'Connell rose to expostulate that whereas the 'mixed' system had been 'met with the unequivocal and unanimous condemnation' of the Irish bishops,

> [t]he principle of the Bill has been lauded by Mr Davis, and was advocated in a newspaper professing to be the organ of the Roman Catholic people of this country [the *Nation*], but which I emphatically pronounce to be no such thing. The section of politicians styling themselves the Young Ireland Party, anxious to rule the destinies of this country, start up and support this measure. There is no such party as that styled 'Young Ireland'. There may be a few individuals who take that denomination on themselves. I am for Old Ireland. 'Tis time that this delusion should be put an end to. Young Ireland may play what pranks they please. I do not envy them the name they rejoice in. I shall stand by Old Ireland; and I have some slight notion that Old Ireland will stand by me.[79]

It seems significant that, in such a context as a Repeal meeting, O'Connell should have identified himself with, and spoken for 'the Roman Catholic people of this country'. Was he too – for all his picture of himself – being sucked into public sectarianism at last? But perhaps the most significant feature of the outburst was his designation (even if only to belittle it as a handful) of a 'Young Ireland party'. So far this had scarcely existed, either in substance or in name, outside on the pages of the hated Madden's book. It was Madden who had coined the phrase, but to little effect as yet. When Smith O'Brien protested in a whisper, O'Connell withdrew the term at once, as 'disclaimed by those to whom it was applied'.[80] But the damage had been done; fatal words had been uttered; its very naming went far towards rendering a schism actual.

As to the rest, the *mores* of the day took over; sentimentality provided a 'resolution'. Davis rose to his feet again, disavowed factionalism, declared that he and his friends were 'bound . . . by a strong affection toward Daniel O'Connell' – and thereupon (in the words of Duffy) 'broke into irrepressible tears'.[81] O'Connell was not to be outdone; he also rose once more, reciprocated the warm expression of personal regard, and throwing his arms about him cried, 'Davis I love you'. One at least of Davis's friends was disgusted by his no less than O'Connell's theatricality. 'Mr O'Connell's attack on Young Ireland', wrote Thomas MacNevin next day, was what I expect from his years and irritability – the candle stinks as it waxes low on the socket. His retraction was shabby: and his hugging of Davis more like the clumsy pantomime of an ox than any display of manly sincerity.

As for Davis, I know not what to say. 'Exit Hibernia in tears'. Ah – what stuff for a politician. What was there in the vulgar assault made on himself and his friends to authorise these pearly drops or this quivering emotion?[82]

But Davis himself was quite satisfied with his 'success'. O'Connell too believed that he had succeeded, that the old lion had both tamed and reconciled his cubs. All this was quite illusory. Not only had the protagonists failed to conjure the divisions away: they eventually ran all the deeper for having been displayed. Once the genii of religious fear and vainglory had been released, within an ailing movement, there was no returning them to their bottles. Peel had, at long last, won his duel with O'Connell. At one blow, he had split both Catholic politics and Repeal.

CHAPTER 11

The Widening Gyre

1845–6

I

The effects of the momentarily-open rupture at Conciliation Hall on 26 May 1845 were not immediately apparent. O'Connell 'had', Gwynn writes, 'lived through so many much more tempestuous and emotional scenes, that he could scarcely have any deep feeling of resentment'.[1] At any rate, he showed no sign of either renewed anger or alarm during the coming months. Conversely, Davis had both publicly repledged his fealty to O'Connell and felt an afterglow of self-satisfaction at the manner in which he had comported himself in the exchange. Moreover, only four days after the 'scene' in Conciliation Hall, a national levée to commemorate the anniversary of O'Connell's imprisonment was held in the Rotunda in Dublin. This, preceded by processions through the streets and attended by delegations from all over Ireland, was an occasion for sentimental demonstrations of renewed loyalty to the Liberator and Repeal. These were repeated at the corresponding celebration in Cork on 8 June 1845, when O'Connell, entering the city on a vast triumphal car, was received with fervid enthusiasm by dignitaries, trades and populace alike: 'The exhibition here was truly magnificent', he wrote, 'It actually exceeded that in Dublin.'[2] It was not difficult, amid such euphoria, to relegate the collision of 26 May to the category of minor and temporary misunderstanding.

The sudden death of Davis on 16 September 1845 at the age of thirty seemed at first to vindicate completely such a view. O'Connell wrote at once from Derrynane in a letter to be read to the Association:

My mind is bewildered and my heart afflicted. The loss of my beloved friend, my noble-minded friend, is a source of the deepest sorrow to my mind. What a blow – what a cruel blow to the cause of Irish nationality! He was a creature of transcendent quality of mind and heart; his learning was universal, his knowledge was as minute as it was general. And then he was a being of such incessant energy and continuous exertion. I, of course, in the few years – if years they be – still left to me, cannot expect to look upon his like again, or to see the place he has left vacant adequately filled up; and I solemnly declare that I never knew any man who could be so useful to Ireland in the present stage of her struggles. His loss is indeed irreparable. What an example he was to the Protestant youths of Ireland! What a noble emulation of his virtues ought to be excited in the Catholic young men of Ireland! And his heart too! It was as gentle, as kind, as loving as a woman's. Yes, it was as tenderly kind as his judgment was comprehensive and his genius magnificent. We shall long deplore his loss. As I stand alone in the solitude of my mountains, many a tear shall I shed in the memory of the noble youth. Oh! How vain are words or tears when such a national calamity afflicts the country. Put me down among the foremost contributors to whatever monument or tribute to his memory shall be voted by the National Association. Never did they perform a more imperative or, alas, so sad a duty!

I can write no more – my tears blind me. . . .[3]

All this was rather in the nature of a lapidary inscription, in which, notoriously, a man is not on oath; and O'Connell was just the person to respond unrestrainedly, even hyperbolically, to the pathos of Davis' death. None the less, with its clear implication that the Repeal cause had been struck a devastating blow, the letter amounted to a public declaration that the disagreements between Davis and O'Connell had been, at most, trivial differences in emphasis.

This was far from true. Religious shibboleths continued to work their poison in the movement after 26 May. O'Connell himself, who habitually attached scurrilous epithets to the objects of his aversion, almost invariably referred to the new Colleges Act as 'infidel' or 'godless'.[4] Naturally such adjectives entered the general currency of Repealers and tended to be transferred – whether carelessly or maliciously – to at least some of those who supported the measure after it had been enacted. O'Connell's son, John, adopted the role of *intransigeant* upon the issue; and as he was at once much of an age (and consequently in something of rivalry) with many of the Young Irelanders; the conductor of proceedings in Conciliation Hall in his father's now-frequent absences; and commonly assumed to be O'Connell's political 'heir', sectarian bitterness was kept fresh and lively throughout the summer of 1845. At the same time, Davis contributed his share before he died. During July and August he drew to Smith O'Brien's attention various signs (as he saw them) that the Repeal movement was degenerating into a mere priests' party. Distinct and hostile factions were becoming ever more evident within the

Association. Even the circumspect secretary, Ray, told Maurice O'Connell on 31 July, apropos the non-denominational colleges and parliamentary reform, 'There is assuredly a difference of opinion on these matters between Mr O'B[rien] and a majority of the people of Ireland.'[5]

Meanwhile, O'Connell had been humiliated during his brief attendance at the House of Commons towards the end of June 1845. 'The Ministry', he wrote to Fitzpatrick from London on the 27th, 'have a most overwhelming majority, especially in favour of any measure opposed by the *old Irish*. In fact, though you may think it vanity, I cannot but assert that the Ministry *seem pleased* to have me so completely in their power, as I necessarily am in the present House of Commons.'[6] He returned to Ireland apparently determined that the parliamentary Repeal party should recover the respect and influence which it had enjoyed in the mid-1830s. His correspondence evidences an unwonted concern with parliamentary representation; and in a letter sent from Derrynane on 8 August 1845 to be read aloud at the next Association meeting in Dublin he set out a plan of revival and renewal. O'Connell's declared objective was the return of sixty to seventy Repeal MPs at the next general election. If this were realistically intended, it meant that he hoped to carry at least twenty of the thirty-two Irish counties, an extremely difficult though not absolutely impossible undertaking. To this end, he proposed a scheme of 'registry wardens', one to be appointed in each parish, with the specific duty of promoting the registration of sympathetic voters. Ray reported to him shortly afterwards that both the mustering of Dublin voters and the preparation of the nation-wide scheme were well in train. 'We have just received', he told O'Connell on 25 August, 'a return from the [Dublin city] Registry, today 19 Repealers to O. . . . We are working the wards well. . . . We are doing all we can to work out the Registry Plan. We have sent the enclosed circular to the Clergy to get "Registry Wardens" named, and the Instruction Papers etc. are printed in quantity.'[7]

But little was achieved. Outside the cities and the 'jurisdiction' of the occasional enthusiast, the 'Plan' was practically ignored. Even O'Connell's intense interest in his own brainchild appears to have been shortlived. When he left Derrynane late in September, it was principally to undertake a short series of general Repeal rallies in the south and west. These were small, decorous affairs, a far cry from the monster meetings of two years before. O'Connell's intention was in part to re-rouse the faithful and in part to preach patience where agrarian disturbances were once more upon the increase. 'Kerry wants a stimulant. Tipperary, if anything, wants restraint', he told O'Brien on 17 September 1845.[8] Between 26 September and 15 October 1845 O'Connell addressed Repeal assemblies and banquets at Killarney, Thurles, Castlebar and Sligo. Everywhere he was greeted with the old deference, and to that extent his little autumn circuit was useful confirmation of his commanding position within the movement. But he was, at best, marking time. Essentially, his home resources for an offensive were exhausted, and he could do little more than await the arrival of some *deus ex machina* – the whigs' return to power perhaps or a general election which would end luckily in the Repealers holding the balance in the House of Commons.

Although O'Connell himself remained publicly sacrosanct, his loss of persistent drive and direction took its toll, and during the third quarter of 1845, the Repeal Association began to suffer badly from the malaise of weakening central power. In Cork, it was said, the local organization was so spiritless that the return of two Repeal members for the city could no longer be assured. In London, a serious quarrel broke out in July between the priest-inspector and some wardens, and several branches were disbanded, at least temporarily. Soon afterwards, the Repealer John Reynolds caused an uproar in Dublin, and provoked O'Connell's direct intervention, by his attacks upon the Repeal-dominated Corporation. O'Connell's favour was fought over in other places. His friend, William O'Donnell, warned him on 9 September that if he accepted the hospitality of the 'advanced' Repealer, Michael Doheny, he would offend other parties in co. Tipperary: 'You can't go to Doheny's. It would not answer . . . his house I would not consent to have you at.'[9] In Limerick, O'Connell became, in effect, the bone of contention between the Repeal mayor, Dr W. H. Geary, and the main body of local Repealers, as both Geary and his opponents strove, in late July, to secure him as guest of honour for a banquet. O'Connell agreed at last on 29 August 1845 to attend a dinner in the city but would fix no date. As he explained to O'Brien some three weeks later, 'You must have perceived in my answer to their [the Limerick Trades'] invitation that I have given myself time to play the long game and I therefore can postpone the dinner till there is a prospect of unanimity amongst all Repealers in Limerick.'[10]

The most serious conflict of all occurred in Waterford, and O'Connell inadvertently added fuel to the blaze when he declared at the Association meeting of 27 October 1845 that he would move a vote of thanks to the local 'radical' Repealer, James Delahunty, for his registration work were it not that to do so might seem as if he were taking sides in the city quarrel. This drew down on him an angry rebuke from his old friend, his Waterford manager and 'fixer' for quarter of a century, Rev. John Sheehan. 'There is no part of your doctrine as an agitator which I admire more', wrote Sheehan on 30 October,

> than your saying that you would not bring about the greatest possible good at the expense of one drop of human blood. This is the true principle of the moral force revolutionist, and the announcement of it has secured for you the active cooperation of thousands amongst those who, looking only to their eternal interests, would not on any other terms consent to be implicated in the turmoil of political agitation.
>
> I am sure that however just may [be] my own abhorrence for the spilling of blood, it is not stronger than your detestation of any course which would bring the bishops and the Catholic clergy into contempt amongst the people ... Read, I pray you, my letter and I ask if I have not established incontestably a case against Mr Delahunty, my own parishioner whom, under an erroneous impression no doubt, you are now sustaining against the Bishop [Foran] and the two parish priests of Waterford. What can you think of a party who cast the vilest and most contumelious imputations upon such a man as Dr Foran? He was lately closing a series of most instructive lectures and he found it necessary to advert in very strong terms to ... the uncharitable and vituperative speeches made at the nocturnal meetings of the Waterford Repeal Association ... He was replied to by one of the party whom you are now sustaining: 'What a pity it is that Dr Foran does [not] take the pledge from Father Mathew' ...
>
> If Mr Delahunty says that without following up the course he is pursuing, you cannot have two Repeal members, for this city, he is making an unfair representation.[11]

Although O'Connell did call on 'the popular party' to apologize for its disrespect to the clergy, he also declared that each side was 'in the wrong to a certain extent', and offered his own services as mediator.[12] It was a far cry from his former easy mastery of the agitation.

These various divisions by no means reflected a simple Old Ireland–Young Ireland dichotomy. In fact, Geary, who was later to lead a Young Ireland faction in Limerick, was at this stage in trouble for his 'whiggish' conduct. Occasionally, there were indications that a clash owed something to antagonism between 'advanced' and 'moderate' elements within the Association. Most clearly did this seem to be the case in Waterford where the traditional clerical leadership was being challenged; moreover, Sheehan's heavy stress on moral force suggests that this too was a ground of battle. On the whole, however, the dissensions did not spring from generational or ideological dispute, but from failure of morale and the consequent diminution in O'Connell's control and direction of the movement.

> Turning and turning in the widening gyre
> The falcon cannot hear the falconer;
> Things fall apart; the centre cannot hold . . .[13]

Moreover, the falconer's voice was no longer clear or decisive. The separate 'knots and bodies' (as Ray called them) within the local Associations were no longer commanded to coalesce; some groups of wardens were beginning to challenge, and even flout, instructions from the centre. 'I greatly dread the relaxation of our Rules', Ray wrote to O'Connell on 8 September 1845 concerning a demand that monies be retained by a branch instead of forwarded as normally to headquarters, 'There is hardly a place where troublesome spirits are not anxious to break through and the great danger is that, if it transpired that any privilege was allowed to Limerick, we would risk speedy disorganisation elsewhere . . . The Rent today is low.'[14] O'Connell's chosen barometer of his agitation's state of health told the essential story: the weekly national Rent now sometimes fell below even £200.

II

In the final months of 1845, O'Connell's attention was drawn away from the Repeal movement proper to two new, but interrelated, factors. The first was the partial failure of the potato crop in Ireland. Its significance was not immediately recognized. In fact, as late as 11 September Fitzpatrick reported to O'Connell that the 'comparatively prosperous state of the country ought to make it [the collection of the Tribute] very successful'.[15] But by the following month the blight was manifest in no less than eleven of the counties. O'Connell himself, moving widely around Munster and Connacht about this time, was among the first to appreciate the extent of the disaster. It was probably at his instigation that Dublin Corporation, on 21 October 1845, set up a special committee to inquire into the causes of the potato failure; at any rate, he dominated its proceedings from the start. His initial objective may have been narrowly political, to seize the opportunity created by the distress to drive home the 'lesson' of Irish misgovernment under British rule. But he was soon horrified by the evidence of suffering which came streaming in: 'my attendance on the Mansion

House committee', he wrote to Smith O'Brien before the year was out, 'has made me acquainted with the frightful certainty of an approaching famine; and you know pestilence always follows famine, the prospect is really frightful'.[16] Immediately, he proposed restricting the output of the breweries and distilleries in order to conserve barley, and the placing of limitations upon the export of other foodstuffs; his next step was to call on the government to provide 'ample means of employment and [put] within the reach of the labouring classes a sufficient quantity of food, to be paid for out of the money they receive as wages'.[17] O'Connell's desperate concern, sense of frustration at his own impotence and fear that an incalculable number would 'perish in Ireland within the next twelve months'[18] are not to be doubted. But, automatically, he translated everything that he experienced into political terms, as well; and the potato blight was of critical importance not only in itself but also in contemporary British politics, because it would compel Peel's ministry to come to a determination on the repeal of the corn laws, an issue which deeply divided the conservatives. This was the second new factor of late 1845.

For some time, Peel and his particular supporters within the cabinet had been moving towards the immediate relaxation of the restrictive legislation; and the incipient Irish famine served powerfully to strengthen the case against 'dear food'. Peel was thus driven to search about for some compromise with the protectionist majority of his own party which would allow the import of cheap grain to Ireland. O'Connell was quick to see a possible advantage in all this. Co-operation with Peel was, as ever, out of the question; but the whigs were likely to move farther and faster towards corn law repeal, which he himself, as a free trade radical, in any event supported. He was doubtless sincere when he declared at the Repeal Association meeting of 3 November 1845, 'If I had only the alternative of keeping the people alive or giving up the repeal, I would give up the repeal.'[19] But it was his rider, that the whigs had not asked him to make any such choice, which told the audience which way the wind was blowing – that a new whig alliance might become practicable politics at last. Conversely, the Young Irelanders (the name was by now in general currency) took alarm; from late November onwards the *Nation* regularly demanded complete independence of the whigs no less than of the tory government.

Having failed to find a new corn laws formula which would leave his cabinet united, Peel resigned office on 6 December 1845, and Lord John Russell was called on to form a new liberal administration.

Through his friend, D. R. Pigot, O'Connell privately informed Russell that he could rely on the support of the Repeal MPs in return for reasonable concessions. O'Connell laid most emphasis upon the need for a reform of the Irish franchise (on which the building up of a strong Repeal party in the House of Commons to some extent depended) and an amendment of the Irish Municipal Corporations Act. On 15 December, he made the substance of his position public when he told a Repeal Association meeting that he was confident that he could make some progress with Lord John Russell.

This precipitated a head-on clash with Smith O'Brien. The corn laws themselves produced a secondary collision. As on most other general issues, O'Brien stood to the right of O'Connell, favouring a gradualist modification of the laws rather than complete repeal. Claiming (quite wrongly) that nine-tenths of the Irish electorate opposed the removal of protection, he demanded that, at the very least, the corn laws remain an 'open question' in the Repeal Association. But the main field of battle was an impending 'whig alliance'. 'I cannot describe to you', O'Brien wrote to O'Connell on 18 December 1845,

> the solicitude which I feel with respect to the policy of the Repeal Party in connection with the recent change of Government. I entertain the most sincere conviction that upon the conduct which we shall adopt during the next three months depend not only our chance of witnessing the accomplishment of the Repeal of the Union but also the character of the Irish nation. If all our exertions, our pledges may I say, our *sacrifices* are to end in placing the Irish nation under the feet of the English Whigs, I cannot justify to myself the part which I have acted nor do I think that the Repeal agitation will have conferred upon Ireland anything but injury and disgrace.

Not merely did O'Brien insist that the Repeal MPs should remain aloof from both British parties, but he also proposed that they should form what was later to be termed an 'independent opposition': the 'alternative which ought be presented to the minister is in my opinion not "If you give us these measures we will support you" but "If you do not give us these measures we will oppose you".' Finally, he excused his 'frankness' by claiming that it was the most effectual mode of countering the current tory newspapers' reports that he and o'Connell were now rivals for the leadership, and that the Repeal Association was being steadily 'O'Brienized'.[20]

Typically, O'Connell dealt with the personal issue first. 'I have passed

50 years of my life in agitation', he replied to Smith O'Brien on 20 December, 'and I never was jealous of any man . . . the more any of my fellow-labourers earned the popular applause and the good opinion of wise men, the more I rejoiced and this feeling it is that makes me exult in your present popularity.'[21] If this seems a very generous, it was also a misleading response. On the one hand, the notion of a duarchy, which O'Connell himself occasionally suggested in writing to O'Brien, could not have been seriously meant. O'Brien was not to be spoken of in the same breath as O'Connell as a popular leader; and his political standing at large still depended on O'Connell's patronage, which in turn sprang from the symbolic value of the adherence of O'Brien, a comparatively able and thoroughly respectable member of the Protestant landowning caste, to the Repeal cause. On the other hand, the Young Irelanders were unquestionably seeking to ensnare O'Brien for their leader, and through him ultimately to dominate the Association. It was also true that O'Brien's stances coincided increasingly with those adopted by the *Nation*. His lack of personal ambition and honourable sense of what was due to the movement as a whole (and perhaps also to O'Connell for past and current favour) continued to hold him back. None the less, circumstances were forcing him gradually towards the role of O'Connell's rival.

As we have seen, the corn laws issue itself divided the two sharply. In his reply of 20 December, O'Connell argued the inevitability of their repeal and the absurdity of calling on the British government to furnish the employment and food needed to stave off mass starvation while yet 'vot[ing] against provisions being as cheap as they might otherwise be'. He added that 'the great majority of the Repealers' agreed with him: this was a safe assertion, they always did! 'However', he told O'Brien, 'as you require that the Corn Law question should be an open question in the Association, I of course at once comply. You are most completely entitled to have your opinion respected to the extent of having no question considered as *closed* which you are convinced ought to be open.'[22]

O'Connell was determined to be conciliatory. He went on to profess his concurrence with O'Brien's policy of complete parliamentary independence, with the sole qualification (if such it was) that 'our neutrality ought not to be a *sulky* neutrality'.[23] But O'Connell's easy acceptance of the formula that every 'good' British measure should be supported and every 'bad' one opposed, irrespective of its whig or tory provenance, meant little, practically. For, to him, government signified much more than pieces of proposed legislation; and a ministry whose decisions he could hope to influence, which was not altogether inconsonant with his general radicalism, and which would allow his party some share in Irish patronage and some voice in the filling of Irish offices, was *ipso facto* to be preferred. As we have seen, he was well into political trading with a prospective whig government at the very time that he proclaimed to Smith O'Brien his continued adherence to 'neutrality'.

It will be obvious that two different political languages were being spoken in the exchange of 18–20 December. O'Brien's was the language of 'principle', or at least of unconscious predeliction or prejudice which presented itself to the locutor as 'principle'. But O'Connell's was the language of advantage. It was characteristic of him that, although an inveterate opponent of the corn laws on free trade 'principle', the argument which first sprang to his mind in December 1845 should have been the crass inexpediency of continued resistance to their repeal. In the same fashion, he had never seen an inconsistency – but rather the contrary – in alternately agitating and shelving the Repeal issue, as occasion served. What matter whether the stick or carrot was employed, provided the donkey moved. Nor had he ever seen a contradiction between taking up a formally 'independent' position in the House of Commons and accommodating a whig government – at a price. For him, whatever he gained as the price of such support, whether in terms of posts, statutes, amendments or advancements, was *not* gained at the expense of ultimate Repeal, but instead brought it a little closer. This complex attitude was epitomized by his comment of 22 December 1845, when he learned that Russell had failed to form a government after all and that Peel would be restored to the prime ministership *malgré lui*, 'If we could have managed to play our cards well in Lord John's Government, we should have *squeezed out* a great deal of good for Ireland without for one moment merging or even postponing Repeal but on the contrary advancing that measure.'[24]

Peel's return to office brought the interchange to a halt, immediately. But meanwhile the seeds of still greater troubles had been sown. John Mitchel, Davis's replacement as leader-writer of the *Nation*, was an Ulster unitarian, suspicious of clericalism generally as well as popish priestcraft, and more violent in both views and language than his predecessor. On 22 November 1845, in response to a London newspaper comment that the railways would greatly speed troop movements about Ireland, he wrote in an editorial,

The military uses (or abuses) of railways are tolerably well understood; but it might be useful to promulgate through the country, to be read by all Repeal Wardens in their parishes, a few short and easy rules, as to the mode of dealing with railways in case of any enemy daring to make a hostile use of them . . . To lift a mile of rail, to fill a perch or two of any cutting or tunnel, to break down a piece of embankment, seem obvious and easy enough . . . Hofer, with his Tyroliens [*sic*], could hardly desire a deadlier ambush than the brinks of a deep cutting upon a railway.[25]

O'Connell was aghast. Not merely had the *Nation* envisaged future armed resistance, but it had also doled out recipes for conducting a guerilla war. This struck at the heart of (in all senses) the very first principle of his politics, the repudiation of physical force in every form. By referring specifically to the Repeal wardens, it had opened up, as well, the prospect of another indictment for sedition. O'Connell had spent a political lifetime striving to secure himself and his movement against just such a prosecution, and his Richmond experiences had deepened, if possible, his horror of incarceration. He immediately protested to the *Nation* and secured the publication of a formal acknowledgement in the following issue that the newspaper 'had neither connexion with, nor control over, Repeal Wardens'.[26] As a further safeguard, O'Connell, at the next meeting of the Repeal Association which he attended, vehemently repudiated the editorial: the safety of the Association, he insisted, must on no account be imperilled by offering the slightest countenance to such statements. But, once more, this was, despite the immediate appearances, unfinished business. Unknowingly – though doubtless he would have been delighted had he known – Mitchel had placed a time-bomb, still more destructive than the issue of truckling to the whigs, in the midst of O'Connell's following.

III

Somehow or other, absurdity kept breaking in upon O'Connell. In the midst of encroaching famine and deepening division he spent much of the last quarter of 1845 in ludicrous denunciation of, and counter-denunciation by, a correspondent of *The Times*. In the autumn of 1845 the newspaper commissioned a barrister, T. C. Foster (thereafter elevated to 'the Commissioner'), to write a series of letters on the condition of the Irish people similar to those which he had recently provided for Wales and the Scottish Highlands. As a matter of course,

O'Connell distrusted *The Times*; he may also have been happy to have a new hare to pursue. Accordingly, he pelted Foster with abuse ('the gutter Commissioner', 'liar', 'scoundrel', 'traducer of my brave people') at the weekly meetings of the Association. It was often a grotesque performance. The 'gutter commissioner', he told the meeting of 27 October,

> introduced himself to my revered and accomplished friend Dean O'Shaughnessy, of Ennis . . . he [Foster] said he saw enough of Ireland to convince him that the Irish were not entitled to a Repeal of the Union . . . Sir, said the Dean, I am not in the habit of being discourteous to any person, but if I were not in my own house I would tell the servant to show you out (cheers). Off went the gutter commissioner . . .[27]

When Foster reported that the Dean had written to confirm that this story was entirely baseless, O'Connell told the next meeting, 'He [Foster] denied altogether that he had been threatened to be kicked out of the house of Dean O'Shaughnessy . . . All, he had to say was that . . . he ought to have been. (Loud laughter and cheers)'.[28] Foster, however, by no means saw himself as a protagonist in a Punch and Judy show. Outraged, he set off to inspect O'Connell's own property in co. Kerry, and in due course provided *The Times* with 'a minute and merciless description of the squalour in which the Liberator's tenants lived', including the graphic detail that there was 'not a pane of glass in the parish [of Derrynanebeg], nor a window of any kind in half the cottages'.[29] Foster's report was probably accurate. W. H. Russell, whom *The Times* sent to confirm Foster's findings, wrote later, 'I believe the tenants of Derrynanebeg were squatters, the evicted refuse of adjoining estates, who flocked to the boggy valley, where they were allowed to run up their hovels of soddened earth and mud.'[30] This would have been quite characteristic of O'Connell's conduct as a proprietor. It was precisely because he allowed his tenants – and squatters – 'to live their lives in their own traditional, slatternly way'[31] that he was popular on his estate. None the less he was stung by Foster's charges into devoting much of December 1845 and the beginning of January 1846 to attempted refutations and the (remarkably successful) drumming up of testimony, from Irish tories as well as whigs, to his merits as an open-handed and indulgent landlord. Among other things, the episode can be seen as an exercise in O'Connell's customary demagogic skills; they had not slackened yet. Burlesque and buffoonery had always been important items in his repertoire for managing the masses; and the politics of the diversion had repeatedly proved useful when – as in his current dealings with the whigs – O'Connell might appear to have been trapped between contradictory commitments. Moreover, he had discerned that this was an occasion – they were rare – for the successful playing of the supra–sectarian card, whereby the latent Anglo-Irish resentment of British assumptions of moral, organizational and social superiority could be temporarily enlisted on his side.

It certainly was the case that the Ascendancy generally was disaffected at the end of 1845 and in the opening months of 1846. 'Just as the possibility of the Whigs returning to power had increased the tension within the Repeal Association,' writes Nowlan, 'so also the break-up of Peel's party weakened the bonds which had secured the body of Irish landlord opinion to English Conservatism.'[32] Smith O'Brien attempted to exploit this disarray by negotiating an agreement with the English tory protectionist, Lord George Bentinck, to accept the temporary import of duty-free grain to Ireland. O'Connell would have none of this. Correctly, he saw O'Brien's move as an attempt to provide the Repeal movement with an alternative to a 'whig alliance'; and, again correctly, he deemed it to be politically inept. There could be no durable combination between Irish nationalists and British diehards and disgruntled landlords. Instead, O'Connell set out from the start of 1846 seriously to court, and be courted by, the liberals. The proper theatre for such operations being Westminster, he returned to the House of Commons on 25 January. Apart from two very short spells of attendance, he had ignored parliament for over three years, since August 1842. He was now to devote himself to it for almost six months on end.

Happily, an ample justification for his about-face lay to hand. Partly because the agrarian crime rate had risen with the onset of distress in 1845 but also because of exaggerated fears that O'Connell's modest, county meetings of October were but the prelude to another massive agitation, Peel was preparing a draconian Irish coercion bill for the coming parliamentary session. O'Connell seized this opportunity. At a meeting of Irish Repeal and liberal MPs in Dublin, which he summoned on the eve of his departure for Westminster, he promised unremitting opposition in parliament to the threatened coercion. Such a programme was by no means the ideal basis for co-operation with Lord John Russell. Like most high whigs, Russell inclined instinctively towards any measure which promised to impose 'firm' government on Ireland. But their common interest in eventually displacing the conservative ministry was sufficiently powerful for Russell to help O'Connell at least to the extent of delaying the progress of Peel's bill – thereby undercutting Peel's argument that its swift passage was, in every sense, a matter of life and death.

It was of course always best to deal with the whigs from a position of strength, and O'Connell used the occasion of a by-election for co. Mayo to demonstrate his continued power in the constituencies. On 2 March 1846, after 'a fierce struggle', his Repeal nominee, J. M. MacDonnell, defeated the strong liberal candidate G. H. Moore (father of the novelist, George Moore), who was both popular locally and a Catholic. O'Connell had called personally for support, contributed to the electoral expenses and, working through MacNicholas, the bishop of Achonry, as well as MacHale of Tuam, enlisted the clergy as his political agents. On 26 February 1846, Moore's mother appealed to O'Connell

> in behalf of your fellow creatures in this country many of whom, unless you exert yourself, will probably become victims to the fury to which I lament to say the priests of our religion are exciting them . . . I do not attempt to interfere with your plans as to the representation of this county. All I implore of you is to use your influence with Doctors McHale and McNicholas to restrain those priests in their respective dioceses who seem so heedless of the consequence of their harangues . . .
>
> [Rev] Mr Coghlan, who has patronised Mr McDonnell in his speech at Swinford, says 'It is not in *tens* nor in *hundreds* but in *thousands* that you should go to the hustings and prevent anyone from voting for Moore.'
>
> Now, sir, it is not in *my* name that I address you but in the name of humanity that I implore you to put a stop to projects which, if carried [into] effect, must cause bloodshed . . .[33]

Clearly, the Repeal party had to strain every nerve in order to defeat Moore; the margin was only seventy votes. 'It was a bold undertaking', O'Connell wrote later to MacHale, 'and would have been fatal if unsuccessful. Your Grace's energy and all-commanding influence, aided by the patriotic clergy, have achieved the most valuable triumph for Ireland since the Clare election.'[34] Though this last was a palpable exaggeration, it is an index of how seriously O'Connell was now setting about the building up of leverage in parliament. He himself participated regularly in the business of the House of Commons throughout the spring of 1846, in pressing for Irish famine relief, in the corn laws debates and, above all, in combating Peel's coercion bill. He compelled a reluctant Maurice to join him at Westminster, writing to him in Derrynane on 26 March,

'You must be here for the second reading of the Coercion Bill immediately after the Easter recess. It is impossible to dispense with your presence';[35] and he busied himself with arranging for the return of his youngest son Daniel at a forthcoming borough by-election. For the first time since leaving Richmond prison, his course seemed really set.

IV

Suddenly O'Brien ran athwart O'Connell's new strategy by another exercise in the politics of principle. On 3 April 1846 he refused to serve on a parliamentary committee, dealing with English railway business, to which he had been appointed. This move originated in a scheme which Davis had mooted, while the 'traversers' were imprisoned in 1844, that the Irish MPs should deliberately absent themselves from parliament in protest. Nothing came of it until, a year later, O'Brien and John O'Connell adopted modified forms of abstention from the Commons; but they did so too late in the summer session of 1845 for any counter-action to be practicable. O'Connell had warmly supported this demonstration; it broke the current political doldrums, if only feebly, and he persuaded himself, if no other constitutional lawyer, that the House of Commons had lost its controlling power over Irish MPs by the Act of Union. From the beginning of 1846, however, O'Connell had changed his tack completely. Parliamentary participation was now the order of the day. Accordingly, John O'Connell accepted committee membership, and O'Brien's adherence to the old resolution was, to say the least, embarrassing.

When O'Brien's contumacy was considered by the Commons on 28 April 1846, O'Connell pleaded that 'it was not the intention of his hon. Friend [Smith O'Brien] to be guilty of any contempt . . . He had merely acted from a mistaken feeling of his duty.'[36] John O'Connell, while praising O'Brien's highmindedness, argued that 'his services to Ireland would have been better rendered in still further opposing the Coercion Bill':[37] he himself had accepted committee membership lest he be rendered 'unable to oppose the Coercion Bill, which he regarded as a higher duty to Ireland'. O'Brien did not anticipate imprisonment for contempt. 'I cannot believe', he wrote to O'Connell in the course of a comparatively cordial discussion of tactics just before the debate, 'that the House will enter into a contention which must be attended with great inconvenience in regard to public business as well as to its results upon public feeling in Ireland. I therefore expect that a motion will be made without parade to substitute another member in my place on the Committee.'[38] Instead, however, he found himself confined in the Tower of London. The train of happenings which would rend the Repeal movement in two had started.

There were of course two views of O'Brien's stand. Like many of his fellow-countrymen, he saw himself as the champion of integrity and consistency, ready 'to encounter every personal hazard in giving effect to the resolve of the Irish nation'.[39] But devoted O'Connellites such as Steele spoke of him as the dupe 'of a perfidious clique, that sought . . . to make him their plastic instrument . . . through his own wayward personal impulses'.[40] As O'Brien could justly claim to have acted in accordance with a Repeal Association resolution of 1845, the real issue was the nature and breadth of O'Connell's authority. This became evident immediately. On 30 April 1846 Ray reported from Dublin to O'Connell:

> There was a very warm discussion in committee today on Mr Smith O'Brien's affair . . . [with] a very full attendance of the *young men* evidently brought together from the circumstances.
>
> Mr Doheny . . . after a flourishing preliminary harangue proposed that a vote should be passed at the [general Association] meeting on Monday [4 April] of sympathy with Mr O'Brien, of approbation of his conduct and of the determination of the Irish people to sustain him and also of their fullest confidence in him etc.
>
> Mr [J. C.] Fitzpatrick, Barrister, opposed Doheny's views . . . He said that Ireland acknowledged you only as Leader, that Mr O'B[rien] had not acted in unison with you but, on the contrary, took an opposite course, that he did not then see how approving of the course in one case could be other than disapproving in the other . . .
>
> I take it almost for granted that we will have a letter from you on Monday to guide us. As things are, it is absolutely necessary we should have your directions public or private as we all fear there will be division at the meeting on Monday.[41]

The meeting was certainly divided, but O'Brien's supporters were heavily outvoted when they proposed that the Association should endorse his defiance of the House of Commons. Evidently, O'Connell had instructed his lieutenants to oppose any move which might identify the Association with illegality, and thereby endanger its existence. Unquestionably, O'Connell feared charges of sedition. But equally, as his publicly expressed hope that O'Brien would soon return to combat the coercion bill made clear, he realized that his command of the Repeal movement was under challenge. As Martin Crean, the assistant secretary of the Association, observed to him after a meeting of the Young Ireland-dominated '82 Club held in Dublin on 9 May, 'I am diffident in giving *you* my opinion but it is my duty to say that the *open* and avowed drift of the majority at the meeting was to set up the "Golden [Calf]" in your stead.'

Although Crean ended his report by assuring O'Connell that 'the *people* will never submit' to the new idolatry,[42] popular support for O'Brien was already manifesting itself in certain places, and particularly in O'Brien's own constituency, Limerick. Repeal meetings in the city and Rathkeale on 9 and 10 May 1846 denounced the pusillanimity of the official policy, and the Rathkeale branch resolved to exclude the O'Connellite *Pilot* from its Reading Room because of its 'unmanly attempt . . . to asperse and misrepresent the conduct of William S. O'Brien'.[43] The Limerick trades went so far as to raise the banner of possible insurrection when they declared that O'Brien would remain true to his pledges 'even if it were necessary to lead his fellow-countrymen to the field in defence of the trampled liberties and prostrated constitution of Ireland'.[44] In all, a considerable proportion of the Limerick activists were moving towards secession from the Association – interestingly, with some priestly support, for O'Brien's imprisonment was precisely the sort of personal suffering to evoke clerical sympathy. To a lesser degree, the same tendencies began to show themselves in other large provincial centres, Cork, Kilkenny and Clonmel.

O'Connell had to deal with all this at a distance, at least three days away in communication-time, and through agents fearful of acting on their own initiative. He was careful, in his public letters, to write no word of disparagement of O'Brien; privately, too, he instructed his Dublin supporters 'not [to] take any part against' him.[45] At the same time, he made it quite clear, though only by implication, that O'Brien's was the mistaken strategy, or at least inferior to that of maintaining the struggle against the coercion bill in the House of Commons. In masterly fashion, he undermined the Young Irelanders' emotional appeals by organizing, through the parochial clergy, a series of petitions against O'Brien's imprisonment. O'Brien's supporters were infuriated, for the 'principle' of his stand was totally ignored; and there were arguments and scuffles at various chapel doors. But O'Connell had chosen his ground well: the petitions (he presented over 200 in all to the Commons) channelled much of the compassionate feeling which the affair had aroused into his own rather than the Young Ireland ranks.

O'Connell certainly suffered from the fact that his was patently the 'unmanly' position; he was abasing himself before instead of defying the British parliament. None the less, it was he who held the master-cards. First, none of his opponents dared as yet an outright challenge to his leadership, and secondly none of them wished to abandon or be driven from the Repeal Association which (the wide circulation of the *Nation* notwithstanding) remained their principal platform and source of influence. It was noteworthy that at both the committee and the general meetings of the Association during May 1846 the Young Irelanders invariably retreated when either O'Connell's authority or the illegality of what they proposed was made the specific issue. Even the most candid and reckless of them, T. F. Meagher, did not fight on after Doheny's motion was replaced by an anodyne resolution of sympathy on 4 May. 'Young Meagher', Ray reported to O'Connell after the next general meeting on 11 May,

> opened a speech, brilliant as usual, by reference to the resolution passed last day which he said he thought fell short of what the Association felt but still perhaps it was the more safe and legal. T. Steele took his opportunity to refer to Meagher's expression and took advantage of its proceeding *from Meagher*. He said that the course taken by the Association had your full approval of its indispensable caution.[46]

Correspondingly, O'Brien himself, despite his anger at his 'abandonment' by O'Connell, decided to use him to raise in the Commons on 22 May 1846 a technical argument (that the committee of selection had been improperly constituted) against his imprisonment. 'I have no hesitation therefore', he wrote to O'Connell early that day, 'in saying that I prefer to owe my discharge to you than to him [unknown] . . . It is . . . of the utmost importance not to me alone but to "Ireland and Repeal" that every possible effort should be made to obtain a successful debate and division tonight.'[47] O'Connell's motion failed, but this mattered little practically, as the Commons discharged O'Brien – *ex gratia* – before the week was out.

It might have seemed as if reconciliation rather than rupture between the two was on the way. But the tide of general politics ran in an adverse direction. By the beginning of June 1846 it was becoming clear that the days of Peel's ministry were numbered, and the whig-liberals likely to succeed him soon in office. In terms of his own objectives, O'Connell's strategy had been vindicated. The corn laws would shortly be repealed, thereby destroying (in the eyes of all members of the Commons except his own faction within the conservative party) the *raison d'être* of Peel's premiership. Mean-while, the Irish coercion bill had been fatally delayed. It was now likely that the whigs, tempted by the prospect of a return to power, and the tory protectionists, eager for vengeance on their 'betrayer', Peel, would combine with O'Connell and the Repeal and radical MPs to defeat it at the third reading. All this foreshadowed an imminent change of government and a new ministry dependent on O'Connell's support. A fresh 'whig alliance' – though O'Connell dared not formally shelve Repeal or admit that he intended the record of 1835–41 to be replayed – was stealing over the horizon.

The Young Irelanders attempted a pre-emptive strike against the threatened entente. On 13 June 1846 the *Nation* published no less than three articles denouncing the rumoured alliance of O'Connell and the whigs, and two days later the brilliant Meagher led a similar attack at the weekly general meeting of the Association. As Crean reported to O'Connell,

> The Young Irelanders mustered strong (as their small number will allow) at the meeting to-day. Young Meagher made a long speech in the course of which he said that suspicions were abroad that Repeal would be sacrificed for Whig patronage and in allusion to Davis he said '*we* looked upon him as our leader and our prophet'. In reply Tom Steele took exception to that phrase in particular and called on Meagher to explain if he meant by 'we' the people of Ireland, [and] that if he did [whether] the people repudiated any leader but 'O'Connell.'[48]

It was said later that 'when the fascination of Meagher's speech was off the meeting were entirely against' the Young Irelanders.[49] At any rate, all of them, including Meagher, retreated when confronted with the question, were they disputing O'Connell's leadership? Next day Ray told O'Connell that, in private conversation, Mitchel had tried to 'explain away' Meagher's 'malevolent' speech. 'He appeared to me', Ray continued, 'very anxious to disengage himself and his party from the imputation of any disrespect towards you. We [Ray and Steele] asked him upon what were the speeches and *Nation* articles founded? Confessedly on rumours in the Tory journals adopted by them; and who had power to make any compromise? as they said – but his pretexts were too shallow.'[50]

Meanwhile O'Connell had decided to put an end to this game of tip-and-run. Although the letter is not extant, it was probably on or about 11 June 1846 that he informed his Dublin lieutenants of his intention. 'In obedience to your desire', Crean responded on 15 June, 'I communicated the purport of your letter to *your friends*. They are delighted at your determination to put down this most mischievous knot',[51] and Steele wrote on the 16th that it had 'given your own Old-Ireland people joy beyond measure that on your return [to Dublin] you intend putting these scamps in their proper position'.[52] It seems likely that the impending change in government was largely responsible for O'Connell's decision to act: bargaining with the whigs would be very difficult if there were still an unchallenged and, in effect, 'licensed' opposition to any such move within the Association. But other factors may have weighed with him, as well. He was genuinely afraid that the current Young Ireland rhetoric might lead to the suppression of the Association. Even references to the 'illegality' of the House of Commons' proceedings against Smith O'Brien seemed dangerous, and were in fact deleted by Ray when presenting correspondence to a general meeting. But it was deviations from the Association's principle of strictly peaceful agitation which alarmed O'Connell most – in addition to providing him with his chosen ground for action. Mitchel's original anticipation, in November 1845, of the possible use of force had been since capped by similar oratorical excursions in the course of protests against O'Brien's confinement in the Tower. Doheny's declaration at a meeting of the Liverpool Repealers on 17 May that there were times when 'the strength of man, contending for principle, must be decided by the issue of his own blood' was probably the most disturbing, as it was delivered by a member of the executive committee to a regular branch meeting of the Association.[53] It was easy to envisage Dublin Castle using such a flourish as the ground for proclaiming the organization. Again O'Connell may well have been influenced by hostile reactions to the coat-trailing of the Young Ireland group. Early in June 1846 Dr Magennis, parish priest of Clones, co. Monaghan, wrote to the secretary of the Association:

I am desirous to tell you with a view of having it communicated to the Liberator and his worthy sons that should this infidel and unprincipled *Young Ireland party* continue to retain their wonted airs of impudent domination, I and every priest and every layman in this vast diocese [Clogher] with the bishop at their head will relinquish all connection with the Association and hold correspondence only with the three I have mentioned.[54]

While Crean's covering observation to O'Connell that Magennis expressed 'the almost unanimous opinions of the clergy of Ireland' was an exaggeration,[55] there could be no doubt that the Church as a whole was rapidly aligning itself against Young Ireland. This was in part a clerical reflection of O'Connell's own changing attitude; but as it developed it presented him with an additional temptation to strike down Young Ireland while the conditions remained favourable.

O'Connell's first move was the dispatch of an open letter from London to the Association on 18 June condemning 'the efforts [of] . . . some of our juvenile members to create dissension', and denying absolutely that the Repeal cause would be 'abandoned, postponed or compromised', even if the whigs came to power: he trusted that this forthright declaration would take away 'some clap-traps from juvenile orators'.[56] It does seem to have left them cowed – outside the columns of the Nation, at any rate. Ray reported that they made no difficulties at the general meetings of the Association on 22 and 29 June 1846. 'I think you will have no further trouble with the Young Irelanders', he told O'Connell on 29 June, 'They see clearly that you are determined to follow up the blow.'[57] And O'Connell did follow up the blow, by returning to Dublin in time for the Association's committee meeting of 11 July – Russell having meanwhile succeeded Peel as prime minister. O'Connell bluntly proposed both the formal confirmation of several earlier resolutions rejecting the use of physical force, and the adoption of a fresh statement which concluded, 'We emphatically announce our conviction that all political amelioration, and the first and highest of all – the Repeal of the Union – ought to be sought for, and can be sought for successfully, only by peaceable, legal, and constitutional means, to the utter exclusion of any other.'[58] To allow his opponents no loophole, O'Connell declared 'the principles of the Association to be the utter & total disclaimer of the contemplation of physical force'.[59] Although Mitchel and Meagher demurred, the remainder of the committee voted obediently for O'Connell's motion. The way was now clear for him to present the same declaration to the general meeting of the Association held two days later. Again he triumphed; only three voices were raised in even qualified opposition, and Meagher was the sole dissenter when O'Connell's motion was put to the meeting, and carried with acclamation. Again O'Connell had left no room for equivocation. He told the meeting that he had so phrased his resolution as 'to draw a marked line between Young Ireland and Old Ireland', and that it specifically required members of the Association to eschew the abstract principle as well as the actual practice of violence.[60]

Having apparently secured his rear, O'Connell returned to London and the business of attempting to influence the shape and direction of Russell's new government. On the surface, he had carried the day with ease by the brutal use of his own 'moral force' – his accumulated authority and habit of command. It was certainly a dextrous and audacious political display by a man almost seventy-one years old. He had dared his 'juvenile' critics to defy him as arbiter of the Repeal Association, and only Meagher had had the final hardihood to do so. He had implicitly challenged Smith O'Brien to choose his side in the affair, and O'Brien, still anxious to avoid an open breach with O'Connell, had absented himself from the critical meetings. O'Connell had chosen his issue with great skill, presenting his opponents as the wanton and dangerous innovators who would sacrifice a formidable movement for a 'principle' which they themselves declared had no bearing on the present or even (so far as they then could see) the future. On the field of battle he had simply rolled them up.

V

The *casus belli* chosen by O'Connell was, however, a mere fragment of the Young Ireland case against him. They had, as R. B. McDowell puts it, 'the advantage of being political puritans'.[61] They loathed what they saw as O'Connell's lack of sensibility, vulgar oratory, coarse populism, financial chicanery, truckling to British enemies and clerical friends, love of sycophants, use of creatures to control the Association, jobbery, duplicity and outworn values. None of these had been conjured away by his triumphs of 11–13 July. It is true that, however willing to wound, the Young Irelanders were yet afraid to strike. In a sense, O'Connell had by now realized his boyhood ambition to be the Father of his Country. At least, he was its father-figure; and for the present no one – not even Meagher – was prepared to disobey a solemn and specific parental order, to be cast adrift in a world without known bearings. But the rebellion was almost ripe; and O'Connell's renewed absence from Dublin from mid-July onwards would prove emboldening.

It should be remembered that, from O'Connell's standpoint, his visit to Dublin to suppress Young Ireland was a mere, if necessary, interruption of his principal task – to secure a more favourable Irish administration and legislative programme from the whigs. On 30 June he had informed O'Brien that he regularly told Russell's emissaries 'that they [the new government] must not only leave the Repeal question open, reinstate all the magistrates [dismissed as members of the Association in 1843] but govern Ireland by Irishmen'.[62] This last was O'Connell's most important immediate concern. He appears to have had a private hand in the appointment of Baron Brady as lord chancellor, of J. J. Murphy as master of chancery, of his friend D. R. Pigot as chief baron of the exchequer, of another friend O'Conor Don as lord of the treasury and perhaps also of Sheil as lord of the mint. Covertly he strove to secure the return of the Irish liberals who had been raised to office by Russell, and hence required re-election. His leading success, in the teeth of Young Ireland protests, was the securing of a clear run for Sheil. 'I have stifled all opposition to Sheil at Dungarvan', he told Pigot, 'The election will not cost him a shilling, and that is what he likes.' He had to play other constituencies warily. 'I have been working in an under channel' in Clonmel, he reported (again to Pigot), for the return of J. H. Monahan, the prospective Irish solicitor-general. He was not prepared, however, to allow Redington, the newly appointed Irish under-secretary, to fill the vacant borough of Dundalk. Not only had Redington been too outspoken an anti-Repealer, but also O'Connell's youngest son, Daniel, was already interested in this constituency. 'I have difficulties enough to encounter', he confessed, 'to keep the Repeal party within bounds without having those difficulties augmented, even in my domestic circle.'[63] But the most important objective of all was to prevent the nomination of a Young Irelander for any of the seats. Even before his excursion to Dublin, he had written to his local mainstay, Edmond Smithwick,

> Kilkenny [county] must return a Repealer, and I cannot possibly permit it to return either a Tory or Whig or an animal more mischievous than either of the others, called a Young Irelander . . . Nothing could afflict me more than any leaning to Meagher after his recent misconduct. I really think him more dangerous than that undermining fellow – Doheny.[64]

O'Connell's attempt to practise a spoils system through sympathetic intermediaries by no means stopped short at high judicial and political office. On 8 July 1846, he had enlisted Pigot's aid to arrange the lower as well as the upper end of the scale satisfactorily. 'There are details', he wrote,

> which will contribute much to the popularity of the new Government. I mean the appointment, under the Castle, of tradesmen, &c. Hitherto they have been almost uniformly violent Orangemen who have got those appointments. These things may be thought trivial: they are not so. They go much farther, sink more deeply than you imagine. Then it may be said to be liberality to leave these persons in their present situations. It is a kind of

liberality that has never been exercised towards the Catholic tradesmen; and whenever an opportunity arose, there never was a more bitter *selector* of Orangeists than that miserable Lord Heytesbury.

I do implore of you, have this matter recommended in the proper quarter, whatever it be, and do have it attended to promptly and distinctly.[65]

Concurrently, O'Connell publicized the Irish measures which he wished the whig administration to adopt. These were familiar: parliamentary reform (of constituencies, franchise and registration), local government reform (of the municipal corporations and grand juries) land reform (in favour of improving tenants and tenants-at-will and punitive of absentee landlords) and an amendment of the Colleges Act. There was nothing immoderate or surprising in this latest Justice for Ireland catalogue, except perhaps the omission of any further design against the Church of Ireland and the inclusion of the university issue, which parliament had settled so recently and with such difficulty. These appear however to have been the nub of the matter for O'Connell at the moment. 'I do not hesitate', he told Russell (through his intermediary, Pigot) on 12 July 1846, 'to place the question of the Protestant church in abeyance but then something must be done respecting education and touching the "*Infidel*" Colleges before Parliament rises.'[66] Who could wonder at the Young Irelanders' outrage when they saw or guessed the true effects, the actual consequences, of O'Connell's continued 'adherence' to the 'principles' of Repeal and independence of the British ministry?

From the standpoint of the *Nation* group, the key to the situation was Smith O'Brien. The *Nation* attempted to save itself by a sort of deathbed moderation. Duffy wrote in its columns on 18 July 1846,

> in the fiery enthusiasm of '43 good men may have thought – did think – that a time was at hand when this country would negotiate best . . . with arms in hand . . . [But] it would be the blindest folly to dream that any means but opinion are within our grasp [now]. We rely on no other. We believe in no other as applicable in the smallest degree to our time and condition.[67]

But O'Connell had already determined to disengage the Association completely from the newspaper, and *within* the Association the Young Irelanders felt impotent without an established national leader to command them. O'Brien was pressed hard on either side. O'Connell made his expectations clear when he wrote to O'Brien, also on 18 July, that it is impossible for me to act with any of the avowed Young Irelanders unless they retract their physical force opinions altogether and submit to the resolutions of the Association. Whilst those resolutions stand approved by all the Committee except two and by the entire meeting of the Association (with only one exception) I am for strictly adhering to them. If they be wrong in anything let them be altered or amended in the usual way; but, until changed by the same authority that passed them, I for one do not think I go too far in requiring the Young Irelanders candidly to adopt them or to cease to cooperate with us.[68]

Meanwhile, Duffy told O'Brien that he had failed his supporters by absenting himself from the fateful general meeting of the Association of 13 July. 'One and all, they [the men to be attacked] believe that, having got into this battle in your defence, you left them, when a crisis came, to take care of themselves.'[69] Slowly, it would seem, O'Brien came to a determination to resist O'Connell's fiat. On 28–9 July, at the first general meeting of the Association which he attended after O'Connell's *coup*, the issue of physical as against moral force was raised again. The ensuing conflict carries the air of a set-piece, as if each party had attempted to pre-arrange its actions and reactions. Meagher, in the course of a scintillating address glorifying armed resistance, was silenced by John O'Connell, from the chair, as in breach of the test of membership of the Association laid down by O'Connell on 15 July. O'Brien protested hotly in the name of liberty of speech. Next Meagher attempted to resume his oration only to be ruled out of order once again. O'Brien then led the chief Young Irelanders and 'a section of the meeting who followed and applauded them' from the hall.[70] The secession had come at last.

The scanty evidence which survives suggests that O'Connell was unperturbed by this denouement. He may well have been relieved, or even satisfied that he achieved his end. Certainly, he would now be free of open rows and dissension within his movement, and free both to secure the political succession for his son John and to bargain with the whigs to best advantage. He had the warmest backing of the Catholic Church in general, and of his own episcopal faction in particular. Cantwell rejoiced in the breach, pronouncing the 'physical force' adherents to 'be regardless of their duty as Christians'; O'Higgins declared proudly that 'we have no physical force men in this diocese [Ardagh]. Neither have we, thank God, any schoolboy philosophers, false and sanguinary Repealers or Voltarian newspapers.'[71] Dr Cane of Kilkenny, long a sympathizer with Young Ireland, warned Duffy:

The priests generally will rejoice to hear you are laid prostrate, and all who abide by their views and follow in their track will echo their sentiments. This is an immense power you have to encounter; and any public meeting anywhere in Ireland, would by its majority rule against you, and with the Association.[72]

Finally, the seceders made no move to set up a counter-organization and O'Brien showed no desire to challenge O'Connell for the national leadership, or even to put himself at the head of the schismatics. Thus O'Connell probably counted himself a net gainer. He had re-attained an obedient – if smaller and shrinking – mass following, and re-awakened clerical – if no other – enthusiasm. The loss of talent, fire and idealism would not have weighed greatly with him. After all, that old and trusty indicator, the Repeal Rent, told him that he was right: the average return almost trebled in the weeks immediately following 29 July 1846.

Beneath the bewildering complexity of stands and shifts in the fourteen months between the original public quarrel between Davis and O'Connell and the final public quarrel between the champions of Young and Old Ireland, one simple pattern is discernible. O'Connell was moving back steadily to the parliamentary method, and, with it, to concern with increasing the numbers and effectiveness of the Repeal party in the House of Commons and, ultimately, helping the whigs back to power. This surely meant that conflict with not only the *Nation* group and its sympathizers but also Smith O'Brien himself was inescapable. The wonder, if any, is that the rupture came so late.

CHAPTER 12

The Dying Fall

1846–7

I

When he returned to Ireland from Westminster early in August 1846 O'Connell may have supposed that another cycle of modest, informal power-sharing was beginning. From Dublin, where he spent the next five weeks, he cannonaded Russell, directly or indirectly, with requests, demands and pleas. He asked, for example, for a peerage for Lord de Freyne's younger brother (so that a 'Catholic' title would not die out), for the reinstatement of the Repeal magistrates dismissed in 1843 and the advancement of various minor officials including six chancery court clerks. He even sought the promotion of his own son Morgan in the registry of deeds. He had persuaded the registrar, Moore, to retire early in order to make way for Morgan, and looked to Pigot to arrange the substitution. 'If you think it has the least appearances of a job', O'Connell added, 'I do not press it in the slightest degree. It seems to me to be nothing more than to allow an officer of forty-eight years' service to retire without personal loss.'[1] Pigot concurred, and Morgan duly became registrar.

This pattern was repeated in much larger matters. On 10 August 1846 O'Connell wrote to Pigot, 'for heaven's sake get rid of the arms Bill or mitigate it exceedingly – no branding'.[2] Three days later he issued another frenzied appeal, 'It gives an irritating topic to your enemies in this city and in the country generally. If possible, get rid of it. *At all events*, get rid of as much as you can of it, especially the branding [clause].'[3] The government proved compliant. The entire bill, proposing to renew an Act against which O'Connell had been inveighing for two years, was dropped almost immediately. On 12 August he begged Russell himself to act at once to counter the effects of blight, now manifest again in co. Cork. O'Connell argued that

the forms of the law and of constitutional guarantees must yield to the pressure of a death-dealing famine. And I also submit whether her Majesty's Government may not feel, at such an awful crisis, it right to consider whether Parliament might not, either by a vote or by a short bill, confer upon the Government extraordinary powers of directing, *without any delay*, the execution of works of public utility and of supplying the immediate means of paying the wages of the labourers employed at such works.[4]

Again the governmental response was favourable. On 17 August 1846, without a division in the House, Russell carried a resolution that £450,000 be made available for public works in Ireland. Meanwhile throughout August 1846 O'Connell had been manoeuvring to secure a candidate for the Clonmel by-election who was both formally a Repealer and a friend to accommodation with the whigs, and found him at last in the liberal Hon. Cecil Lawless, who joined the Association at the eleventh hour. In due course Lawless was returned, unopposed, though the deal itself bordered on the scandalous.

Thus, O'Connell's brokerage brought in a small but steady political revenue at first. Although Russell might declare that he favoured non-Repealers for preferment, Dublin Castle, under the lord lieutenancy of O'Connell's old friend, Duncannon (now the Marquis of Bessborough), was anxious to placate him whenever possible, in the belief that his influence alone stood between it and serious disorder. But O'Connell was grossly mistaken if he concluded from this that he had succeeded, in effect, in putting back the clock ten years, and essentially restored the conditions and relationships of 1836. First, he was now encountering, for the first time in his political career, a systematic and continuous nationalist critique of his policies and conduct and a coherent and growing opposition to his type and use of leadership. This is not to say that Irish middle-class 'juvenility' was ranged against him *en bloc*. Almost as many of the young Catholic and liberal Protestant bourgeoisie had supported as resisted him in the Association. *Pace* the cynical observation that the 1848 Revolutions were really about jobs in the civil service, the young men of the mid-1840s, whether O'Brienite or O'Connellite, generally ended up as successful public servants, politicians, judges, journalists, lawyers, doctors or engineers. None the less, it was the Young Irelanders who dominated in their generation, especially in tongue, pen, vision and fervour. Forty years before, O'Connell had been foremost of the foremost in just such a thrusting forward of the ardent young. His role reversal was politically expensive as well as most painful to consider.

Secondly, O'Connell's physical strength was failing. It is difficult to say precisely how and when his decline in health became precipitous. Evidently, he went downhill badly in the course of his usual autumn retreat (September–October) at Derrynane. Soon after he reached Kerry he wrote of the pain he suffered as signifying 'the breaking up of [my] constitution'.[5] O'Neill Daunt was shocked by the bodily deterioration in O'Connell when he met him again in Dublin at the beginning of November 1846:

> I was greatly struck with the physical decay of O'Connell. I had not seen him in public for many months, and the change was painfully manifest. His intellect was as strong as ever, but his voice was extremely weak. How different were his faint and feeble accents from the stirring trumpet tones in which I had heard him, on the banks of the Boyne in 1840, rallying the Repealers of Drogheda around him! I doubt if he could now be heard six yards off.[6]

Even the faithful Steele admitted, about the same time, 'It is sad to contemplate the vast difference between the O'Connell of 1843 and the O'Connell of 1846.'[7] O'Connell assured Fitzpatrick that he could still make himself audible if he chose, that 'he purposely economizes his vocal powers'.[8] But in fact he would never again be heard by the Irish masses: the agitator-general was dead already.

Finally, the times were out of joint, politically. As Nowlan notes, 'Had there been no failure of the potato crop for a second time in the autumn of 1846, the course of political development in Ireland might well have confirmed the victory O'Connell appeared to have won in 1846. But that second and, as it proved, total failure of the crop had a most disturbing effect on political calculations.'[9] Russell and his cabinet failed to grasp the magnitude of the calamity – in fact, Russell told O'Connell on 14 August 1846 that he inferred from the paucity of Irish harvest labourers in Britain 'that they found employment in their own country'![10] In any event, the whigs were in general inhibited by their economic and social preconceptions from embarking on state expenditure and intervention to anything like the degree called for by the Irish crisis. As this crisis deepened, O'Connell seemed, more and more, to have backed the wrong horse, so far as both Irish necessity and Irish opinion were concerned. With all this, there would certainly be no return to the prosperous liberal partnership of the preceding decade.

II

On his arrival in Dublin, O'Connell had immediately grasped the significance of the already widespread second blight. Only nine days later he told Russell that the people of Cork 'are not merely menaced but actually engulfed' by starvation, and that 'there is the greatest danger of outbreaks . . . of the population driven to despair from the want of food'.[11] Instinctively, he slipped into the part of responsible landlord, which was to be his predominant approach to the Irish situation during his remaining months of life. On 27 August he pressed Maurice, at Derrynane, to make provision 'to meet the coming emergencies' on the estate, in particular, to store 'Indian corn' and 'American saved beef', which was 'cheap and good and would make excellent rations occasionally for the labourers'.[12] O'Connell's first-hand experience of the distress, when he reached Derrynane for his long vacation, increased his apprehension. After three weeks there, he told Fitzpatrick, 'It would be the absurdest of all absurd things to think of a Tribute in such times as these. They are indeed more awful than you have any notion of. All our thoughts are engrossed with the two topics – endeavouring to keep the people from outbreaks and endeavouring to get food for them. I tell you danger is in our path.'[13] Meanwhile O'Connell used his political weight on behalf of the suffering peasantry of Iveragh. Finding that the necessary public works sanctioned at the baronial presentments for the locality under the new Labour Rate Act had not begun because of administrative delays, and that by bureaucratic ineptitude the government meal depot for the area had been fixed at the impossibly distant Dingle, he put successful pressure on the new chief secretary, Henry Labouchere, to get wages and food moving at last towards the necessitous. So much was O'Connell caught up in the role of humane proprietor that he not only continued to demand a tax upon absentee landlords but also, on 25 September 1846, mooted the idea of joint action by the resident Irish gentry. The famine had become 'so all-absorbing a subject as to banish all politics unconnected with the distress'.[14] A fortnight later, he issued a public call for the formation of 'a central body of Irish landholders meeting in Dublin, and conferring with all parts of Ireland, as well as with the government'.[15] His prime objective was the extension of the provisions of the Labour Rate Act to reproductive works (that is, works benefitting individuals) instead of unreproductive only. Perhaps because of O'Connell's pressure, Bessborough, quite suddenly, allowed the extension. Thereupon O'Connell withdrew from his own initiative – prematurely as things turned out, for the new scheme was practically unworkable. At this stage, he was determined, almost to the point of obsession, to work hand-in-hand with both government and fellow-landlords rather than by mass-action, let alone agitation. In agreeing, on 13 October 1846, to a meeting at Fermoy with some of the co. Cork gentry, clergy and relief committee representatives, he wrote, 'It is scarcely necessary for me to add that my arrival in Fermoy should not be accompanied by any popular demonstration. Our meeting will be constituted by gentlemen of every sect and persuasion and of course should not be tinged by anything of a party or even a political nature.'[16] After he and the remainder of the Fermoy deputation, bearing their list of complaints and applications, had seen Bessborough and his officials on 30 October, O'Connell even expressed sympathy with the administrators of relief who had so many difficulties to contend with!

As befitted one 'standing above' party, O'Connell's range of favour-seekers extended far beyond his customary clientele during the autumn of 1846. He continued to advance his own family in a minor way, asking that Maurice be restored to the deputy-lieutenancy of co. Kerry and that his 'clansman and very dear friend',[17] Jeremiah O'Connell, receive the commission of the peace. Other applications for unknown young men were imperative because of their source. When his well-tried episcopal supporter, Browne, called on 'the father of our country' to seek an assistant barristership for 'the son-in-law of one of my oldest and dearest friends',[18] O'Connell could not but respond. Old Irelanders such as William O'Connell or Thomas Arkins pressed him to find government employment for their sons; he helped to secure a lunacy commission inspectorate for his family friend and personal physician, Dr John Nugent; and rank-and-file Repealers enlisted his aid to secure humble jobs at the disposal of the Post Office or Dublin Castle. But he was equally energetic on behalf of the sons of liberal or whig friends, or even tories. A Church of Ireland minister, a neighbour in Kerry, called confidently for his help in securing the transfer of a living, 'It strikes me now that you are on the spot [in Dublin], that an application from you to the Government would have a good effect.'[19] O'Connell also went to great pains to get an extended leave of absence for R. G. MacDonnell, the Chief Justice of Gambia, solely because of his friendship for his father, 'an old circuit companion of mine ... though ... a Protestant Parson and ... a wicked anti-Repealer'. In pressing this case on the colonial under-secretary, O'Connell concluded, 'You cannot imagine how much you would gratify and delight me if you could assist this young gentleman in his purposes. It will be conferring a great personal obligation upon me.'[20]

Thus O'Connell made little attempt to operate an informal spoils system – except to exclude from office, so far as he was able, Young Irelanders and malignant Orangemen. He openly welcomed the appointments of sympathetic non-Repealers (particularly Catholics) and lauded the government which advanced them. In O'Connell's eyes, at this point in the political cycle, each such appointment was regarded as an advance, however small, towards national self-government rather than the shameful acceptance of a whig douceur. 'It was said', he declared at the general Association meeting of 3 August,

> that there were a great many young men of talent – Repealers in principle – but who were afraid to join the Association lest they should thereby deprive themselves of the chance of obtaining the honors and dignities of their professions. (Hear, hear.) . . . Ought we not all be delighted that an opportunity should be given to such men to come amongst us? Ought we not to be grateful to the government that gives it, as we ought to vituperate the government that refuses it?[21]

Contrariwise, the seceders were denounced. 'Talk to me of the paltry Young Ireland party – faugh! There is only one man among them whose loss I regret – that is Smith O'Brien.'[22] Throughout August 1846 O'Connell attempted – publicly – to woo O'Brien back. But the condition which he laid down for the prodigal's return, unreserved concurrence 'in the principles of moral force and moral force alone',[23] seemed simultaneously to present a bar to its ever taking place. Moreover, O'Connell introduced another apple of discord when on 31 August he secured a resolution from the Association withdrawing Repeal Reading Room subscriptions to the *Nation*. Quoting recent editorials envisaging the use of physical force and constitutional separation from Great Britain, he added that

> whoever seeks to repeal a law by force – whoever incites to the use of physical force for such a purpose, is in point of law guilty of high treason. It would be most culpable in me, as counsel for the Association and people of Ireland, to enter into any compromise with the men who hold and preach up those physical force doctrines.
> They were guilty of no overt act, to be sure, and I am glad of it – they only endeavoured to incite others.[24]

That was the end of the malcontents so far as O'Connell was concerned: he now felt quite free to play the statesman.

For a considerable time, the Young Irelanders accepted the situation at O'Connell's valuation. They remained politically inert for more than two months after their withdrawal from Conciliation Hall. In fact, the first move on their behalf came not from any member of the inner group, but from Cane of Kilkenny who on 26 September wrote to Ray proposing that O'Connell make an attempt to win back the secessionists: the breach with Young Ireland, he believed, would ultimately destroy the Repeal movement. Cane was curtly dismissed by the Association's management; and no one in the *Nation* group followed up his initiative or took any step either to counter, or come to terms with, O'Connell during September–October 1846. They seemed content to adopt O'Brien's proposal to Duffy in October that 'a portion of the *Nation* [be] dedicated to . . . propaganda . . . with the bold heading "Young Ireland" over its leading column'.[25]

Once again however the terrific consequences of the Irish potato blight turned the course of events. From late September onwards, rapidly rising food prices and unemployment rates in the cities drove numbers of artisans and urban labourers into revolt against an Association now calling (against John O'Connell's and probably O'Connell's own better judgment) for 'PATIENCE, PEACE, AVOIDANCE OF CRIME, CONFIDENCE IN ALMIGHTY GOD, AND RESIGNATION TO HIS HOLY WILL'.[26] The most dangerous manifestation of insubordination was probably a Dublin 'remonstrance' presented to (but ignominiously rejected by) the Association on 26 October 1846, protesting against not only the suppression of free speech on the peace issue, but also O'Connell's collaboration with the whigs. Although the Old Irelander Arkins might dismiss the movers of the remonstrance as 'the low chartists and discontented of Dublin',[27] and Ray describe them as 'an assemblage of obscure creatures not half a dozen of whom do we know',[28] at least one-third of the Repeal wardens of the city were among the signatories. Meanwhile similar outbursts took place in Cork and Limerick during October, often with angry interchanges between the protestors and loyal O'Connellites. These may well have been an additional reason for O'Connell's insistence that his return progress from Derrynane to Dublin in late October be treated as a 'private' journey.

How was O'Connell to react to the implicit pressure, which all this contained, to seek a reconciliation with the Young Irelanders? The received account (mainly *per* Duffy) is of a faltering old man, in Dublin once again in November 1846, so impressed by the growing strength of the opposition as to sanction an approach to O'Brien and his friends – only to have his scheme dashed cruelly by his son John. Duffy 'quoted' an anonymous 'eye-witness' of the crucial scene as to O'Connell's final utterance, 'You see, Sir Colman [O'Loghlen], I am powerless; there is my best beloved son; you hear what he has said; nothing can now be done.'[29] It is true that O'Connell's immediate entourage was fiercely opposed to a *détente*, although John O'Connell did not speak quite so intransigently as Ray or Crean. But others of O'Connell's close friends, such as the much-respected O'Loghlen, were generally bent on reconciliation. Even O'Neill Daunt asked Smith O'Brien privately on 14 October 1846, 'is there no mode in which you can arrange your difference with Mr O'C[onnell], so as to work once more in the Conciliation Hall? . . . If you can manage to fulfil (as I trust and think you can) the earnest popular wish [that you do so], pray command me in any way in which I could aid in achieving a reunion.'[30] Moreover, O'Connell was well aware of the local pressures being placed on his supporters. In late November, for example, the parish priest of Kilkee, co. Clare, in recommending a young man spoke of him as still adhering to 'the old and experienced *pilot*' though 'strongly prompted by different influences to join the Young Ireland party'.[31] Thus, O'Connell was being pulled not in one but in two directions by his trusted followers. There seems no reason to believe that he was materially influenced by either section. In fact, there is no worthwhile evidence at all that he was as yet either incapable of or unwilling to form his own judgment, or that, until late November 1846, he ever wavered in his determination to ignore the secessionists and protesters.

On 20 November, however, one of O'Connell's most steadfast Repeal bishops, Blake of Dromore, intervened with an appeal for unity which could not be ignored. Blake's first letter (to O'Connell initially but meant to be read aloud later to the Association) has not survived; but its substance may be inferred from O'Connell's reply: 'Such a letter, coming from you and making light of the difference between us and the seceders, would be considered by the public and made use of by the seceders as an approval of their physical-force principles; as an approval, in short, of the illegality and treasonable nature of their principles.' O'Connell assured Blake that there was

> no practicable sacrifice that I would not make for the purpose of reconciliation . . . But there are things which I cannot do, and which you are certainly the last man living to advise me to do, namely, to sacrifice

principle and to risk and put in jeopardy the liberties and even the lives of all the members of the Association.

The point hinges upon this. We, the sincere Repealers, have placed the basis of our exertions on this: the carrying the Repeal by peaceable, legal and constitutional means and by *none other*. The seceders, on the contrary, insist that, in case we do not succeed by peaceable and legal means, we should reserve to ourselves the use in any favourable opportunity of the sword.

Now, my venerated Lord, I solemnly, as a lawyer of many years' standing, assure your Lordship, with the most perfect truth, that the plan of the seceders would, if we were to accede to or even tolerate it in the Association, involve every member of the Association, including your Lordship, in the guilt of high treason.[32]

O'Connell's consistency is worth noting here. For fully a year, ever since Mitchel's original 'indiscretion' of November 1845, he had held unwaveringly to the line that any endorsement, however remote or contingent, of physical force would destroy the Repeal organization. Moreover, he had always argued, the slightest countenancing of violence in Ireland would set in motion a process which could only end in blood.

Blake responded to O'Connell's desperate plea to withdraw his letter ('If I were in your presence, I would go on my knees to ask this favour'[33]) by substituting a milder version. Even this, however, called on O'Connell

> *to heal those dissensions which distract, and afflict, and strike with dismay the public mind*: and I hope that all *sincere* Repealers – and they are still very many, even *among the seceders* – will, ... meet your efforts for *reconciliation*, as acts of condescension on your part, and when re-entered into Conciliation Hall, will not only adhere inviolably to your peaceable course ... but will also strenuously ... second your glorious efforts.[34]

Such strong pressure called for some response from O'Connell, all the more so as, by now, the pitiful inadequacy of the government's efforts to halt the spread of disease and starvation over the west and south was manifest. O'Connell would soon have to distance himself – to a degree, at least – from Russell's execrated administration; in addition to its mishandling of the famine crisis, it had rejected out of hand any amendment of the Colleges Act, to which the clerical Repealers still attached first importance. In fact, some of the more forward of the Young Irelanders (who as a group remained even yet wedded to political 'education' rather than political action) had begun to fear that O'Connell would 'scoop' them by abandoning the whigs and launching a national campaign against the ineffectuality and parsimony of the official measures.

A public meeting called by the Dublin 'remonstrants' on 2 December 1846 proved the final turn of the screw for O'Connell. After passing several now-familiar anti-O'Connellite motions, the meeting, which attracted some Young Ireland attendance, resolved to re-assemble in January with the purpose of forming an independent repeal movement. O'Connell responded immediately to this threat. At the next general meeting of the Association (7 December) he deplored the gross failure of the government to cope with the Irish crisis, and proposed the constitution of a national front to press immediate reforms upon parliament and the cabinet. In particular, he called for a junction of the Irish gentry and middle classes and he proposed that a representative committee should consider and try to resolve the whole disputed issue of the peace resolutions. O'Connell had seized the initiative. It was he who emerged as generous and magnanimous in the public estimation.

Divided between those who believed that O'Connell's overture was genuine and those who suspected him of seeking to entrap them, and between those who wished to bargain frankly and those who insisted that every grievance of theirs be met, the Young Irelanders fared ill when their delegates met O'Connell on 15 December 1846. The negotiations quickly failed, but O'Connell retained whatever credit for large-mindedness survived. Although he laid down that the peace resolutions must be accepted (or at least legally adjudicated) before any other item was discussed, he 'conceded' that the peace issue might be limited to Anglo-Irish relations. Contrariwise, the Young Irelanders simply presented a long list of demands, among them, a prohibition on the acceptance of government places; complete freedom of discussion within the Association; the exclusion of paid officers from, and the reconstitution of, its committee; the regular publication of its accounts; the restoration of the *Nation* to Repeal Reading Rooms; and neutrality on 'sectarian' issues. The Young Irelanders were, not altogether unfairly, seen as asking for the impossible – unconditional surrender; and initially at least, they bore the brunt of the blame for the continuance of disunion in the repeal ranks.

It must not be forgotten, however, that reunion with the seceders was, even if sincerely sought, a secondary matter for O'Connell. His primary objectives, as he had developed them at the Association meeting of 7 December 1846, were to arouse the world at large to a knowledge of the frightful character of the Irish calamity and to produce a combination of the Irish gentry to confront Russell's government. This is made clear by O'Connell's draft letter of 10 December to the editor F. W. Conway, seeking to enlist the aid of the *Dublin Evening Post* 'to arouse the fears and excite the attention of the resident landed proprietors of Ireland. They are by no means sufficiently alive to the horrible state of the country.' O'Connell felt warranted in calling on them 'to meet, to consult, to deliberate' at once. As he predicted, with dreadful accuracy, Ireland was only at the threshold of her horrors.

> A NATION, it is starving. If there be any exceptions, they are so few and so far between that they are not worth mentioning or being noticed. I repeat, the nation is starving, and to the all-prevalent famine is now superadded dysentery and typhus in their worst shapes. Nothing can be more appalling than the spread of these diseases. The typhus is setting in in its worst shape.[35]

Oppressed by this black awareness of the impending catastrophe, O'Connell paid scant attention to Repeal or conventional politics of any kind after 15 December. Instead, he was (he believed) his country's last best hope as a rallying-point for the critically important landed classes, as well as for the nation as a whole.

O'Connell had been forced back briefly into domestic politics as the inadequacy of the government's response to the famine, and the threat of an independent repeal movement, became unmistakable. Even then, he had deplored rather than denounced the meagreness of Russell's measures, and striven to present the nationalist division as a legal rather than a political issue. 'I stand altogether upon the law', he told the Young Irelander, T. D. Reilly, just before the negotiations of 15 December, 'My sole difficulty rests upon the legal objection to the admission of the seceders.' In the same letter, while offering to seek and abide by other eminent counsels' opinion, he set out his argument succinctly:

> I take these propositions to be clear in law: – First: That any assembly admitting any species of physical force as part of its means of obtaining a repeal of an Act of Parliament is an unlawful assembly, liable to be dispersed by any magistrate, and its members punished by indictment.
>
> Secondly: That any such assembly is not only unlawful, but that any acts done by it in furtherance of its objects constitute a treasonable fact, rendering the members liable to conviction and execution for treason . . .
>
> It follows, if I be right, that the seceders cannot safely be admitted into

the Repeal Association unless upon the fullest and most explicit disclaimer of resorting to any physical force means to achieve the Repeal of the Union.

In order to be enabled to receive the seceders into the Association again it should be ascertained whether, beyond a doubt, I am right in point of law or not.[36]

After the negotiations failed, O'Connell attempted to keep the matter on the same neutral ground. On 17 December he reiterated to Smith O'Brien his 'professional' opinion that the 'physical force question' involved the personal safety of the Association's members.

I should vote for the readmission ... of very many of the seceders if they would disavow the physical force principle; or if, without that disavowal, the Association would still be a legal assembly ... it was to ascertain this point, and this alone, that I proposed the legal conference as a preliminary step to a complete conciliation.[37]

The seceders, divided before the meeting with O'Connell, were at one afterwards in proclaiming him to have been disingenuous. Mitchel declared, 'I never for one moment believed the proposal to be *bona fide*'[38] and Duffy described it as 'a move which had for its object solely to put us in the wrong'.[39] Certainly, O'Connell's 'move' had served his immediate interest. It was he who could present himself to the people as the spurned bearer of the olive branch. But this is not necessarily to say that his conduct was deceitful. That any step, even a rhetorical leaning, towards physical force would endanger the Repeal movement had been (as we have seen) his *idée fixe* from the beginning. Age and frailty could only have tightened his grip upon his supposed security. Moreover, he had put his bargaining position to the hazard. None of the four counsel – O'Hagan, O'Hea, O'Loghlen and Dillon – to whom he proposed to refer the legal issue was a 'servile' O'Connellite, or even (apart from O'Loghlen) an especial friend. It was not inconceivable that the seceding faction might have accepted his nominations for the adjudicating panel or even that, in due course, the joint opinion of the panel might have run counter to his 'professional' interpretation. At any rate, whether and in whatever proportion O'Connell intermixed guile and candour, he certainly strove to minimize his own *political* involvement, and resumed, as rapidly as he could, his role as high priest of a stricken people.

Apart from a few sad, unmeaning genuflections to Repeal – such as, 'How different would the scene be if we had our own Parliament, taking care of our people, of our own resources!'[40] – his sole significant foray into politics proper from then on was undertaken, characteristically, in the cause of Catholic equality. On 22 January 1847 he complained to the new Irish lord chancellor, Brady, that the Dublin magistracy was almost entirely Protestant in composition, adding 'I respectfully submit to your Lordship the propriety of a prompt measure to remedy this grievance.'[41] Brady, whose elevation owed something to O'Connell's good offices, dutifully complied. Almost all the Dublin magistrates appointed during 1847 were Catholics, probably drawn from the list which O'Connell had attached to his submission. There was a certain fitness in his final specifically political excursion being 'Emancipatory'.

III

Technically, O'Connell was himself an absentee landlord throughout 1846 except for a few weeks in the early autumn. His proprietorship was exercised through the resident Maurice. Maurice was also his agent, John Primrose Jr having been replaced some time before, still owing O'Connell a considerable sum on the estate accounts. Possibly Primrose was removed, not for inefficiency, but in order to prepare Maurice for the management of his succession. If so, O'Connell left little to his son's discretion, even though he sensed by the beginning of October 1846 that his end was near.

It was ironic that O'Connell, who had suffered his uncle Hunting Cap's domination for almost half a century, should have meted out much the same treatment to his eldest son, albeit with counterbalancing affection. Maurice, forty-three years old in 1846, was still painfully subservient to as well as dependent on his father. By another irony, O'Connell, who had lived for at least two decades in a Brazilian jungle of unmet obligations and overdue promissory notes, now harangued his son ceaselessly on the evils of accepting bills. Unfortunately for Maurice, O'Connell had a case. 'Don't conceal from me the fact', he wrote to Maurice on 19 August 1846, 'if you have been accepting accommodation bills for any person, and in any event I do most strongly insist that you will not accept an accommodation bill for any person, without my express permission.'[42] Over the next three months, both from Dublin and at Derrynane, O'Connell badgered the wretched Maurice for a full account of his indebtedness. 'I cannot think you would equivocate with me',[43] he told him on 5 November —doubtless meaning the opposite. Maurice's reply tells its own sad story of his father's domination:

I am sufficiently blameable for my conduct with regard to those bills, without any addition particularly of the charge of seeking to deceive you. The bill of Ally [Alice] Primrose's you allude to was mentioned in my letters ... I mentioned it to you *here*. I stated it to you in the very commencement of this unhappy business. Most assuredly I had and have no design of deceiving you, and in this instance the evidence is multiplied that such could not be my intention.

With regard to my letter from *Hillgrove* [John Primrose's house] I neither drew nor accepted any bill, nor took a pen in my hand [there] at all unless to write unlucky [*sic*] letter to you ...[44]

Evidently Maurice's bills (according to one list which may have been incomplete) amounted to almost £2000, and O'Connell forbade him ever to accept another 'without letting me know it while I live'.[45] As a melancholy coda bearing witness to the unhappy relationship between the two, we may add Maurice's reply when, after O'Connell's death, one of his executors refused to sanction a heavy expenditure he had proposed: 'I have been too long trained to suppress and sacrifice my own feelings, in order to give way to my dear father's wishes and orders, to suffer much from my struggle against them at present.'[46]

As one might guess from this, O'Connell was no 'absentee' in spirit, but a most exacting principal when managing his property from a distance. Even before the end of August 1846, he upbraided Maurice harshly for not keeping him *au fait* with the state of the potato crop at home and the steps which he was taking 'to meet the coming emergencies';[47] at the same time he ordered reserves of provisions to be fetched from Cork by the family sloop. During his month's stay at Derrynane, O'Connell busied himself with local relief work and the sanctioning of a pier or breakwater to be built close by his house. The distress which he witnessed on every side drove all else – at least temporarily – from his mind. Even after his return to Dublin on 28 October, it continued to obsess him. Government acquiescence in his initiatives did not necessarily mean government action. Maurice had, for example, to complain to him on 18 November,

The outcry for work at Cahir[civeen] continues still loud and vehement and the orders of the Board of Works are, I understand, causing fresh impediments, the last 'ukase' being that no one who has the grass of a cow is to get labour. This would confine the market indeed in this district. All are nearly equally without provisions, and though the cowless creature may be something lower in the scale, yet the wants of the others are equally pressing. The result of all these changeable orders, all nearly equally ridiculous, is delay and while the Board are balancing straws, the people starve.[48]

O'Connell settled this – so far as it could be settled at the mere centre of bureaucracy – by calling on the Board in Dublin and obtaining an immediate assurance that the 'ukase' was quite unauthorized.[49] This was typical of the fashion in which he used his own standing to inaugurate, expedite or sustain official relief measures in his own barony. Regarding him now as the great bulwark against peasant violence, the Irish administration certainly jumped when O'Connell cracked the whip. He secured British naval transport to carry his own food purchases to Cahirciveen in December; and it was only with lengthy and laborious apology that the Board rejected his extra-ordinary request to purchase the entire government supply of meal and biscuit at its depot in the town. Meanwhile, to the end of 1846 and into 1847 he maintained his barrage of minute instructions to Maurice for both immediate action and preparation for the still more fearful future. Characteristically, these included such peremptory admoni-tions as: 'Take care to have the accounts most accurately kept. Go through the form of giving a ticket to every man employed, and give it previous [to] or on the day of his beginning to work. Be vigilant in matter of form as well as in substance.'[50]

O'Connell was torn between his own increasing impoverishment and the calls of the needy on and about his property. Following the initial rise in the Repeal Rent after the secession of 2 July, it fell away almost to nothing, and O'Connell was compelled to make capital payments from his own resources in order to keep the organization in being. On 16 October Ray thanked him for a draft for £453; he added that the 'balance [in the "account" between O'Connell and the Association] must by this time be very much in your favour and I am uneasy lest you may be inconvenienced by advances. Still, without drawing upon you we cannot go on.'[51] O'Connell had moreover to offer abatement of rents even though it was from rents that Maurice's debts were meant, in the first instance, to be paid. The Derrynane food stores also tied up capital, and these would be sold below cost price at whatever the labourers could afford at the time of sale. Though O'Connell attempted to strike the right balance in his injunctions, he almost always came down finally on the side of mercy. 'I wish you to be as abundant to the people as you possibly can, recollecting however that we have dreadful times before us',[52] he ended his letter to Maurice of 5 December. A few days later, he wrote in one of his last surviving instructions to his son, 'Of course, you should get as much money as you possibly can for corn and bread. If it were nothing else but to help you to pay off the rascally bills. But I know you will not be harsh to the people.'[53]

From mid-August 1846, when the widespread failure of the potato crop became certain, O'Connell's 'politics' tended to be his experiences of and at Derrynane writ large. The prospect of famine (and behind it the spectre of food riots, social disorder and bloodshed) dwarfed all else; and the government, with its power to say yea or nay to the creation of employment, and its command of money and administrative machinery, became the treasury of last resort rather than a body to be coaxed or bullied politically in the normal way. Correspondingly, O'Connell's domestic politics wore the air of *de haut en bas* in place of his customary popular mobilization. He spoke for and attempted to weld together the 'responsible' classes (and especially those with specific responsibilities for their properties such as himself) to engage the common enemy, mass starvation. It is true that he used his own peculiar influence (at this stage) with the Irish administration largely in the interests of his native barony – and possibly at the expense of other districts. But this emblemized his personalization – in every sense – of the great crisis, and represented, in his eyes, the behaviour proper to every dutiful and feeling master of the fates of others. Truckling to the whigs seemed now an empty charge: to whom should not one truckle if it meant the saving of human lives?

IV

After the abortive negotiations of 15 December 1846 – and despite the setting up at last of a rival Young Ireland political organization, the Irish Confederation, on 13 January 1847 – the popular suffering became once more, and remained, O'Connell's engrossing public interest. He stayed in Dublin until the end of January, still attempting to muster the property of Ireland, and (through Bessborough) the Irish executive, in the cause of much larger and more urgent relief. It was London, however, that commanded the resources; and O'Connell, despite his confession to Fitzpatrick on 11 January 1847 that 'he felt himself gradually failing in bodily strength',[54] decided on an appeal in person to the House of Commons. His hope (if he really had hoped) was immediately extinguished. He wrote to Ray from London on 6 February that

> there is, alas! but little prospect of substantial relief on that enormously large scale which is absolutely necessary to prevent hundreds of thousands of the Irish people from perishing of *famine and pestilence* . . .
> I trust in God that my health will enable me to take that active part which

I desire on behalf of the famishing people. I intend, please God, on Monday [8 February], in sadness and sorrow, to develope my views of what is necessary to save Ireland. The obstacles in the House of Commons are manifold, and there seems to be an ignorance of the real state of horror in which Ireland is plunged. How I wish that it were possible to make Parliament comprehend the enormous and hideous extent of the calamity which cries for a remedy.[55]

Three days later he confirmed to Fitzpatrick that there was 'every reason to despond', adding, however, 'If it be in my power I shall say a few words this evening.'[56] It was barely in his power. He could scarcely stand in the House for trembling, or be heard even in the total silence of a pitying respect. At last he cast himself – as his British mockers had long cast him – as the Big Beggarman. In effect, he held out his hands for alms. He attempted no argument, attributed no blame, threw his country upon the mercy of its foes. The Irish people, the report of his speech ran,

> were starving in shoals, in hundreds – aye, in thousands and millions. Parliament was bound, then, to act not only liberally but generously – to find out the means of putting a stop to this terrible disaster . . . He had not said one word to produce irritation – he had not uttered one word of reproach . . . She [Ireland] was in their hands – in their power. If they did not save her, she could not save herself. He solemnly called on them to recollect that he predicted with the sincerest conviction, that one-fourth of her population would perish unless Parliament came to their relief.[57]

O'Connell's terrible prophecy was fulfilled. If famine-induced emigration is added to famine-induced mortality in making the computation, over two million Irish persons 'perished' in the years 1845–52.

O'Connell made one last call on Lord John Russell – again a mendicant, but this time on behalf of his faithful, but now bereft, Fitzpatrick. He won the promise of a sinecure, the assistant registrarship of deeds in Dublin, a promise that was honoured later when the government could arrange for the current incumbent to retire on full salary. This was part of the process of winding up his life, which O'Connell had begun already when he told Fitzpatrick of his anxiety 'to settle some matters that might cause difficulty in the event of his death'.[58] He was powerless to make better provision for his children. Pierce Mahony, who was trustee for certain of his property, attempted to improve the family's prospects by some form of settlement backed by the further insurance of O'Connell's life. O'Connell was cut to the quick by this *bêtise*. His life, he replied, was 'certainly not insurable'; Mahony should never have presented him with 'such a document . . . I have neither health nor money to embark in the transaction'.[59] Early in February 1847, he added a codicil to his will reducing his bequest to the Repeal Association from £1000 to £630; the bequest carried the pathetic rider, 'I implore that it may be received ... as in full satisfaction of any demand that body may or could have on me. In short that if more be in anywise due of me that it may be fully and freely remitted to me so as to leave no kind of debt to the association weighing on my soul.'[60] Two and a half weeks later, O'Connell sent Fitzpatrick his final instructions about the disposition of his assets, including the sale of 'another' £1000 of stock. 'My illness', he went on, 'is very expensive, and the times are indeed bad.' The scatter of orders to his trusted agent included, apparently, the destruction of his mementos of Rose McDowell. O'Connell told Fitzpatrick that he would find in the 'standing desk in my bedchamber ... a correspondence with a lady which you may read yourself because it contains nothing disreputable. Of course, when you have read it, destroy it.'[61] Nothing, it seems, survived of Mary except the caches of loving letters.

O'Connell began his next letter to Fitzpatrick, 'They deceive themselves, and consequently deceive you, who tell you I am recovering';[62] earlier he had written, 'Poor Nugent is so anxious to have me well that he mistakes his wishes for his opinions.' At first O'Connell had hoped to regain his homeland before he died and in particular to be 'within the reach of [the Rev] Dr Miley', his friend and confessor. 'But', he added despairingly, 'that is idle as I am not strong enough to return to Ireland in such weather as this.'[63] Within a few days, however, the convergence of his physicians' wish that he should seek a warmer climate, a pious scheme that he make a pilgrimage to the Holy City, and Fitzpatrick's tactful application to Archbishop Murray that Miley be released to act as chaplain on the way, issued in a plan to take O'Connell, by easy stages, to Rome. O'Connell was overjoyed at Miley's 'kind, kind' acquiescence. On 16 February, he asked Fitzpatrick to make 'with him whatever arrangements are the most suitable and the most respectful for his coming over here. I would not hurry him but the sooner he finds it his convenience to come, infinitely the better ... Of course you will insist upon his accepting the full amount of his expenses on the journey.'[64] When he reached London, however, Miley discovered that it was spiritual comfort that O'Connell sought rather than a chaplain for a pilgrimage which he was now most reluctant to undertake. Miley joined forces with the physicians in cajoling him to go. Meanwhile he reported, 'Prayer is his [O'Connell's] only occupation. It is at once most edifying and affecting to witness his demeanour in this respect, not alone by day, but by night also. He is perfectly prepared for death, and had rather not be diverted from the thought of it.'[65] Not until 6 March did O'Connell leave London, and even then it was merely to repair to Hastings to build up his strength for the journey being urged upon him. There the sun broke through and his spirits lightened; he recalled that several of the O'Connells had passed ninety years of age; and calls of courtesy from leading English Catholics were at least diverting, if all too patently valedictory. But there were also signs of occasional agitation. On 12 March, for example, he added two codicils to his will on a single day. Later, Fitzpatrick and Christopher Fitz-Simon arrived at Hastings to bid farewell and accompany O'Connell on the first stage of what would be a *via dolorosa* – to Folkestone where he was to embark on the cross-channel steamer on 22 March. 'O'Connell', Fitzpatrick reported to his sister, 'is very reluctant now to travel, except by railway, [but] this comparatively short drive will be so rapidly accomplished that I trust he will be sufficiently reconciled to it.'[66] Before O'Connell took ship, he 'gave me [Fitzpatrick] his blessing, designating me "the best of *all* his friends" '.[67] It was a long- and hard-earned reward. As a political enemy had once observed, Fitzpatrick 'was the tortoise that sustained the elephant that sustained the world of Irish agitation'.[68]

When O'Connell had last crossed the English Channel in 1823, it had been alone – but to join his wife and children to holiday in Paris. Now he was supported by Miley, his son Daniel and his manservant Duggan – but had only a destination, and no meaningful aim, in view. It was as if O'Connell were attempting to run from death – or, rather, as if his guardsmen were hurrying him ahead of a pursuing doom. The 'frequent, though not continuous, fits of depression',[69] which Fitzpatrick had noted even while O'Connell was in Hastings, deepened after he reached France. An abbé who waited on him in Boulogne was struck by his unremitting gloom. The travel itself, however – by steamer on a flat-calm sea and on short runs by rail – was comparatively easy until Paris was reached on 26 March 1847. There at last homage could be paid, in person, to the avatar of Liberal Catholicism on the Continent. Archbishop Affre of Paris (destined to die on the barricades in the Revolution of 1848) called on him at his hotel in the rue de Rivoli. So too did a deputation from the celebrated Society for the Defence of Religious Freedom. Montalembert, who led it, read the tribute.

We are come to salute in you the Liberator of Ireland – of that nation which has always excited in France fraternal feelings. But you are not only *the Man of one Nation*, you are the Man of all *Christendom*. Your glory is not only Irish; it is Catholic. Wherever Catholics begin anew to practise civic virtues, and devote themselves to the conquest of their legislative rights under God, it is your work. Wherever religion tends to emancipate itself from the thraldom in which several generations of sophists and lawyers have placed it, to you, after God, it is indebted.

In his weakness, O'Connell answered that he was almost silenced 'by sickness and emotion', and could only say that the demonstration of respect was 'one of the most significant events of my life'.[70] It was also the last public happening. How ironic that the European accolades, dammed up for quarter of a century, should have fallen in the end on indifferent ears and a mind absorbed by imminent demise.

From Paris on, travel had to be by road. The dragging of the dying man, over a five-week period, to Marseilles became increasingly macabre. At the Lapalise stage, near Vichy, Fr Miley reported on 8 April to Fitzpatrick that

> his strength, his appetite, and his spirits are daily sinking. For me to attempt any description of the harrowing anxieties I endure under these most depressing circumstances would be utterly vain. Some nights I do not undress at all. Just now, being much depressed, having headache and indigestion, I went out, while Daniel and Duggan were both with him. I was not away twenty minutes, and, when returning, I was met by two messengers, and coming into the room found him in the greatest alarm at my absence. In fact, I cannot be out of his sight a moment.[71]

At Lyons, where the journey was broken for eleven days, O'Connell recovered sufficiently to walk abroad on a few occasions. But, lost in despondency, he seemed scarcely to notice the reverential crowds who followed him; he made no answer to their expressions of sympathy or admiration. It was Miley who bore the brunt of the misery about this time. 'Never have I had such a struggle', he wrote from Lyons on 16 April,

> as from 2 to 4 o'clock last night to keep him in bed or prevent the alarm being given to the whole hotel. At the moment it would have been most unfortunate that any but his own should have seen him . . .
>
> The doctors give hope, but so terrible are his mental agitations, so pertinaciously does he cling to the most gloomy ideas and prospects, that it is next to a miracle that either mind or body can hold out against it. I fear I am myself beginning to sink. Even by day I cannot leave him to walk in the open air for fifteen minutes; as for the night, all its griefs and terrors are on

me, for he will not be satisfied unless I am by his bed; and by day and by night nothing will he ever hear or speak or think of for a moment but his own maladies and misfortunes.[72]

Marseilles was reached on 2 May 1847, and Genoa, by sea, three days later. There after a brief flare of better health and spirits, O'Connell collapsed, physically and mentally. A fearful consciousness of the past and terror of the coming judgment destroyed his nights; by day he was ceaselessly agitated. His entourage, and Miley in particular, pressed him vainly to move on to Rome. Miley complained angrily to Fitzpatrick that the solemn 'compact' which O'Connell had made with him at Hastings, in Fitzpatrick's presence – namely, to throw 'his own mighty will' into the effort of attaining the final goal – was being broken. 'And yet', wrote Miley, 'so entirely unworthy of him does it appear to me, that I cannot and will not abandon the hope . . . of yet persuading him.'[73] This was not perhaps as wantonly blind or cruel as it might seem for the Genoese doctors had (like their French counterparts) spoken initially of improvement. But by 8 May O'Connell's state was desperate. He ceased to eat. Intermittently he became delirious. He shouted defiance of a phantasmagoric Peel and exulted that Repeal was safely in his box. Duggan's diary entry for 11 May reads: 'Asked me had Mr Wyse brought forward his motion and who seconded it. That Wyse was mad, and to call him there be a division. No food: worse to-day.'[74] He begged Duggan repeatedly to make sure that he was dead before he allowed him to be buried. In between O'Connell clung to Miley for reassurance. Then, forty-eight hours before he died, calm fell on him, and thenceforward he spoke (wrote Miley) only of 'his eternal interests and the bright hopes of eternity'. At 2 am on 15 May 1847 he received the last sacrament in a scene worthy of the brush of Goya though it received nothing better than an ill-drawn oleograph.

The Cardinal Archbishop [of Genoa] having been confined to his bed ever since our arrival here (he is eighty-eight years old), the vicar-general, attended by his curates and the clerics of his church, and followed by several of the faithful, though it was the dead of night, carried the adorable viaticum with the solemnities customary in Catholic countries, and reposed it in the tabernacle, which we had prepared in the chamber of the illustrious sufferer. The Liberator joined fervently and as audibly as his exhausted powers would permit in the prayers which we had been reciting for an hour before . . . he was perfectly in possession of his mind while receiving the last rites . . . his hands were clasped in prayer, except when he stretched them out to receive the sacred unction.[75]

At 9.35 pm that evening O'Connell died. By 9.35 pm many hundreds of other Irish people had died on 15 May 1847. Most had perished of the direct or indirect effects of the great famine, which in another sense had also borne O'Connell down. It made no difference in the grave.

> Scepter and crown
> Must tumble down,
> And in the dust be equal made
> With the poor crooked scythe and spade.[76]

But perhaps the poor starved ones had been the luckier. O'Connell had had to die publicly over many weeks. His priest, and his son and servant, formed a grotesque species of immediate audience. Their surrounding presence led him on to express, instead of consuming inwardly, his terrors and to indulge in an abasing scrupulosity and despair, which his companions must strive to counter. But even this course may have had its natural, to say nothing of any other, use. On 14 May, Miley wrote that O'Connell 'has been long prepared for death; he has *familiarized* himself with the contemplation of his last end'.[77] This may have been the necessary cost-price for his final hours of quiet and submission.

Towards the end, he asked that his heart be sent to Rome. So it was, encased in a silver urn. Symbolically, this seems quite wrong. It should surely have been laid in the Irish ground from which it had drawn, and to which it gave back so much.

References

CHAPTER 1
A Sort of Plateau
1830

1 1 March 1831, M. R. O'Connell (ed.), *The Correspondence of Daniel O'Connell* (Dublin, 1972-80), vol. iv, p. 131.
2 O'Connell to Mary O'Connell, 2 June 1831, ibid., p. 328.
3 W. T. Fagan, *The Life and Times of Daniel O'Connell* (Cork, 1847-8), vol. ii, pp. 179-80.
4 O'Connell to Mary O'Connell, 28 Nov. 1800, O'Connell, *Correspondence*, vol. i, p. 34.
5 [13 March 1832], ibid., vol. iv, p. 404.
6 Mary O'Connell to O'Connell [17 March 1830], ibid., p. 141.
7 [1] and 2 March [1830], ibid., pp. 130-1, 133.
8 24 July [1830], ibid., p. 191.
9 'Her affections were remarkable for feminine strength and fervour. Her intellect was of a masculine order, and good sense was its chief attribute.' Fagan, *Life and Times of O'Connell*, op. cit., vol. ii, p. 582.
10 2 March [1830], O'Connell, *Correspondence*, vol. iv, pp. 132-3.
11 [17 March 1830], ibid., p. 140.
12 [1 Dec. 1830], ibid., p. 240.
13 26 May 1831, ibid., p. 326.
14 2 June 1831, ibid., pp. 327-8.
15 5 Dec. 1830, ibid., pp. 242-3.
16 W. J. O'N. Daunt, *Personal Recollections of the late Daniel O'Connell M.P.* (London, 1848), vol. i, p. 250.
17 O'Connell to Mary O'Connell, 2 March 1831, O'Connell, *Correspondence*, vol. iv, p. 283.
18 O'Connell to Mary O'Connell, 28 Feb. 1831, ibid., pp. 281-2.
19 10 March 1831, ibid., p. 290.
20 [5 March 1831], ibid., p. 286.
21 26 May 1831, ibid., p. 326.
22 O'Connell to Richard Barrett, 29 Oct. 1832, ibid., p. 461.
23 14 Dec. 1839, ibid., p. 291.
24 Fagan, *Life and Times of O'Connell*, op. cit., vol. ii, pp. 626-7.
25 W. H. Curran, *Sketches of the Irish Bar; with Essays, Literary and Political* (London, 1855), vol. i, pp. 172-4.
26 *Freeman's Journal*, 29 Oct. 1829.
27 ibid., 2 Nov. 1829.
28 ibid., 29 Oct. 1829.
29 M. MacDonagh, *The Life of Daniel O'Connell* (London, 1903), p. 204.
30 *Freeman's Journal*, 29 Oct. 1829.
31 ibid., 3 Nov. 1829.
32 ibid., 2 Nov. 1829.
33 ibid., 3 Nov. 1829.
34 MacDonagh, *Life of O'Connell*, op. cit., p. 204.
35 *Freeman's Journal*, 29 Oct. 1829.
36 10 May 1830, O'Connell, *Correspondence*, vol. iv, p. 163.
37 24 June 1830, ibid., p. 175.
38 Aug. 1830, ibid., pp. 194-5.
39 Jane Austen, *Mansfield Park* (London, 1948), ch. 34, pp. 277-8.
40 Daunt, *Personal Recollections*, op. cit., vol. ii, p. 44.
41 ibid., vol. i, pp. 127-8.
42 O'Connell to P. V. Fitzpatrick, 4 Sept. 1837, O'Connell, *Correspondence*, vol. vi, p. 84.
43 Seamus MacCall, *Thomas Moore* (London, 1935), p. 101.
44 15 March 1820, O'Connell, *Correspondence*, vol. ii, p. 243.

45 A. Houston, *Daniel O'Connell: His Early Life, and Journal, 1795 to 1802* (London, 1906), pp. 119–20.

46 16 Feb. 1830, O'Connell, *Correspondence*, vol. iv, p. 129.

47 11 Sept. 1829, ibid., p. 95.

48 *Hansard*, n.s. vol. xxii, col. 799.

49 ibid., n.s. vol. xxiv, col. 794.

50 13 July 1833, *Daniel O'Connell Upon American Slavery* (New York, 1860), p. 47.

51 *Liberator*, 7 Aug. 1840, quoted in Gilbert Osofsky, 'Abolitionists, Irish Immigrants, and the Dilemmas of Romantic Nationalism', *American Historical Review*, vol. 80, no. 4, Oct. 1975, p. 893.

52 *Liberator*, 6 Dec. 1839, quoted in Osofsky, 'Abolitionists, Irish Immigrants, and the Dilemmas of Romantic Nationalism', op. cit., p. 892.

53 Osofsky, 'Abolitionists, Irish Immigrants, and the Dilemmas of Romantic Nationalism', op. cit., p. 891.

54 17 June 1840, O'Connell, *Correspondence*, vol. vi, p. 337.

55 20 June 1840, ibid., pp. 338–40.

56 W. E. Gladstone, 'Daniel O'Connell', *Nineteenth Century*, vol. 25, no. 143, Jan. 1889, pp. 156–7.

57 11 Sept. 1829, O'Connell, *Correspondence*, vol. iv, p. 95.

58 J. O'Connell (ed.), *The Select Speeches of Daniel O'Connell M.P.* (Dublin, 1867), vol. i, p. 376.

59 M. F. Cusack (ed.), *The Speeches and Public Letters of the Liberator* (Dublin, 1875), vol. ii, p. 285.

60 Daunt, *Personal Recollections*, op. cit., vol. i, p. 76.

61 ibid., p. 156.

62 ibid., p. 78.

63 O'Connell to the Ministers and Office-Bearers of the Wesleyan Methodist Societies of Manchester, 1 Aug. 1839, *Freeman's Journal*, 5 Aug. 1839.

64 O'Connell to Christopher Fitz-Simon, 11 Sept. 1830, O'Connell, *Correspondence*, vol. iv, pp. 203–5.

65 Pope Gregory XVI, 'Mirari vos', 15 Aug. 1832, in Colman J. Barry (ed.), *Readings in Church History* (Westminster, 1965), vol. iii, p. 41.

66 O'Connell to a friend in Rome, 1837, O'Connell, *Correspondence*, vol. vi, p. 1.

67 Daunt, *Personal Recollections*, op. cit., vol. i, p. 75.

68 Helen Coldrick, 'Daniel O'Connell and Religious Freedom', PhD thesis, Fordham University, 1974, p. 106.

69 13 Feb. 1838, *Hansard*, 3rd series, vol. xl, cols 1085–6.

70 ibid., col. 1097.

71 ibid., col. 1086.

72 T. Moore, 'The Song of O'Ruark', *The Poetical Works of Thomas Moore*, (ed.) Willia:.. Rossetti (London, [1882]), p. 367.

CHAPTER 2

The Houseman

1830–1

1 C. Greville, *The Greville Memoirs; a journal of the reigns of King George IV and King William IV*, (ed.) H. Reeve (London, 1875), vol. ii, p. 100.

2 March 1833, A. Aspinall (ed.), *Three Early Nineteenth Century Diaries* (London, 1952), p. 314.

3 O'Connell to James Sugrue, 21 May 1829, O'Connell, *Correspondence*, vol. iv, p. 67.

4 4 Feb. 1830, *Hansard*, n.s. vol. xxii, col. 94.

5 O'Connell to Charles Sugrue, 20 May 1829, O'Connell, *Correspondence*, vol. iv, p. 63.

6 Greville, *Greville Memoirs; journal of reigns of King George IV and*

King William IV, op. cit., vol. i, p. 275.

7 9 Feb. 1830, O'Connell, *Correspondence*, vol. iv, p. 124.

8 11 Feb. 1830, Lord Broughton (J. C. Hobhouse), *Recollections of a Long Life, with additional extracts from his private diaries*, (ed.) Lady Dorchester (London, 1909–11), vol. iv, p. 8.

9 Fagan, *Life and Times of O'Connell*, op. cit., vol. ii, p. 315.

10 *Dublin Evening Post*, 18 Jan. 1827, quoted in F. O'Ferrall, 'O'Connellite Politics and Political Education', PhD thesis, Trinity College, Dublin, 1978, p. 310.

11 O'Connell to C. Sinclair Cullen, 16 Feb. 1830, O'Connell, *Correspondence*, vol. iv, p. 130.

12 Richard Scott to O'Connell, 24 April 1830, ibid., p. 156.

13 *Dublin Evening Post*, 29 June 1830.

14 25 June 1830, O'Connell, *Correspondence*, vol. iv, p. 177.

15 21 April 1830, ibid., p. 155.

16 24 June 1830, ibid., p. 175.

17 20 April 1830, ibid., p. 154.

18 O'Connell to Richard Barrett, 8 July 1830, ibid., p. 187.

19 ibid.

20 P. V. Fitzpatrick to O'Connell, 3 Oct. 1830, ibid., p. 212.

21 O'Connell to R. N. Bennett, 5 Oct. 1830, ibid., p. 213.

22 *Freeman's Journal*, 12 Oct. 1830.

23 11 Oct. 1830, O'Connell, *Correspondence*, vol. iv, pp. 213–14.

24 Fagan, *Life and Times of O'Connell*, op. cit., vol. ii, p. 54.

25 *Freeman's Journal*, 20 Oct. 1830.

26 *Dublin Evening Post*, 30 Oct. 1830.

27 3 Nov. 1830, O'Connell, *Correspondence*, vol. iv, pp. 221–2.

28 31 Aug. 1830, ibid., p. 200.

29 3 Sept. 1830, ibid., pp. 201–3.

30 A. Macintyre, *The Liberator: Daniel O'Connell and the Irish Party, 1830–47* (London, 1965), p. 79.

31 P. V. Fitzpatrick to O'Connell, 3 Oct. 1830, O'Connell, *Correspondence*, vol. iv, pp. 211–12.

32 O'Connell to Bishop MacHale, 3 Dec. 1830, ibid., p. 241.

33 *Hansard*, 3rd series, vol. i, col. 329.

34 ibid., col. 327.

35 6 Feb. 1829, O'Connell, *Correspondence*, vol. iv, p. 7.

36 O'Connell to R. N. Bennett, 31 Dec. 1830, ibid., p. 247.

37 1 Dec. 1830, ibid., p. 240.

38 Lord Anglesey to Lord Melbourne, 21 Dec. 1830, Plas Newydd Papers, quoted in Marquess of Anglesey, *One Leg. The Life and Times of Henry William Paget, First Marquess of Anglesey* (London, 1961), p. 378.

39 Lord Anglesey to Lord Holland, 11 Dec. 1830, Ilchester MS, quoted in Anglesey, *One Leg*, op. cit., p. 245.

40 Lord Cloncurry, *Personal Recollections of the Life and Times, with Extracts from the Correspondence of Valentine Lord Cloncurry* (Dublin, 1849), pp. 411–12.

41 O'Connell to Edward Dwyer, 29 Nov. 1830, O'Connell, *Correspondence*, vol. iv, p. 237.

42 1 Dec. 1830, ibid., p. 239.

43 *Freeman's Journal*, 11 Jan. 1831.

44 Thomas Wallace to O'Connell, 19 Jan. 1831, O'Connell, *Correspondence*, vol. iv, p. 257.

45 Macintyre, *The Liberator*, op. cit., p. 23.

46 7 Feb. 1831, O'Connell, *Correspondence*, vol. iv, p. 269.

47 Edward Dwyer to O'Connell, 26 Feb. 1831, ibid., p. 279.

48 5 March 1831, *Freeman's Journal*, 8 March 1831.

49 5 March 1831, O'Connell, *Correspondence*, vol. iv, p. 286.

50 8 March 1831, ibid., p. 287.
51 10 March 1831, Greville, *Greville Memoirs; journal of reigns of King George IV and King William IV*, op. cit., vol. ii, p. 125.
52 Lord Grey to Sir Francis Burdett, 3 April 1831, M. W. Patterson, *Sir Francis Burdett and his times 1770–1844* (London, 1931), vol. ii, p. 586.
53 21 Feb. 1831, *Hansard*, 3rd series, vol. ii, col. 816.
54 12 May 1830, ibid., n.s., vol. xxiv, col. 651.
55 Jonathan Swift, 'A Letter to a Young Gentleman, lately entered into Holy Orders', 9 Jan. 1720, in *Satires and Personal Writings*, (ed.) W. A. Eddy (London, 1932), p. 273.
56 *Freeman's Journal*, 23 Oct. 1830.
57 ibid., 24 Oct. 1830.

CHAPTER 3
Systole and Diastole
1831–2

1 29 April 1831, O'Connell, *Correspondence*, vol. iv, p. 309.
2 2 May 1831, ibid., p. 313.
3 Maurice Fitzgerald to John Croker, 23 Feb. 1831, Croker Papers, Duke University Library.
4 O'Connell to Bishop Doyle, 16 June 1831, O'Connell, *Correspondence*, vol. iv, p. 335.
5 O'Connell to Richard Barrett, 2 July 1831, ibid., p. 337.
6 ibid., p. 338.
7 ibid.
8 18 June 1832, *Hansard*, 3rd series, vol. xiii, col. 805.
9 ibid., vol. v, col. 1122.
10 Fagan, *Life and Times of O'Connell*, op. cit., vol. ii, p. 67.
11 5 Oct. 1831, O'Connell, *Correspondence*, vol. iv, p. 355.
12 8 Oct. 1831, ibid., p. 357.
13 Lord Grey to Sir Francis Burdett, 22 Oct. 1831, Patterson, *Sir Francis Burdett*, op. cit., vol. ii, p. 596.
14 W. J. Fitzpatrick, *The Life, Times and Correspondence of the Right Rev. Dr Doyle* (Dublin, 1880), vol. ii, p. 334.
15 19 Oct. 1831, O'Connell, *Correspondence*, vol. iv, pp. 359–60.
16 O'Connell to Lord Duncannon, 4 Dec. 1831, ibid., p. 370.
17 *Pilot*, 25 Nov. 1831.
18 O'Connell to Lord Duncannon, 4 Dec. 1831, O'Connell, *Correspondence*, vol. iv, p. 371.
19 *Pilot*, 7 Dec. 1831, quoted in ibid., p. 388 n. 1.
20 Lord Duncannon to O'Connell, 28 Nov. 1831, O'Connell, *Correspondence*, vol. iv, p. 366.
21 26 Dec. 1831, ibid., p. 389.
22 8 March 1831, *Hansard*, 3rd series, vol. iii, col. 181.
23 28 June 1831, ibid., vol. iv, col. 423.
24 22 June 1831, ibid., col. 247.
25 O'Connell to Charles Rivers Carroll, 21 Feb. 1829, *Morning Register*, 26 Feb. 1829.
26 4 March 1831, *Hansard*, 3rd series, vol. iii, col. 21.
27 4 July 1831, ibid., vol. iv, cols 652–3.
28 3 Jan. 1832, O'Connell, *Correspondence*, vol. iv, pp. 396–7.
29 22 Jan. 1832, ibid., p. 400.
30 11 Feb. 1832, ibid., p. 401.
31 13 March 1832, ibid., p. 404.
32 *Freeman's Journal*, 26 March 1832.
33 ibid., 22 March 1832.
34 O'Connell to James Dwyer, 17 May 1832, O'Connell, *Correspondence*, vol. iv, p. 417.
35 19 March 1832, ibid., p. 405.
36 O'Connell to the *Newry Examiner*, 10 July 1832, quoted in ibid., p. 427.
37 19 July 1832, O'Connell, *Correspondence*, vol. iv, p. 427.

38 25 Oct. 1832, ibid., p. 460.
39 4 Aug. 1832, ibid., p. 434.
40 17 July 1832, ibid., pp. 425–6.
41 O'Connell to P. V. Fitzpatrick, 17 July 1832, ibid., p. 426.
42 P. V. Fitzpatrick to O'Connell, 21 July 1832, ibid., p. 432.
43 O'Connell to Mr Galloway, 28 June 1832, ibid., p. 424.
44 O'Connell to the editor, *Pilot*, 18 July 1832.
45 O'Connell to John Primrose, 17 July 1832, O'Connell, *Correspondence*, vol. iv, p. 426.
46 19 July 1832, ibid., p. 431.
47 O'Connell to P. V. Fitzpatrick, 29 Aug. 1832, ibid., pp. 441–2.
48 ibid., p. 442.
49 29 Sept. 1832, ibid., pp. 454–5.
50 O'Connell to P. V. Fitzpatrick, 7 Nov. 1832, ibid., p. 464.
51 O'Connell to P. V. Fitzpatrick, 22 Sept. 1832, ibid., p. 451.
52 ibid.
53 20 Dec. 1832, ibid., pp. 477–8.
54 ibid., p. 476.
55 14 April 1832, ibid., p. 413.
56 18 April 1832, ibid., p. 414.
57 O'Connell to O'Conor Don, [22 April 1832], ibid., p. 415.
58 21 July 1832, ibid., p. 432.
59 19 July 1832, ibid., p. 431.
60 O'Connell to John Primrose jr, 17 July 1832, ibid., p. 427.
61 30 March 1832, ibid., p. 407.
62 O'Connell to Mary, [4 April 1832], ibid., p. 409.
63 11 Aug. 1832, ibid., p. 436.
64 31 March 1832, ibid., p. 408.
65 [3 April 1832], ibid., p. 409.
66 ibid.
67 26 Dec. 1832, ibid., pp. 480–1.
68 25 Nov. 1831, ibid., p. 363.
69 Note in Grove Jones' letter book, quoted in ibid., p. 400, n. 1.
70 29 April 1832, O'Connell, *Correspondence*, vol. iv, p. 415.

CHAPTER 4

The Uses of Repeal

1833–4

1 27 Nov. 1832, O'Connell, *Correspondence*, vol. iv, p. 471.
2 *Nation*, 4 March 1843.
3 10 Geo. IV c. 7.
4 J. Levy (ed.), *A Full and Revised Report of the Three Days' Discussion in the Corporation of Dublin on the Repeal of the Union* (Dublin, 1843), pp. 191–2.
5 *Freeman's Journal*, 10 May 1832.
6 O'Connell to P. V. Fitzpatrick, 10 Jan. 1833, O'Connell, *Correspondence*, vol. v, p. 2.
7 Macintyre, *The Liberator*, op. cit., p. 57.
8 14 Jan. 1833, O'Connell, *Correspondence*, vol. v, p. 3.
9 Diary of E. J. Littleton, 3 Feb. 1833, Aspinall (ed.), *Three Early Nineteenth Century Diaries*, op. cit., p. 293.
10 O'Connell to P. V. Fitzpatrick, 21 Feb. 1833, O'Connell, *Correspondence*, vol. v, p. 11.
11 O'Connell to P. V. Fitzpatrick [c. 22 March 1833], ibid., p. 21.
12 Diary of Denis Le Marchant, Feb. 1833, Aspinall (ed.), *Three Early Nineteenth Century Diaries*, op. cit., p. 295.
13 [15 Feb. 1833], O'Connell, *Correspondence*, vol. v, p. 8.
14 Diary of Lord Ellenborough, 15 Feb. 1833, Aspinall (ed.), *Three Early Nineteenth Century Diaries*, op. cit., p. 302.
15 Anglesey memorandum on Illegal Confederacies, 6 Jan. 1833, H. O. Papers 100/241, ff. 79–81.
16 17 Feb. 1833, O'Connell, *Correspondence*, vol. v, p. 9.
17 Athlone Trades Political Union to O'Connell, 4 March 1833, ibid., p. 13.
18 Diary of E. J. Littleton, 26 Feb.

1833, Aspinall (ed.), *Three Early Nineteenth Century Diaries*, op. cit., p. 308.

19 O'Connell to P. V. Fitzpatrick, 6 March 1833, O'Connell, *Correspondence*, vol. v, p. 14.

20 O'Connell to P. V. Fitzpatrick, 11 March 1833, ibid., p. 16.

21 O'Connell to P. V. Fitzpatrick, 21 March 1833, ibid., p. 20.

22 O'Connell to P. V. Fitzpatrick, 27 April 1833, ibid., p. 26.

23 O'Connell to Richard Barrett, 7 June 1833, ibid., p. 40.

24 O'Connell to P. V. Fitzpatrick, 18 April 1833, ibid., p. 25.

25 O'Connell to Richard Barrett, 7 June 1833, ibid., p. 33.

26 O'Connell to P. V. Fitzpatrick, 1 June 1833, ibid., p. 35.

27 O'Connell to Richard Barrett, 7 June 1833, ibid., p. 40.

28 O'Connell to P. V. Fitzpatrick, 13 June 1833, ibid., pp. 42–3.

29 O'Connell to P. V. Fitzpatrick, 22 June 1833, ibid., pp. 48–9.

30 O'Connell to P. V. Fitzpatrick, 26 June 1833, ibid., p. 50.

31 W. Stokes, *William Stokes: his life and work* (London, 1898), p. 104.

32 5 July 1833, O'Connell, *Correspondence*, vol. v, p. 51.

33 Diary of E. J. Littleton, Aspinall (ed.), *Three Early Nineteenth Century Diaries*, op. cit., pp. 351–2.

34 20 Oct. 1833, O'Connell, *Correspondence*, vol. v, p. 82.

35 *Freeman's Journal*, 7 Nov. 1833.

36 Daunt, *Personal Recollections*, op. cit., vol. i, p. 18.

37 O'Connell to P. V. Fitzpatrick, 13 June 1833, O'Connell, *Correspondence*, vol. v, p. 43.

38 O'Connell to Michael Staunton, 9 April 1834, ibid., p. 120.

39 O'Connell to P. V. Fitzpatrick, [c. 10 April 1834], ibid., p. 122.

40 Robert Huish, *The Memoirs private and political of Daniel O'Connell Esq., M.P., his Times and Contemporaries* (London, 1836), p. 709.

41 24 April 1834, O'Connell, *Correspondence*, vol. v, p. 126.

42 25 April 1834, *Hansard*, 3rd series, vol. xxiii, col. 40.

43 8 May 1834, O'Connell, *Correspondence*, vol v, p. 132.

44 O'Connell to P. V. Fitzpatrick, 7 May 1834, ibid., p. 129.

45 Patterson, *Sir Francis Burdett*, op. cit., vol. ii, p. 621.

46 7 May 1834, O'Connell, *Correspondence*, vol. v, pp. 129–30.

47 O'Connell to P. V. Fitzpatrick, 8 May 1834, ibid., p. 131.

48 W. J. Fitzpatrick (ed.), *Correspondence of Daniel O'Connell The Liberator* (London, 1888), vol. i, p. 433.

49 O'Connell to P. V. Fitzpatrick, 30 May 1834, O'Connell, *Correspondence*, vol. v, p. 138.

50 17 June 1834, ibid., p. 145.

51 Macintyre, *The Liberator*, op. cit., p. 133.

52 O'Connell to Richard Barrett [c. 11 July 1834], O'Connell, *Correspondence*, vol. v, p. 151.

CHAPTER 5
St Martin's Summer
1834–6

1 31 July 1834, O'Connell, *Correspondence*, vol. v, pp. 158–9 n. 1.

2 ibid., p. 158.

3 O'Connell to P. V. Fitzpatrick, 6 Aug. 1834, ibid., p. 162.

4 O'Connell to P. V. Fitzpatrick, 9 Aug. 1834, ibid., p. 164.

5 20 Aug. 1834, ibid., p. 167.

6 O'Connell to P. V. Fitzpatrick, 25 Aug. 1834, ibid., p. 168.

7 O'Connell to the People of Ireland,

25 Aug. 1834, *Freeman's Journal*, 28 Aug. 1834.

8 27 Aug. 1834, O'Connell, *Correspondence*, vol. v, p. 169.

9 2 Oct. 1834, ibid., p. 189.

10 2 Sept. 1834, ibid., pp. 171–2.

11 Lord Duncannon to O'Connell, 8 Sept. 1834, ibid., p. 180.

12 Edward Ellice to O'Connell, 16 Sept. 1834, ibid., p. 183.

13 11 Nov. 1834, ibid., p. 199.

14 O'Connell to Thomas Mooney, 13 June 1834, ibid., p. 143.

15 *Freeman's Journal*, 2 July 1834.

16 ibid.

17 8 July 1834, O'Connell, *Correspondence*, vol. v, pp. 149–50.

18 Sir Matthew Slattery, *The National Bank 1835–1970* (London, n.d.), p. 5.

19 Minutes of the National Bank of Ireland, in possession of the Royal Bank of Scotland, Committee meeting of 15 Oct. 1834.

20 8 July 1834, O'Connell, *Correspondence*, vol. v, p. 150.

21 ibid.

22 O'Connell to P. V. Fitzpatrick, 25 Aug. 1834, ibid., pp. 167–8.

23 Fagan, *Life and Times of O'Connell*, op. cit., vol. ii, pp. 503–4.

24 O'Connell to P. V. Fitzpatrick, 17 Nov. 1834, O'Connell, *Correspondence*, vol. v, p. 201.

25 18 Nov. 1834, ibid., p. 202.

26 *Freeman's Journal*, 21 Nov. 1834.

27 21 Nov. 1834, O'Connell, *Correspondence*, vol. v, p. 204.

28 James Birch to the Duke of Wellington, 22 [Nov. 1834], Apsley House MS, in A. Aspinall, *Politics and the Press c. 1780–1850* (London, 1949), p. 483.

29 25 Nov. 1834, O'Connell, *Correspondence*, vol. v, p. 207.

30 Fagan, *Life and Times of O'Connell*, op. cit., vol. ii, p. 326.

31 R. D. Craig to E. J. Littleton, Dec. 1834, Teddesley MS, quoted in R. B. McDowell, *Public Opinion and Government Policy in Ireland 1801–1846* (London, 1952), p. 162.

32 3 Dec. 1834, O'Connell, *Correspondence*, vol. v, p. 216.

33 8 Dec. 1834, ibid., p. 222.

34 C. Fitzmaurice to O'Connell, 19 Dec. 1834, ibid., p. 237.

35 28 Nov. 1834, ibid., p. 212.

36 5 Dec. 1834, ibid., p. 217.

37 20 Jan. 1835, ibid., p. 263.

38 13 Feb. 1835, ibid., p. 270.

39 Lord Duncannon to Lord Melbourne, 18 Dec. 1834, Melbourne Papers, 230, quoted in Macintyre, *The Liberator*, op. cit., p. 140.

40 Lord Duncannon to Lord Russell, [17 Feb. 1835], quoted in Spencer Walpole, *The Life of Lord John Russell* (London, 1889), vol. i, p. 222.

41 John O'Connell, *Recollections and Experiences during a parliamentary career from 1833 to 1848* (London, 1849), vol. i, p. 135.

42 19 Feb. 1835, O'Connell, *Correspondence*, vol. v, p. 271.

43 O'Connell to P. V. Fitzpatrick, 27 March 1835, ibid., p. 287.

44 *Mirror of Parliament*, 1835, vol. i, p. 121.

45 John Earl Russell, *Recollections and Suggestions 1813–1873* (London, 1875), p. 135.

46 10 April 1835, O'Connell, *Correspondence*, vol. v, p. 288.

47 ibid.

48 O'Connell to P. V. Fitzpatrick, 14 April 1835, ibid., p. 289.

49 Fagan, *Life and Times of O'Connell*, op. cit., vol. ii, pp. 371–2.

50 22 April 1835, O'Connell, *Correspondence*, vol. v, pp. 296–7.

51 W. E. H. Lecky, *Leaders of Public Opinion in Ireland* (new edn,

London, 1903), vol. ii, p. 157.

52 'Prefatory Letter on Music', *Irish Melodies, The Poetical Works of Thomas Moore*, (ed.) W. M. Rossetti (London, 1911), p. 329.

53 11 March 1835, O'Connell, *Correspondence*, vol. v, p. 281.

54 O'Connell to —, 16 March 1835, ibid., p. 283.

55 25 March 1835, ibid., p. 285.

56 4 Sept. 1835, ibid., p. 330.

57 21 April 1835, ibid., p. 295.

58 20 April 1835, *Hansard*, 3rd series, vol. xxvii, col. 1009.

59 1 May 1835, O'Connell, *Correspondence*, vol. v, p. 300.

60 J. R. O'Flanagan, *Life and Times of Daniel O'Connell with Sketches of his Contemporaries* (Dublin, 1875), vol. ii, p. 589.

61 *The Times*, 6 May 1835.

62 Lady Salisbury, 1 Nov. 1835, Salisbury MS, quoted in Macintyre, *The Liberator*, op. cit., p. 157.

63 M. A. G. O Tuathaigh, *Thomas Drummond and the Government of Ireland 1835–41* (Dublin, 1977), p. 4.

64 Terence de Vere White, 'English Opinion', in M. Tierney (ed.), *Daniel O'Connell. Nine Centenary Essays* (Dublin, 1949), p. 215.

65 30 June 1836, *Hansard*, 3rd series, vol. xxxiv, col. 1097.

66 4 Sept. 1835, O'Connell, *Correspondence*, vol. v, p. 329.

67 Ó Tuathaigh, *Thomas Drummond*, op. cit., p. 18; *Pilot*, 4 Nov. 1840.

68 11 May 1835, O'Connell, *Correspondence*, vol. v, pp. 303–4.

69 4 Dec. 1835, ibid., p. 345.

70 8 Dec. 1835, ibid., p. 347.

71 4 Sept. 1835, ibid., p. 330.

72 11 Sept. 1835, ibid., p. 332.

73 O'Connell to P. V. Fitzpatrick, 4 Sept. 1835, ibid., p. 329.

74 23 June 1835, ibid., p. 314.

75 25 July 1835, ibid., p. 321.

76 31 Dec. 1835, ibid., p. 349.

77 31 July 1835, *Hansard*, 3rd series, vol. xxix, cols 1316–17.

78 Thomas Spring Rice to Sir John Newport, 19 Aug. 1835, Monteagle Papers 551, p. 96.

79 O'Connell to James Aytoun, 18 Aug. 1835, O'Connell, *Correspondence*, vol. v, p. 327.

80 11 Sept. 1835, ibid., p. 331.

81 MacDonagh, *Life of O'Connell*, op. cit., pp. 253–4.

82 O'Connell to P. V. Fitzpatrick, 4 Sept. 1835, O'Connell, *Correspondence*, vol. v, p. 330.

83 *The Annual Register, a record of world events*, 1835, p. 367.

84 O'Connell to John Hill Burton, 3 Dec. 1835, O'Connell, *Correspondence*, vol. v, p. 343.

85 14 Dec. 1835, ibid., p. 348.

86 *Freeman's Journal*, 1 Feb. 1836.

87 Lecky, *Leaders of Public Opinion*, op. cit., vol. ii, p. 157.

88 Fagan, *Life and Times of O'Connell*, op. cit., vol. ii, p. 496.

89 O'Connell to Arthur French, 28 June 1837, Fitzpatrick, *Correspondence*, vol. ii, p. 105.

90 *Freeman's Journal*, 1 Feb. 1836.

91 Fagan, *Life and Times of O'Connell*, op. cit., vol. ii, p. 333.

92 'The dream of those days', *The Poetical Works of Thomas Moore* (London, 1853), vol. iv, p. 103.

93 O'Connell to Arthur French, 28 June 1837, Fitzpatrick, *Correspondence*, vol. ii, p. 105.

94 Fagan, *Life and Times of O'Connell*, op. cit., vol. ii, p. 496.

95 O'Connell to P. V. Fitzpatrick, 31 July 1834, O'Connell, *Correspondence*, vol. v, pp. 158–9 n. 1.

CHAPTER 6

Liaisons

1836–8

1 7 June 1835, O'Connell,

Correspondence, vol. v, p. 309.

2 O'Connell to Alexander Raphael, 1 June 1835, ibid., p. 308.

3 Alexander Raphael to O'Connell, 28 July 1833, ibid., p. 323.

4 5 Aug. [1835], ibid., p. 325.

5 O'Connell to Alexander Raphael, 3 Aug. 1835, ibid., p. 324.

6 Report of the Select Committee on Carlow Election Petition, 11 March 1836, *Commons Papers*, 1836, vol. xl, p. iii.

7 Fagan, *Life and Times of O'Connell*, op. cit., vol. ii, p. 593.

8 ibid.

9 ibid.

10 *Annual Register, a record of world events*, 1836, p. 30.

11 Fagan, *Life and Times of O'Connell*, op. cit., vol. ii, p. 527.

12 O'Connell to Arthur French, 18 Aug. 1836, *The Times*, 29 Aug. 1836.

13 9 May 1836, *Hansard*, 3rd series, vol. xxxiii, cols 734–5.

14 M. R. O'Connell, *Irish Times*, 6 Aug. 1975, and 'Daniel O'Connell and his family', in D. McCartney (ed.), *The World of Daniel O'Connell* (Dublin, 1980), p. 23.

15 *The Times*, 22 Sept. 1836.

16 Quoted in ibid., 23 Sept. 1836.

17 ibid., 22 Sept. 1836.

18 O'Connell to Joseph D. Mullen, 9 March 1836, O'Connell, *Correspondence*, vol. v, p. 356.

19 22 March 1836, ibid., p. 361.

20 O'Connell to Richard Sullivan, 10 March 1836, ibid., p. 357.

21 O'Connell to P. V. Fitzpatrick, 13 May 1836, ibid., p. 371.

22 ibid., p. 372.

23 ibid.

24 Fagan, *Life and Times of O'Connell*, op. cit., vol. ii, p. 537.

25 *Blackwood's Magazine*, July 1836, p. 116.

26 O. MacDonagh, *Early Victorian Government* (New York, 1977), p. 58.

27 *The Times*, 11 May 1836.

28 O'Connell to P. V. Fitzpatrick, 13 May 1836, O'Connell, *Correspondence*, vol. v, p. 371.

29 Fagan, *Life and Times of O'Connell*, op. cit., vol. ii, p. 577.

30 ibid., p. 585.

31 E. Holt, *Protest in Arms: the Irish Troubles, 1916–1923* (London, [1960]), p. 300.

32 13 Sept. 1835, O'Connell, *Correspondence*, vol. v, p. 333.

33 O'Connell to Mary O'Connell, 30 May 1836, ibid., p. 376.

34 4 Sept. 1836, ibid., p. 393.

35 6 Sept. 1836, ibid., p. 395.

36 6 Sept. 1836, ibid., p. 396.

37 9 Sept. 1836, ibid.

38 4 Sept. 1836, ibid., p. 393.

39 9 Sept. 1836, ibid., p. 397.

40 O'Connell to P. V. Fitzpatrick, 26 Oct. 1836, ibid., pp. 400–1.

41 ibid., p. 400.

42 O'Connell to William Howitt, 7 Nov. 1836, ibid., p. 402.

43 O'Connell to P. V. Fitzpatrick, 26 June 1833, ibid., p. 50.

44 25 Dec. 1834, ibid., p. 242.

45 4 Feb. 1836, *Hansard*, 3rd series, vol. xxxi, col. 98.

46 Sir Robert Peel to Duke of Wellington, 10 Feb. 1836, C. S. Parker, *Sir Robert Peel from his private papers* (London, 1899), vol. ii, p. 322.

47 Greville, *The Greville Memoirs; a journal of the reigns of King George IV and King William IV*, op. cit., vol. iii, 10 March 1836, p. 347.

48 16 May 1836, Fitzpatrick, *Correspondence*, vol. ii, p. 58.

49 *Hansard*, 3rd series, vol. xxxiii, col. 734.

50 Russell Papers, PRO 30/22/2B.

51 2 July 1836, O'Connell, *Correspondence*, vol. v, pp. 384–5.

52 *Hansard*, vol. xxxiv, cols 1097–8.

53 2 July 1836, O'Connell, *Correspondence*, vol. v, p. 383.
54 O'Connell to P. V. Fitzpatrick, 2 July 1836, ibid., p. 386.
55 Fagan, *Life and Times of O'Connell*, op. cit., vol. ii, p. 669.
56 29 Dec. 1886, O'Connell, *Correspondence*, vol. v, pp. 412–13.
57 Fagan, *Life and Times of O'Connell*, op. cit., vol. ii, pp. 529–30.
58 Preface to 'John Bull's Other Island', *Prefaces by Bernard Shaw* (London, 1938), p. 457.
59 O'Connell to P. V. Fitzpatrick, 18 Feb. 1837, O'Connell, *Correspondence*, vol. vi, p. 16.
60 *Hansard*, 3rd series, vol. xxxvi, col. 486.
61 26 May 1837, O'Connell, *Correspondence*, vol. vi, p. 38.
62 3 June 1837, ibid., p. 42.
63 O'Connell to Archbishop MacHale, 31 May 1837, ibid., p. 39.
64 ibid., 4 June 1837, p. 46.
65 *Freeman's Journal*, 1 July 1837.
66 1 July 1837, O'Connell, *Correspondence*, vol. vi, p. 54.
67 O'Connell to a kinsman in Tralee, 11 July 1837, ibid., p. 61.
68 21 April 1837, ibid., pp. 31–2.
69 4 Sept. 1837, ibid., p. 84.
70 O'Connell to Arthur French, General Association, 19 Oct. 1837, *Freeman's Journal*, 25 Oct. 1837.
71 20 Nov. 1837, *Hansard*, 3rd series, vol. xxxix, col. 69.
72 O'Connell to J. Arthur Roebuck, 23 Sept. 1837, O'Connell, *Correspondence*, vol. vi, p. 86.
73 Joshua Scholefield to O'Connell, 16 Dec. 1837, ibid., p. 106.
74 1 Jan. 1838, ibid., pp. 120–1.
75 SPOI, CSO, RP, Outrage reports, 9/257 (1837), head office of police, 6 Nov. 1837, quoted in F. A. D'Arcy, 'The artisans of Dublin and Daniel O'Connell, 1830–47: an unquiet liaison', *Irish Historical Studies*, vol. xvii, Sept. 1970, p. 231.
76 *Freeman's Journal*, 7 Nov. 1837.
77 D'Arcy, 'The artisans of Dublin and Daniel O'Connell', op. cit., p. 228.
78 *Freeman's Journal*, 11 Dec. 1833.
79 ibid., 22 Nov. 1837.
80 William O'Hanlon to the National Trades Political Union, 16 Dec. 1837, NLI MS1364 (18).
81 *Freeman's Journal*, 27 Dec. 1837.
82 ibid., 9 Jan. 1838.
83 ibid.
84 ibid.
85 ibid.
86 Richard Whately to N. Senior Esq., 25 Jan. 1838, E. J. Whately, *Life and Correspondence of R. Whately* (London, 1866), vol. i, p. 414.
87 James Cosgrave to O'Connell, [c. 21 Dec. 1837], O'Connell, *Correspondence*, vol. vi, p. 115.
88 O'Connell to George Julian Harney, 24 Dec. 1837, ibid., p. 118.
89 *Freeman's Journal*, 27 Nov. 1841.
90 ibid., 21 Oct. 1842.
91 W. B. Yeats, 'Nineteen Hundred and Nineteen', *The Collected Poems of W. B. Yeats* (London, 1963), p. 235.

CHAPTER 7
Declinations
1838–41

1 10 Feb. 1838, O'Connell, *Correspondence*, vol. vi, p. 133.
2 9 Feb. 1838, *Hansard*, 3rd series, vol. xl, col. 948.
3 *Freeman's Journal*, 19 Dec. 1837.
4 O'Connell to Archbishop MacHale, [c. 18 Feb. 1838], O'Connell, *Correspondence*, vol. vi, p. 136.
5 10 Feb. 1838, ibid., p. 133.
6 27 Feb. 1838, ibid., p. 139.
7 O'Connell to John Primrose jr, 4 May 1838, ibid., p. 159.

8 Fagan, *Life and Times of O'Connell*, op. cit., vol. ii, p. 536.

9 26 April 1838, O'Connell, *Correspondence*, vol. vi, p. 156.

10 O'Connell to P. V. Fitzpatrick, 15 Feb. 1838, ibid., p. 134.

11 Fagan, *Life and Times of O'Connell*, op. cit., vol. ii, p. 636.

12 4 May 1838, O'Connell, *Correspondence*, vol. vi, pp. 157–8.

13 James Sheil to O'Connell, 28 March 1837, ibid., p. 27.

14 25 Sept. 1837, ibid., p. 90.

15 Curran, *Sketches of the Irish Bar*, op. cit., vol. i, p. 165.

16 O'Connell to a kinsman in Kerry, 27 March 1837, O'Connell, *Correspondence*, vol. vi, p. 26.

17 19 Feb. 1837, ibid., p. 18.

18 O'Connell to Richard Barrett, 25 Feb. 1837, ibid., p. 20.

19 15 June 1838, ibid., p. 170.

20 18 June 1838, ibid., pp. 170–1.

21 O'Connell to P. V. Fitzpatrick, 15 June 1838, ibid., p. 170.

22 11 Aug. 1838, ibid., p. 174.

23 O'Connell to Viscount Morpeth, 10 June 1838, ibid., pp. 166–7.

24 *Freeman's Journal*, 20 Aug. 1838.

25 6 Sept. 1838, O'Connell, *Correspondence*, vol. vi, p. 175.

26 O'Connell to F. W. Conway, 15 Sept. 1838, ibid., p. 178.

27 30 Sept. 1838, ibid., pp. 185–6.

28 28 Oct. 1838, ibid., p. 196.

29 7 Oct. 1838, ibid., p. 189.

30 O'Connell to F. W. Conway, 15 Sept. 1838, ibid., p. 178.

31 23 Oct. 1838, ibid., p. 195.

32 D. Pigot to O'Connell [c. 27 Sept. 1838], ibid., p. 181.

33 3 Jan. 1839, ibid., p. 202.

34 ibid.

35 6 Feb. 1839, ibid., p. 213.

36 3 Jan. 1839, ibid., p. 204.

37 O'Connell to Archbishop MacHale, 4 Oct. 1838, ibid., p. 187.

38 O'Connell to Rev. Dr Thomas O'Brien Costello, 16 May 1839, ibid., p. 247.

39 7 May 1839, ibid., p. 238.

40 9 May 1839, ibid., p. 241.

41 10 May 1839, ibid., p. 242.

42 11 May 1839, ibid., p. 243.

43 O'Connell to Joseph Parkes, 14 May 1839, ibid., p. 246.

44 O'Connell to P. V. Fitzpatrick, 28 June 1839, ibid., p. 252.

45 O'Connell to P. V. Fitzpatrick, 5 Aug. 1839, ibid., p. 263.

46 6 Aug. 1839, ibid., p. 264.

47 O'Connell to Lord Ebrington, 8 Aug. 1839, ibid., p. 269.

48 7 Aug. 1839, ibid., pp. 266–7.

49 8 Aug. 1839, ibid., pp. 267–8.

50 O'Connell to P. V. Fitzpatrick, 21 Aug. 1839, ibid., p. 277.

51 *Freeman's Journal*, 15 Nov. 1839.

52 Lord Ebrington to Lord J. Russell, 8 Sept. 1839, PRO 30/22/3D.

53 29 Nov. 1839, O'Connell, *Correspondence*, vol. vi, p. 287.

54 23 Dec. 1839, ibid., p. 292.

55 13 Dec. 1839, ibid., p. 291.

56 17 Jan. 1840, ibid., p. 296.

57 29 Jan. 1840, ibid., p. 298.

58 3 Feb. 1840, ibid., p. 300.

59 4 Feb. 1840, ibid., p. 302.

60 O'Connell to R. L. Sheil, 29 Oct. 1839, ibid., p. 285.

61 22 Feb. 1840, ibid., p. 313.

62 8 April 1840, ibid., p. 320.

63 ibid., p. 321.

64 11 April 1840, ibid., p. 324.

65 *Freeman's Journal*, 15 April 1840.

66 30 May 1840, O'Connell, *Correspondence*, vol. vi, p. 333.

67 O'Connell to P. V. Fitzpatrick, 30 June 1840, ibid., p. 344.

68 McDowell, *Public Opinion and Government Policy in Ireland*, op. cit., p. 175.

69 30 July 1840, O'Connell, *Correspondence*, vol. vi, pp. 349–50.

70 14 Aug. 1840, ibid., pp. 352–3.

71 *Freeman's Journal*, 1 Oct. 1830.

72 6 Nov. 1840, O'Connell,
  Correspondence, vol. vi, p. 377.
73 21 Nov. 1840, ibid., pp. 379–80.
74 O'Connell to Archbishop MacHale,
  30 Nov. 1840, ibid., p. 385.
75 O'Connell to P. V. Fitzpatrick, 8
  Dec. 1840, ibid., p. 388.
76 ibid., p. 389.
77 4 Dec. 1840, ibid., p. 387.
78 6 Sept. 1840, ibid., pp. 358–9.
79 11 Sept. 1840, ibid., p. 361.
80 9 Sept. 1840, ibid., p. 360.
81 26 Jan. 1841, ibid., vol. vii, p. 12.
82 O'Connell to P. V. Fitzpatrick, 10
  Feb. 1841, ibid., p. 20.
83 O'Connell to P. V. Fitzpatrick, 19
  Feb. 1841, ibid., p. 23.
84 O'Connell to Archbishop Slattery,
  17 Jan. 1841, ibid., p. 8.
85 ibid., p. 36.
86 8 May 1841, ibid., p. 50.
87 29 April 1841, ibid., p. 44–5.
88 19 Feb. 1841, ibid., p. 23.
89 ibid.
90 O'Connell to P. V. Fitzpatrick, 4
  May 1841, ibid., p. 46.
91 7 May 1841, ibid., p. 48.
92 ibid., p. 49.
93 ibid.
94 O'Connell to P. V. Fitzpatrick, 9
  June 1841, ibid., p. 86.
95 17 May 1841, ibid., p. 62.
96 Fitzsimon to O'Connell, 25 May
  1841, ibid., p. 72.
97 26 [and 28] May 1841, ibid., p. 75.
98 O'Connell to John O'Connell, 29
  May 1841, ibid., p. 78.
99 ibid.
100 P. V. Fitzpatrick to O'Connell, 10
  May 1841, ibid., p. 53.
101 *Freeman's Journal*, 22 May 1841.
102 O'Connell to Richard More
  O'Ferrall, 15 June 1841,
  O'Connell, *Correspondence*, vol.
  vii, p. 91.
103 21 May 1841, ibid., p. 67.
104 9 June 1841, ibid., pp. 85–6.
105 Annals, St Leo's, Carlow.
106 O'Connell to ——, 18 June 1841,
  O'Connell, *Correspondence*, vol.
  vii, pp. 94–5.
107 13 July 1841, ibid., p. 105.
108 O'Connell to Edmond Smithwick,
  19 July 1841, ibid., p. 107.

CHAPTER 8
Divagations
1841–2

1 17 July 1841, O'Connell,
  Correspondence, vol. vii, p. 106.
2 Sir Robert Peel to Sir James
  Graham, 19 Oct. 1843, Parker, *Sir
  Robert Peel*, op. cit., vol. iii, p. 65.
3 Sir Robert Peel to Sir James
  Graham, 2 Jan. 1842, *The papers of
  Sir James Graham* (Brighton,
  Sussex, Harvester Press Microform
  Publications), General Series 1820–
  1860, Bundle 46.
4 *Freeman's Journal*, 27 Oct. 1841.
5 ibid., 2 Nov. 1841.
6 John O'Connell to O'Connell, 22
  Oct. 1841, O'Connell,
  Correspondence, vol. vii, p. 122.
7 *Freeman's Journal*, 19 Oct. 1841.
8 ibid.
9 John O'Connell to O'Connell, 4
  Nov. 1841, O'Connell,
  Correspondence, vol. vii, p. 125.
10 ibid.
11 *Freeman's Journal*, 9 Dec. 1841.
12 W. Shakespeare, *Measure for
  Measure*, Act II, scene ii, l. 107.
13 *Freeman's Journal*, 23 Dec. 1841.
14 ibid., 24 March 1842.
15 ibid., 24 Aug. 1842.
16 ibid., 2 Nov. 1842.
17 ibid., 17 Aug. 1842.
18 O'Connell to P. V. Fitzpatrick, 20
  Sept. 1842, O'Connell,
  Correspondence, vol. vii, p. 175.
19 *Freeman's Journal*, 2 Nov. 1842.
20 O'Connell to Betsey Ffrench, 4 Dec.
  1841, O'Connell, *Correspondence*,
  vol. vii, p. 127.
21 *Freeman's Journal*, 17 Aug. 1842.

22 25 July 1842, O'Connell, *Correspondence*, vol. vii, p. 169.
23 ibid.
24 29 July 1842, ibid., p. 171.
25 6 Aug. 1842, ibid., pp. 172–3.
26 9 May 1842, ibid., p. 157.
27 9 Sept. 1842, ibid., p. 173.
28 O'Connell to Thomas Lyons, 17 Sept. 1842, ibid., p. 174.
29 7 Jan. 1843, ibid., p. 183.
30 W. E. Gladstone quoted in John Morley, *The Life of William Ewart Gladstone* (London, 1911), vol. i, p. 332.
31 Daunt, *Personal Recollections*, op. cit., vol. i, p. 228.
32 ibid., p. 304.
33 ibid., p. 87.
34 ibid., p. 303.
35 O'Connell to Rev. W. A. O'Meara OFM, 9 Sept. 1841, O'Connell, *Correspondence*, vol. vii, pp. 114–15.
36 From John Dryden, *The Hind and the Panther*, part 1, ll. 64–71, in O'Connell to O'Meara, 9 Sept. 1841, O'Connell, *Correspondence*, vol. vii, p. 115.
37 O'Connell to Betsey Ffrench, 28 June 1839, O'Connell, *Correspondence*, vol. vi, pp. 253–4.
38 O'Connell to Betsey Ffrench, 8 July 1839, ibid., pp. 258–9.
39 O'Connell to John Primrose Sr, 7 Aug. 1832, ibid., vol. iv, pp. 434–5.
40 17 Aug. 1832, ibid., p. 439.
41 O'Connell to Betsey Ffrench, 8 July 1839, ibid., vol. vi, p. 259.
42 ibid.
43 Daunt, *Personal Recollections*, op. cit., vol. i, p. 238.
44 Memoir by Mrs C. Fitz-Simon, quoted in MacDonagh, *Life of O'Connell*, op. cit., pp. 120–1.
45 O'Connell to Betsey Ffrench, 28 June 1839, O'Connell, *Correspondence*, vol. vi, p. 253.
46 O'Connell to Betsey Ffrench, 8 July 1839, ibid., p. 258.
47 [20 March 1841], ibid., vol. vii, p. 31.
48 Christopher Fitz-Simon to O'Connell, 24 May 1841, ibid., p. 72.
49 27 Jan. 1841, ibid., p. 13.
50 Christopher Fitz-Simon to O'Connell, 28 April 1841, ibid., p. 43.
51 9 Dec. 1840, ibid., vol. vi, pp. 390–1.
52 Committee Book of the Board of the National Bank of Ireland, in the possession of the Royal Bank of Scotland.
53 18 Dec. 1837, O'Connell, *Correspondence*, vol. vi, p. 108.

CHAPTER 9
The Big Bang
1843

1 O'Connell to the People of Ireland, 1 Jan. 1843, *Nation*, 7 Jan. 1843.
2 *Freeman's Journal*, 6 May 1843.
3 J. B. Atkins, *The Life of Sir William Howard Russell* (London, 1911), vol. i, p. 30.
4 *Freeman's Journal*, 10 June 1843.
5 *Nation*, 17 June 1843.
6 ibid.
7 'Report on Waterford', n.d., Loyal National Repeal Association correspondence, MS 3143, NLI.
8 MacDonagh, *Life of O'Connell*, op. cit., pp. 301–2.
9 24 March 1843, O'Connell, *Correspondence*, vol. vii, p. 193.
10 MacDonagh, *Life of O'Connell*, op. cit., p. 319.
11 ibid., pp. 309–10.
12 *Freeman's Journal*, 14 June 1843; MacDonagh, *Life of O'Connell*, op. cit., p. 315.
13 R. Pares, *George III and the Politicians* (Oxford, 1953), p. 30.
14 Lord De Grey to Sir Robert Peel, 6 May 1843, Parker, *Sir Robert Peel*, op. cit., vol. iii, p. 47.

15 *The Politics of Repeal* (London, 1965), p. 46.
16 *Nation*, 20 May 1843.
17 ibid., 1 July 1843.
18 16 June, 7 July 1843, *Hansard*, 3rd series, vol. lxx, cols. 53, 810–11.
19 *Nation*, 20 May 1843.
20 Sir James Graham to Lord Stanley, 16 July 1843, Graham Papers, op. cit., General Series 1820–1860, Bundle 63.
21 Lord Palmerston to Lord Russell, 22 Dec. 1843, Russell Papers, PRO 30/22/4C.
22 9 Sept. 1843, O'Connell, *Correspondence*, vol. vii, p. 224.
23 14 Sept. 1843, ibid., pp. 224–5.
24 *Nation*, 7 Oct. 1843.
25 *Politics of Repeal*, op. cit., pp. 55–6.
26 Sir Robert Peel to Sir James Graham, 16 Oct. 1843, Graham Papers, op. cit., General Series 1820–1860, Bundle 66B.
27 *Nation*, 14 Oct. 1843.
28 Warrant of arrest, *Nation*, 21 Oct. 1843.
29 *Life of O'Connell*, op. cit., p. 329.
30 *Nation*, 18 Nov. 1843.
31 ibid., 9 Dec. 1843.
32 9 Dec. 1843, O'Connell, *Correspondence*, vol. vii, p. 227.

CHAPTER 10
The Fall-Out
1844–5

1 MacDonagh, *Life of O'Connell*, op. cit., p. 333.
2 *Punch*, vol. vi, Jan.–June 1844, p. 248.
3 H. Shaw, *Authenticated Report of the Irish State Trials 1844* (Dublin, [1844]), p. 475.
4 ibid., p. 479.
5 *Freeman's Journal*, 31 May 1844.
6 *Hansard*, 3rd series, vol. lxxii, col. 930.
7 16 Feb. 1844, O'Connell, *Correspondence*, vol. vii, p. 241.
8 O'Connell to P. V. Fitzpatrick, 25 March 1844, ibid., p. 242.
9 19 March 1844, ibid., p. 246.
10 O'Connell to P. V. Fitzpatrick, 25 March 1844, ibid., p. 249.
11 *Freeman's Journal*, 3 June 1844.
12 C. G. Duffy, *Young Ireland. A Fragment of Irish History 1840–45* (London, 1896), vol. ii, p. 60.
13 22 April 1844, O'Connell, *Correspondence*, vol. vii, p. 254.
14 1 May 1844, ibid., p. 255.
15 MacDonagh, *Life of O'Connell*, op. cit., p. 354.
16 Duffy, *Young Ireland*, op. cit., vol. ii, p. 81.
17 21 June 1844, O'Connell, *Correspondence*, vol. vii, p. 258.
18 Daniel O'Connell jr to the Repeal Association, *Freeman's Journal*, 2 July 1844.
19 1 Aug. 1844, O'Connell, *Correspondence*, vol. vii, p. 261.
20 MacDonagh, *Life of O'Connell*, op. cit., p. 344.
21 O'Connell to R. L. Sheil, 19 June 1844, O'Connell, *Correspondence*, vol. vii, p. 256.
22 ibid.
23 1 Aug. 1844, ibid., p. 261.
24 MacDonagh, *Life of O'Connell*, op. cit., p. 347.
25 11 Aug. 1844, O'Connell, *Correspondence*, vol. vii, pp. 262–3.
26 19 Feb. 1844, *Hansard*, 3rd series vol. lxxii, cols. 1185–6.
27 *Freeman's Journal*, 9 Sept. 1844.
28 ibid.
29 ibid.
30 *Nation*, 14 Sept. 1844.
31 ibid.
32 ibid.
33 John Mitchel, *The Last Conquest of Ireland (perhaps)* (Glasgow, [1876]) p. 56.
34 3 Oct. 1844, O'Connell,

Correspondence, vol. vii, p. 273.

35 O'Connell to P. V. Fitzpatrick, 8 Oct. 1844, ibid., p. 275.

36 Northern Whig, 17 Oct. 1839.

37 1 Oct. 1844, O'Connell, Correspondence, vol. vii, p. 272.

38 12 Oct. 1844, ibid., p. 276.

39 3 Oct. 1844, O'Connell to P. V. Fitzpatrick, ibid., p. 273.

40 12 Oct. 1844, ibid., p. 276.

41 Freeman's Journal, 15 Oct. 1844.

42 1 Oct. 1844, O'Connell, Correspondence, vol. vii, p. 272.

43 12 Oct. 1844, ibid., p. 278.

44 8 Oct. 1844, ibid., p. 275.

45 29 Oct. 1844, ibid., p. 285.

46 Daunt, Personal Recollections, op. cit., vol. ii, pp. 220–1.

47 O'Connell to T. M. Ray, read at Repeal Association meeting of 11 Nov. 1844, Freeman's Journal, 12 Nov. 1844.

48 9 June 1845, O'Connell, Correspondence, vol. vii, p. 319.

49 9 Jan. 1844, ibid., p. 235.

50 ibid., pp. 235–6.

51 ibid., p. 237.

52 ibid.

53 Charles Greville, The Greville Memoirs (second part); a journal of the reign of Queen Victoria 1837 to 1852, (ed.) H. Reeve (London, 1885), vol. ii, p. 221.

54 Cabinet memorandum by Sir Robert Peel, 17 Feb. 1844, Parker, Sir Robert Peel, op. cit., vol. iii, p. 106.

55 Nation, 31 Aug. 1844.

56 Freeman's Journal, 11 Jan. 1845.

57 To the Clergy and Faithful of the Archdiocese of Tuam, First Sunday in Advent, The Letters of the Most Rev. John MacHale (London, 1847), p. 583.

58 Lord Eliot to Lord Heytesbury, n.d., Parker, Sir Robert Peel, op. cit., vol. iii, p. 132.

59 Lord Heytesbury to Sir Robert Peel, 20 Dec. 1844, ibid., p. 144.

60 Freeman's Journal, 3 Dec. 1844.

61 2 Feb. 1845, O'Connell, Correspondence, vol. vii, pp. 303–4.

62 O'Connell to Archbishop MacHale, 19 Feb. 1845, ibid., p. 306.

63 Nation, 17 May, 31 May 1845.

64 O'Connell to P. V. Fitzpatrick, 27 June 1845, O'Connell, Correspondence, vol. vii, p. 322.

65 ibid.

66 O'Connell to Pierce Mahoney, 25 April 1845, ibid., p. 314.

67 O'Connell to Pierce Mahony, 26 April 1845, ibid., p. 316.

68 MacDonagh, Life of O'Connell, op. cit., p. 351.

69 Pilot, 15 Jan. 1845.

70 ibid., 24 Jan. 1845.

71 Rev. F. J. Nicholson to O'Connell, 24 May 1845, O'Connell, Correspondence, vol. vii, p. 317.

72 O'Connell to Rev. W. A. O'Meara, O.F.M., 9 Sept. 1841, ibid., pp. 114–15.

73 O'Connell to William Smith O'Brien, 2 April 1844, ibid., p. 252.

74 Young Ireland and 1848 (Oxford, 1949), p. 23.

75 Smith O'Brien Papers, NLI MS 435, item 1371.

76 O'Connell to Thomas Davis, 30 Oct. 1844, O'Connell, Correspondence, vol vii, pp. 286–7.

77 1 Dec. 1844, C. G. Duffy, Thomas Davis. The Memoirs of an Irish Patriot 1840–1846 (London, 1890), p. 308.

78 Duffy, Young Ireland, op. cit., vol. ii, p. 175.

79 ibid., p. 177.

80 ibid.

81 ibid.

82 Thomas MacNevin to Smith O'Brien, 27 May 1845, Smith O'Brien Papers, NLI MS 441, item 2288.

CHAPTER 11
The Widening Gyre
1845–6

1 *Young Ireland and 1848*, op. cit., p. 45.
2 O'Connell to William Smith O'Brien, 9 June 1845, O'Connell, *Correspondence*, vol. vii, p. 319.
3 O'Connell to T. M. Ray, 17 Sept. 1845, ibid., p. 342.
4 *Nation*, 17 May, 31 May 1845.
5 O'Connell Papers, NLI MS 13646(24).
6 27 June 1845, O'Connell, *Correspondence*, vol. vii, p. 322.
7 25 Aug. 1845, ibid., pp. 332–3.
8 17 Sept. 1845, ibid., p. 341.
9 9 Sept. 1845, ibid., p. 338.
10 17 Sept. 1845, ibid., 341.
11 30 Oct. 1845, ibid., pp. 345–6.
12 *Nation*, 8 Nov. 1845.
13 W. B. Yeats, 'The Second Coming', *The Poems*, (ed.) Richard Finneran (London, 1984), p. 187.
14 T. M. Ray to O'Connell, 8 Sept. 1845, O'Connell, *Correspondence*, vol. vii, pp. 336–7.
15 11 Sept. 1845, ibid., p. 340.
16 20 [and 22] Dec. 1845, ibid., p. 352.
17 ibid.
18 ibid.
19 Nowlan, *Politics of Repeal*, op. cit., p. 97.
20 18 Dec. 1845, O'Connell, *Correspondence*, vol. vii, pp. 349–50.
21 20 Dec. 1845, ibid., p. 351.
22 ibid., pp. 352–3.
23 ibid., p. 353.
24 O'Connell to William Smith O'Brien, 22 Dec. 1845, ibid., p. 353.
25 *Nation*, 22 Nov. 1845.
26 ibid., 29 Nov. 1845.
27 ibid., 1 Nov. 1845.
28 ibid., 8 Nov. 1845.
29 *History of the Times: The Tradition Established 1841–1884* (London, 1939), vol. ii, p. 9.
30 Atkins, *Life of Sir William Howard Russell*, op. cit., vol. i, pp. 33–4.
31 MacDonagh, *Life of O'Connell*, op. cit., p. 380.
32 *Politics of Repeal*, op. cit., p. 99.
33 26 Feb. 1846, O'Connell, *Correspondence*, vol. viii, p. 7.
34 15 April 1846, ibid., pp. 12–13.
35 26 March 1846, ibid., p. 10.
36 *Hansard*, 3rd series, vol. lxxxv, col. 1161.
37 28 April 1846, ibid., col. 1170.
38 28 April 1846, O'Connell, *Correspondence*, vol. viii, p. 15.
39 William Smith O'Brien to secretary of Liberal Club in co. Limerick, 6 May 1846, Smith O'Brien Papers, NLI MS 436, item 1570.
40 Thomas Steele to O'Connell, 9 May 1846, O'Connell, *Correspondence*, vol. viii, p. 23.
41 30 April 1846, ibid., pp. 16–17.
42 9 May 1846, ibid., p. 22.
43 *Nation*, 16 May 1846.
44 *Limerick Reporter*, 8 May 1846.
45 Edward Brodrick to O'Connell, 15 May 1846, O'Connell, *Correspondence*, vol. viii, p. 30.
46 11 May 1846, ibid., p. 24.
47 22 May 1846, ibid., p. 38.
48 15 June 1846, ibid., p. 46.
49 T. M. Ray to O'Connell, 16 June 1846, ibid., p. 48.
50 ibid., p. 47.
51 15 June 1846, ibid., p. 48.
52 16 June 1846, ibid.
53 *Nation*, 23 May 1846.
54 Quoted in Martin Crean to O'Connell, 15 June 1846, O'Connell, *Correspondence*, vol. viii, p. 46.
55 ibid.
56 *Nation*, 27 June 1846.
57 29 June 1846, O'Connell, *Correspondence*, vol. viii, p. 60.
58 *Nation*, 18 July 1846.
59 Minute (in T. M. Ray's

handwriting) of the committee meeting is in the Smith O'Brien Papers, NLI MS 437, item 1660.

60 *Nation*, 18 July 1846.

61 McDowell, *Public Opinion and Government Policy in Ireland*, op. cit., p. 254.

62 30 June 1846, O'Connell, *Correspondence*, vol. viii, p. 61.

63 8 July 1846, ibid., p. 63.

64 23 June 1846, ibid., p. 56.

65 8 July 1846, ibid., p. 63.

66 12 July 1846, ibid., p. 67.

67 *Nation*, 18 July 1846.

68 18 July 1846, O'Connell, *Correspondence*, vol. viii, p. 70.

69 Cahirmoyle Correspondence, quoted in C. G. Duffy, *Four Years of Irish History 1845–1849* (London, 1883), p. 200.

70 Duffy, *Four Years of Irish History*, op. cit., p. 239.

71 ibid., p. 245.

72 ibid., p. 241.

CHAPTER 12
The Dying Fall

1846–7

1 O'Connell to David R. Pigot, 4 Aug. 1846, O'Connell, *Correspondence*, vol. viii, p. 79.

2 10 Aug. 1846, ibid., p. 81.

3 13 Aug. 1846, ibid., p. 83.

4 12 Aug. 1846, ibid., pp. 82–3.

5 Dr John Nugent to O'Connell, 13 Oct. [1846], ibid., p. 126.

6 *Personal Recollections*, op. cit., vol. ii, pp. 255–6.

7 ibid., p. 253.

8 ibid., p. 256.

9 *Politics of Repeal*, op. cit., pp. 110–11.

10 14 Aug. 1846, O'Connell, *Correspondence*, vol. viii, p. 84.

11 12 Aug. 1846, ibid., p. 82.

12 27 Aug. 1846, ibid., p. 87.

13 5 Oct. 1846, ibid., p. 110.

14 Public letter to T. M. Ray, 2 Oct. 1846, *Freeman's Journal*, 6 Oct. 1846.

15 ibid.

16 O'Connell to Stephen Barry, 13 Oct. 1846, O'Connell, *Correspondence*, vol. viii, p. 125.

17 O'Connell to Maziere Brady, 24 Sept. 1846, ibid., p. 98.

18 Bishop George J. P. Browne to O'Connell, 27 Nov. 1846, ibid., p. 146.

19 Rev. Barry Denny to O'Connell, 28 Sept. 1846, ibid., p. 103.

20 O'Connell to Benjamin Hawes, 19 Oct. 1846, ibid., pp. 133–4.

21 *Nation*, 8 Aug. 1846.

22 ibid., 12 Sept. 1846.

23 ibid., 15 Aug. 1846.

24 ibid., 5 Sept. 1846.

25 Smith O'Brien Papers, NLI MS 3444, quoted in Gwynn, *Young Ireland and 1848* op. cit., p. 86. This particular MS does not appear to be among the Smith O'Brien papers any longer.

26 Address of Loyal National Repeal Association to the People of Ireland, *Freeman's Journal*, 3 Oct. 1846.

27 Thomas Arkins to O'Connell, 26 Sept. 1845, O'Connell, *Correspondence*, vol. viii, p. 101.

28 T. M. Ray to O'Connell, 10 Oct. 1846, ibid., p. 119.

29 C. G. Duffy, *Four Years of Irish History* (London, 1883), p. 338.

30 Smith O'Brien Papers, NLI MS 437, item 1691.

31 Rev. Michael Comyn to O'Connell, 26 Nov. 1846, O'Connell, *Correspondence*, vol. viii, p. 145.

32 21 Nov. 1846, ibid., pp. 141–2.

33 ibid., p. 142.

34 Bishop Michael Blake to Repeal Association, 22 Nov. 1846, *Nation*, 28 Nov. 1846.

35 10 Dec. 1846, O'Connell, *Correspondence*, vol. viii, pp. 152–3.

36 12 Dec. 1846, Fitzpatrick, *Correspondence*, vol. ii, p. 394.
37 17 Dec. 1846, ibid., p. 397.
38 John Mitchel to William Smith O'Brien, 30 Dec. 1846, Smith O'Brien Papers, NLI MS 437, item 1747.
39 C. G. Duffy to William Smith O'Brien, 26 Dec. 1846, Smith O'Brien Papers, NLI MS 434, item 1303.
40 O'Connell to T. M. Ray, 13 Feb. 1847, Fitzpatrick, *Correspondence*, vol. ii, p. 407.
41 22 Jan. 1847, O'Connell, *Correspondence*, vol. viii, p. 161.
42 19 Aug. 1846, ibid., p. 86.
43 5 Nov. 1846, ibid., p. 137.
44 16 Nov. 1846, ibid., p. 140.
45 21 Nov. 1846, ibid., p. 143.
46 Maurice O'Connell to Pierce Mahony, 17 Dec. 1848, Rathcon Papers, quoted in M. R. O'Connell, 'O'Connell: Income, Expenditure and Despair', *Irish Historical Studies*, vol. xvii, Sept. 1970, p. 219 n. 3.
47 27 Aug. 1846, O'Connell, *Correspondence*, vol. viii, p. 87.
48 18 Nov. 1846, ibid., pp. 140–1.
49 Maurice O'Connell to O'Connell, 18 Nov. 1846, O'Connell to Maurice O'Connell, 21 Nov. 1846, ibid., pp. 140, 143.
50 5 Nov. 1846, ibid., p. 138.
51 16 Oct. 1846, ibid., p. 129.
52 5 Dec. 1846, ibid., p. 149.
53 10 Dec. 1846, ibid., p. 154.
54 Memo of Fitzpatrick, 11 Jan. 1847, Fitzpatrick, *Correspondence*, vol. ii, p. 399.
55 6 Feb. 1847, ibid., pp. 401–2.
56 8 Feb. 1847, O'Connell, *Correspondence*, vol. viii, p. 162.
57 8 Feb. 1847, *Hansard*, 3rd series, vol. lxxxix, cols 944–5.
58 Memo of Fitzpatrick, 11 Jan. 1847, Fitzpatrick, *Correspondence*, vol. ii, p. 399.
59 11 Feb. 1847, O'Connell, *Correspondence*, vol. viii, pp. 163–4.
60 Certified copy of O'Connell's will, O'Connell MS, University College, Dublin..
61 1 March 1847, O'Connell, *Correspondence*, vol. viii, p. 165.
62 3 March 1847, ibid., p. 165.
63 12 Feb. 1847, ibid., p. 164.
64 16 Feb. 1847, ibid.
65 Rev. John Miley to P. V. Fitzpatrick, 22 Feb. 1847, Fitzpatrick, *Correspondence*, vol. ii, p. 408.
66 19 March 1847, ibid., p. 410.
67 P. V. Fitzpatrick to his sister, 22 March 1847, ibid., p. 411.
68 Remigius Sheehan, quoted in ibid., p. 404.
69 P. V. Fitzpatrick to his sister, 22 March 1847, ibid., pp. 410–11.
70 MacDonagh, *Life of O'Connell*, op. cit., pp. 404–5.
71 8 April 1847, Fitzpatrick, *Correspondence*, vol. ii, p. 412.
72 Rev. John Miley to P. V. Fitzpatrick, 16 April 1847, ibid., p. 413.
73 April/May 1847, ibid., p. 414.
74 Duggan's diary, 11 May 1847, ibid., p. 415 n. 8.
75 Rev. John Miley to Morgan O'Connell, 15 May 1847, W. B. MacCabe, *The Last Days of O'Connell* (Dublin, 1847), p. 87.
76 James Shirley, 'The Contention of Ajax and Ulysses for the Armour of Achilles', scene iii, *The Dramatic Works and Poems of James Shirley*, (ed.) William Gifford (London, 1833), vol. vi, p. 397.
77 Rev. John Miley to P. V. Fitzpatrick, 14 May 1847, Fitzpatrick, *Correspondence*, vol. ii, p. 416.

Appendix I

Chief Officers of the Irish Administration, 1830–47

LORD-LIEUTENANTS

Duke of Northumberland (Mar. 1829).
Marquess of Anglesey (Dec. 1830).
Marquess Wellesley (Sept. 1833).
Earl of Haddington (Jan. 1835).
Earl of Mulgrave (May 1835).
Viscount Ebrington (Apr. 1839).
Earl De Grey (Sept. 1841).
Lord Heytesbury (July 1844).
Earl of Bessborough (July 1846).

CHIEF SECRETARIES

Lord Francis Leveson-Gower (June 1828).
Sir Henry Hardinge (July 1830).
Lord Stanley (Nov. 1830).
Sir John Cam Hobhouse (Mar. 1833).
Edward John Littleton (May 1833).
Sir Henry Hardinge (Dec. 1834).
Viscount Morpeth (Apr. 1835).
Lord Eliot (Sept. 1841).
Sir Thomas Francis Fremantle (Feb. 1845).
Earl of Lincoln (Feb. 1846).
Henry Labouchere (July 1846).

UNDER SECRETARIES

William Gregory (Oct. 1812).
Sir William Gossett (Dec. 1830).
Thomas Drummond (July 1835).
Norman Macdonald (May 1840).
Edward Lucas (Sept. 1841).
Richard Pennefather (Aug. 1845).
Thomas Redington (July 1846).

Appendix II

Assessment by Dr B. J. O'Neil of the causes of O'Connell's death, based on the findings of the post-mortem examination and the medical report of Dr Lacour who attended O'Connell during the last four weeks of his life.

In my opinion, O'Connell's illness and death can be attributed to the surgery he underwent two years before.

O'Connell had had troublesome haemorrhoids for years. In time, these painful lesions began to discharge to such an extent that he sought the services of a well known English surgeon. The operation certainly stopped the discharge (presumably pus and mucus), but O'Connell himself, his close friends and some eminent physicians considered that, from then on, his health began to diminish. By the autumn of 1846, his body had become noticeably weaker and his limbs and movements more feeble. Even his voice faded to a whisper. In the opinion of Professor Chomel and Dr Oliffe who examined him in Paris six weeks before his death, his by then diminished appetite, unsteady gait, failing intellect and depression were caused by a slow cerebral congestion, which symptoms had begun with head pains shortly after the surgery to his haemorrhoids. We may conjecture, but with near-certainty, that the operation caused a bacteraemia, whereupon organisms lodged in the frontal lobe of his brain. His body fought back and put a fibrous wall around the embolism, but the body's defence in such cases is not perfect. There is always surrounding oedema and inflammation. This causes increased pressure in the cranium and would account for the progressive symptomatology up to the last eight days of O'Connell's life.

During his last two months he suffered intense bronchitis and generalized weakness, anorexia, difficulty in moving his arms, trembling of the right arm and coldness of the hand, and his face was very much injected. On 7 May 1847 he suffered a violent headache, and his speech became quick and his movements spasmodically rapid. Two days later he was in a slight state of delirium, with impeded speech, bounding pulse and marked injection of the face. I consider that this state was the result of meningitis, which progressed and killed him after a further five days. In these last days his speech became more difficult and he was unable to swallow; and on the night of 13 May he went into a violent delirium. Some hours before his death, his mind cleared, a common occurrence in these terminal deliriums, and he died peacefully.

Post mortem showed the layers of the arachnoid connected together by adhesions resembling those of the pleura. The pia mater was densely adherent so that several gyra were glued together; it was also very vascular in its whole extent. This was the general inflammation of the covering of the brain. The cerebral matter was firm. The pia mater could be peeled off easily except over the anterior lobe of the right hemisphere. A space, the size of a walnut, was transformed into a greyish thick fluid, in the midst of which was a little blood. There was congestion in the rest of the brain, as if it had been sprinkled with blood. The other findings were congested lungs, sound heart and ossification of the aorta. The post mortemist stated the cause of death as 'ramolissement' of the brain, arising from the disease which he had contracted two years previously.

In my opinion there is no doubt that O'Connell died of a brain abscess, deriving from the surgery of two years previously, which eventually caused oedema of the brain giving him symptoms of intracranial pressure, culminating in a terminal meningitis leading to his death.

Select Bibliography

I PRIMARY SOURCES

1 MANUSCRIPTS
Graham Papers (Brighton, Sussex, Harvest Press Microform Publications).
Monteagle Papers. National Library of Ireland.
O'Connell Papers. National Library of Ireland.
O'Connell MS, University College, Dublin, Archives.
Peel Papers, British Library.
Annals, Sisters of Mercy, St Leo's, Carlow.
Records of Home Office relating to Ireland, H.O.100, Public Record Office.
Records of the National Bank of Ireland, in the possession of the Royal Bank of Scotland.

2 PARLIAMENTARY PAPERS
Report of the Select Committee on the Carlow Election Petition, 11 March 1836, *House of Commons Papers*, 1836, vol. xl.

3 PARLIAMENTARY DEBATES
Hansard, T. C., *Parliamentary Debates*, new and 3rd series.

4 PUBLISHED SELECT DOCUMENTS AND LETTERS
Aspinall, A. (ed.), *Three Early Nineteenth Century Diaries* (London, 1952).
Cusack, M. F. (ed.), *The Speeches and Public Letters of the Liberator*, 2 vols (Dublin, 1875).
Fitzpatrick, W. J. (ed.), *Correspondence of Daniel O'Connell the Liberator*, 2 vols (London, 1888).

Fitzpatrick, W. J., *The Life, Times and Correspondence of the Right Rev. Dr Doyle*, 2 vols (Dublin, 1880).
Gooch, G. P. (ed.), *The later correspondence of Lord John Russell, 1840–78*, 2 vols (London, 1925).
Hudson, D. (ed.), *The Diary of Henry Crabb Robinson, An Abridgement* (London, 1967).
MacHale, J., *Letters of the Most Reverend John MacHale, 1820–34* (Dublin, 1893).
O'Connell, J. (ed.) *The Life and Speeches of Daniel O'Connell*, 2 vols (Dublin, 1846).
O'Connell, J. (ed.) *The Select Speeches of Daniel O'Connell*, 2 vols (Dublin, 1854).
O'Connell, M. R. (ed.), *The Correspondence of Daniel O'Connell*, 8 vols (Dublin, 1972-80).
Russell, R. (ed.), *The early correspondence of Lord John Russell, 1805–40*, 2 vols (London, 1913).

5 NEWSPAPERS
Dublin Evening Post
Freeman's Journal (Dublin)
Morning Register
Nation
Pilot
The Times

6 CONTEMPORARY PRINTED SOURCES
The Charitable Bequests Act. A letter to the most Reverend Doctor Murray – By a lay Roman Catholic (Dublin, 1844).
Cloncurry, Lord Valentine Browne

(Lawless), *Personal Recollections of the Life and Times, with Extracts from the Correspondence of Valentine Lord Cloncurry* (Dublin, 1849).

Courtenay, Ellen, *A Narrative of the Most Extraordinary Cruelty, Perfidy and Depravity Perpetrated against Her by Daniel O'Connell Esq.* (London, 1837).

Curran, W. H., *Sketches of the Irish Bar*, 2 vols (London, 1855).

Cusack, M. F., *The Liberator: his Life and Times, Political and Social*, 2 vols (Kenmare, n.d.).

Daunt, W. J. O'N., *Personal Recollections of the late Daniel O'Connell, M.P.*, 2 vols (London, 1848).

Daunt, W. J. O'N., *A Life Spent for Ireland* (London, 1896).

de Beaumont, G. (trans. W. C. Taylor), *L'Irlande, Sociale, Politique et Religeuse*, 2 vols (London, 1839).

Duffy, C. G., *Four Years of Irish History 1845–1849* (London, 1883).

Duffy, C. G., *Thomas Davis. The Memoirs of an Irish Patriot 1840–1846* (London, 1890).

Duffy, C. G., *Young Ireland. A Fragment of Irish History 1840–45*, 2 vols (London, 1896).

Fagan, W., *The Life and Times of Daniel O'Connell*, 2 vols (Cork, 1847–8).

Greville, C., *The Greville Memoirs: a Journal of the reigns of King George IV and King William IV*, (ed.) H. Reeve, 3 vols (London, 1875).

Greville, C., *The Greville Memoirs (second part): a Journal of the Reign of Queen Victoria from 1837 to 1852*, (ed.) H. Reeve, 3 vols (London, 1885).

Hobhouse, J. (Lord Broughton), *Recollections of a Long Life, with Additional Extracts from His Private Diaries*, (ed.) Lady Dorchester, 6 vols (London, 1909–11).

Houston, A., *Daniel O'Connell, His Early Life, and Journal, 1795 to 1802* (London, 1906).

Huish, R., *Memoirs Private and Political of Daniel O'Connell* (London, 1836).

Levy, J. (ed.), *A Full and Revised Report of the Three Days' Discussion in the Corporation of Dublin on the Repeal of the Union* (Dublin, 1843).

Luby, T. C., *The Life, Opinions, Conversations and Eloquence of Daniel O'Connell* (New York, 1872).

MacCabe, W. B., *The Last Days of O'Connell* (Dublin, 1847).

Madden, D. O., *Ireland and its Rulers since 1829* (London, 1844).

O'Connell, D. (ed.), *A Full report of the Proceedings of the Great Meeting of the Catholics of London. With an Address to the English People, and the Letters to the Wesleyan Methodists* (London, 1839).

O'Connell, D., *Instructions for the Appointments of Repeal Wardens and Collectors of the Repeal Fund, their Duties, &c.* (Dublin, 1843).

O'Connell, D., *A Letter to the Duke of Wellington* (London, 1835).

O'Connell, D., *Liberty and Intolerance. An Address to the Wesleyan Methodists, being a Reply to the Manifesto, lately published by the Methodists of Manchester, on national education* (Sheffield, 1839).

O'Connell, D., *Liberty or Slavery. Daniel O'Connell on American Slavery. Reply to O'Connell by S. P. Chase* [Cincinnati?, 1864].

O'Connell, D., *Daniel O'Connell upon American Slavery* (New York, 1860).

O'Connell, D., *A Memoir on Ireland, Native and Saxon, 1172–1660,* vol. i [no more published], (Dublin, 1843).

O'Connell, D., *Speech on Justice to Ireland (1836).*

O'Connell, J., *Recollections and Experiences from a Parliamentary Career from 1833 to 1848,* 2 vols (London, 1849).

O'Connell, M. J., *The Last Colonel of the Irish Brigade,* 2 vols (London, 1892).

O'Flanagan, J. R., *Bar Life of O'Connell* (London, 1875).

O'Flanagan, J. R., *Life and Times of Daniel O'Connell* (Dublin, 1875).

Peel, (Sir) R., *Memoirs by Sir Robert Peel,* (eds) Earl Stanhope and E. Cardwell, 2 vols (London, 1857–8).

Shaw, H., *Authenticated Report of the Irish State Trials 1844* (Dublin, [1844]).

Sheil, R. L., *Sketches, Legal and Political,* (ed.) M. W. Savage, 2 vols (London, 1855).

A Special Report of the Proceedings in the Case of the Queen against Daniel O'Connell, J. O'Connell in the Court of Queen's Bench, Ireland, 1843 and 1844, on an indictment for conspiracy and misdemeanours, (ed.) J. Flanedy (Dublin, 1844).

Stokes, W., *William Stokes: his life and journal* (London, 1898).

Thackeray, W. M., *The Irish Sketch Book* (Collins edn, London and Glasgow, n.d.).

Whately, E. J., *Life and correspondence of Richard Whately,* 2 vols (London, 1866).

Venedey, J. (trans. W. B. McCabe), *Ireland and the Irish during the Repeal Year 1843* (Dublin, 1844).

II SECONDARY SOURCES

1 BOOKS AND ARTICLES

Anglesey, Marquess of, *One-Leg, The life and letters of William Henry Paget, first Marquess of Anglesey, KG, 1768–1854* (London, 1961).

Atkins, J. B., *The Life of Sir William Howard Russell,* 2 vols (London, 1911).

Aspinall, A., *Lord Brougham and the Whig Party* (Manchester, 1927).

Aspinall, A., *Politics and the Press c.1780–1850* (London, 1949).

Auchmuty, J. J., *Sir Thomas Wyse, 1791–1862: the life and career of an educator and diplomat* (London, 1939).

Aydelotte, W. O., 'The House of Commons in the 1840s', *History,* 1954.

Broderick, J. F., *The Holy See and the Irish Repeal Movement, 1829–47* (Rome, 1951).

Clarke, R., 'The Relations between O'Connell and the Young Irelanders', *Irish Historical Studies,* vol. iii, 1942.

Connolly, S. J., *Priests and People in Pre-Famine Ireland, 1780–1845* (Dublin, 1982).

D'Arcy, F. A., 'The Artisans of Dublin and Daniel O'Connell, 1830–47', *Irish Historical Studies,* vol. xvii, 1970.

Dunlop, R., *Daniel O'Connell and the Revival of National Life in Ireland* (London, 1900).

Edwards, R. D., 'The contribution of Young Ireland to the development of the Irish National idea', in S. Pender (ed.) *Féilscríbhinn Tórna* (Cork, 1947).

Edwards, R. D. and Williams, T. D., *The Great Famine* (Dublin, 1956).

Edwards, R. D., *Daniel O'Connell and his world* (London, 1975).

Farrell, B., *The Irish Parliamentary Tradition* (Dublin, 1973).

Gash, N., *Sir Robert Peel, The Life of Sir Robert Peel after 1830* (London, 1972).

Gladstone, W. E., 'Daniel O'Connell', *Nineteenth Century*, vol. 25, no. 143, Jan. 1889.

Good, W. J., 'O'Connell and Repeal', *Dublin Review*, vol. 184, 1929.

Graham, A. H., 'The Lichfield House Compact, 1835', *Irish Historical Studies*, vol. xii, 1961.

Gwynn, D., *Daniel O'Connell and Ellen Courtenay* (Oxford, 1930).

Gwynn, D., *Daniel O'Connell* (rev. edn., Oxford 1947).

Gwynn, D., *O'Connell, Davis and the Colleges Bill* (Oxford, 1948).

Gwynn, D., *Young Ireland and 1848* (Cork, 1949).

Hall, F. G., *The Bank of Ireland, 1783–1946* (Dublin, 1949).

Hill, J., 'Nationalism and the Catholic Church in the 1840s: Views of the Dublin Repealers', *Irish Historical Studies*, vol. xix, 1975.

Hill, J., 'The Protestant response to Repeal: the case of the Dublin working class', in F. S. L. Lyons and R. A. J. Hawkins (eds), *Ireland under the Union: Varieties of Tension* (Oxford, 1980).

Hoppen, K. T., *Elections, Politics, and Society in Ireland* (Oxford, 1984).

Inglis, B., 'O'Connell and the Irish Press, 1800–42', *Irish Historical Studies*, vol. viii, 1952.

Inglis, B., *The Freedom of the Press in Ireland, 1784–1841* (London, 1954).

Kennedy, B. A., 'Sharman Crawford on the repeal question, 1847', *Irish Historical Studies*, vol. vi, 1949.

Kerr, D., *Peel, Priests and Politics* (Oxford, 1982).

Lecky, W. E. H., *Leaders of Public Opinion in Ireland*, 2 vols (New York, 1912).

Lefevre, G. S., *Peel and O'Connell* (London, 1887).

Lynch, P. and Vaizey, J., *Guinness's Brewery in the Irish Economy 1759–1876* (Cambridge, 1960).

Lyne, G. J., 'Daniel O'Connell, Intimidation and the Kerry Elections of 1835', *Kerry Archaeological and Historical Society*, vol. iv, 1974.

MacCaffrey, L. J., *Daniel O'Connell and the Repeal Year* ([Lexington, 1966]).

McCartney, D. (ed.), *The World of Daniel O'Connell* (Dublin, 1980).

MacDonagh, M., *The Life of Daniel O'Connell* (London, 1903).

MacDonagh, O., 'The Contribution of O'Connell', in B. Farrell (ed.), *The Irish Parliamentary Tradition* (Dublin, 1973).

MacDonagh, O., 'The Politicization of the Irish Catholic Bishops 1800–50', *Historical Journal*, vol. 18, no. 1, 1975.

MacDonagh, O., 'Ambiguity in Nationalism – the case of Ireland', *Historical Studies*, vol. 19, no. 76, 1981.

MacDonagh, O., 'O'Connell and Repeal, 1840–1845', in M. Bentley and J. Stevenson (eds), *High and Low Politics in Modern Britain* (Oxford, 1983).

MacDonagh, O., 'The Victorian Bank, 1824–1914', in F. S. L. Lyons (ed.), *Bicentenary Essays. Bank of Ireland 1783–1983* (Dublin, 1983).

MacDonagh, O., *States of Mind: a Study of Anglo-Irish Conflict 1780–1980* (London, 1983).

McDowell, R. B., *Public Opinion and Government Policy in Ireland 1801–1846* (London, 1952).

MacIntyre, A., *The Liberator: Daniel O'Connell and the Irish Party,*

1930–47 (London, 1965).

MacManus, M. J. (ed.), *Thomas Davis and Young Ireland* (Dublin, 1945).

Moley, R., *Daniel O'Connell, Nationalism Without Violence: an essay* (New York, 1974).

Monypenny, W. F. and Buckle, G. E., *The Life of Benjamin Disraeli, Earl of Beaconsfield*, 6 vols (London, 1910–20).

Mulvey, H. F., 'The Correspondence of Daniel and Mary O'Connell', in M. R. O'Connell (ed.), *The Correspondence of Daniel O'Connell* (Shannon and Dublin, 1972–80), vol. i.

Murphy, M., 'Repeal, Popular Politics and the Clergy of Cork', *Journal of the Cork Historical and Archaeological Society*, vol. lxxxii, 1977.

Nowlan, K. B., 'The Meaning of Repeal in Irish History', *Historical Studies IV* (Dublin 1963).

Nowlan, K. B., *The Politics of Repeal: a study of the relations between Great Britain and Ireland, 1842–50* (London, 1965).

Nowlan, K. B. and O'Connell, M. R. (eds), *Daniel O'Connell: Portrait of a Radical* (Belfast, 1984).

O'Brien, J., *The Catholic Middle Classes in Pre-Famine Cork* (O'Donnell Lecture, NUI, 1979).

O'Brien, R. B., *Fifty years of concession to Ireland, 1831–81* (London, n.d.).

O'Brien, R. B., *Thomas Drummond, under-secretary in Ireland, 1835–40: Life and Letters* (London, 1889).

O'Connell, B. M., *O'Connell Family Tracts*, nos 1–3 (Dublin, 1947–51).

O'Connell, M. R., 'Daniel O'Connell: Income, Expenditure and Despair', *Irish Historical Studies*, vol. xvii, 1970.

O'Connell, M. R., 'Daniel O'Connell and Religious Freedom', *Thought*, vol. 50, no. 197, June 1975.

O'Connell, M. R., 'O'Connell as Lawyer and Landlord', Thomas Davis Lecture for Radio-Telefís Eireainn, spring 1975.

O'Connell, M. R., 'Daniel O'Connell and his family', *Irish Times*, 6 Aug. 1975.

O'Connell, M. R., 'O'Connell Reconsidered', *Studies*, vol. lxiv, 1975.

O'Connell, M. R., 'O'Connell, Young Ireland and Violence', *Thought*, vol. 52, 1977.

O'Connell Centenary Record 1875 (Dublin, 1878).

Ó Faoláin, S., *King of the Beggars: A Life of Daniel O'Connell* (London, 1938).

O'Ferrall, F., 'The Growth of Political Consciousness in Ireland', *Irish Economic and Social History*, vol. i, 1979.

O'Ferrall, F., *Daniel O'Connell* (Dublin, 1981).

O'Ferrall, F., 'Daniel O'Connell and Henry Cooke: the conflict of civil and religious liberty in Modern Ireland', *Irish Review*, vol. i, 1986.

O'Higgins, R., 'Irish Trade Unions and Politics', *Historical Review*, vol. iv, 1961.

Osofsky, G., 'Abolitionists, Irish Immigrants, and the Dilemmas of Romantic Nationalism', *American Historical Review*, vol. 80, no. 4, Oct. 1975.

Ó Tuathaigh, G., *Ireland before the Famine, 1798–1848* (Dublin, 1972).

Ó Tuathaigh, M. A. G., *Thomas Drummond and the Government of Ireland 1835–41* (O'Donnell Lecture, NUI, 1977).

Parker, C. S., *Life and letters of Sir James Graham, second baronet of Netherby, 1792–1861*, 2 vols (London, 1907).

Parker, C. S., *Sir Robert Peel from*

his private papers, 3 vols (London, 1899).

Patterson, M. W., *Sir Francis Burdett and his Times (1770–1844)*, 2 vols (London, 1931).

Riach, D. C., 'Daniel O'Connell and American anti-slavery', *Irish Historical Studies*, vol. xx, 1976.

Slattery, M., *The National Bank 1835–1970* (London, n.d.).

Tierney, M. (ed.), *Daniel O'Connell. Nine Centenary Essays* (Dublin, 1949).

Trench, C. C., *The Great Dan. A Biography of Daniel O'Connell* (London, 1984).

Tyrrell, A., *Joseph Sturge and the Moral Radical Party in Early Victorian Britain* (London, 1987).

Walpole, S., *The Life of Lord John Russell*, 2 vols (London, 1889).

Walsh, W. J., 'The Board of Charitable Donations and Bequests', *Irish Ecclesiastical Record*, 3rd series, vol. xiv.

Walsh, W. J., *O'Connell, Archbishop Murray and the Board of Charitable Bequests* (Dublin, 1916).

Whyte, J. H., 'Daniel O'Connell and the repeal party', *Irish Historical Studies*, vol. xi, no. 44, Sept. 1959.

Whyte, J. H., 'The Influence of the Catholic Clergy on Elections in Nineteenth Century Ireland', *English Historical Review*, vol. lxxv, 1960.

Woodham-Smith, C., *The Great Hunger: Ireland 1845–9* (London, 1962).

2 THESES

Coldrick, Sister H., 'Daniel O'Connell and Religious Freedom', PhD thesis, Fordham University, 1974.

O'Ferrall, F., 'O'Connellite Politics and Political Education', PhD thesis, Trinity College, Dublin, 1978.

Bibliographical Note

Much the most important contemporary biographical sources for O'Connell's life are Fagan's *Life and Times*, O'Neill Daunt's *Personal Reminiscences* and *Life Spent in Ireland*, and the detailed annotations in W. J. Fitzpatrick's collection of the *Correspondence*. Fagan was close to O'Connell and his Cork 'manager' during the 1830s; O'Neill Daunt was his personal secretary for several years; and W. J. Fitzpatrick was the nephew of P. V. Fitzpatrick, O'Connell's friend and agent. M. MacDonagh's *Life* includes some contemporary comment on O'Connell not otherwise extant, and Gavan Duffy in *Four Years of Irish History* provides some first-hand accounts of the 'traversers'' sojourn in Richmond prison.

Among earlier biographies of O'Connell, Dunlop's *Daniel O'Connell and the Revival of National Life*, Ó Faoláin's *King of the Beggars* and O'Ferrall's *O'Connell* are outstanding, the first for its immediately post-Parnellite perspective, the second for its remarkable psychological insight and empathy, and the third as a very well-balanced brief biographical essay. Lecky's analysis of O'Connell's career and personality in *Leaders of Public Opinion* is full and fair, and Gladstone's 1889 review article extraordinarily perceptive.

Three excellent studies, MacIntyre's *The Liberator*, McDowell's *Public Opinion and Government Policy* and Nowlan's *Politics of Repeal*, provide between them a thorough background to the relevant politics and political organizations of the years 1830–47. Ó Tuathaigh's *Drummond and the Government of Ireland* and Broderick's *Holy See and the Irish Repeal Movement* are particularly useful monographs on the Irish Administration, 1835–41, and the political attitudes of the Catholic hierarchy, respectively. Although O'Ferrall's *Catholic Emancipation* lies outside the period under consideration, it illuminates a political methodology which O'Connell was to repeat and perfect in later years.

A number of articles in learned journals or volumes of collected essays give authoritative accounts of various facets of O'Connell's conduct or situation during his last seventeen years. Chief among them are D'Arcy's 'Artisans of Dublin and O'Connell', Graham's 'Lichfield House Compact', J. Hennig, 'Continental Opinion' in Tierney (ed.), *O'Connell: Nine Centenary Essays*, Inglis's 'O'Connell and the Irish press', Mulvey's 'Correspondence of Daniel and Mary O'Connell', M. R. O'Connell's 'O'Connell: Income, Expenditure and Despair', 'O'Connell and his family' and 'O'Connell and Religious Freedom', Osofsky's 'Abolitionists, Irish Immigrants, and the Dilemmas of Romantic Nationalism', Riach's 'O'Connell and American anti-slavery', K. F. Roche's 'Revolution and Counter-Revolution' in Tierney (ed.), *O'Connell: Nine Centenary Essays*, H. Rollet's 'The Influence of O'Connell's Example on French Liberal Catholicism' in McCartney (ed.), *The World of O'Connell*, Walsh's 'Board of Charitable Donations and Bequests' and Whyte's 'O'Connell and the repeal party'.

Biographical Notes

Biographical Notes were supplied in *The Hereditary Bondsman: Daniel O'Connell, 1775–1829* for many of the persons also mentioned in this book. In these cases, the reader is referred to the entries in the earlier volume.

James ABERCROMBY (1776–1858)
MP for Midhurst 1807–12, for Calne 1812–30, for Edinburgh 1832–9. Judge advocate general 1827–8. Chief baron of the exchequer (Scotland) 1830–2. Master of the mint in 1834. Speaker of the House of Commons 1835–9. Created Baron Dunfermline in 1839.

William ABRAHAM (1792–1837)
Bishop of Waterford and Lismore 1830–7.

John Charles (Spencer) styled Viscount ALTHORP (1782–1845)
MP for Oakhampton 1804–6, for St Albans 1806, for Northamptonshire 1806–34. A lord of the treasury 1806–7. Chancellor of the exchequer and leader of the House of Commons 1830–4. Succeeded as third Earl Spencer in 1834.

William (Arden), second baron ALVANLEY (1789–1849)
Officer in the Coldstream Guards, later Capt. 50th Reg. of Foot. Succeeded as second baronet in 1804.

Marquess of ANGLESEY, see *The Hereditary Bondsman*

Thomas ARKINS
Repeal warden. Merchant tailor in Dublin.

Anthony Ashley Cooper, Lord ASHLEY, seventh earl of Shaftesbury (1801– 1885)
MP 1826–46, 1847–51. 1828 commissioner of the board of control, 1834 board of the admiralty. Refused later offer of cabinet positions. A philanthropist concerned with the treatment of lunatics, of workers in factories and mines, and of chimney sweep apprentices; and with the education of the poor, working class dwellings and religious societies.

Thomas ATTWOOD (1783–1856)
A Birmingham banker and political reformer. MP for Birmingham 1832–40.

Walter J. BALDWIN JP (1774–1835)
Eldest son of James Baldwin, Clohina, co. Cork, and first cousin of O'Connell. Author of pamphlet, *An Appeal to Common Sense and to Religion on the Catholic Question* ... (1823).

John BANIM (1798–1842)
Irish novelist, dramatist and poet. He wrote the O'Hara Tales with his brother Michael. His other works include *The Celt's Paradise, Damon and Pythias* and *Boyne Water*.

Michael BANIM (1796–1874)
He wrote the O'Hara Tales with his brother John, and organized the family's business affairs. He worked hard for Catholic Emancipation. In 1852 he was appointed postmaster in Kilkenny.

Richard BARRETT (d.1854)
Editor and proprietor of the *Pilot* newspaper which he established in 1827 to support O'Connell.

R. N. BENNETT see *The Hereditary Bondsman*

William George Frederic Cavendish
BENTINCK (1802–48)
Officer in 10th hussars. 1822–5
private secretary to Canning, his
uncle. 1825 joined the 2nd life
guards. 1828–48 MP for Lynn.
Leading defender of the corn laws. In
1846 he organized the protectionists
as a third political party.

Ralph BERNAL (d.1854)
Whig MP 1818–52. Chairman of
committees 1833–41, 1847–52.
Well-known art collector.

John William (Ponsonby) Earl of
BESSBOROUGH see *Duncannon, Lord*

Charles BIANCONI (1786–1875)
Promoter of passenger and mail car
system in Ireland from 1815. Mayor
of Clonmel 1845 and 1846. 1863
appointed deputy lieutenant.

James BIRCH
Journalist. Proprietor of *World*
newspaper, founded in Dublin in
1840. After it had become a Dublin
Castle organ, he took an action
against the Irish chief secretary for
insufficient payment for his services.

Francis BLACKBURNE (1782–1867)
Attorney-general for Ireland 1831–5,
1841–2. Master of the rolls 1842–6.
Chief justice of queen's bench 1846–
52. Lord chancellor of Ireland 1852,
1866. Lord justice of appeal in
Ireland 1856.

Mark BLAKE
MP for co. Mayo 1840–6.

Michael BLAKE (1775–1860)
Parish priest of Townsend Street
1831–3. Catholic bishop of Dromore
1833–60.

Charles BOYTON (1799–1844)
Church of Ireland rector of Conwall,
co. Donegal from 1833.

Maziere BRADY (1796–1871)
Solicitor-general 1837–9. Attorney-
general 1839–40. Chief baron of the
exchequer 1840–6. Judge of the
court of chancery 1846–66. Lord

chancellor of Ireland 1846–52,
1853–8, 1859–66. Created a baronet
1869.

Maurice BRENAN
New Street, Killarney. Son of John
Brenan and Ellen, youngest daughter
of Charles Sugrue. A close relative of
O'Connell.

Lord BROUGHAM see *The Hereditary
Bondsman*

George Joseph Plunket BROWNE (c.
1790–1858)
Bishop of Galway 1831–44. Bishop
of Elphin 1844–58

William BROWNE
MP for co. Kerry 1830–1, 1841–7.

Henry BRUEN (d. 1852)
MP for co. Carlow 1812–31, 1835–
7, Dec. 1840–52. Colonel in Carlow
militia.

Charles BULLER (1806–1848)
Liberal politician and pamphleteer.
MP for West Looe, Cornwall 1830–
1, for Liskeard 1832–48. Secretary to
governor-general of Canada in 1838.
Judge-advocate-general 1846. Chief
poor law commissioner in 1847.

Sir Francis BURDETT see *The
Hereditary Bondsman*

Patrick BURKE (c. 1776–1843)
Coadjutor of Elphin 1819–27, bishop
of Elphin 1827–43.

Charles BURTON (1760–1847)
Born in Northamptonshire. Called to
the Irish bar in 1792. Became a
justice of the King's Bench in 1820.
As a judge in the state trials of 1844
he passed sentence on O'Connell.

Lt. Col. Hon. Pierce BUTLER D. L.
(1774–1846)
MP for co. Kilkenny 1832–46.
Colonel in co. Kilkenny militia.

Isaac BUTT (1813–79)
Chair of political economy TCD
1836–41. Called to the Irish bar in
1838. Elected alderman of the new
Dublin corporation, as a
conservative, in 1841. Established
Protestant Guardian newspaper in

Dublin. 1844 called to the inner bar. Defended Smith O'Brien and others in the state trials of 1848. MP for Harwich 1852, liberal-conservative MP for Youghal 1852–65. Called to the English bar in 1859. 1865–9 defence counsel for Fenian prisoners. President of the Amnesty Association in 1869. MP for Limerick city and leader of the Home Rule party 1871–9.

George Gordon BYRON (1788–1824) Poet. He succeeded as sixth lord in 1798. He spoke in the House of Lords three times 1812–13, but any political ambition was extinguished by his literary success. His works include *Childe Harold, Don Juan, The Waltz*, the *Giaour*, the *Bride of Abydos*, and *The Corsair*. Despite his aristocratic origins, he was critical of the cant and immorality of the ruling classes at home and abroad. He started a journal called the *Liberal* in 1822, but it only lasted four numbers.

John CAMPBELL (1779–1861) Solicitor-general of England 1832–4. Knighted 1832. Attorney-general of England 1834, 1835–41. Lord chancellor of Ireland June–Oct. 1841. Chief justice 1850–9. Chancellor of England 1859–61. Legal biographer.

Robert CANE (1807–1858) Surgeon. Mayor of Kilkenny 1845 and 1849. Chief promoter of Repeal in Kilkenny. He did not take part in the 1848 insurrection but was arrested and imprisoned for a time. In 1853 he originated the Celtic Union, a semi-political and semi-literary society.

John CANTWELL (1792–1866) Catholic bishop of Meath 1830–66.

Hon. Henry CAULFIELD D. L. (1779–1862) Younger son of first earl of Charlemont. MP for co. Armagh 1802–7, 1815–18 and 1820–30.

Lord CLONCURRY see *The Hereditary Bondsman*

William COBBETT see *The Hereditary Bondsman*

Richard COBDEN (1804–1865) 1838–46 he was a key figure in the Anti-Corn Law League. MP for Stockport 1841–7, for West Riding 1847–57, for Rochdale 1859–65. He negotiated a commercial treaty with France 1859–60. In 1861 he returned to Paris as chief commissioner for working out the scale of duties on particular articles.

Thomas COEN (d. 1847) Coadjutor of Clonfert 1816–31, bishop of Clonfert 1831–47.

John COGHLAN (d. 1863) Parish priest, Kilmovee, Ballaghaderreen from 1846.

Thomas [O'] CONNOR Merchant in Dublin.

Frederick William CONWAY (1782–1853) Editor *Freeman's Journal* 1806–12, editor Dublin weekly *Messenger* 1808–12. Editor and proprietor of the *Dublin Evening Post* 1814–53.

Marcus COSTELLO (born c. 1801) First president of the National Trades Political Union 1831–c. 1833. Attorney-general of Gibraltar 1842–68. A Protestant.

Patrick COSTELLO (d. 1858) Solicitor. Engaged in Catholic agitation and anti-tithe campaign. MP for Waterford city 1848–52.

Philip Cecil CRAMPTON (1782–1862) Professor of law TCD 1816–34. MP for Milborne 1831–2. Solicitor-general for Ireland Dec. 1830–4. Judge of the court of king's bench 1834–59.

William Sharmon CRAWFORD (1781–1861) 1811 sheriff of Down. MP for Dundalk 1835–7, Rochdale 1841–52. Strong advocate of tenant-right and radical parliamentary reform.

Gerald CREAN
 Brother of Martin Crean. Secretary to
 the Education Society. Printer,
 stationer and account book
 manufacturer.

Martin CREAN (c. 1802–67)
 Acting-secretary of the Repeal
 Association for part of 1846.
 Associated with the glass
 manufacturing industry.

Paul CULLEN (1803–1878)
 Rector of the Irish College, Rome
 1832–48; of the Propaganda College,
 Rome 1848–9. Archbishop of
 Armagh 1849–52, of Dublin 1852–
 78. Cardinal in 1866. From 1850
 on he dominated the Irish Catholic
 hierachy.

William Henry CURRAN (1789–1858)
 Called to the Irish bar 1816.
 Insolvency commissioner in Ireland.
 Bencher of King's Inns, Dublin 1848.
 Author of Life of John Philpot
 Curran (his father), and Sketches of
 the Irish Bar.

Patrick CURTIS see The Hereditary
 Bondsman

Col. Hon. George Lionel Dawson
 DAMER (1788–1856)
 Third son of the first earl of
 Portarlington. MP for Portarlington
 1835–47. Comptroller of the
 household 1841–7.

William Joseph O'Neill DAUNT
 (1807–94)
 Convert to Roman Catholicism.
 Returned for Mallow, in the general
 election of 1832 but unseated on the
 petition of the tory candidate. 1841–
 2 secretary to O'Connell, as lord
 mayor of Dublin. Daunt was Repeal
 director for Leinster, and head
 Repeal warden for Scotland, and
 much involved in Repeal Association
 proceedings in 1845–6.

Thomas Osborne DAVIS (1814–45)
 Poet and journalist. Called to the bar
 in 1838. 1839 he joined the Repeal
 Association. In 1841 he was joint

editor of the Dublin Morning
 Register with John Dillon. July 1842
 he, Dillon and Duffy founded the
 Nation, to which he was a leading
 contributor, 1842–5.

George Robert DAWSON (1790–1856)
 Private secretary to Robert Peel. MP
 for co. Londonderry 1815–30, for
 Harwich 1830–2. Under-secretary of
 state for the home department
 1822–7. Financial secretary to the
 treasurer 1828–30. In 1830 he was
 made a privy councillor.

Arthur (French), Baron DE FREYNE
 (1786–1856)
 Whig MP for co. Roscommon
 1821–32. 1839 created Baron de
 Freyne of Artagh. Having no male
 issue, he was in 1851 created Baron
 de Freyne of Coolavin, with a special
 remainder, failing direct heirs, to his
 brothers. Lieutenant of co.
 Roscommon 1854–6.

John (French), Baron DE FREYNE
 (1788–1863)
 Rector of Grange Sylvae, co.
 Kilkenny. Succeeded as Baron de
 Freyne of Coolavin in 1856.

Thomas Philip DE GREY, second earl
 De Grey (1781–1859)
 He became the second earl De Grey
 in 1833. First lord of the admiralty
 1834–5; lord lieutenant of Ireland
 1841–4.

James DELAHUNTY (1808–1885)
 Waterford merchant. Alderman of
 Waterford 1842–5. Coroner of co.
 Waterford 1850–67. MP for
 Waterford City 1868–74; for co.
 Waterford 1877–80.

Thomas DENMAN see The Hereditary
 Bondsman

Cornelius DENVIR (1791–1866)
 Professor of mathematics and natural
 philosophy at Maynooth 1813–26.
 Parish priest of Downpatrick 1826–
 35. Bishop of Down and Connor
 1835–65.

Duke of DEVONSHIRE see The
 Hereditary Bondsman

John Blake DILLON (1816–1866)
A member of the Young Ireland movement. With Davis and Duffy he founded the *Nation* in 1842. He took part in the 1848 rebellion, escaped to the US and returned to Ireland in 1855 after the amnesty. He helped to found the National Association and became its first secretary. MP for co. Tipperary 1865–6.

Benjamin DISRAELI (1804–1881)
Man of letters and statesman. Became an MP in 1837, and in 1848 leader of the conservative party in the House of Commons. Chancellor of the Exchequer 1852, 1858–9, 1866–8. Prime minister 1868, 1874–80. In 1876 he was created earl of Beaconsfield.

Michael DOHENY (1805–1862)
A leading member of the Repeal Association. Contributed prose and verse to the *Nation*. After the 1848 insurrection he escaped to New York, where he was admitted to the bar. Became a colonel of the 9th New York State militia regiment, and wrote *The History of the American Revolution* and *The Felon's Track: a Narrative of '48*.

John DOHERTY see *The Hereditary Bondsman*

Richard DOWDEN
Merchant at Cork. Mayor of Cork 1845.

James Warren DOYLE see *The Hereditary Bondsman*

Thomas DRUMMOND (1797–1840)
Engineer. He invented the lime-light or Drummond light, and a form of heliostat. Head of the boundary commission for the great Reform bill. In 1833 he became secretary to Lord Althorp. Under-secretary for Ireland 1835–40.

Charles Gavan DUFFY (1816–1903)
Joined the *Morning Register*, Dublin in 1836. 1839–41 first editor of the Belfast *Vindicator*. With Davis and Dillon he founded the *Nation* and edited it 1842–9. MP for New Ross 1852–5. Emigrated to Australia in 1855 and settled in Melbourne. In 1856 he stood for the first Victorian parliament under responsible government. Minister for Lands 1858–9, 1861–3. In 1868 he helped to found the Melbourne *Advocate*. 1871–2 premier of Victoria. Became Speaker in 1877. 1880 returned to Europe.

John William Ponsonby, styled Lord DUNCANNON (1781–1847)
Styled Lord Duncannon until 1844. Created Baron Duncannon (UK) in 1834. Succeeded as fourth earl of Bessborough in 1844. MP for various English constituencies 1805–26, 1832–4, for co. Kilkenny 1826–32. Home secretary July–Dec. 1834. Lord lieutenant of Ireland July 1846–May 1847.

Edward DWYER see *The Hereditary Bondsman*

Hugh Fortescue, styled Viscount EBRINGTON (1783–1861)
MP almost continuously 1804–39. Went to the House of Lords in 1839 in his father's barony of Fortescue. Succeeded as second earl Fortescue in 1841. Lord lieutenant of Ireland 1839–41. Lord steward of the household 1846–50.

Maria EDGEWORTH (1767–1849)
Novelist. Her works include *Castle Rackrent, Belinda, Essay on Irish Bulls* (with her father), *Tales of a Fashionable Life, Patronage, Harrington* and *Ormond*. She finished and published her father's *Memoirs*.

Edward Granville (Eliot) styled Lord ELIOT (1798–1877)
MP for Liskeard 1824–32, for East Cornwall 1837–45. Chief secretary for Ireland 1841–5, postmaster general 1845–6, lord lieutenant of Ireland 1853–5. Styled Lord Eliot

1823–45, succeeded as third earl of
St Germans in 1845.

Edward Law, second baron
ELLENBOROUGH (1790–1871)
Tory MP for St Michael's 1813–18.
Chief clerk of Pleas, King's Bench,
1812–38. Privy councillor 1828.
Privy seal 1828–9. President of the
board of control 1828–30, 1834–5,
1841, 1858. Governor general of
India 1841–4. Created Viscount
Southam and Earl of Ellenborough in
1844. First lord of the admiralty
1846.

Edward ELLICE (1781–1863)
MP for Coventry almost continually
1818–63. Secretary to the treasury
and liberal whip 1830–3. Secretary at
war 1833–4.

John Richard ELMORE M.D. (d. 1860)
A member of the London Board of
Directors of the National Bank.
Friend and physician of O'Connell.

George Hampden EVANS
MP for co. Dublin 1832–41.

William Trant FAGAN (1801–1859)
Merchant at Cork. Alderman in
Cork, mayor in 1844. MP for city of
Cork 1847–51, 1852–9. Author of
The Life and Times of Daniel
O'Connell.

Thomas FEENY (d. 1873)
1839 appointed administrator of the
diocese of Killala, as Bishop of
Ptolemais. 1848–73 bishop of
Killala.

Robert Cutlar FERGUSON (1768–1838)
Barrister. MP for Kirkcudbright
Stewartry 1826–38. Judge advocate-
general 1834–8. Fined and
imprisoned in 1799 for his alleged
part in the attempted rescue of
Arthur O'Connor at Maidstone in
1798.

Elizabeth (Betsey) FFRENCH
(O'CONNELL) see The Hereditary
Bondsman

Nicholas FFRENCH (d. 1842)
In 1831 he married O'Connell's

youngest daughter, Betsey. He was
appointed a stipendiary magistrate in
Oughterard, co. Galway in 1836.

Lord Thomas FFRENCH (1765–1814)
see The Hereditary Bondsman

William Francis FINN (1784–1862)
MP for co. Kilkenny 1832–7. Son of
a rich Carlow merchant who owned
Finn's Leinster Journal, Kilkenny.
Married O'Connell's sister Alicia
1812.

Edward Michael FITZGERALD
Secretary of Carlow liberal club.

Vesey FITZGERALD see The Hereditary
Bondsman

James Coleman FITZPATRICK (c.
1818–80)
Called to the Irish bar in 1842. Chief
justice of the Gold Coast in 1857–61.
Judge of British Kaffraria 1861–72.
Judge of Supreme Court of Cape of
Good Hope 1872–79. Author of The
pope, his rights and duties (1860).

Patrick Vincent FITZPATRICK see The
Hereditary Bondsman

Christopher FITZ-SIMON see The
Hereditary Bondsman

Nicholas FITZ-SIMON (b. 1806)
MP King's co. 1832–41; knighted
1841; a magistrate in Dublin Castle
from 1841.

Nicholas FORAN (d. 1855)
Ordained 1808. President St John's
College, Waterford 1814–18. Parish
priest, Lismore 1824–9, Dungarvan
1829–37. Bishop of Waterford and
Lismore 1837–55.

Thomas Campbell FOSTER (1813–82)
Barrister and legal writer.
Parliamentary reporter for the Times.

Arthur FRENCH (born c. 1802)
Secretary of the General Association.
First cousin to Arthur French, created
Baron de Freyne in 1839.

Edmund FRENCH O. P. (d. 1852)
Bishop of Kilmacduagh and
Kilfenora 1824–52.

John Matthew GALWEY (c. 1790–
1842)

Merchant, shipowner and landowner. 1832–5 MP co. Waterford. J.P., grand juror, co. Waterford.

William GODWIN see *The Hereditary Bondsman*

Isaac GOLDSMID see *The Hereditary Bondsman*

Thomas GOOLD see *The Hereditary Bondsman*

William GOSSETT (d. 1848)
Private secretary to the lord lieutenant. MP for Truro 1820–6. Under-secretary for Ireland 1830–5. Knighted in 1831.

Henry GOULBURN see *The Hereditary Bondsman*

Sir James Robert George GRAHAM (1792–1861)
MP almost continually 1818–21, 1826–61. First lord of the admiralty 1830–4, 1852–5. Home secretary 1841–6.

Henry GRATTAN (1789–1859)
Biographer of his father Henry Grattan. J.P., barrister, landowner and owner-editor of the *Freeman's Journal* until 1830. MP for Dublin City 1826–30, for co. Meath 1831–52.

Charles GREVILLE (1794–1865)
1821–59 clerk to the privy council. He had close relations with the Duke of Wellington, the Duke of Bedford, Lord Palmerston and Lord Clarendon and was sometimes used as a negotiator during ministerial changes.

Charles (Grey), second earl GREY see *The Hereditary Bondsman*

Gerald GRIFFIN (1803–40)
Dramatist, novelist and poet. He was a law student at the University of London for a time. In the late 1830s he joined the congregation of the Irish Christian Brothers.

Francis HALY (1781–1855)
Administrator of Mountrath 1813–22. Parish priest of Kilcock 1822. Bishop of Kildare and Leighlin from 1838.

Sir Henry HARDINGE (1785–1856)
Secretary at war 1828–30, 1841–4; Irish secretary July–Nov. 1830, Dec. 1834–April 1835; governor-general of India 1844–8. In 1846 he was created Viscount Hardinge of Lahore and of Durham. His army career culminated in his becoming field marshal in 1855.

John HARDY (1773/4–1855)
Barrister. Bencher 1840, reader 1850. Recorder of Leeds 1806–33. MP for Bradford 1832–7, 1841–7.

Benjamin HAWES (1797–1862)
MP for Lambeth 1832–47, for Kinsale 1848–52. Under-secretary for the colonies 1846–51. 1851–7 deputy secretary for the war department. Knighted 1856. 1857-62 permanent under-secretary for war.

Joseph HAYES
Merchant at Cork. Alderman of Cork.

William A'Court, first baron HEYTESBURY (1779–1860)
Succeeded his father as second baronet in 1817. Ambassador to Portugal 1824–8, to Russia 1828–32. In 1828 he was created Baron Heytesbury of Heytesbury, Wiltshire. Lord lieutenant of Ireland 1844–6. Governor of the Isle of Wight until 1857.

Sir John Cam HOBHOUSE, second baronet (1786–1869)
MP for Westminster 1820–33, for Nottingham 1834–47, for Harwich 1848–52. Succeeded as second baronet in 1831. 1832 became a privy councillor. Secretary of war 1832–3, chief secretary for Ireland March–April 1833, first commissioner of woods and forests 1834, president of the board of control 1835–41, 1846–52. Friend and executor of Byron. Created Baron Broughton in 1851.

Henry Richard (Vassall Fox) third baron HOLLAND (1773–1840)

Lord privy seal 1806–7, chancellor of duchy of Lancaster 1830–4, 1835–40.

Robert HOLMES (1765–1859)
Called to the Irish bar in 1795. Opposed the enactment of the Union. Married Robert Emmet's sister Mary and was imprisoned on suspicion during Emmet's rebellion. He declined to receive any favours from the government, refusing various offers of legal offices.

Joseph HUME (1777–1855)
A Radical. MP in 1812 and almost continuously 1818 to 1855. Leading advocate of Catholic Emancipation and economical reform.

Henry HUNT see *The Hereditary Bondsman*

Robert HUTTON
Presbyterian coachbuilder and merchant. MP for Dublin city 1837–41. Member of the Council of University College, London and of the British Association. Elected a fellow of the Geographical Society in 1813.

Sir John Kingston JAMES (1784–1869)
Created a baronet in 1823. Lord mayor of Dublin in 1822 and 1841.

Edward JONES M.D.
Physician to the lunatic asylum, Waterford. Appointed a magistrate for Waterford city 1837.

Leslie Grove JONES (1779–1839)
He served in the army throughout the Peninsular War, becoming captain and lieutenant-colonel in 1813. His pamphlet, 'Principles of Legitimacy' was published in 1827. During the reform agitation he wrote strong letters to the *Times* signed 'Radical'.

Sir Richard KEANE bt
MP for co. Waterford 1832–5.

James KEATINGE (1783–1849)
Appointed provincial coadjutor with right of succession 6 Dec. 1818; bishop of Ferns, 1819–49.

Richard KEATINGE (1793–1876)
K.C. in 1835. Appointed Queen's serjeant in 1842, judge of the prerogative court 1843. Judge of the probate court 1858–68.

George Bourke [O'] KELLY (1760–1843)
Acton, Middlesex. Married in 1799 Mary, second daughter of Peter Pentheny MD, Tara, co. Meath.

Valentine (Browne), second earl of KENMARE (1788–1853)
Styled Viscount Castlerosse 1801–12. Became second earl of Kenmare in 1812.

Patrick KENNEDY (d. 1850)
Coadjutor 1835–6, bishop of Killaloe 1836–50.

John KENNY (1792–1879)
Parish priest, Kilrush, co. Clare 1828–48. Parish priest, Ennis and dean of Killaloe 1848–79.

Knight of KERRY see *The Hereditary Bondsman*

Charles William (FitzGerald), marquess of KILDARE (1819–1887)
Styled marquess of Kildare till 1874 when he succeeded as fifth duke of Leinster. A Commissioner of National Education 1841 until his death. High sheriff for co. Kildare 1843. Liberal MP for co. Kildare 1847–52. Chancellor of the Queen's University of Ireland 1870–81. President of the Royal Dublin Society 1874 till his death.

Abraham Bradley KING see *The Hereditary Bondsman*

Henry LABOUCHERE (1798–1869)
Liberal MP from 1826. 1832–41 he held a number of ministerial posts. Chief secretary for Ireland 1846–7. 1847–52 president of the board of trade. 1855–8 secretary of state for the colonies. Created Baron Taunton in 1859.

(Jean-Baptiste-) Henri LACORDAIRE (1802–61)
Leading ecclesiastic in the Catholic revival in France following the 1789

revolution. Ordained as a priest in 1827. Co-founder of *L'Avenir*, a journal advocating separation of church and state. Joined the Dominican order at Rome in 1838. Reestablished the Dominican order in France in 1843. Head of French Dominicans 1850–4. In favour of a Republican France. Criticized Napoleon III. Elected to the French Academy in 1860.

Patrick LALOR (d. 1856)

1832–5 Repeal MP for Queen's County. Prominent in anti-tithe movement as a Catholic farmer with a large estate. Father of James Fintan Lalor, the Young Irelander.

Hon. George LAMB (1784–1834)

Brother of Lord Melbourne. Author of many essays and articles. MP for Westminster 1819–20, for Dungarvan 1826–34; under-secretary of the home department 1830–4.

Henry LAMBERT, J.P., D.L. (1786–1861)

MP for co. Wexford 1831–5.

(Hughes-) Félicité (-Robert de) LAMENNAIS (1782–1854)

Priest and liberal Catholic philosophical and political writer. Co-founder of the newspaper *L'Avenir* in 1830. Publication was suspended in Nov. 1831, and after a vain appeal to the pope, its principles were condemned in the encyclical, *Mirari Vos*. Lamennais then attacked the papacy, which led to his severance from the church. He served in the Constituent Assembly after the 1848 revolution.

Lord LANSDOWNE see *The Hereditary Bondsman*

Patrick M. LAVELLE (c. 1802–1837)

Proprietor and editor of the *Freeman's Journal* from 1830 till his death.

Cecil John LAWLESS (1820–53)

Second son of second baron Cloncurry. MP for Clonmel 1846–53.

Nicholas Philpot LEADER see *The Hereditary Bondsman*

Augustus Frederick (Fitzgerald), third duke of LEINSTER see *The Hereditary Bondsman*

Denis LE MARCHANT (1795–1874)

Secretary to Lord Brougham in 1830. Appointed clerk of the crown in chancery in 1834. Secretary to the board of trade 1836–41. He was also joint secretary to the treasury in 1841. Created a baronet in 1841. MP for Worcester 1846–7; under-secretary for the home department 1847; secretary of the board of trade 1848; chief clerk to the House of Commons 1850–71.

Lord Francis LEVESON-GOWER (1800–57)

Second son of first duke of Sutherland. MP almost continuously 1822–46. A lord of the treasury 1827, under-secretary of state for the colonies 1828, chief secretary for Ireland 1828–30, secretary at war 1830. Created Earl of Ellesmere in 1846. Assumed the surname Egerton in 1833.

Edward John LITTLETON, first baron Hatherton (1791–1863)

MP for Staffordshire 1812–32, for South Staffordshire 1832–5. Chief secretary for Ireland 1833–4. He became a member of the privy council in 1833. Created Baron Hatherton of Hatherton in 1835. Lord lieutenant of Staffordshire 1854–63.

Robert Banks (Jenkinson), second earl of LIVERPOOL see *Hereditary Bondsman*

Edward LUCAS (1787–1871)

MP for co. Monaghan 1834–41. Under-secretary to the lord lieutenant 1841–5.

Baron LYNDHURST see *The Hereditary Bondsman* under Sir John Singleton Copley.

Thomas Babington MACAULAY (1800–59)

Historian. Commissioner in bankruptcy 1828–31. MP for Calne 1830–3, for Edinburgh 1839–47, 1852–6. Commissioner for the board of control 1832. On the supreme council of India Dec. 1833–Jan. 1838. Secretary of war 1839–41. He became lord rector of the university of Glasgow in 1848. Raised to peerage 1856.

William Bernard MacCABE (1801–91) Author and historian. Journalist in Ireland 1823–35. Published a 3 volume Catholic History of England 1847–54.

Joseph Myles MacDONNELL (1796–187?) Sometime JP. MP for co. Mayo 1846–7.

Richard Graves MacDONNELL (1814–81) Called to the Irish bar in 1838, to the English bar in 1841. Chief justice of Gambia 1843–7. 1847–72 colonial governor in Gambia, St Lucia, St Vincent, South Australia, Nova Scotia and Hong Kong.

Rose McDOWELL (c. 1821–1902) Eldest daughter of Robert McDowell, merchant, of Belfast.

Nicholas McEVOY (1800–60) Curate 1830–40, administrator 1841–5 and parish priest of Kells 1845–60. Active in support of tenant rights in co. Meath.

John MacHALE (1791–1881) Lecturer in theology at St Patrick's College, Maynooth 1814–25; titular bishop of Moronia and coadjutor bishop of Killala 1825–34; archbishop of Tuam 1834–81.

Peter MacLAUGHLIN (c. 1760–1840) Catholic bishop of Raphoe 1802-19; administrator of Derry 1819–24; bishop of Derry 1824–40.

Cornelius MacLOGHLIN see The Hereditary Bondsman

Charles McNALLY (d. 1864) Coadjutor bishop 1843–4, bishop of Clogher 1844–64.

Major William MacNAMARA see The Hereditary Bondsman

Patrick MacNICHOLAS (c. 1781–1852) Bishop of Achonry 1818–52.

Daniel Owen MADDEN (1815–59) Worked for the Press newspaper. Author of many works including Ireland and its Rulers since 1829, The Age of Pitt and Fox and a memoir of H. Grattan.

Francis MAGENNIS (d. 1847) Parish priest of Clones 1842–7.

Edward MAGINN D.D. (1802–49) Curate in Moville, co. Donegal 1825–9. Parish priest of united parishes of Fahan and Deysertegny 1829–45. He was appointed coadjutor to the bishop of Derry in 1845. Bishop of Ortosia 1846–9. An enthusiastic supporter of Repeal.

James MAHER (1793–1874) Parish priest of Killeshin, co. Carlow from Jan. 1841. An uncle of Cardinal Cullen and one of the most distinguished Irish priests of his time.

James O'Gorman MAHON see The Hereditary Bondsman

Pierce MAHONY see The Hereditary Bondsman

Father Theobald MATHEW (1790–1856) Ordained in 1814 as a Capuchin priest and worked in Cork at the 'Little Friary'. In 1838 he began his campaign for total abstinence, travelling throughout Ireland. In 1843 he went to London and travelled in the USA 1849–51. In 1848 he was named by the clergy of the diocese for the vacant bishopric of Cork but the choice was not ratified by the Vatican. A pension was granted to him through the influence of Lord John Russell.

Thomas Francis MEAGHER (1823–67) Young Irelander, and a founder of

the Irish Confederation in 1847.
Transported to Van Dieman's Land
in 1849 for his part in the 1848
insurrection. In 1852 he escaped to
USA and lectured and worked as a
journalist there 1852–4. Admitted to
the bar in 1855. In the US federal
army from 1861. 1862 became a
brigadier general. Enrolled as a
Fenian in 1863. Temporary governor
of Montana 1866 until his death.

John Chambre (Brabazon), tenth earl of
MEATH (1772–1851)
Lord lieutenant of co. Dublin 1831–
51. Created Baron Chaworth (UK)
1831.

William (Lamb), second viscount
MELBOURNE see *The Hereditary
Bondsman*

John MILEY, D.D. (1805–61)
Curate Marlborough St, Dublin
1835–49. Rector of the Irish College,
Paris 1849–59. Parish priest, Bray
1859–61. Historian.

Joseph (Leeson), fourth earl of
MILLTOWN (1799–1866)
He was styled Viscount Russborough
1801–7. Succeeded to the earldom in
1807.

John MITCHEL (1815–75)
Young Irelander. Admitted as a
solicitor in 1840. Assisted in editing
the *Nation* 1845–7. Founded the
United Irishman in 1848.
Transported to Van Dieman's Land
for sedition in 1848. In 1853 he
escaped to San Francisco where he
was editor of various journals and
papers. He was imprisoned for five
months because of his articles in
defence of the southern cause in the
American Civil War. Elected MP for
co. Tipperary in 1875, but his
election was disallowed after his
death.

James Henry MONAHAN (1804–78)
Solicitor-general for Ireland 1846–7.
Attorney-general 1847. Chief justice
of the common pleas 1850–76. 1867
he presided at the special commission
for the trial of the Fenian prisoners at
Cork and Limerick.

Charles de MONTALEMBERT (1810–70)
Orator, politician and historian who
was a leader in the struggle against
absolutism in church and state in
France in the nineteenth century. He
began his political career with the
newspaper *L'Avenir*. He helped
found a Catholic school in 1831 for
which he was prosecuted. Wrote for
L'Univers Religieux. After the 1848
revolution he swung the Catholic
party behind Louis Napoleon, an act
which he later regretted. He came
into conflict with the Church for his
insistence that it encourage civil and
religious liberties.

George Henry MOORE J.P. (1811–70)
MP for co. Mayo 1847–57, 1868–
70. Father of George Moore, the
novelist.

George Ogle MOORE (born c. 1779)
Called to the bar 1800. MP for
Dublin city 1826–31. Deputy
registrar of deeds 1802–31, registrar
of deeds 1831–46.

Louisa MOORE
A Catholic. Daughter of Hon. John
Browne and grand-daughter of the
first earl of Attamont.

Thomas MOORE see *The Hereditary
Bondsman*

George William Frederick (Howard)
styled Lord MORPETH (1802–64)
1825–48 known as Lord Morpeth.
Succeeded as seventh earl of Carlisle
in 1848. MP 1826–41, 1846–8.
Chief secretary of Ireland 1835–41.
Chief commissioner of woods and
forests 1846–50. Lord lieutenant of
East Riding 1847–64. Chancellor of
the duchy of Lancaster 1850–2. Lord
lieutenant of Ireland 1855–8, 1859–
64.

Lucretia MOTT (1793–1880)
Quaker preacher and reformer,
advocate of women's rights and
abolition of slavery.

Constantine Henry (Phipps), second
earl of MULGRAVE (1797–1863)
MP almost continually 1818–30. In
1831 he succeeded as earl of
Mulgrave. Governor of Jamaica
1832–4. Lord privy seal July–Dec.
1834. Lord lieutenant of Ireland
1835–9. Created marquess of
Normanby in 1838. Secretary of state
for war and the colonies 1839.
Secretary of state for the home
department 1839–41. Ambassador to
Paris 1846–52. 1854–8 minister at
the court of Tuscany.

Joseph Denis MULLEN
Trimming manufacturer. Sometime
governor of the Four Courts
Marshalsea. A prominent member of
the Catholic Association. A director
of the Royal Canal Co. from c. 1821.

Frederick W. MULLINS (1804–54)
MP for co. Kerry 1831–7.

Philip Henry MUNTZ (1811–88)
Merchant in Birmingham. Chief
promoter of incorporation of the
borough in 1837, mayor 1839 and
1840. MP for Birmingham 1868–85.

John Joseph MURPHY
Attorney of Murphy and Ruthven,
solicitors, 13 College Green, Dublin.

William MURPHY (d. 1849)
A rich Dublin salesmaster, who had
taken part in the 1798 rebellion.

Daniel MURRAY see The Hereditary
Bondsman

Thomas Lamie MURRAY
Managing director of the National
Bank.

Francis Joseph NICHOLSON (1803–55)
He joined the Discalced Carmelites in
1825. Consecrated coadjutor
archbishop of Corfu in 1846,
succeeding in 1852.

John NUGENT M.B. (1806–99)
Travelling physician to O'Connell.
An original member of the Reform
Club, London. Inspector of
commissioners of control of lunacy,
Ireland 1846–90. Knighted 1890.

Cornelius O'BRIEN (1782–1860)
He became an attorney in 1811. MP
for co. Clare 1832–47, 1852–7.

William Smith O'BRIEN (1803–64)
MP for Ennis as tory
Emancipationist 1828–31. MP for
co. Limerick as liberal and Repealer
1835–49. A leader of the Young
Ireland movement and of the 1848
rising, for his part in which he was
transported to Tasmania in 1849.
Returned to Ireland 1856.

Catherine (Kate) O'CONNELL
(daughter) see The Hereditary
Bondsman

Charles O'CONNELL (1805–77)
Cousin of O'Connell. He married
Kate, O'Connell's second daughter.
MP for co. Kerry 1832–4. Appointed
resident magistrate in April 1847.

Daniel O'CONNELL (son) see The
Hereditary Bondsman

Elizabeth (Betsey) O'CONNELL
(daughter) see The Hereditary
Bondsman

Ellen O'CONNELL (daughter) see The
Hereditary Bondsman

James O'CONNELL (brother) see The
Hereditary Bondsman

John O'CONNELL (brother) see The
Hereditary Bondsman

John O'CONNELL (son) see The
Hereditary Bondsman

Mary O'CONNELL (wife) see The
Hereditary Bondsman

Maurice O'CONNELL (son) see The
Hereditary Bondsman

Morgan O'CONNELL (son) see The
Hereditary Bondsman

Morgan John O'CONNELL (1811–75)
Eldest son of O'Connell's brother
John. MP for co. Kerry 1835–52. In
1865 he married Mary Anne,
daughter of Charles Bianconi.

Feargus Edward O'CONNOR (1794–
1855)
Chartist leader. Son of Roger
O'Connor, a United Irishman. MP
for co. Cork 1832–5, for

Nottingham borough 1847–52. He founded the central committee of radical unions in 1836, and the London Democratic Association in 1837. Established the *Northern Star*, a weekly radical paper in 1837. In 1840 he was found guilty of seditious libel and imprisoned for eighteen months. In 1846 he inaugurated the 'Chartist Co-operative Land Company', and in 1847 a journal called *The Labourer*.

Denis O'CONOR (1794–1847)
O'Conor Don from 1831. MP for co. Roscommon 1831–47. A lord of the treasury 1846–7.

Laurence O'DONNELL (d. 1855)
Bishop of Galway 1844–55.

William O'DONNELL
Retired merchant. The Cottage, Carrick-on-Suir, co. Tipperary.

Andrew Carew O'DWYER (1800–77)
MP for Drogheda 1832–5, reelected 1835 but unseated on petition. 1837 appointed filacer of the exchequer.

Richard More O'FERRALL (1797–1880)
MP for co. Kildare 1830–47, 1859–65; for co. Longford 1851–2. A lord of the treasury 1835–9. Secretary of the admiralty 1839–41. A secretary of the treasury in 1841. Governor of Malta 1847–51.

Thomas O'HAGAN (1812–85)
Called to the Irish bar 1836. Edited the *Newry Examiner* 1836–40. He defended Gavan Duffy in 1842 and 1843–4. Assistant barrister of co. Longford 1847–57, of co. Dublin 1857–9, 1859 third serjeant, 1861 solicitor-general, 1862 attorney-general, 1865 judge of the court of common pleas in Ireland. Lord chancellor of Ireland 1868–74. Created Baron O'Hagan in 1870.

James O'HEA (1809–82)
Called to the Irish bar 1838. One of the defending counsel in state trial of 1844. Crown prosecutor in co.

Limerick 1860–82 and the county and city of Cork 1849–82.

Patrick O'HIGGINS (d. 1854)
Merchant in Dublin. Became known as 'the Irish Chartist'.

William O'HIGGINS (1793–1853)
Bishop of Ardagh and Clonmacnoise 1829–53. An especially active supporter of Repeal.

Colman Michael O'LOGHLEN (1819–77)
Second baronet. Called to the bar 1840. 1856–9 chairman of Carlow quarter sessions. 1859–61 chairman of Mayo quarter sessions. 1863–77 MP for Clare. 1865 third serjeant-at-law for Ireland, 1866 second serjeant-at-law for Ireland. 1868–70 judge advocate general. Subsequently emigrated to Australia.

Michael O'LOGHLEN (1789–1842)
Called to the bar in 1811. K.C. in 1830. MP for Dungarvan 1835–7. Solicitor-general Oct. 1834–Jan. 1835, April–Sept. 1835. Attorney-general Aug. 1835–Nov. 1836. Baron of the court of exchequer Nov. 1836–Jan. 1837. Master of the rolls 1837–42. Created a baronet in 1838. He was the first Catholic law officer and the first Catholic judge since the reign of James II.

Margaret O'MARA (d. 1874)
Daughter of Thomas O'Mara and Margaret (née Callan) formerly Mrs T. Fitz-Simon. Half sister of Christopher Fitz-Simon. In 1845 she married James Netterville Blake M.D. (d. 1847). In 1854 she married William Bowman.

Terence O'SHAUGHNESSY (1763–1848)
Parish priest of Ennis and Dean of Killaloe, 1820–48.

Henry John (Temple), third viscount PALMERSTON (1784–1865)
A lord of the admiralty 1807–9. Secretary at war 1809–28. Secretary for foreign affairs 1830–4, 1835–41,

1846–51. Home secretary 1852–5. Prime minister 1855–8, 1859–65.

Sir Henry PARNELL bt see *The Hereditary Bondsman*

Joseph PEASE (1772–1846)
A rich Yorkshire woollen merchant. A Quaker who strongly supported the anti-slavery cause.

Sir Robert PEEL bt see *The Hereditary Bondsman*

Richard PENNEFATHER (1773–1859)
Chief baron of the Irish exchequer 1821–59.

Louis PERRIN (1782–1864)
Called to the Irish bar 1806. MP for Dublin city May–Aug. 1831, for co. Monaghan 1832–5, for Cashel Jan.–Aug. 1835. Third serjeant-at-law 1832–5; first serjeant Feb.–April 1835. Attorney-general April–Aug. 1835. Justice of the King's Bench 1835–60.

David Richard PIGOT (1797–1873)
Called to the bar in 1826, created K.C. in 1835. MP for Clonmel 1839–46. Solicitor-general 1839–40. Attorney-general 1840–1. Chief baron of the exchequer 1846–73.

Hon. Frederick George Brabazon PONSONBY (1815–95)
Called to the bar in 1840. Succeeded in 1880 as sixth earl of Bessborough. A liberal in politics. A member of the commission to inquire into the land system in Ireland 1880–1 (known as the Bessborough commission).

Caleb POWELL J.P. (1793–1881)
Called to the Irish bar 1817. MP for co. Limerick 1841–7. Sheriff of Limerick in 1858.

John PRIMROSE jr see *The Hereditary Bondsman*

Peter PURCELL (d. 1846)
Founded the *Monitor*, a Dublin liberal journal in 1838.

Thomas Rodney PURDON
Governor of the Richmond Bridewell, South Circular Road, Dublin at the time of O'Connell's imprisonment in 1844.

Michael QUIN (1796–1843)
Editor of *Monthly Review* 1825–32, *Catholic Journal* 1828–9, first editor of *Dublin Review* 1836. Barrister.

Alexander RAPHAEL (1775–1850)
English merchant born in India. Converted to Roman Catholicism from Judaism. Sheriff of London in 1834. He was elected MP for Carlow 1835, but was unseated on petition. MP for St Albans 1847–50. He opposed Jewish emancipation.

Thomas Mathew RAY (1801–81)
Secretary of the National Trades Political Union Dublin. Secretary of the Precursor Society 1838–40. Secretary of the Repeal Association from April 1840. Tried and sentenced with O'Connell in 1844 state trials. Assistant registrar of deeds in Ireland 1865–80.

Thomas Nicholas REDINGTON (1815–62)
MP for Dundalk 1837–46. Under-secretary for Ireland 1846–52. Later knighted.

Thomas Devin REILLY (1824–54)
Wrote for the *Nation* and *United Irishman*. He escaped to New York in 1848 and contributed to Irish-American newspapers. He edited the *Democratic Review* and later the *Washington Union*.

John REYNOLDS (1794–1868)
Secretary in Ireland of National Bank 1834–41. Appointed managing director of the Land Investment Co. of Ireland in 1841. MP for Dublin city 1847–52. Lord mayor of Dublin 1850.

Thomas REYNOLDS
Merchant. Vice-president of the National Trades Political Union.

John RICHARDS (1790–1872)
K.C. in 1830. Solicitor-general 1835–6. Attorney-general Nov. 1836–Feb. 1837. Baron of the exchequer 1837–49.

David ROCHE (1791–1865)

MP for Limerick city 1832–44. Created a baronet in 1838. Agent to Edward Bourchier Hartapp.

David Robert ROSS, J.P., D.L. (1797–1851)
High sheriff of co. Down in 1837. MP for Belfast 1842–7. Lieutenant governor of Tobago in 1851.

Lord John RUSSELL (1792–1868)
Home secretary 1835–9; colonial secretary 1839–41; prime minister 1846–52, 1865–6. Created Earl Russell in 1861.

William Henry RUSSELL (1820–1907)
Reporter in Ireland for the *Times* during part of the Repeal campaign. Celebrated Crimean war correspondent. Knighted in 1895.

Edward Southwell RUTHVEN (1772–1836)
He assumed the name Ruthven, instead of Trotter, in 1800. MP for Downpatrick 1806–7, 1830–2; for Dublin City 1832–6 when he was unseated on petition, after his death.

Joshua SCHOLEFIELD (1775–1844)
Radical MP for Birmingham 1832–44. Banker, merchant and manufacturer. Vice president of the Political Union during the reform agitation 1830–2. Director of the National Provincial Bank of England and the London Joint-Stock Bank.

Bindon SCOTT
Cahircon, Kildysert, co. Clare. Married Frances Percy in 1810. Their daughter Mary married O'Connell's son, Maurice, in 1832.

Sir Walter SCOTT (1771–1832)
Scottish poet, novelist, historian, antiquarian, editor and biographer. His works include *The Lay of the Last Minstrel, Marmion, The Lady of the Lake,* the *Waverley* novels, *The Bride of Lammermoor, Ivanhoe* and the *Life of Napoleon.* In 1805 he became a secret partner in the Border Press with James and John Ballantyne. This company failed in

1825, leaving him enormously in debt.

William SCOTT
Sheriff of Dublin in 1830.

Frederick SHAW (1799–1876)
MP for Dublin city 1830–2; for Dublin University 1832–48. Recorder of Dundalk 1826–8. Recorder of Dublin 1828–76. Succeeded his brother as third baronet in 1869.

John SHEEHAN (d. 1854)
Parish priest, St Patrick's, Waterford 1828–54.

Remigius SHEEHAN (d. 1847)
Cork attorney. Converted from Catholicism to Church of Ireland. 1824 became editor of the *Dublin Evening Mail.* Proprietor of the *Star of Brunswick* which he established about 1828 to combat the Emancipation movement. Made a freeman of th city of Dublin in 1828.

Richard Lalor SHEIL see *The Hereditary Bondsman*

John (Talbot), Earl of SHREWSBURY see *The Hereditary Bondsman*

Michael SLATTERY (1785–1857)
Professor of philosophy at Carlow College, 1809–15. Parish priest of Cashel 1815–33. President of St Patrick's College, Maynooth 1833–4. Archbishop of Cashel 1834–57.

Edmond SMITHWICK (1800–76)
Brewer. Alderman of Kilkenny 1843, mayor of Kilkenny 1844, 1864, 1865.

Thomas SPRING-RICE see *The Hereditary Bondsman*

Edward George Geoffrey Smith STANLEY (1799–1869)
Lord Stanley from 1834, succeeded as fourteenth earl of Derby in 1851. MP from 1822. Under-secretary for the colonies 1827–8; chief secretary for Ireland 1830–3, secretary of state for the colonies 1833–4, 1841–5; prime minister 1852, 1858–9, 1866–8.

Michael STAUNTON see *The Hereditary Bondsman*

Thomas STEELE (1788–1848)
Raised money for and joined revolt against Ferdinand VII of Spain 1823–4. Enthusiastic supporter and admirer of O'Connell. His position as a Protestant landlord increased his value to O'Connell. He was appointed 'head pacificator' by O'Connell.

William STOKES (1804–78)
Physician. In 1837 he published a treatise on *Diseases of the Chest* and in 1854 *Diseases of the Heart and Aorta*. In 1861 he was elected FRS and appointed physician in-ordinary to Queen Victoria. 1874 President RIA.

Sir Edward Burtenshaw SUGDEN (1781–1875)
Solicitor-general of England 1829–30; lord chancellor for Ireland Dec. 1834–April 1835, 1841–6; lord chancellor of England 1852. In 1852 created Baron St Leonards. Author of legal textbooks.

James SUGRUE see *The Hereditary Bondsman*

Richard SULLIVAN (c. 1795–1855)
Merchant at Kilkenny, engaged in brewing, malting and milling. MP for Kilkenny city 1832–6. Resigned his seat in favour of O'Connell. Mayor of Kilkenny 1837–8.

Nicholas Aylward VIGORS (1785–1840)
MP for Carlow borough 1832–4, for co. Carlow 1837–40. Protestant landowner. Army officer.

Thomas WALLACE see *The Hereditary Bondsman*

Francis Andrew WALSH (c. 1805–52)
Called to the bar 1836. Professor of law at Queen's College, Cork 1845–51. A powerful speaker at temperance meetings.

Henry WARBURTON (1784–1858)
Radical politician. MP for Bridport 1826–41, for Kendal 1843–7.

Richard Colley (Marquess) WELLESLEY see *The Hereditary Bondsman*

Arthur (Wellesley) duke of WELLINGTON see *The Hereditary Bondsman*

Richard WHATELY (1787–1863)
He became principal of St Alban Hall, Oxford in 1825. 1829–31 professor of political economy. In 1831 he was appointed archbishop of Dublin, and took his seat in the House of Lords in 1833. Head of the commission to administer the new system of 'united national education' 1831–53. He presided over the royal commission on the condition of the Irish poor 1833–6.

William WOODLOCK (b. 1801)
Attorney in Dublin, employed by O'Connell.

Thomas WYSE see *The Hereditary Bondsman*

John Ashton YATES (1782–1863)
MP for co. Carlow 1837–41.

Apart from using such conventional sources as the *Dictionary of National Biography*, the *Handbook of British Chronology*, Dod's *Parliamentary Companion*, and *The Complete Peerage of England, Scotland, Ireland, Great Britain and the United Kingdom* (ed. Hon. Vicary Gibbs, London, 1910), I have drawn largely on the annotations in M. R. O'Connell, ed., *Correspondence*, as well as those in Macintyre, *The Liberator*, and *Parliamentary Results in Ireland*, 1801–1922 (ed. B. M. Walker, Dublin, 1978), in compiling these Notes.

Index

Details of O'Connell's relationships are indexed under the names of the people involved, e.g. his relationship with his eldest son, Maurice, is indexed under O'Connell, Maurice.
Noblemen appear under their titles.
Titles of books are listed under the name of the author.
The method of alphabetical arrangement is letter-by-letter.
Sub-headings are arranged in chronological order where possible.